T0291376

Value Proposition to Tourism Coopetition

BUILDING THE FUTURE OF TOURISM

Series Editor: Anukrati Sharma

The world is entering the third millennium in which great changes are expected in all areas of human interest, life and activity. These changes have been brought on by past and present man-made events, which have had both positive and negative consequences. The coming millennium will be marked by significant social, political, demographic and technological changes, and will definitely differ from the last century. The future will bring more leisure time, a higher standard of living and a better quality of life for us all. This series examines recent and the most probable changes and gives a wide range of visionary insights, as well as operational takeaways.

Forthcoming Volumes

Meaningful Tourism: Strategies and Futuristic Development
Pankaj Kumar Tyagi, Vipin Nadda, and Ajit Kumar Singh

Value Proposition to Tourism Coopetition: Cases and Tools

EDITED BY

ADRIANA FUMI CHIM-MIKI

Federal University of Campina Grande, Brazil
University of Aveiro, Portugal

AND

RUI AUGUSTO DA COSTA

University of Aveiro, Portugal

United Kingdom – North America – Japan – India – Malaysia – China

Emerald Publishing Limited
Emerald Publishing, Floor 5, Northspring, 21-23 Wellington Street, Leeds LS1 4DL

First edition 2025

British Library Cataloguing in Publication Data
A catalogue record for this book is available from the British Library

ISBN: 978-1-83797-828-1 (Print)
ISBN: 978-1-83797-827-4 (Online)
ISBN: 978-1-83797-829-8 (Epub)

INVESTOR IN PEOPLE

Contents

List of Figures and Tables

Figures

Tables

List of Abbreviations

ABRATUR	International Academy for the Development of Tourism Research in Brazil
ADXTUR	Agência para o Desenvolvimento Turístico das Aldeias do Xisto
ARCTISEN	Culturally Sensitive Tourism in the Arctic
CDs	Constitutive Definitions
CEs	Constitutive Elements of Analysis
CIPD	Innovative Planning and Development
CITUR	Centre for Tourism Research, Development and Innovation
CNPq	National Council for Scientific and Technological Development
CooPM	Coopetition Players Mapping
CooTB	Coopetition Toolbox
CooVP	Coopetition Value Proposition
DEs	Descriptions of the Elements
DMOs	Destination Management Organisation
DO	Denomination of Origin
FAPEMIG	Minas Gerais State Research Support Foundation
FGI	Focus Group Interview
FGV EAESP	Fundação Getúlio Vargas, São Paulo School of Business Administration
GI	Geographical Indication
GIS	Geographic Information Systems
GOF	Goodness of Fit
GOVCOPP	Research Unit on Governance, Competitiveness and Public Policies
HGTUR	Hospitality, Gastronomy and Tourist Services

IAD	Institutional Analysis and Developed
iCOOL	Coopetition Local Index
ICT	Information and Communication Technologies
IDIs	In-depth Interviews
IDSC-BR	Sustainable Development Index of Cities – Brazil
KPIs	Key Performance Indicators
LPBM	Board of Town Planners Malaysia
MIP	Malaysian Institute of Planners
ML	Machine Learning
MTur	Ministry of Tourism
NGOs	Non-governmental Organisations
ODs	Operational Definitions
OLS	Ordinary Least Squares
PLAGET	Tourism Destination Planning and Management
RBV	Resources-based Theory
SBS	Stellenbosch Business School
SDGs	Sustainable Development Goals
SMEs	Small- and Medium-sized Enterprises
TMC - UFPR	Tourism, Marketing and Competitiveness Research Group
TTDI	Travel and Tourism Development Index
TVA	Turismo: Visão e Ação
UCC	UNESCO Creative Cities
UCCN	UNESCO Creative Cities Network
UFCG	Federal University of Campina Grande, Brazil
UFSC	Federal University of Santa Catarina
UFV	Universidade Federal de Viçosa
UNISUL	University of Southern Santa Catarina
UNIVALI	University of Vale do Itajaí

About the Editors

Adriana Fumi Chim-Miki, Federal University of Campina Grande, Brazil and Aveiro University, Portugal, holds a PhD in Tourism, Economics, and Management from the University of Las Palmas de Gran Canaria, Spain. She is a Full Researcher at the Research Unit on Governance, Competitiveness and Public Policies (GOVCOPP), University of Aveiro, Portugal. She is a Professor at the Faculty of Management and Accounting at the Federal University of Campina Grande, Brazil. She has co-authored many articles on coopetition and tourism, and she is the coordinator of the research group Coopetition Network Lab, registered by CNPq (National Council for Scientific and Technological Development) from Brazil.

Rui Augusto da Costa holds a PhD in Tourism from University of Aveiro. He is an Assistant Professor in the Tourism Area in the Department of Economics, Management, Industrial Engineering and Tourism at University of Aveiro, Portugal. He's the Director of the Bachelor in Tourism Management and Planning, and a Full Researcher at Tourism and Development Research Group in the Research Unit on Governance, Competitiveness and Public Policy. He develops his research in planning and project in Tourism, destinations' competitiveness, governance and public policy, tourism technologies and monitoring and evaluation in tourism destinations. He participates as a coordinator and a researcher in several international and national research projects funded by international and national organisations. He's the author and co-author of several articles in national and international journals. He's an Associate Editor of the Journal of Tourism & Development (indexed in SCOPUS), a member of the Editorial Board of Event Management Journal and a member of the Organizing Committee of the International Conference INVTUR and also an internship coordinator in tourism (Bachelor and Master).

About the Contributors

Maria Saju Abraham is a Research Intern at Cardiff Business School, United Kingdom. Her research expertise is in circularity and its application in the Tourism and hospitality sector. With a special focus on the food and drinks sector, she has conducted research exploring technological applications to reduce food waste in restaurants.

Sofia Almeida is an associate professor and tourism director at Faculty of Social Sciences and Technology - Campus Lispolis, Universidade Europeia, Portugal. Sofia is also integrated researcher at Universidade Europeia; CETRAD-Centro de Estudos Transdisciplinares para o Desenvolvimento, Universidade de Trás os Montes e Alto Douro.

Marcia Mariluz Amaral holds a Master's degree in Tourism and Hospitality from the Universidade do Vale do Itajaí (Univali), Brazil, and a Bachelor's degree in Accountancy from Feevale, complemented by a specialisation in Business Management from FACCAT. Her research interests include wine tourism, gastronomy tourism, business management and regional development.

Sara Joana Gadotti dos Anjos, is a Professor of the Postgraduate Master's and Doctoral Programme in Tourism and Hospitality at the University of Vale do Itajaí, Brazil (Univali). She is a a Research Productivity Researcher at CNPq – National Council for Scientific and Technological Development. Sara is the Regional Editor for South America of the Journal of Hospitality and Tourism Insights. Her research interests include innovation in hotel and restaurant, motivation, human resources, tourist behaviours, management of destination excellence, hotel management and quality service.

Rosa M. Batista-Canino holds a PhD in management. She is a Full Professor at the Universidad de Las Palmas de Gran Canaria, Spain. She has been the Head of Global Entrepreneurship Monitor Canarias' research team since 2003 and is part of the GEM-Spain team. She led the Global University Entrepreneurial Spirit Student's Survey at ULPGC and for six years she led the research team 'Entrepreneurship, Digital Firms and Innovation'. She developed cooperation projects, and training projects for entrepreneurs, R&D and business development in countries such as Cape Verde, Chile, Colombia, Cuba, Brazil, Morocco and

Mexico. Also, she is co-editor of several books and articles on tourism, coopetition and entrepreneurship.

Mariana Carvalho is an Invited Adjunct Professor at the Coimbra Education School - Polytechnic Institute of Coimbra (Portugal). She holds a PhD in Tourism and a Master's Degree in Tourism Management and Development from the University of Aveiro (Portugal), and a degree in Tourism from the University of Coimbra. She integrates the Research Unit of CITUR (Centre for Tourism Research, Development and Innovation). She is the author and co-author of published papers and chapters in the field of Tourism and the tourist experience and she has participated in research projects related to rural, cultural and experience co-creation in tourism. Her main research areas of interest are experience co-creation, food and wine tourism, the tourist experience, rural tourism, cultural and creative tourism.

Jin Hooi Chan is a Professor of Sustainable Strategy, Innovation & Entrepreneurship at Greenwich Business School, University of Greenwich, United Kingdom. He is also an Associate Researcher at the Energy Policy Research Group, University of Cambridge. He holds a PhD degree in Management Studies from Judge Business School, University of Cambridge. As a multidisciplinary researcher, he builds on the study of industrial organisation, industrial policy, entrepreneurship and innovation and covers sustainability, creative, heritage/culture, tourism and hospitality and cleantech industries. He holds several international research grants (funded by ESRC/AHRC, UK), the British Academy, EU Interreg and other national funders worldwide.

Tatiane Pellin Cislaghi is currently a Professor in Management and International Trade at Federal Institute of Education, Science and Technology of Rio Grande do Sul, Bento Gonçalves Campus, Brazil. She holds a PhD degree in Administration from Unisinos University, Porto Alegre, Brazil. She was a visiting student in the Kassel University, Germany (2018). Her main research interests are related to governance of agri-food chains in an emerging country context (organic supply chain), internationalisation, strategic management, supply chain management, buyer–supplier relationship, inter-organisational relationship, inter-organisational governance and logistics (international logistics; humanitarian logistics). She has published in Supply Chain Management: *An International Journal, British Food Journal, Brazilian Journal of Management – ReA UFSM, International Business and Management Review – Internext*, etc.

Wojciech Czakon, Jagiellonian University, Poland. He obtained his PhD in Management from The Karol Adamiecki University of Economics in Katowice, Poland. He is a Full Professor of strategy at the Faculty of Management and Communication of the Jagiellonian University in Krakow, Poland. His research revolves around inter-organisational phenomena, strategies and structures. In particular, he published many articles and books on coopetition at various levels of analysis and in various empirical settings. His recent publications focus on coopetition behavioural underpinnings like trust, perceptions and preferences. He co-organised workshops and conference tracks on coopetition and co-edited the books *Routledge Companion to Coopetition Strategies, Strategic Management and Myopia: Challenges and Implications* and *Managing Tourism in a Changing World: Issues and Cases.*

Katarzyna Czernek-Marszałek is an Associate Professor, the head of the Department of Management Theory at the University of Economics in Katowice, Poland. Her research interests include inter-organisational relationships (especially cooperation and coopetition) and their determinants (e.g. trust and social embeddedness). Her empirical research focuses on the tourism sector. Her works also concern qualitative research methodology. Her research was published in journals such as *Industrial Marketing Management, Tourism Management, Journal of Destination Marketing & Management, Annals of Tourism Research, Journal of Travel Research* and *Current Issues in Tourism.*

Maya Damayanti, PhD, is an Associate Professor at Department of Urban and Regional Planning, Universitas Diponegoro, Indonesia. She was awarded PhD in urban tourism development from the University of Queensland, Australia, with research topic on coopetitive behaviours of the informal tourism economy. Her current research area includes urban management, governing the tourism commons and community-based tourism.

João Domingues is a researcher at Faculty of Social Sciences and Technology - Campus Lispolis, Universidade Europeia, Portugal.

Milad Ebrahimi is a master's degree graduate in Financial Management from Yazd University in Iran. He works as a researcher in the field of financial management. His areas of interest include behavioural finance, sustainability and marketing. He has also published articles in these areas. Additionally, he has experience in teaching various financial management courses.

Magnus Emmendoerfer, Universidade Federal de Viçosa (UFV), Brazil, holds a PhD in Human Sciences: Sociology and Politics from Universidade Federal de Minas Gerais, Brazil. He has a postdoctorate in management, public policy, creative tourism and entrepreneurship from universities in the Netherlands, Portugal and United States. He is a Full Professor in the Graduate Programme in Public Administration, UFV. He is a General Coordinator of UNESCO Chair Creative Economy & Public Policies (CEPP). He is the co-editor of 20 books and has several articles published as well as having authored 62 book chapters to date.

Luiz Carlos da Silva Flores, University of Vale do Itajaí, Brazil, is a Research Productivity Researcher CNPq – National Council for Scientific and Technological Development. He holds a Postdoctorate from the University of Algarve (Portugal), in the area of Tourism; PhD in Production Engineering; and master's in Administration from the Federal University of Santa Catarina (UFSC). He is a Professor-researcher of the postgraduate programme in Tourism and Hospitality, Masters and Doctorate, and a Professor of the Administration course, at undergraduate level - University of Vale do Itajaí, Brazil, linked to the Hospitality, Gastronomy and Tourist Services (HGTUR) and Tourism Destination Planning and Management (PLAGET) research groups, working in the areas of management, organisation, marketing of tourism and services and organisational strategy.

Anna-Emilia Haapakoski is a University Teacher in Tourism Research at the Faculty of Social Sciences, University of Lapland, Finland. Her research interests lie in philosophy and approaches of slow, sustainability and contemporary mobilities with an emphasis on tourism and localities. Most recently, she has been involved with the project 'Towards sustainable accessibility' focusing on sustainable tourism development in Lapland (led by Kideve, Kittilä development, funded by EAKR).

Elahe Hosseini holds a PhD in Organizational Behavior and Human Resource Management, Yazd University, Iran. Her research interest is about organisation behaviour, human resource management and social and entrepreneurship activities to develop entrepreneurship in developing countries. Also, she has several publications in international journals and participated in several conferences in some countries. She serves as an editor, a member of the editorial board in a series of distinguished journals such as *the Iranian Journal of Management Studies* and *International Journal of Management and Enterprise Development*.

Hairul Nizam Ismail is currently a Professor and the Director of Centre for Innovative Planning and Development (CIPD) in the Faculty of Built Environment and Surveying, UTM, Malaysia. He is also a Registered Town Planner under Board of Town Planners Malaysia (LPBM) and Corporate Member of Malaysian Institute of Planners (MIP) since 2012. Hairul's main research interests are in the fields of urban tourism, urban planning and tourism in developing countries. His academic interests address the issue of tourism planning and urban planning and expanding to the area such as tourism image, tourist behaviour, volunteerism, tourism entrepreneurship and transgenerational business in tourism as well as have published on themes relating to this area.

Elisabeth Kastenholz is an Associate Professor with aggregation at the Department of Economics, Management, Industrial Engineering and Tourism at the University of Aveiro (Portugal), where she teaches Tourism and Marketing-related subjects since 1994, also integrating the University's Research Unit Governance, Competitiveness and Pubic Policies (GOVCOPP). She holds a PhD in Tourism Studies, an MBA, a Licenciatura in 'Tourism Management and Planning' and a bachelor in 'Public Administration - Specificity Foreign Affairs' (Germany). She is member of the Deutsche Gesellschaft für Tourismuswissenschaft e.V. and of the Portuguese Society of Rural Studies. She has coordinated and participated in 16 research projects, in the fields of accessible, senior, social rural, nature, cultural and sustainable tourism, innovative tourism education, cross-border tourism initiatives and regional development. Her current research interests lie in sustainable tourism destination marketing, consumer behaviour in tourism (focus on destination image and destination experience), sustainable and regenerative tourism, accessible tourism, rural tourism and related topics like food and wine, slow and nature-based tourism.

Nadine Leder is a Lecturer in Logistics and Operations Management at Cardiff Business School, United Kingdom. Her research expertise is in Circular Economy & Circular Business Models and the implementation of circular and sustainable practices in Operations and Supply Chain Management. Nadine has conducted research in a variety of industry sectors, including the Tourism and Hospitality, Food and Drink, Construction, Plastics and Waste and Resource sectors.

Sari Lenggogeni is a Founder and Director of Tourism Development Center, Universitas Andalas, West Sumatera, Indonesia. She is also a Chairwoman of West Sumatra Tourism Board, Indonesia. She was awarded a PhD from the School of Tourism, University of Queensland, Brisbane, Australia. Her research interests include tourism crises and disaster management, tourism marketing, psychology of tourism, halal tourism and tourist behaviour. She was an expert team of tourism working group KEIN RI presidential advisory board in Indonesia (2016–2019). In collaboration with University of Queensland, Australia, Sari and team won the Australia Indonesia Institute grant from DFAT, Australia in 2022. Sari is also an ad hoc reviewer for Q1 Scopus-Indexed Tourism Journal including *Tourism Management, Annals of Tourism Research, Current Issues in tourism,* etc. She is an experienced expert leader for tourism policy and planning in Indonesia. She is a speaker in international and national tourism conferences/guest lectures.

Rogério João Lunkes is a Professor in the Accounting Department and the Graduate Program in Accounting, Administration, and Management Planning and Control at the Federal University of Santa Catarina (Brazil). She has a BS in Accounting and a master's degree and PhD in Production Engineering and Systems from the Federal University of Santa Catarina (Brazil). She has completed her postdoctorate work in accounting at the University of Valencia (Spain) and the University of Macerata (Italy). She has written several books and book chapters as well as published articles in international journals, including the *Journal of Cleaner Production, Environmental Monitoring and Assessment, Auditing and Accountability Journal, Business Strategy and the Environment, European Accounting Review, Journal of Applied Accounting Research, Sustainability, International Journal of Contemporary Hospitality Management,* and *International Journal of Hospitality Management.* PQ-1D Researcher at CNPq, the National Council for Scientific and Technological Development.

Kettrin Farias Bem Maracajá is an Associate Professor at the Federal University of Rio Grande do Norte, Brazil, Currais Novos, in the Tourism course. She is a Researcher and Professor on temporary assignment at the Academic Unit of Administration and Accounting at the Federal University of Campina Grande. She is a Permanent Professor at Postgraduate Program in Administration, Federal University of Campina Grande, Brazil (UFCG). She is a Permanent Professor of the Postgraduate Program in Natural Resources Engineering and Management, Federal University of Campina Grande, Brazil (UFCG). She is the Coordinator of the Environment, tourism and sustainability (GEATS) Research Group Faculty of Administration and Accounting (UAAC/UFCG). She is a member of the International Academy for the Development of Tourism Research in Brazil (ABRATUR). She is a member in the Tourism, Marketing and Competitiveness Research Group (TMC) - UFPR. She has published in many scientific journals. She participates in research lines in the areas of tourism management, general administration, wine tourism, sustainability, environmental education, competitiveness in tourist destinations and water footprint.

Márcio Ribeiro Martins is an Adjunct Professor at the Instituto Politécnico de Bragança (IPB), Portugal. He has a PhD in Tourism from the University of Aveiro. His main research areas are the spatiotemporal behaviour of tourists, tourist tracking technologies and backpacker tourism. He has also collaborated with the Polytechnic Institute of Viseu as a Visiting Assistant Professor at the Lamego School of Technology and Management, where he teaches the 'Geography, Landscape and Geotourism' course in the Tourism, Cultural and Heritage Management degree programme. He is currently an integrated member of CITED - IPB's Centre for Transdisciplinary Research in Education and Development, a collaborating member of the Centre for Research, Development and Innovation in Tourism (CITUR) and of IPB's Management Applied Research Unit (UNIAG). He is the author of a book, several book chapters and several scientific articles in international journals (Scopus/WoS), and has also participated in granted research projects.

Elias Mediotte, Universidade Federal de Viçosa (UFV), Brazil, holds a PhD in Public Administration, with a stay-research period at the Universidad Complutense de Madrid (UCM) in Spain. He has a Postdoctorate in public governance from UFV and started another in tourism at the Federal University of Ouro Preto (UFOP). He is a Research Member of UNESCO Chair CEPP. His research interests are Governance, placemaking, Creative Cities, and Sustainability.

Jefferson Marlon Monticelli is an Assistant Professor at Unisinos University, Business School, in Brazil. He holds a Postdoctorate at the Department of Production and Operations Management at Fundação Getúlio Vargas, São Paulo School of Business Administration (FGV EAESP), São Paulo, Brazil. He holds a Doctorate and Master's degree in Business Administration from Unisinos University, Porto Alegre, Brazil. He was a visiting student in the Department of Business Studies, Uppsala University, Sweden, during his Doctorate. His main research interest is related to coopetition, institutional theory, international business, entrepreneurship and family business. He has published in *Global Strategy Journal, Industrial Marketing Management, Journal of Business & Industrial Marketing, International Journal of Emerging Markets, International Journal of Entrepreneurial Behaviour & Research*, etc.

André Pedrosa completed his Bachelor's degree in Geography from the University of Porto and his master's degree in Tourism Management and Planning from the University of Aveiro. Since 2017, he has been engaged in research at the University of Aveiro and is currently pursuing a Doctoral Programme in Tourism. His doctoral research focuses on critical success factors for tourism route development. Additionally, he has been engaged in the publication and presentation of research on topics related to tourism and has been teaching Physical and Human Geography of Portugal at the University of Aveiro since 2020. His work encompasses cycling tourism, nature tourism, tourist routes and geographic information systems in tourism.

Mohd Alif Mohd Puzi is currently a Senior Lecturer from Program of Urban and Regional Planning in the Faculty of Built Environment and Surveying, Malaysia. Mohd Alif's main research interests are in the fields of urban planning, tourism planning and urban economic. His academic interests highlight areas such as tourism entrepreneurship and transgenerational entrepreneurship that has influence towards the peripheral community development. His current research interest is exploring the tourism from business and economic perspectives.

Rauno Rusko is a University Lecturer at the University of Lapland, Finland. His research activities focus on cooperation, coopetition, strategic management, digitising and social media, supply chain management and entrepreneurship mainly in the branches of information communication technology, forest industry and tourism. In addition to several book chapters, his articles appeared in *the European Management Journal*, *Forest Policy and Economics*, *International Journal of Business Environment*, *Industrial Marketing Management*, *International Journal of Innovation in the Digital Economy* and *International Journal of Tourism Research* among others.

Aidin Salamzadeh is the Vice Dean of the Faculty of Business Management at the University of Tehran, in Iran. His interests are startups, new venture creation and entrepreneurship. Aidin serves as an associate editor for the *Humanities and Social Sciences Communications* (Nature.com); *Journal of Enterprising Communities*; Revista de Gestão; *Innovation Management Review* (Emerald), *Entrepreneurial Business and Economics Review*, *Journal of Women's Entrepreneurship and Education* as well as *The Bottom Line* (Emerald). Besides, he is a reviewer in numerous distinguished international journals. Aidin is a member of the European SPES Forum (Belgium), the Asian Academy of Management (Malaysia), Ondokuz Mayis University (Turkey) and the Institute of Economic Sciences (Serbia). He co-founded the Innovation and Entrepreneurship Research Lab (London).

Joice Denise Schäfer is a Professor in the Accounting Department and the Graduate Program in Management Planning and Control at the Federal University of Santa Catarina (Brazil). Has a BS in Accounting from the State University of Western Paraná, a master's degree in Accounting and a PhD in Administration from the Federal University of Santa Catarina (Brazil).

Juulia Tikkanen is a Researcher at the University of Lapland at the Faculty of Social Sciences, Finland. Her research interests in tourism research are related to sustainable tourism in the Arctic. Recently, she has explored tourism degrowth in the context of Arctic tourism. Currently, she works in a European Union's

Horizon 2020-funded project, ArcticHubs, where various issues related to land use in the Arctic industries and livelihoods, including tourism, have been studied.

Petra Vašaničová, University of Presov, Faculty of Management and Business, Presov, Slovakia. She is an Associate Professor at the Faculty of Management and Business, University of Presov. Her research mainly focuses on tourism competitiveness and development and coopetition in tourism. Her research interest is the study of how tourism activity among European countries is interconnected, how to predict the financial distress of companies in the tourism sector and how network theory can help us understand the interconnectedness of tourism activity in Europe. Since 2015, she has published more than 140 studies, including papers in journals or proceedings, monographs and textbooks. Her publications also deal with business, finance, management and marketing.

Jako Volschenk, Stellenbosch Business School (SBS), South Africa. He holds a PhD in Business Administration and Management from the SBS. Currently, he is an Associate Professor of Strategy and Sustainability at the Stellenbosch Business School, South Africa. He is the author of several publications covering virtuous inter-organisational relationships, renewable energy, sustainability, coopetition and environmental consumer behaviour. His research in inter-organisational behaviour aims to understand how value is created and appropriated in different contexts and involving different stakeholders, especially focused on coopetition strategy.

Dagmara Wójcik, PhD, is an Assistant Professor in the Department of Management Theory at the University of Economics in Katowice, Poland. Her research interests include strategic management issues, i.e. inter-organisational cooperation, and coopetition in particular, in the creative industries such as the performing arts. She is also a researcher involved in individual and team projects subsidised by the National Science Centre, the Ministry of Science and Higher Education and the European Commission.

Foreword

It is my pleasure to write this foreword for this book which is edited by Adriana Fumi Chim-Miki and Rui Augusto da Costa. This book distinguishes itself by presenting coopetition cases within the hospitality and tourism (H&T) industry. It also offers practical tools for applying this strategy, making it valuable for both practitioners and scholars across various sectors, particularly the H&T industry. Based on my knowledge, this is one of the few books focusing on coopetition within these sectors. Coopetition is an increasingly significant paradigm in management literature, and dedicating a book to the H&T industry is particularly timely. This strategy is gaining traction in the management practices of tourism destinations and their firms. Therefore, I congratulate the editors and the authors for their efforts and contribution to the field.

The concept of cooperating with competitors has expanded into a broad value network, becoming an important framework for analysing networks, clusters, alliances and partnerships. Cooperation and competition have always been fundamental behaviours of businesses, organisations and individuals. Nowadays, these behaviours often merge, particularly in the tourism economy, where coopetition is essential. Understanding this strategy and defining mechanisms for its successful implementation is crucial, and this book significantly contributes to that endeavour.

This book illustrates various ways in which value is created through tourism coopetition. It is a particularly apt perspective for tourism, where value is generated by a joint effort of firms, entrepreneurs, governments, tourists, support institutions and synergy with other industries. In this book, the cases presented demonstrate how coopetition can foster tourism development in diverse contexts, involving different players and network structures. The chapters also highlight the connections and, at times, overlap between coopetition and other important theories. Despite its primary focus on coopetition, this book adopts a multidisciplinary approach and multi-level analysis characteristic of the H&T industry.

Another potential advantage of this book is its ability to offer practical solutions. The cases illustrate how coopetition strategies are implemented among businesses and organisations in tourism destinations. They explore problems, identify key players, define shared goals and demonstrate co-value creation. The book chapters address some of the challenges in the H&T industry and propose solutions based on coopetition strategy. Additionally, the book provides direct tools for implementing coopetition, such as the Coopetition Value Proposition, the Coopetition Players Mapping and the Coopetition Toolbox, offering practical solutions for practitioners.

This book emphasises the diverse values created by tourism coopetition at both private and public levels, contributing to economic, environmental and social positive impacts on firms and tourism destinations. Its effects on sustainability are also highlighted through discussions on the circular economy, multi-governance and sociocultural preservation. In summary, this book showcases the efforts of various authors to provide an integrative view of coopetition knowledge and practices in the tourism and hospitality industry. It is a valuable resource for researchers and practitioners alike, aiding the advancement of the coopetition paradigm. I hope the readers find this book enlightening and inspiring.

Dr Fevzi Okumus
CFHLA Preeminent Chair Professor
University of Central Florida's Rosen College of Hospitality Management, USA

Chapter 1

Introduction: The Value Proposition to Tourism: The Coopetition Era

Adriana Fumi Chim-Miki[a] and Rui Augusto da Costa[b]

[a]Federal University of Campina Grande, Brazil
[b]University of Aveiro, Portugal

Abstract

This chapter is the introduction to this book. Thus, it leads the reader to the coopetition theme as a value proposition for developing the tourism sector. We synthesise the coopetition mindset to tourism and show why this behaviour became a paradigm. The chapter provides an overview of this book's content, highlighting each chapter's singularity and supporting the statement: we live in the coopetition era.

Keywords: Tourism coopetition; coopetition era; value proposition; tourism networks; coopetition mindset

Book Introduction

Welcome to the coopetition era. Twenty-eight years after the publication of Brandenburger and Nalebuff's (1996) book that highlights coopetition as a new mindset, we can consider coopetition a paradigm in consolidation thanks to the efforts of various researchers in many areas. This new mindset, coopetition, has become a characteristic of society, an essential strategy for organisations, and an intrinsic behaviour of networks, clusters and tourism destinations.

Coopetition is a sub-area of strategy that grows daily, being applied and studied in different contexts, as it has become the construct that better explains current market relationships (Monticelli et al., 2022). Cooperating and competing are two fundamental and natural characteristics of human beings and, therefore, an essential aspect of society and its organisations. Nevertheless, cooperation and competition were previously seen as antagonistic processes and behaviours. This dual perspective generated a partial understanding of society and firm dynamics.

Value Proposition to Tourism Coopetition, 1–7
doi:10.1108/978-1-83797-827-420241001

Coopetition brings together cooperation and competition, breaking the dichotomous viewpoint and providing a more realistic perspective of social, business and individual dynamics. We are coopetitive by nature.

The coopetition paradigm was adapted to many contexts and received contributions from scholars of different areas. Tourism was one of these areas that adopted coopetition as it expresses the intrinsic behaviour of the tourism destination (Chim-Miki et al., 2023). The diversity of the tourism destination is a fruitful environment for studying coopetition. As Crick (2018) highlighted, the study context can shape the construction of a paradigm. In most industries, coopetition is a strategy for creating competitive advantages through the complementarity of firms' resources, knowledge and capabilities (Czakon et al., 2020). The organisations create different types of coopetition networks and outcomes.

Tourism expanded the meaning of coopetition. It is not more the simplistic view of cooperating with competitors. Coopetition in tourism is from the broad perspective of the value network created by Brandenburger and Nalebuff (1996), who claimed coopetition is defined as competitive cooperation between competing, complementary, substitute companies, suppliers and customers. However, tourism goes further since the tourism value network includes support organisations, government and society (Chim-Miki & Batista-Canino, 2018). The interplay between participants in this broad value network co-creates collective and individual competitive advantages, that is, for the tourism destination and its firms and residents. Ultimately, coopetition in tourism creates different types of value that are appropriated by players and can be managed by destination organisations to create benefits for society, achieving the status of value devolution (Chim-Miki et al., 2023; Volschenk et al., 2016). Thus, tourism brings two extensions to the theory of coopetition: the expansion of the value network and the expansion of the coopetition value cycle. What was a cycle of creation and appropriation of value is becoming the creation, appropriation and devolution of value (Chim-Miki et al., 2023). These extensions demonstrate that tourism coopetition studies are contributing to consolidating this paradigm. Tourism scholars generated a broad theoretical and empirical focus demonstrating the power of the coopetition strategy.

This book was structured to highlight the interplay in tourism and how dynamics between key stakeholder groups can create value. New strategies are shaping the world of organisations to produce a more inclusive development in society. Managers keep the focus on resources but broaden the look on relational capabilities. The model of competing alone is losing ground to competition in partnership. Therefore, participating in a network becomes vital for organisations. Indeed, the competitive advantage gained an ally in the coopetition behaviour (Crick et al., 2021). In some sectors, such as tourism, coopetition is an intrinsic and emergent behaviour that, if well planned, can generate coopetitive advantages for the destination and its stakeholders. Tourism coopetition is a dyadic behaviour of cooperating and competing simultaneously between two or more players to develop the tourism destination as an integral product (Chim-Miki & Batista-Canino, 2017). This book delves into the diverse strategies for cultivating and fortifying coopetition networks within the realm of tourism, as perceived by stakeholders in the tourism value network, as illustrated in Fig. 1.1. Through the lens of carefully chosen real-world

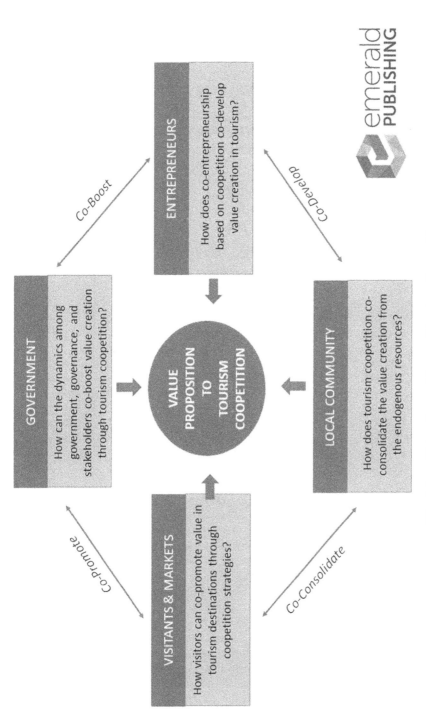

Fig. 1.1.   Value Proposition to Tourism Coopetition.

examples in tourism, it explores avenues for co-developing, co-producing, co-promoting and co-entrepreneurship within the framework of coopetition strategies. By addressing key questions such as how to collaboratively innovate and deliver products and services to the tourism sector, the book provides a comprehensive examination of coopetition's role. Additionally, it furnishes a compelling value proposition for embracing coopetition in tourism, along with practical tools and actionable insights to leverage coopetition within the industry effectively.

Book Part 1, named *Co-boost the Tourism Destination: Public Policies to Foster Coopetition Networks*, covers four chapters with real cases of tourism coopetition from the Government's perspective. Studies in Part 1 helped answer the question: How can the dynamics among government, governance and stakeholders co-boost value creation through tourism coopetition? The authors from South Africa, Poland, Brazil, Portugal and Slovakia provided ways to implement a coopetition strategy in the tourism destination and insights into the successful interplay between public–private organisations under a coopetition strategy to develop tourism destinations.

A roadmap to implement coopetition networks between public and private organisations with a governance system aimed at intensifying the generation of value for society is presented in Chapter 2. This chapter is a tool for tourism professionals, DMOs and public governments. The roadmap presented has six steps to build a coopetition network and a toolkit to manage the implementation and its outcomes. Cross-border coopetition is usually due to shared tourist attractions or similar characteristics among destinations; however, it is under-studied. Chapter 3 explores this topic using a sample of European countries that are externally heterogeneous but internally homogeneous, as they are tourism competitors but could cooperate to improve value generation. Chapter 4 illustrated how the values created by coopetition can be appropriate at Common, Private, Privately captured common or Public levels. It shows a taxonomy of different types of value generated by the coopetition strategy considering seven types of capital: Financial, Manufactured, Intellectual, Human, Social, Natural and Cultural. In addition, Chapter 5 investigates coopetition under Multilevel Governance in UNESCO-designated tourism destinations. The authors of Chapter 5 underscore the complexity of integrating coopetition within UNESCO Creative Cities (UCC) governance and its implications for the UCC identity and sustainable value creation. Tourism is a sector with an atomised offer.

Book Part 2 is titled *Co-create Tourism Business and Products: Co-entrepreneurs Using Coopetition Strategies*. It is dedicated to the question: How does co-entrepreneurship based on coopetition co-develop value creation in tourism? Part 2 includes four chapters with cases of tourism entrepreneurs' networks and tools that provide operational takeaways of coopetition strategy. Authors from Indonesia, Malaysia, Finland, Brazil and Spain highlighted variables and dimensions that influence the coopetition among tourism firms.

Destinations have many small firms, and coopetition is a strategy that helps them create value and overcome challenges. Chapter 6 uses the institutional analysis and developed (IAD) framework to study the small-scale accommodation in Indonesia and Malaysia. It shows that Small and Medium-sized

Enterprises (SMEs) establish coopetition as a symbiosis relationship towards a win-win condition to guarantee better tourism satisfaction with limited resources. However, the coopetition is mediated by cultural and local rules. Chapter 7 combines coopetition and slow (city) tourism to show how tourism entrepreneurs can rethink local development's value(s). Service agglomerations and shopping centres shared co-location, creating intentional and unintentional coopetition in a singular case characterised as the Santa Claus Village. Complementarily, Chapter 8 analysed, under the coopetition lens, the formal and informal control mechanisms among businesses that contribute to developing tourism destinations as integrated products as co-entrepreneurship. The insights from this chapter provided directions for helping DMOs to manage the coopetition networks at the tourism destinations. The last Chapter of Book Part 2 presents a management tool that considers the tourism destination as a co-entrepreneurship. Chapter 9 provides an aggregate index to measure the coopetition level, a tool named the Local Coopetition Index (i-COOL), which is helpful to destination managers to identify the variables to improve the coopetition strategy efficiency and thus improve the value creation for all stakeholders.

Book Part 3 is *Co-consolidate the Tourism Destination: Endogenous Resources and the Coopetition Behaviour at the Host Society*. Part 3 covers four chapters with essay and cases from the host society as an essential player in the tourism coopetition networks. It focuses on the question: *How does tourism coopetition co-consolidate the value creation from the endogenous resources?* Authors from Brazil, United Kingdom and Portugal provided insights and examples of the interplay among stakeholders to regional destination development based on a coopetition strategy towards social progress.

Chapter 10 pointed out how coopetition can support the transition towards sustainability and, thus, preserve destination resources. The authors examined the potential and practice of coopetition strategies among SMEs in 10 (inter-) national reusable cup-sharing schemes. The chapter provides a conceptual framework for coopetition levels to support organisations in implementing organisational innovations such green solutions. The endogenous resources of a territory generate different industries, and many synergise with tourism, shaping a network of intersectoral local coopetition. One example is the winescape. Wine culture, its rural landscape, resources and firms cooperate with tourism stakeholders. Through the coopetition strategy, they generate value for rural communities, develop tourism destinations and preserve traditions. Chapters 11 and 12 show the coopetitive force of wine tourism. A literature review on the wine tourism ecosystem shows the interplay between the wine industry and wine tourism, highlighting the intentional and unintentional cooperation, associative and cluster effects. Chapter 11 proposes a model capturing coopetition layers in shared wine territories. It is a valuable tool for business and regional governance. In a complementary way, Chapter 12 explores the barriers created by coopetition to wine tourism in the context of preserving the identity of a geographical indication (GI). A longitudinal study over 10 years showed that the coopetition network used barriers to leverage the region's sustainable development, reducing the uncontrolled expansion of the sector to maintain the endogenous resources and local identity, the wine culture. It is another way to create value from coopetition. Finally, Chapter 13 is an essay on coopetition that highlights different types of competitive relationships between adversaries, based on game theory, and evidenced the player's interdependency to remind us that organisations must balance cooperation and competition to thrive in a complex and interconnected global tourism marketplace. Undoubtedly, the set of endogenous resources, players and territory can create value to co-consolidate the tourism destination through coopetition strategies.

Book Part 4 is *Co-promote the Tourism Sector: Including the Visitors in the Coopetition Process to Co-produce the Destination.* It is dedicated to the question: How visitors can co-promote value in tourism destinations through coopetition strategies? Part 4 has four chapters with real cases that illustrate how visitors are coopetition players and cocreators of the tourism destinations and value. Authors from Iran, Portugal and Poland bring studies of the interplay between visitors and tourist destinations towards memorable experiences and the different types of value co-created from coopetition networks.

Residents and tourism are essential players in the coopetition network. They are co-creators of the value of the tourism experience. Chapter 14 shows how the residents' voices, shared knowledge and social media brand engagement improve coopetition among tourism destinations. This study's findings demonstrated how residents are coopetitors that co-promote sustainability and rural destination attractiveness. Also, in the context of rural tourism, Chapter 15 highlighted how residents can co-create experiences with visitors. They can be part of a coopetition strategy to create value. In this chapter, the authors demonstrated that experience co-creation positively impacts visitors' satisfaction. By the coopetition approach, they identified that players in the tourism industry recognised the importance of cooperation in generating competitive advantages aligned with sustainable rural tourism experiences. Chapter 16 explores another side of the social dynamics in the tourism coopetition networks. This chapter analysed a common product in the tourism destination that is a natural coopetition networks: the touristic routes. The authors showed that social relationships affect coopetition among players and help to understand some problems that can hinder or foster value creation. Chapter 17 also concentrates on the role of tourists as co-promoters of tourism destinations but in another way, mediated by technology. The authors indicated how DMOs can analyse tourism consumption to identify the best coopetition network to promote a balanced tourism flow. Chapter 16 analysed visitors' spatiotemporal behaviour using the geotagged data from the Social Media Flickr photos to identify visitors' trajectories and model the changes and trends. Tourists create value through the tourism footprint captured by the coopetition network to promote a sustainable regional tourism destination.

The book closes with a conclusion chapter providing a footprint of tourism coopetition. It presented an overview of the studies scholars have delivered through research on tourism and hospitality sectors focused on coopetition, including the places studied and approaches. This trail of tourism coopetition studies is building an evolutionary path of destination competitiveness towards the tourism destination *coopetitiveness paradigm*.

We extend our heartfelt gratitude to the 37 authors whose contributions have enriched this volume. Many of them are esteemed scholars who have long championed the advancement of coopetition theory, thus playing a pivotal role in shaping its evolution.

References

Brandenburger, A. M., & Nalebuff, B. J. (1996). *Co-opetition: A revolutionary mindset that combines competition and cooperation in the marketplace.* Harvard Business School Press.

Chim-Miki, A. F., & Batista-Canino, R. M. (2017). Tourism coopetition: An introduction to the subject and a research agenda. *International Business Review, 26*(6), 1208–1217.

Chim-Miki, A. F., & Batista-Canino, R. M. (2018). Development of a tourism coopetition model: A preliminary Delphi study. *Journal of Hospitality and Tourism Management, 37*, 78–88.

Chim-Miki, A. F., da Costa, R. A., & Oliveira-Ribeiro, R. (2023). Tourism coopetition for a better world: A cycle of creation, appropriation, and devolution of social value. *Current Issues in Tourism*, 1–15.

Crick, J. M. (2018). Studying coopetition in a wine industry context: Directions for future research. *International Journal of Wine Business Research, 30*(3), 366–371.

Crick, J. M., Karami, M., & Crick, D. (2021). The impact of the interaction between an entrepreneurial marketing orientation and coopetition on business performance. *International Journal of Entrepreneurial Behavior & Research, 27*(6), 1423–1447.

Czakon, W., Klimas, P., & Mariani, M. (2020). Behavioral antecedents of coopetition: A synthesis and measurement scale. *Long Range Planning, 53*(1), 101875.

Monticelli, J. M., Garrido, I. L., Vieira, L. M., Chim-Miki, A. F., & Carneiro, J. (2022). Can competitors cooperate? The impact of formal institution agents in promoting coopetition among emerging market exporters. *Journal of Business & Industrial Marketing, 37*(9), 1915–1932.

Volschenk, J., Ungerer, M., & Smit, E. (2016). Creation and appropriation of socio-environmental value in coopetition. *Industrial Marketing Management, 57*, 109–118.

Part One

Co-boost the Tourism Destination: Public Policies to Foster Coopetition Networks

Chapter 2

A Roadmap to Build Tourism Coopetition: Oneway to Coopetitiveness

Adriana Fumi Chim-Miki[a] and *Rui Augusto da Costa*[b]

[a]Federal University of Campina Grande, Brazil
[b]University of Aveiro, Portugal

Abstract

The chapter constitutes a conceptual paper aimed at furnishing a roadmap for the implementation of a coopetition strategy within tourism destinations. This endeavour was prompted by numerous inquiries from industry practitioners seeking guidance on integrating coopetition into their operations. The roadmap delineates six sequential steps for establishing a robust coopetition network, complemented by a toolkit designed to oversee the implementation process and its ensuing outcomes. Key components of this toolkit include the Coopetition Value Proposition, Coopetition Players Mapping and the Coopetition Toolbox, each serving as indispensable resources for navigating the intricacies of coopetition strategy in the tourism sector. In amalgamating theoretical insights with practical applications, our approach not only deepens comprehension of coopetition within the context of strategic management but also equips stakeholders with the requisite tools to harness coopetition's potential for generating social, economic and environmental value. Furthermore, our methodology transcends the boundaries of the tourism industry, offering a versatile framework adaptable to diverse sectors. Through this concerted effort, we endeavour to facilitate the transition of tourism destinations towards the coopetitiveness paradigm, wherein collaboration and competition intertwine to propel sustainable growth and innovation. Ultimately, our chapter serves as a guiding beacon for tourism stakeholders, offering a structured pathway towards embracing coopetition as a cornerstone of strategic management, thus fostering prosperity and resilience amidst evolving market dynamics.

Keywords: Tourism coopetition; coopetition journey map; coopetition roadmap; strategic management; tourism networks

Value Proposition to Tourism Coopetition, 11–24
Copyright © 2025 Adriana Fumi Chim-Miki and Rui Augusto da Costa
Published under exclusive licence by Emerald Publishing Limited
doi:10.1108/978-1-83797-827-420241002

Introduction

Coopetition is a growing subarea of the strategy as it expresses the dynamics of current markets, in which relationships present a hybrid behaviour of cooperation and competition simultaneously (Chim-Miki et al., 2023). The theoretical roots of coopetition originate from several consolidated strategic management theories (Klimas et al., 2023). However, in recent decades, studies in different sectors have brought theoretical and empirical implications outlining a theoretical body to support this construct as a current paradigm. Specifically in tourism, coopetition *was defined as a dyadic behaviour of cooperation and competition simultaneously, which occurs between two or more tourism actors in a destination, to promote their development as an integral product* (Chim-Miki & Batista-Canino, 2017, p. 384). The tourism destination is a network that integrates multiple players distributed across several subnets, comprising a mosaic of multilevel coopetition. The type of participants and their positions in the tourism value chain defines the configurations of coopetition networks, which can be horizontal, vertical or mixed (Bengtsson & Kock, 2014). The network configuration can also reach individual, intra-organisational, inter-organisational or inter-network levels (Rusko, 2018).

The motivation for coopetition generally comes from the outputs, the shared goal. In tourism, scholars indicate coopetition networks for innovation (Yavuz & Çemberci, 2022), governance (Damayanti et al., 2019), co-marketing (Wang & Krakover, 2008), management of shared resources (Czernek & Czakon, 2016; Kylänen & Rusko, 2011) or synergy between industries, for example, the wine industry and tourism (Crick, 2018), and others. The literature offers several models of tourism coopetition, validating this strategy's outputs, elements and characteristics (e.g. Chim-Miki & Batista-Canino, 2018; Della Corte & Aria, 2016; Kylänen & Rusko, 2011). As coopetition scholars, we are on the road towards consolidating this paradigm. However, as managers, we still feel a certain degree of abstraction. Questions arise, such as: Who should be the players in the coopetition network? Where do I start implementing the coopetition strategy? How do we guarantee and monitor the effects of coopetition? These questions and others have arisen in many conferences about coopetition in tourism that we delivered in recent years. These questions motivated us to dedicate this chapter to providing a perspective from theory to practice of how coopetition can materialise as a strategic management and tool.

The chapter is a conceptual paper that aims to provide a roadmap for implementing a coopetition strategy at the tourism destination. We offered six steps to build a coopetition network and a toolkit to manage the implementation and its outcomes: the Coopetition Value Proposition, the Coopetition Players Mapping and the Coopetition Toolbox. Despite focusing on the toolkit, the chapter has theoretical and practical implications. It builds coopetition as a sub-area of strategic management in tourism. Our roadmap highlighted the power of coopetition to create social, economic and environmental value. We are helping the transition of tourism competitiveness to tourism coopetitiveness, a new paradigm.

Why Using Strategic Management Based on Coopetition?

Coopetition has exceeded its initial limits, which defined it as cooperating with competitors. The concept's expansion comes from the understanding that there is competition for different benefits in most relationships but varies according to the objectives and players. If some cooperation also occurs in this relationship, coopetition is configured. Therefore, different dynamics and players may be involved, whether they are direct competitors in the market or not. For firms and tourism destinations, coopetition can generate diverse competitive advantages (Köseoğlu et al., 2019). In this sense, Cygler et al. (2014) highlighted that the greater the number of networks the firm participates in, the greater its chances of survival.

In tourism, there are three main reasons to conduct strategic management based on coopetition. Firstly, coopetition is an intrinsic, emerging and fundamental strategy (Chim-Miki & Batista-Canino, 2017; Czernek-Marszałek, 2018). The tourism destination comprises several small businesses, requiring different activities and sectors that are often complementary. The interdependence among players in the tourism destination includes the public and private sectors and the society (Oliveira-Ribeiro et al., 2022). Therefore, the tourism destination facilitates coopetition behaviour. However, the coopetition must be intentional and planned to move from natural and emergent behaviour to strategy. Second, besides the complementarity and interdependence among players to create an integrated tourism offer, tourism often have synergy with other industries. For example, to create Wine tourism, Olive tourism, Creative tourism, Industrial tourism, etc. These synergies conducted under the coopetition strategy can generate better outcomes (Crick, 2018). Third, tourism development is usually conducted through destination management organisations (DMOs) and governmental agencies, and the tourism destination has various business associations. These organisations bring together stakeholders to participatory management models, provide the integration of players and search to guarantee positive outcomes for firms, governments and society. In other words, DMOs and business associations become hubs of tourist coopetition (Chim-Miki et al., 2024).

Building Coopetition Tourism Destinations: Roadmap and Tools

According to Grängsjö (2003), destination development depends on whether tourism actors work with or against one another. Indeed, the best way is to mix these behaviours, creating coopetition strategies since they contribute to higher competitiveness (Grauslund & Hammershøy, 2021). Coopetition can be an intrinsic behaviour in a tourism destination, but it needs to be planned to achieve a strategy's status and guarantee positive outputs. Despite DMOs and tourism associations being the hubs of coopetition (Chim-Miki et al., 2024), engaging players in the coopetition strategy is challenging for destination managers. Scholars indicated some conditions to foster the coopetition networks, such as previous experiences of managers on cooperation projects (Czakon et al., 2020), mutual trust (Czernek-Marszałek, 2018), partners with complementarity and interdependency level (Chim-Miki et al., 2017), networks with rules and objectives defined (Damayanti et al., 2017), the value perceived (Almeida et al., 2023), minimisation of risks (Monticelli et al., 2022), etc. Considering the literature indications, we propose a roadmap with six steps for a tourism destination to create and implement a coopetition strategy. The steps are associated with a toolkit to assist the coopetition development (Table 2.1).

The tourism destination is an ecosystem formed by multiple coopetition networks cooperating and competing simultaneously. Many of these networks are led by tourism associations, making the destination a system of multi-level mediated coopetition (Chim-Miki et al., 2024). A strategic fit within and between networks is necessary to foster cooperation (Czakon et al., 2020). Tourism destination development is the core shared objective among stakeholders, but more is needed to consolidate the coopetition network. Therefore, to improve the willingness to coopetition, it is recommended to establish specific

Table 2.1. Roadmap to Building Tourism Coopetition.

Step	Coopetition Toolkit
(1) Identify a shared goal towards a problem solution as a common objective to achieve. Identify the competitive advantage associated with this shared goal at the different levels: Firms, public government, destination (city) and society (residents).	Coopetition value proposition
(2) Identify the interest groups impacted by the process (firms, employees, institutions, clients, suppliers, distributors, community, etc)	Coopetition players mapping
(3) Understand and outline current interactions between interest groups. Identify the players essential in overcoming the liability of newness and proposing a shared vision in the early stage.	
(4) Organise workshops where interest groups share experiences, imagine opportunities for improvement and design the network rules.	
(5) Co-build platforms or schemes for implementing the ideas and allow new interactions.	Coopetition toolbox
(6) Co-define the ways to follow-up the payoffs. Establish the milestones, timeline and KPI of the network.	

common objectives by generating different coopetitive networks (Chim-Miki et al., 2024). This way, the strategic fit grows, the definition of ideal partners is much more straightforward and strategies co-create. We create a set of toolkits to assist the manager, and players understand why coopetition is essential and how to promote the interplay at the tourism destination.

Creating the Coopetition Value Proposition

Coopetition involves a cycle of cooperation in a network to create value and competition to absorb the collective value created by the network. This cycle in the business context is known as the value creation and appropriation cycle (Ritala & Tidström, 2014). The expansion of this cycle to reach levels of creation-appropriation-return of value to society was identified in social business coopetition networks (Nascimento et al., 2023), in sustainable tourism (Nguyen et al., 2022) and tourism destinations focused on development centred in society (Chim-Miki et al., 2023). This line of studies demonstrated that tourism coopetition networks can create economic and socio-environmental value (Volschenk et al., 2016).

That means the value created from coopetition in tourism can go beyond creating a competitive advantage for firms, generating benefits for all stakeholders. To achieve this collective outcome is necessary to plan the coopetition strategy focusing on the value proposition. In this sense, step 1 of the roadmap into tourism coopetition represents the kick-off of the coopetition strategy. To support Step 1, we developed the Coopetition Value Proposition toolkit (Fig. 2.1). It is a framework for identifying what problem will be addressed by coopetition, what collective value the network will generate and how far the benefits can be

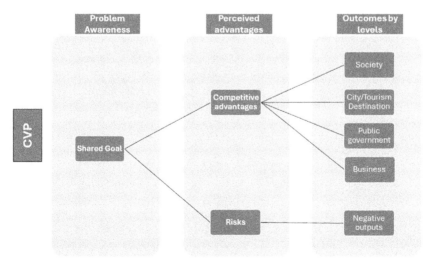

Fig. 2.1.   Coopetition Value Proposition (CVP).

captured among stakeholders. Having a clear shared goal towards a problem solution as a common objective in the network improves the player's engagement in the coopetition. Also, it improves the perceived advantage among players, that is, identifies the competitive advantage associated with this shared goal at the different levels: firms, public government, destination (city) and society (residents). According to Czakon (2018), there is a value creation potential at the core of coopetition network; however, to achieve it, the players need to understand the value net scope, the challenges and the shared value generation and capture.

Designing the Coopetition Network: The Coopetition Players Mapping

Coopetition networks go beyond cooperating with competitors. Czakon (2018) underlines that the more players in the value network, the more value can be created. However, to guarantee coopetition results for the destination and the partners, it is essential to establish the connection among players, common goals and payoffs (Czakon et al., 2020). That means choosing the adequate configuration for the coopetition network (Temel et al., 2023). The literature points out some network configurations, for instance, vertical – among complementary and suppliers firms; horizontal – among direct competitors or firms that offer substitute products and services; or mixed networks – that include competitors, complementary firms, suppliers and supportive organisations (Oliveira-Ribeiro et al., 2022).

Some scholars argue the importance of identifying the adequate composition of the coopetition network since diversifying the objectives and the type of partners can reduce the outputs because it increases the network complexity (Temel et al., 2023). Other scholars pointed out that some network configurations can produce better results. For instance, Feng and Sivakumar (2016) claimed that vertical and third-party collaborations are more beneficial than horizontal collaboration in the services industry. However, mixed networks, with partners of different activities or sectors, are necessary for developing the tourism destination. It can hinder the coopetition strategy implementation. To overcome this obstacle, finding the ideal number and profile of partners according to aligned interests is needed. That is, to guarantee a strategic fit (Czakon et al., 2020).

Thus, Steps 2 and 3 are towards identifying the different groups impacted by the coopetition and what is the interplay among them. Therefore, Step 2 determines the interest groups to be included in the coopetition network, for example, the firms, employees, institutions, clients, suppliers, distributors, community, etc. Step 3 maps the interactions between interest groups: how they can co-create value, what type of value they co-create, which ways to co-develop the value and why they co-produce value. That mapping of the tourism coopetition dynamics helps identify the essential players to guarantee an adequate network structure to the network goals and, thus, the strategic fit. We developed the Coopetition Players Mapping toolkit (Fig. 2.2) to support the implementation of Steps 2 and 3 in creating a tourism coopetition network. The Coopetition Players Mapping is a diagram to identify the central players related to the goal defined in the

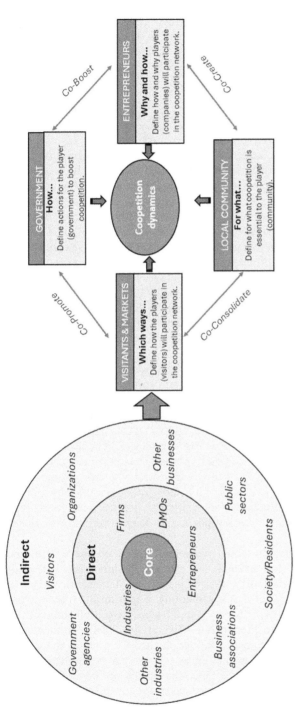

Fig. 2.2.   Coopetition Players Mapping (CPM).

Coopetition Value proposition and who are the direct and indirect players in the tourism ecosystem related to the value proposition. In sequence, this toolkit helps map how the interplay among them can co-create value, co-promote, co-consolidate and co-boost tourism development at the destination.

Co-build Tourism Coopetition Schemes: The Coopetition Toolbox

At this point, we have the definition of a value proposition and players for the coopetition networks. In the sequence, planning and running the coopetition strategy is necessary. Bengtsson et al. (2010) claimed that coopetition can be a context, process or result. However, coopetition is a loop of context, process and result in the tourism destination. It is a natural context for coopetition due to the interdependency and complementarity of businesses, institutions and society in creating a tourism destination. Also, it is a process since coopetition is a basic strategy in the tourism sector that usually operates in cooperative-competition networks. The development of the tourism sector results from a coopetition strategy that produces various competitive advantages for the destination and its stakeholders. Therefore, Steps 4–6 build this coopetition loop. To support these steps, we developed the toolkit named Coopetition Toolbox (Fig. 2.3), which provides a scheme to manage the implementation of strategic coopetition in tourism destinations, considering it as a context, process and result in the logic of project management.

In Step 4, on the Coopetition Player's Mapping results, workshops should be organised among the interest groups to provide a forum to share experiences, imagine opportunities for improvements of the tourism destination and co-design the network rules. Coopetition is working together with competitors; that is, there is intrinsic tension and risks (Kylänen & Rusko, 2011). One dark side of coopetition is opportunism, risks such as knowledge overlap and conflicts of interest among stakeholders (Yu, 2019); sometimes, intrinsic tension reduces coopetition outcomes (Kylänen & Rusko, 2011). Thus, it is necessary to create some mechanisms to minimise the risks and tensions. Establishing clear rules for participating in the network, defining individual objectives and tasks and formalising agreements are recommended to consolidate the coopetition strategy in the tourism destination.

Also, the network structure should be defined based on the Coopetition Player's Mapping results. For example, in tourism, business associations or DMOs can be the central hub of networks and players, mediating tensions among players and between tourism subnets and promoting fit adjustments. This network architecture promotes Mediated coopetition and fosters the consolidation of this strategy in the tourism destination (Chim-Miki et al., 2024). This network architecture is typical in destinations with consolidated Convention Bureaus or a strong business association. Other times, many subnets can shape the structure without a central hub. This network architecture usually occurs in destinations with various active business associations, such as hotel associations, travel agencies associations, tour guide cooperatives, etc. Another usual configuration

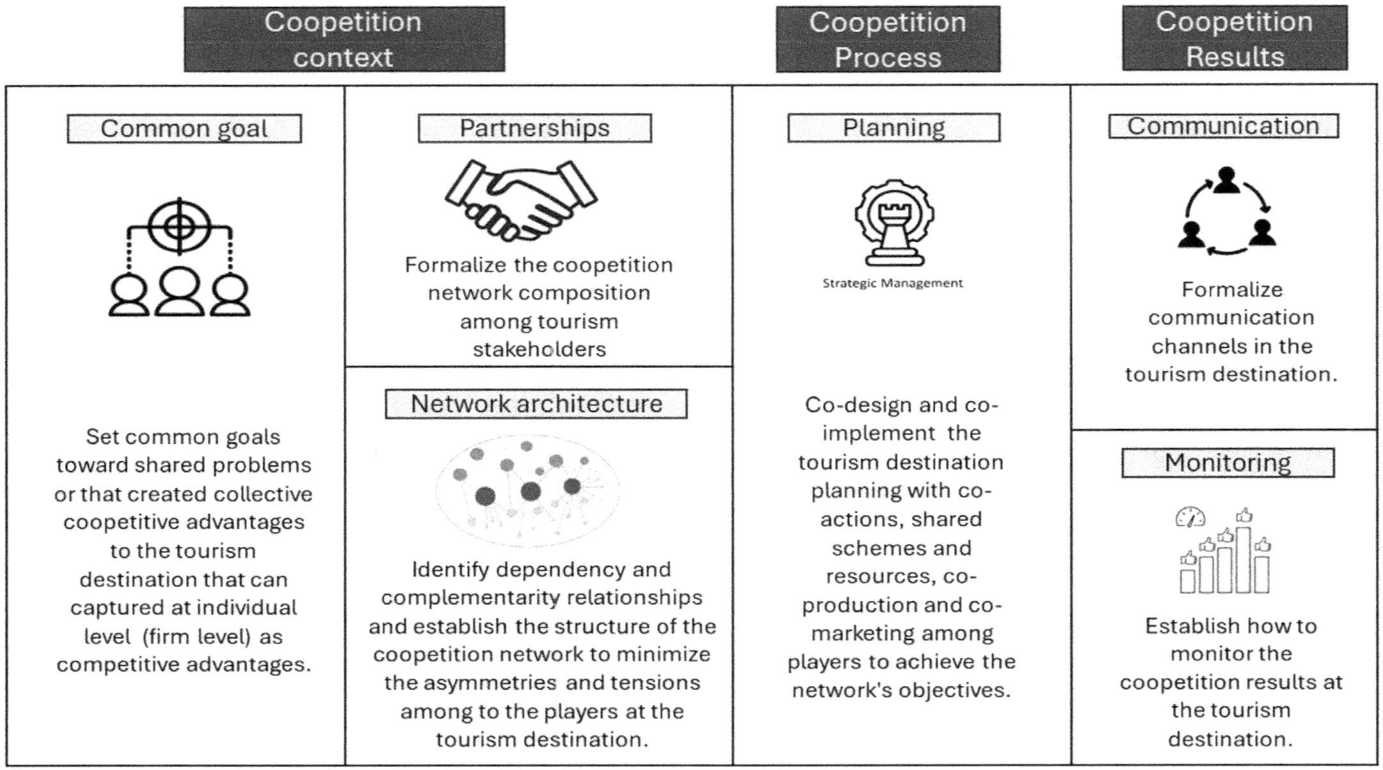

Fig. 2.3. Coopetition Toolbox (CTB).

occurs when the destination highly depends on a specific tourism attractive or firm. The network tends to be shaped around these players. Despite the existence of a hub, it is not a mediated coopetition; it is a hierarchical coopetition. Different network architectures can be established; the choice depends on the tourism destination configuration, coopetition objectives, potential players and the dynamics among them.

Co-create tourism products and experiences, innovations, events, attractiveness and social solutions from tourism development is co-planning and co-design in Step 5 from the Coopetition Value Proposition results. In Step 5, the shared goal of the value proposition should be divided into specific objectives, and potential players will co-create the coopetition strategy, that is, different shared schemes that can be implemented to achieve the value proposition. Also, the partners should co-build platforms or ways, technological or non-technological, to implement the co-marketing, ideas, and allow new interactions. Different shared schemes can co-exist using subnets to co-produce and co-boost coopetition results. For example, creating an integrative tourism circuit among small cities in the region to boost staycation can generate a coopetition network with economic and social value creation for firms, destinations, and residents during the low season. Staycation is characterized by residents' trips around 80 miles from home during the vacations. Another example is a shared scheme to improve the workability of residents in the tourism sector in which schools and universities supported by governments and local firms created special programs to provide tourism skills. Foz do Iguaçu destination, in Brazil, created an example of this. The shared scheme of this destination was named 'Youth Trail' because it was directed at the social problem of reducing poverty among young people of low-income families. The shared scheme was associated with a tourism skill programme course, internships in local firms and the possibility of keeping a job there (Chim-Miki et al., 2016).

Finally, in Step 6, it is necessary to create methods to monitor the coopetition results. Thus, the players should co-define the ways to follow up the payoffs. The specific objectives can be distributed in a timeline and linked to the network's milestones and key performance indicators (KPIs). The organisation of Step 6 follows the project management structure. Each partner needs to understand their role in the results. The objectives should be divided into tasks assigned to the players or group of players. Coopetition in tourism is an independent and complementary network; therefore, the outputs feedback the process. Despite coopetition being a long-term and permanent strategy at the destination, it should be conducted through many undertakings with timelines. It improves how the players perceive the advantages and produces various cycles of creation-appropriation-social value devolution from tourism. Engagement is enhanced if the players obtain payoffs. The KPIs depend on the Coopetition value Proposition and players in the networks. For instance, it can be an increase in the percentage of market share, the launching of new tourism products, an increase in tourist spending at the destination, the creation of tourism infrastructure, the participation of small businesses, social empowerment, etc. The indicators should express the creation of the collective value and the appropriation of value at the individual level by the stakeholders in the network and the host society. Another essential issue is establishing ways to flow communication inside the network, through the network and by the network. Better communication promotes coopetition results, stimulates engagement, the flow of ideas and ways to dialogue. Canals should be created to communicate with partners, DMO managers, public government, entrepreneurs, tourists and host society. Coopetition is co-creation. Thus, communication among players inside and outside of the network is needed.

Conclusion

This chapter provided a roadmap for implementing a coopetition strategy at the tourism destination to generate *coopetitiveness*. There is a consensus in the literature that coopetition is an intrinsic behaviour in tourist destinations. However, destinations must go beyond emergent behaviour and transform it into a planned strategy to ensure better results for the destination and its stakeholders. Coopetition is the current paradigm driving the transition from the Porter era of competitiveness models to the era of *Coopetitiveness* Models (Chim-Miki & Batista-Canino, 2018).

Tourism coopetitiveness is the ability to generate co-value in the tourism destination through a joint action that optimises the use of resources based on a coopetition strategy that manages the destination as a tourism co-entrepreneurship towards a shared goal generating co-production, tourism attractiveness and social and economic and environmental benefits.

This chapter designed six steps supported by a toolkit to manage the implementation and its outcomes. It is a roadmap to create networks focused on coopetition strategy for tourism destinations that can be used by the DMOs, tourism associations, public government or groups of tourism stakeholders. The first tool is the Coopetition Value Proposition (CVP), which outlines the coopetition mindset. It directs the efforts towards problem-solving thinking based on coopetition and clarifies the payoffs to each group of stakeholders. Then, CVP acts on important variables pointed out by the literature as motivators of coopetition: the perceived advantage (Almeida et al., 2023), shared goal (Oliveira-Ribeiro et al., 2022), competitive advantages (Czakon et al., 2020) and outcomes to society, firms, public government and the tourism destinations. As Volschenk et al. (2016) has named it, the outcomes can be the public and private value from coopetition. Also, the CVP leads to thinking about the risks and possible negative outputs from coopetition, which can be minimised or prevented while implementing the coopetition strategy. In Game Theory, the payoff defines the cost-benefit of each strategy. Therefore, it is essential to identify the positive and negative outcomes of the competition value Proposition.

The second tool is the Coopetition Players Mapping (CPM), which identifies the potential and more adequate participants for the competition stakeholders. It needs to be aligned with the value proposition; there is the network objective. As indicated in the literature, the suitable network composition improves the outcomes and facilitates the fit adjustment (Czakon, 2018). Also, there are core players that can act as hubs of coopetition (Chim-Miki et al., 2024). Direct and indirect players create a coopetition dynamic to create value in the destination. Understanding these dynamics and players provides an overview of the opportunities and ways to create social, economic and environmental value for the destination and its stakeholders.

The third tool is the Coopetition Toolbox (CTB), which makes the coopetition strategy more tangible to the managers. It synthesises the steps to plan and implement shared schemes towards the coopetition value proposition with the mapped players. The setting indicates core aspects to plan the coopetition considering the context, process and results. It outlines the importance of dividing the shared goals into tasks, formalising the partnerships, defining the network architecture, co-design shared schemes to implement in the tourism destination, provide communication channels and ways to measure the coopetition results.

This roadmap and its toolkits were developed to bring coopetition from the theory to the practice in tourism destinations. We look to respond to the most frequent question that we listen to during our conferences with tourism practitioners: How should I start the coopetition? How can I develop the coopetition strategy? How can I engage the stakeholders? How can I make work the coopetition in the tourism destination?

Despite the chapter's practical approach, the coopetition toolkit has a theoretical implication. Tourism and management are applied social sciences, and theoretical assumptions must be the background to managerial implications. Theoretically, our roadmap highlighted the power of coopetition to create social, economic and environmental value. We are helping to build the tourism coopetitiveness, a new paradigm. For academic research, our approach helps analyse the maturity level of coopetition in the networks and perform case studies. It is important to note that we focused on tourism destinations; nevertheless, our approach is helpful to any industry.

We invite scholars and practitioners to apply the Coopetition roadmap using this baseline toolkit in different tourism destinations and modalities, creating improvements to support the destinations' transition from competitiveness to *coopetitiveness*. Thus, it is a way to promote society-centred tourism development by generating coopetitive advantages that improve the creation of value from tourism, which covers economic, social, cultural and environmental value at both levels, public and private.

References

Almeida, S., Morgado, P. S., Costa, C., Simões, J. M., & Seabra, C. (2023). Revealing cooperative behaviour arrangements within hotel marketing consortia. *Tourism Management Perspectives, 46*, 101089. https://doi.org/10.1016/j.tmp.2023.101089

Bengtsson, M., Eriksson, J., & Wincent, J. (2010). Co-opetition dynamics – an outline for further inquiry. *Competitiveness Review: An International Business Journal, 20*(2), 194–214. https://doi.org/10.1108/10595421011029893

Bengtsson, M., & Kock, S. (2014). Coopetition—Quo vadis? Past accomplishments and future challenges. *Industrial Marketing Management, 43*(2), 180–188. https://doi.org/10.1016/j.indmarman.2014.02.015

Chim-Miki, A. F., & Batista-Canino, R. M. (2017). Tourism coopetition: An introduction to the subject and a research agenda. *International Business Review, 26*(6), 1208–1217. https://doi.org/10.1016/j.ibusrev.2017.05.003

Chim-Miki, A. F., & Batista-Canino, R. M. (2018). Development of a tourism coopetition model: A preliminary Delphi study. *Journal of Hospitality and Tourism Management, 37,* 78–88. https://doi.org/10.1016/j.jhtm.2018.10.004

Chim-Miki, A. F., Batista-Canino, R. M., & Medina-Brito, P. (2016). Coopetición en un destino turístico de frontera entre Argentina, Brasil y Paraguay: el caso Poloiguassu. *Semestre Económico, 19*(40), 145–174. https://doi.org/10.22395/seec. v19n40a6

Chim-Miki, A. F., da Costa, R. A., & Okumus, F. (2024). Investigating the strategic role of business associations in willingness toward tourism coopetition. *Current Issues in Tourism,* (1–18). https://doi.org/10.1080/13683500.2024.2333910

Chim-Miki, A. F., da Costa, R. A., & Oliveira-Ribeiro, R. (2023). Tourism coopetition for a better world: A cycle of creation, appropriation, and devolution of social value. *Current Issues in Tourism,* 1–15. https://doi.org/10.1080/13683500. 2023.2254448

Crick, J. M. (2018). Studying coopetition in a wine industry context: Directions for future research. *International Journal of Wine Business Research, 30*(3), 366–371. https://doi.org/10.1108/IJWBR-11-2017-0067

Cygler, J., Gajdzik, B., & Sroka, W. (2014). Coopetition as a development stimulator of enterprises in the networked steel sector. *Metalurgija, 53*(3), 383–386.

Czakon, W. (2018). Network coopetition. In *Routledge companion to coopetition strategies* (pp. 47–57). Routledge.

Czakon, W., Klimas, P., & Mariani, M. (2020). Behavioral antecedents of coopetition: A synthesis and measurement scale. *Long Range Planning, 53*(1), 101875. https:// doi.org/10.1016/j.lrp.2019.03.001

Czernek, K., & Czakon, W. (2016). Trust-building processes in tourist coopetition: The case of a Polish region. *Tourism Management, 52,* 380–394. https://doi.org/10. 1016/j.tourman.2015.07.009

Czernek-Marszałek, K. (2018). Cooperation evaluation with the use of network analysis. *Annals of Tourism Research, 72,* 126–139. https://doi.org/10.1016/j.annals. 2018.07.005

Damayanti, M., Scott, N., & Ruhanen, L. (2017). Coopetitive behaviours in an informal tourism economy. *Annals of Tourism Research, 65,* 25–35. https://doi.org/ 10.1016/j.annals.2017.04.007

Damayanti, M., Scott, N., & Ruhanen, L. (2019). Coopetition for tourism destination policy and governance: The century of local power?. In *The future of tourism: Innovation and sustainability* (pp. 285–299).

Della Corte, V., & Aria, M. (2016). Coopetition and sustainable competitive advantage. The case of tourist destinations. *Tourism Management, 54,* 524–540. https:// doi.org/10.1016/j.tourman.2015.12.009

Feng, C., & Sivakumar, K. (2016). The role of collaboration in service innovation across manufacturing and service sectors. *Service Science, 8*(3), 263–281. https:// doi.org/10.1287/serv.2016.0135

Grängsjö, Y. I. F. (2003). Destination networking: Co-opetition in peripheral surroundings. *International Journal of Physical Distribution & Logistics Management, 33*(5), 427–448. https://doi.org/10.1108/09600030310481997

Grauslund, D., & Hammershøy, A. (2021). Patterns of network coopetition in a merged tourism destination. *Scandinavian Journal of Hospitality and Tourism, 21*(2), 192–211. https://doi.org/10.1080/15022250.2021.1877192

Klimas, P., Ahmadian, A. A., Soltani, M., Shahbazi, M., & Hamidizadeh, A. (2023). Coopetition, where do you come from? Identification, categorization, and configuration of theoretical roots of Coopetition. *Sage Open, 13*(1), 21582440221085003. https://doi.org/10.1177/215824402210850

Köseoğlu, M. A., Yildiz, M., Okumus, F., & Barca, M. (2019). The intellectual structure of coopetition: Past, present and future. *Journal of Strategy and Management, 12*(1), 2–29. https://doi.org/10.1108/JSMA-07-2018-0073

Kylänen, M., & Rusko, R. (2011). Unintentional coopetition in the service industries: The case of Pyhä-Luosto tourism destination in the Finnish Lapland. *European Management Journal, 29*(3), 193-205. https://doi.org/10.1016/j.emj.2010.10.006

Monticelli, J. M., Garrido, I. L., Vieira, L. M., Chim-Miki, A. F., & Carneiro, J. (2022). Can competitors cooperate? The impact of formal institution agents in promoting coopetition among emerging market exporters. *Journal of Business & Industrial Marketing, 37*(9), 1915–1932. https://doi.org/10.1108/JBIM-10-2020-0482

Nascimento, L. D. S., da Costa Júnior, J. C., Salazar, V. S., & Chim-Miki, A. F. (2023). Coopetition in social entrepreneurship: A strategy for social value devolution. *International Journal of Emerging Markets, 18*(9), 2176–2197. https://doi.org/10.1108/IJOEM-09-2020-1062

Nguyen, T. Q. T., Johnson, P., & Young, T. (2022). Networking, coopetition and sustainability of tourism destinations. *Journal of Hospitality and Tourism Management, 50*, 400–411. https://doi.org/10.1016/j.jhtm.2022.01.003

Oliveira-Ribeiro, R., Chim-Miki, A. F., & de Araújo Machado, P. (2022). Coopetition at society level: A scale validation. *International Journal of Business Administration, 13*(4), 19–37. https://doi.org/10.5430/ijba.v13n4p19

Ritala, P., & Tidström, A. (2014). Untangling the value-creation and value-appropriation elements of coopetition strategy: A longitudinal analysis on the firm and relational levels. *Scandinavian Journal of Management, 30*(4), 498–515. https://doi.org/10.1016/j.scaman.2014.05.002

Rusko, R. (2018). Coopetition for destination marketing: The scope of forging relationships with competitors. In *Tourism planning and destination marketing* (pp. 75–98). Emerald Publishing Limited.

Temel, S., Mention, A. L., & Yurtseven, A. E. (2023). Cooperation for innovation: More is not necessarily merrier. *European Journal of Innovation Management, 26*(2), 446–474. https://doi.org/10.1108/EJIM-10-2020-0392

Volschenk, J., Ungerer, M., & Smit, E. (2016). Creation and appropriation of socio-environmental value in coopetition. *Industrial Marketing Management, 57*, 109–118. https://doi.org/10.1016/j.indmarman.2016.05.026

Wang, Y., & Krakover, S. (2008). Destination marketing: Competition, cooperation or coopetition?. *International Journal of Contemporary Hospitality Management, 20*(2), 126–141. https://doi.org/10.1108/09596110810852122

Yavuz, F., & Çemberci, M. (2022). The moderator role of trust in the relationship between coopetition and incremental innovation: Evidence from tourism industry. *Geo Journal of Tourism and Geosites, 44*(4), 1292–1299. https://doi.org/10.30892/gtg.44413-945

Yu, P. L. (2019). Interfirm coopetition, trust, and opportunism: A mediated moderation model. *Review of Managerial Science, 13*(5), 1069–1092. https://doi.org/10.1007/s11846-018-0279-y

Chapter 3

Cross-border Tourism Coopetition Among European Countries: Insights From the Travel and Tourism Development Index

Petra Vašaničová

University of Presov, Slovakia

Abstract

Coopetition is a phenomenon characterised by the simultaneous presence of cooperation and competition within a networked relationship. The current body of literature provides real instances of coopetitive networks within the tourism sector. Conversely, many countries possess the potential to initiate new examples. This research aims to identify European countries that are externally heterogeneous but internally homogeneous and thus point out competing countries that could cooperate in the tourism sector. This study contributes to the literature on cross-border tourism coopetition from a theoretical perspective of possible cooperation among 32 competing European countries using existing secondary data from the Travel and Tourism Development Index (TTDI). The results of cluster analysis show a six-group solution. Although there are many challenges and issues, the positive outlook lies in the potential for coopetition among analysed countries, which could contribute to regional tourism growth. This study proposes several recommendations essential to cross-border tourism coopetition.

Keywords: Tourism; coopetition; competitiveness; travel and tourism development index; cross-border coopetition

Introduction

Coopetition refers to a behaviour that gives rise to a networked connection in which both collaboration and competition exist simultaneously (Chim-Miki & Batista-Canino, 2017b). It occurs within a framework where diverse resources

Value Proposition to Tourism Coopetition, 25–39

Copyright © 2025 Petra Vašaničová

Published under exclusive licence by Emerald Publishing Limited

doi:10.1108/978-1-83797-827-420241003

complement each other in the coopetition network (Lorgnier & Su, 2017). Coopetition can potentially reduce competition-related risks through the advantages of cooperation (Chim-Miki & Batista-Canino, 2017a). A tourism destination has many characteristics mentioned in the literature that favour fostering coopetition partnerships (Della Corte & Sciarelli, 2012). Chim-Miki and Batista-Canino (2017a) emphasised interdependence, complementarity, common goals and co-location.

Individual countries are usually considered to be separate tourism destinations that compete with each other. However, there is a possibility of connecting two or more countries and creating a more important tourism destination to increase international success. The main motivations of countries to develop tourism can differ depending on the economic, strategic, social and legal goals that are given by the overall functioning of a country. Coopetition can help overcome various economic, technological and other changes resulting from future trends and existing, identifiable determinants of tourism development. Encouraging cooperation between countries could prevent the loss of valuable resources in times of crisis and strengthen regional and local social and economic systems. Existing literature mentioned real examples of coopetitive networks in tourism; on the other hand, many countries have the potential to create new coopetitive networks. The question is, which competitors could cooperate? One approach is to determine this based on secondary tourism competitiveness and development data.

Our research aims to identify European countries that are externally heterogeneous but internally homogeneous, and thus point out competing countries that could cooperate in the tourism sector. This chapter provides valuable insights into the theoretical concept of coopetition among 32 European countries, as it exists for this region. Therefore, the chapter provides valuable insights into networks among countries generating, theoretical and managerial implications for coopetition at an understudied level: the macro level. It explores the possibilities of configuration coopetition networks among the 32 European countries.

Literature Review

Historically, global borders have been viewed as obstacles, but they also present opportunities for cross-border cooperation and advancement in border landscapes (Timothy et al., 2016). Tourism has been known for influencing alterations in the geopolitical dynamics of nations by fostering cross-border cooperation, shared infrastructure and even exchanges in sovereign territory (Timothy et al., 2014).

Numerous factors contribute to the diversification in tourism, encompassing both horizontal distinctions, based on attributes, and vertical distinctions, based on quality. Firstly, geographic location can be seen as a source of inherent horizontal diversity. When a location is linked to natural and cultural/historical features, two distinct destinations must be acknowledged as separate tourism products with unique attributes. It increases the probability of two-way trade in international tourism services. Governments can enhance this type of diversification by developing tourism resources that are not strictly tied to location. These resources could include special events, a wide array of available activities, entertainment options and shopping opportunities (Nowak et al., 2012). Secondly, in tourism, vertical diversification may hold greater significance than horizontal diversification. Empirical studies have highlighted the strategic importance of quality and innovation in determining the appeal of a particular tourism destination (Cracolici & Nijkamp, 2009).

Regional tourism integration within the European Union enhances economic ties in the tourism sector and optimises the network structure. This optimisation of the tourism economic connection network fosters advancements in the level of tourism integration (Xie et al., 2021). Existing studies deal with real examples of coopetitive tourism networks, for example, Iguassu (Brazil, Argentine, Paraguay) (Chim-Miki & Batista-Canino, 2017a), Shrines of Europe (France, Portugal, Poland, Italy, Austria, Germany) (Stefko & Nowak, 2014), European Quartet – One Melody (Visegrad group countries) (Vasanicova et al., 2022), Central European Region initiative (Austria, Slovakia, Czechia, Hungary) (Finka et al., 2020), Bayerischer Wald/Šumava (Germany and Czechia) (Mayer et al., 2019), Bothnian Arc (Baltic Sea Region – Sweden and Finland) (Ioannides et al., 2006), the Culturally Sensitive Tourism in the Arctic – ARCTISEN (Canada, Denmark, Finland, Greenland, New Zealand, Norway and Sweden) (Olsen et al., 2019), Nordic Region (Timothy et al., 2016), Cross-border Programme Macedonia – Albania (Seferaj, 2014), Eastern Partnership Territorial Cooperation Programs (Romania, Moldova, Ukraine) (Sokolovskyy, 2022), many cooperation projects co-financed by Interreg (Durand, 2022; Mayer et al., 2019).

Scholarly research has examined the phenomenon of cross-border cooperation (or collaboration) among countries (Durand, 2014; Durand, 2022; Kropinova, 2020; Kropinova, 2021; Lovelock & Boyd, 2006; Mayer et al., 2019; Nezirović et al., 2016; Seferaj, 2014; Sokolovskyy, 2022; Stoffelen et al., 2017; Timothy & Saarinen, 2013; Şlusarciuc & Tokar, 2021). On the other hand, there is currently a lack of literature (only, e.g., Molak & Soukopová, 2022; Pitelis et al., 2018; Ferreira et al., 2014) that specifically utilise the term cross-border coopetition and investigate the collaborative and competitive dynamics in international relations and economic interactions. This study uses secondary data to contribute to the literature on cross-border tourism coopetition from the theoretical perspective of possible cooperation among competing European countries.

Data and Methodology

The research sample, a comprehensive representation of the European tourism landscape, encompasses 32 countries. This includes eight from Western Europe, seven from Southern Europe, six from Northern Europe and 11 from Balkans and Eastern European countries. The complete list of countries can be found in results session, underscoring the broad scope of this study.

Data used for the analysis are obtained from the Travel and Tourism Development Index (TTDI) (Uppink Calderwood & Soshkin, 2022). The TTDI is a valuable and adaptable instrument for leaders and professionals to evaluate the performance of their travel and tourism development, management and long-term strategies. It considers various factors contributing to destinations and travel markets' overall resilience and sustainability. Using insights from the index, public and private leaders of the tourism sector can gain valuable information to guide the development of innovative practices, solutions and policies. TTDI can become a tool to ensure that the returns from travel and tourism are managed to safeguard the diverse assets upon which the sector is built. It has the potential to significantly contribute to global inclusive economic development, facilitate cultural exchange and generate employment opportunities. The TTDI has 17 pillars and 112 indicators distributed into several dimensions. In this chapter, we suggested a coopetition network composition using a cluster analysis based on the following TTDI pillars, which are directly linked to travel and tourism:

- Prioritisation of Travel and Tourism (pillar 6): Active promotion and investment by governments and investors in the development of the Travel and Tourism sector create a conducive environment for cross-border coopetition, facilitating collaboration between countries to maximise tourism's economic and social benefits.
- Air Transport Infrastructure (pillar 9): International and domestic air route capacity and quality as they play a crucial role in supporting cross-border coopetition by facilitating travel, trade, economic development, regional integration, tourism promotion and cultural exchange.
- Ground and Port Infrastructure (pillar 10): The availability of efficient and accessible ground and port transportation to important business centres and tourist attractions is essential for promoting cross-border coopetition by facilitating business connectivity, promoting tourism accessibility, enhancing regional integration, supporting trade and investment and encouraging cross-border mobility.
- Tourist Service Infrastructure (pillar 11): Convenient access to accommodation and car rental services simplifies cross-border travel logistics for tourists, reducing barriers to entry and encouraging more people to explore destinations beyond their home country. This increased mobility fosters cross-border coopetition by promoting cultural exchange, cross-cultural understanding and collaboration among tourism stakeholders.
- Natural Resources (pillar 12): Natural resources in a country can serve as drivers for cross-border coopetition by promoting shared resource management, transboundary environmental conservation, joint infrastructure development and cross-border tourism promotion.
- Cultural Resources (pillar 13): Cultural resources in a country play a vital role in supporting cross-border coopetition by promoting cultural exchange and understanding, heritage tourism promotion, cross-border education and research and creative industries collaboration.
- Travel and Tourism Demand Pressure and Impact (pillar 17): Visitor stays, tourism seasonality, proxies for the dispersion of tourism and the distribution of Travel and Tourism economic benefits to local communities play crucial

roles in supporting cross-border coopetition by promoting multi-destination travel, mitigating seasonality challenges, fostering balanced regional development and empowering local communities in border regions.

The method was cluster analysis, and the data were scaled from 1 to 7 according to the TTDI standard. The cluster analysis simplifies the object's dimensional complexity by consolidating multiple variables into a single representation that indicates the object's membership in a predefined group. This study uses a hierarchical cluster analysis that creates a system of groups and subgroups so that each group can contain several lower-order subgroups and be part of a higher-order group (Vasanicova et al., 2022). Ward's method was the basis for clustering. This method leads to clusters of the same size and shape. Clusters are formed by maximising intra-cluster homogeneity. A dendrogram (hierarchical tree) will visually illustrate the outcomes. The number of clusters shown on the dendrogram will be reduced using the stopping rule with the Duda-Hart $Je(2)/Je(1)$ index associated with the pseudo-T^2. The number of clusters that are most different from each other is determined using the highest value of the Duda-Hart index, which also has the lowest pseudo-T^2 value (Duda et al., 2000; Vasanicova et al., 2022). The outcomes will be derived using the Stata software.

Results and Discussion

Fig. 3.1 shows the resulting dendrogram and corresponding cartogram. Because several smaller clusters were formed using Ward's method, the Duda-Hart $Je(2)/Je(1)$ index decides on the final number of clusters. The calculation was performed for one to 15 possible groups, while the optimal number is associated with the highest possible level of the index associated with the lowest value of pseudo-T^2. Table 3.1 shows the results of the stopping rule, while a six-group solution has been chosen. Table 3.2 shows the classification of European countries into resulting clusters (with the country's code used in Fig. 3.1).

The resulting clusters can be interpreted according to cluster centroids that represent the mean value of the relevant pillar in each cluster (see Table 3.3).

Cluster 1: Spain, Italy, France, Germany. Cluster 1 represents European countries with the best position in the TTDI (in the top 10 from 117 analysed economies). The means analysed pillars reached the highest values for the Cultural Resources, Natural Resources and Air Transport Infrastructure pillars. Countries also have good positions in Tourist Service Infrastructure and ground and Port Infrastructure. It comprises nations with an extensive history and culture, abundant natural resources and a flourishing tourism sector. These countries boast coastal access, making them appealing destinations for summer vacations, and are distinguished by mountainous landscapes like the Alps or the Pyrenees. Furthermore, tourism emphasises exploring cultural monuments, not only in the capitals of these countries. Spain, France and Italy are the most representative Mediterranean tourist destinations with a long history of tourism development (Kožić et al., 2019). Travel agencies currently offer Mediterranean journeys

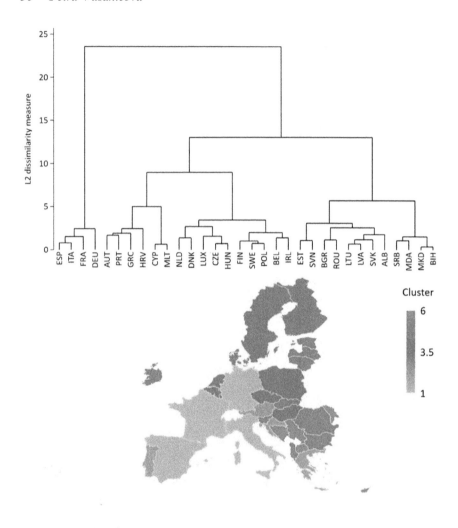

Fig. 3.1.   Dendrogram of Cluster Analysis and Corresponding Cartogram. *Source:* Elaborated by the authors by processing in Stata and Excel.

starting in France (Paris), continuing in Spain (Madrid), and ending in Italy (Rome). Tours are also offered to Germany and France, frequently accompanied by the inclusion of the Netherlands or Switzerland. The interconnection among the countries is evident in the context of wine tourism. Regarding wine production, in 2019, Germany ranked in Europe after Italy, France and Spain (Tafel & Szolnoki, 2021).

Table 3.1. Stopping Rule – Duda-Hart Index.

Number of Clusters	*Je*(2)/*Je*(1)	Pseudo-T^2
1	0.5541	24.15
2	0.6870	11.85
3	0.6036	9.19
4	0.5692	7.57
5	0.4307	5.29
6	*0.6715*	*3.91*
7	0.6225	3.64
8	0.4248	4.06
9	0.5328	3.51
10	0.5247	1.81
11	0.3440	3.81
12	0.5050	2.94
13	0.4373	1.29
14	0.3836	3.21
15	0	.

Source: Own processing using Stata.

Cluster 2: Austria, Portugal, Greece, Croatia. Countries in cluster 2 have the best position in tourist service infrastructure and are also in the leading place in the prioritisation of travel and tourism. Apart from Austria, these are countries with access to the sea. Mediterranean countries, Greece and Croatia, are supposed to be the most developed 'sun and sea' tourism destinations (Kožić et al., 2019). Travel agencies provide combined tours to Croatia and Greece, with Montenegro also linked to these destinations. Croatian, Portuguese and Greek cities have benefits from cruise tourism, like profit for the local community, jobs, fees, etc. (Kovačić & Silveira, 2020). According to Vindobona (2023), economic relations between Austria and Portugal have recently intensified significantly. In 2022, the number of Austrian branches in Portugal alone increased by one-third.

Cluster 3: These southern European countries lead in the prioritisation of travel and tourism, as well as the pressure of demand and impact of travel and tourism. In addition, they have a high level of Tourist Service Infrastructure. Cyprus and Malta often cooperate with educational institutions and provide training and practices in tourism and hospitality. These well-visited nations are renowned for their captivating scenery, rich history and lively cultural atmospheres (Gauci et al., 2013). Both places offer a superior standard of living, excellent quality of life and tax advantages that would attract investors. According to Theocharous et al. (2020), collaboration boosts tourism demand

Table 3.2. Belonging the Country to the Cluster.

Code	Country	Code	Country	Code	Country
Cluster 1		*Cluster 3*		*Cluster 5*	
ESP	Spain	CYP	Cyprus	EST	Estonia
ITA	Italy	MLT	Malta	SVN	Slovenia
FRA	France	*Cluster 4*		BGR	Bulgaria
DEU	Germany	NLD	Netherlands	ROU	Romania
Cluster 2		DNK	Denmark	LTU	Lithuania
AUT	Austria	LUX	Luxembourg	LVA	Latvia
PRT	Portugal	CZE	Czech Republic	SVK	Slovak Republic
GRC	Greece	HUN	Hungary	ALB	Albania
HRV	Croatia	FIN	Finland	*Cluster 6*	
		SWE	Sweden	SRB	Serbia
		POL	Poland	MDA	Moldova
		BEL	Belgium	MKD	North Macedonia
		IRL	Ireland	BIH	Bosnia and Herzegovina

Source: Own processing using Stata.

among these countries by enhancing tourist trust and confidence through mutual understanding, stability and safety.

Cluster 4: Netherlands, Denmark, Luxembourg, Czech Republic, Hungary, Finland, Sweden, Poland, Belgium, Ireland. According to the resulting cluster centroids, these countries excel in Ground and Port Infrastructure and Tourist Service Infrastructure. These countries are distinguished by a tourism emphasis primarily directed towards their capitals and their associated cultural and

Table 3.3. Cluster Centroids.

Cluster	Pillar 6	Pillar 9	Pillar 10	Pillar 11	Pillar 12	Pillar 13	Pillar 17
1	4.22	5.07	5.22	5.54	4.67	6.19	3.71
2	4.53	4.07	4.58	6.04	3.27	3.40	3.45
3	5.11	4.02	3.61	5.48	1.71	2.04	4.17
4	3.98	3.90	5.38	4.17	2.25	2.85	3.92
5	4.35	2.74	4.25	4.22	2.12	2.22	3.54
6	3.28	2.55	3.22	3.39	1.59	1.83	3.55
Total	4.15	3.62	4.60	4.57	2.53	3.00	3.71

Source: Own processing using Stata.

historical monuments. The shared destination management strategy among these countries may involve developing comprehensive sightseeing tour packages in their respective capitals. Considering the geographical positioning of the countries within the cluster, our suggestion is to design separate sightseeing tours for Poland, the Czech Republic and Hungary. Despite not being a part of this cluster, Slovakia could be incorporated to maintain policy coherence among the countries of the Visegrad group. Studies by Michalkó et al. (2022), Zemanová (2022), Antošová et al. (2020) and Finka et al. (2020) point out the tourism cooperation in this region. A cruise could be attractive for the Netherlands, Denmark, Finland and Sweden because the capitals have a port. Kropinova (2020) and Olsen et al. (2019) examine the role of tourism in mentioned Baltic countries and highlight the role of cross-border cooperation. The connection of Luxembourg, Belgium and Ireland can be found in business tourism. These countries are visited on business trips; they are trade crossings and industrial centres (e.g. Ireland). In this regard, we can highlight, for example, Luxembourg and Belgium, which have a dominant position in banking and finance, and various institutions of the European Union are located here. Cross-border cooperation between Luxembourg and Belgium was the point of studies of Durand (2022), Mayer et al. (2019), Durand (2014) and Timothy and Saarinen (2013).

Cluster 5: Estonia, Slovenia, Bulgaria, Romania, Lithuania, Latvia, Slovak Republic, Albania. These analysed countries have less tourism development and do not stand out in any of the measured indicators. The countries are characterised by year-round tourism and several natural resources, for example, Rila National Park in Bulgaria, the Transylvania region in Romania, the Accursed Mountains in Albania, the Tatras in Slovakia or the Alps in Slovenia. While Estonia, Latvia and Lithuania, three nations situated along the Baltic Sea, may appear surprisingly diverse, they share a common history that unites them. The unspoiled landscapes along the Baltic coast, the vibrant culture and traditions and the heritage left by past superpowers collectively make the Baltics an appealing tourist destination. According to Spiriajevas (2013), cooperation among Lithuania, Latvia and Estonia to advance international tourism development relies on a public–private partnership. Moreover, for many years, the Baltic States have joined forces in promoting tourism to create a unique historical image and establish the Baltic region as a prominent destination, emphasising spa tourism. Health tourism, encompassing trips to spas, thermal baths, hot springs, spa and wellness accommodations, as well as hospitals and clinics for surgical and medical treatments, along with spiritual or holistic retreats, has emerged as a shared trademarks for the Baltic countries. Collaborative partnerships and clusters are discussed as strategies to exchange best practices, enhance quality and establish branding, aiming to boost the competitiveness of destinations in health and wellness tourism (Cottrell & Cottrell, 2015). Kropinova (2021) describes cooperation among countries in the Baltic Sea Region in more detail. Bulgaria and Romania share an intertwined history marked by complete isolation from the rest of the world for a continuous 50-year period under the Communist regime.

Cluster 6: Serbia, Moldova, North Macedonia, Bosnia and Herzegovina. Upper-middle-income Balkans and Eastern European countries of cluster 6 have the worst mean position among analysed pillars of the TTDI. Within the TTDI, they were ranked 70–95. Cooperation would be possible between Serbia, Bosnia and Herzegovina, as they are neighbouring countries (e.g. Nezirović et al., 2016; Mulalic, 2019). North Macedonia could be included in the trip if Montenegro and Albania were also visited (Seferaj, 2014). Porfido (2020) discusses the possibilities of tourism in the mentioned region. Moldova holds significant tourist potential, primarily stemming from the distinctive geomorphological features of its territory. It includes an exceptional variety of landscape reserves, scenic views and unique geological landmarks with European and global significance. Unfortunately, collaboration with other countries in the cluster is restricted, primarily due to the distant geographical placement. Existing literature shows possible cooperation with Romania and Ukraine (Sokolovskyy, 2022; Stanciu, 2022; Buchko, 2021; Şlusarciuc & Tokar, 2021).

Some countries from clusters 5 to 6 lack a distinctive tourist image in many parts of the world. These countries are often considered synonymous with their capital city or nationalities, failing to recognise the differences between these nations. Employing more flexible governance methods could aid in addressing these challenging trends, promote collaboration among various countries and facilitate establishing networks addressing shared issues, problems and actions. Creating networks and cooperation among stakeholders from the mentioned countries poses a considerable challenge. These networks are anticipated to comprehend and meet the demands of highly globalised territorial development and inherently grasp local societies' internal needs.

Despite the difficulties, coopetition yields numerous advantages. Combining the resources, marketing efforts, staffing and infrastructure of involved countries reduces costs. It enhances the resilience of the destinations when confronted with financial risks (Carson et al., 201 4; Lovelock & Boyd, 2006; Ioannides et al., 2006). Moreover, when two destinations are jointly marketed, each with distinct yet complementary features, it results in regional-scale economies. This collaboration enables smaller destinations to achieve critical mass in tourism by offering appealing packages to tourists from diverse backgrounds (Lovelock & Boyd, 2006; Shepherd & Ioannides, 2020). Furthermore, collaborative efforts in cross-border tourism can support a sustainable approach to regional tourism development, particularly when the two adjacent countries have a shared resource, such as a wildlife reserve (Stoffelen et al., 2017). Through collaboration, destinations on each side can strive towards a shared vision, effectively treating the cross-border region as a unified entity for planning and management purposes (Pinheiro, 2009).

Unfortunately, the coopetition process is sluggish and intricate due to legal frameworks, varying levels of political will, uneven budget limitations and cultural disparities among the involved parties. On the other hand, European cross-border tourism coopetition could be supported by a European Union project funding arm known as Interreg (Shepherd & Ioannides, 2020).

Conclusion

The insights presented have implications for tourism policymakers, both in the public and private sectors, regarding macroeconomic policies, tourism develop-ment initiatives and marketing practices, such as image and brand restoration. Indicative measures involve running public relations campaigns, utilising pub-licity and optimising media use as part of collaborative regional marketing ini-tiatives and efforts. A thorough understanding of the underlying indicators causing tourism connections among analysed countries could enable stakeholders to take proactive and collective measures to ensure the sustainability of their tourism sector. Measures built on specific tactics and strategies could guide tourism destinations in cooperation between their countries. The establishment and funding of global and regional tourism monitoring observatories, in collab-oration with other international agencies, can improve communication quality and the exchange of information (Theocharous et al., 2020).

Often, the problem in coopetition could be a need for more cooperation between the national and local governments in the absence of a second-tier government, such as a decentralised regional authority, which poses several management challenges. It is essential to foster local partnerships and coopera-tion, extending beyond tourism enterprises to include cooperation actions with other local stakeholders. Collaboration and trust form the foundation of many transnational initiatives, requiring partners to be adaptable and motivated to accomplish shared goals.

One of the main difficulties in analysed countries was the size and heteroge-neity of actors. The scale of cooperation might be different in each cluster. Therefore, it is important to find and build on common interests. Although there are many challenges and issues, the potential coopetition among several European countries and the potential for tourism growth in this region is positive.

In conclusion, several recommendations and proposals are essential to pro-mote cross-border tourism coopetition:

- Engaging in proactive communication with domestic stakeholders to build and uphold a positive image is crucial.
- Regular and transparent reassessment of the vision serves as a crucial correc-tive mechanism.
- Focusing on shared interests and objectives promotes commitment to aligning political priorities. Emphasising shared points and themes of common interest can promote mutual trust and ensure the sustainability of cooperation. There should be a harmonious balance between competitive and cooperative ele-ments, avoiding disruptive interference. Regions should be receptive to initi-ating fresh partnerships, drawing insights from exemplary practices across diverse fields of activity and consistently enhancing their capacity for innovation.
- Collaborating partners should coordinate their activities mutually and engage in informal structures and channels. This pertains to the coordination of actions within the framework of an effective governance system, encompassing

both vertical and horizontal coordination of activities within the territory and transcending borders.
- Parallel communication and collaboration frameworks have the potential to fortify and supplement official decision-making bodies.
- Beyond an ambitious brand-building process, it is crucial to establish frameworks for advancing the shared interests of stakeholders within coopetitive regions. A successful regional brand should be consistently founded on an alignment of perspectives between internal stakeholders (residents) and the expectations of external actors (tourists, visitors and investors).

This research underscores the importance of cross-border tourism coopetition as a significant driver of tourism growth and development. By focusing on this aspect, the chapter enhances the understanding of coopetition dynamics within the tourism context and offers valuable insights for practitioners and policy-makers seeking to capitalise on cross-border collaborations. This study enriches the existing body of cross-border coopetition literature.

Acknowledgement

This research was supported by the Scientific Grant Agency of the Ministry of Education, Science, Research, and Sport of the Slovak Republic and the Slovak Academy of Sciences, grant No. 1/0241/25–VEGA.

References

Antošová, G., Vogl, M., & Schraud, M. (2020). Challenges for the Visegrad Group–the coronavirus crises and its impact on tourism. *Visegrad Journal on Bioeconomy and Sustainable Development, 9*(1), 28–32.

Buchko, Z. (2021). Transborder recreational tourism complexes (TBRTC) as a result of international collaboration. *Prace Komisji Geografii Przemysłu Polskiego Towarzystwa Geograficznego, 35*(3), 76–89.

Carson, D. A., Carson, D. B., & Hodge, H. (2014). Understanding local innovation systems in peripheral tourism destinations. *Tourism Geographies, 16*(3), 457–473.

Chim-Miki, A. F., & Batista-Canino, R. M. (2017a). The coopetition perspective applied to tourism destinations: A literature review. *Anatolia, 28*(3), 381–393.

Chim-Miki, A. F., & Batista-Canino, R. M. (2017b). Tourism coopetition: An introduction to the subject and a research agenda. *International Business Review, 26*(6), 1208–1217.

Cottrell, S., & Cottrell, J. R. (2015). The state of tourism in the Baltics. *Scandinavian Journal of Hospitality and Tourism, 15*(4), 321–326.

Cracolici, M. F., & Nijkamp, P. (2009). The attractiveness and competitiveness of tourist destinations: A study of Southern Italian regions. *Tourism Management, 30*(3), 336–344.

Della Corte, V., & Sciarelli, M. (2012). Can coopetition be source of competitive advantage for strategic networks. *Corporate Ownership and Control, 10*(1), 363–379.

Duda, R. O., Hart, P. E., & Stork, D. G. (2000). *Pattern classification*. John Wiley & Sons.

Durand, F. (2014). Challenges of cross-border spatial planning in the metropolitan regions of Luxembourg and Lille. *Planning Practice and Research, 29*(2), 113–132.

Durand, F. (2022). What types of cultural cooperation exist in European cross-border areas?. *Geografiska Annaler: Series B, Human Geography, 104*(4), 307–326.

Ferreira, J. J., Raposo, M. L., & Fernandes, C. I. (2014). Inter-firm cross border co-opetition: Evidence from a two-country comparison. In M. Peris-Ortiz & J.-M. Sahut (eds), *New challenges in entrepreneurship and finance: Examining the prospects for sustainable business development, performance, innovation, and economic growth* (pp. 35–55). Springer.

Finka, M., Husár, M., & Jašso, M. (2020). CENTROPE initiative – Lessons learned and inspirations for the Western Balkans. *Annual Review of Territorial Governance in the Western Balkans, 2,* 150–167.

Gauci, J. B., Attard, C., Camilleri, S. P., Cauchi, M., & Gatt, A. (2013). Collective accommodation establishments in Corfu, Cyprus, and Malta: A comparative study of online prices. *Anatolia, 24*(3), 319–336.

Ioannides, D., Nilsson, P. Å, & Billing, P. (2006). Transboundary collaboration in tourism: The case of the Bothnian Arc. *Tourism Geographies, 8*(2), 122–142.

Kovačić, M., & Silveira, L. (2020). Cruise tourism: Implications and impacts on the destinations of Croatia and Portugal. *Pomorstvo: Scientific Journal of Maritime Research, 34*(1), 40–47.

Kožić, I., Sorić, P., & Sever, I. (2019). Interdependence of international tourism demand for Mediterranean countries: Impact of demand shocks. *International Journal of Tourism Research, 21*(1), 97–107.

Kropinova, E. G. (2020). The role of tourism in cross-border region formation in the Baltic Region. In G. Fedorov, A. Druzhinin, E. Golubeva, D. Subetto, & T. Palmowski (eds), *Baltic Region—The region of cooperation* (pp. 83–97). Springer.

Kropinova, E. (2021). Transnational and cross-border cooperation for sustainable tourism development in the Baltic Sea Region. *Sustainability, 13*(4), 2111.

Lorgnier, N., & Su, C. J. (2017). Considering coopetition strategies in sport tourism networks: A look at the nonprofit nautical sports clubs on the northern coast of France. *European Sport Management Quarterly* Value co-creation in sport management, *14*(1), 87–109.

Lovelock, B., & Boyd, S. (2006). Impediments to a cross-border collaborative model of destination management in the Catlins, New Zealand. *Tourism Geographies, 8*(2), 143–161.

Mayer, M., Zbaraszewski, W., Pieńkowski, D., Gach, G., & Gernert, J. (2019). Cross-border politics and development in the European Union with a focus on tourism. In *Cross-border tourism in protected areas. Geographies of tourism and global change.* Springer.

Michalkó, G., Németh, J., Tokodi, P., Kamal Abboud, T., & Birkner, Z. (2022). The potential of the Visegrad Cooperation (V4) for the safe restarting of tourism in the region following the COVID-19 epidemic. *Scientia et Securitas, 2*(4), 452–458.

Molak, M. W., & Soukopová, J. (2022). Can institutionalization be considered a trap in defining functional cross-border areas? Coopetition and local public services in borderlands. *NISPAcee Journal of Public Administration and Policy, 15*(2), 122–153.

Mulalic, M. (2019). Prospects for trilateral relations between Turkey, Serbia, and Bosnia and Herzegovina. *Insight Turkey*, *21*(2), 129–148.

Nezirović, S., Bidžan-Gekić, A., Avdić, B., & Gekić, H. (2016). Cross border cooperation between Bosnia and Herzegovina and Serbia in the case of tourism development in municipalities of middle Podrinje. In *Proceedings of 2nd International Tourism and Hospitality Management Conference* (pp. 121–133).

Nowak, J. J., Petit, S., & Sahli, M. (2012). Intra-tourism trade in Europe. *Tourism Economics*, *18*(6), 1287–1311.

Olsen, K., Abildgaard, M. S., Brattland, C., Chimirri, D., Bernardi, C. D., Edmons, J. , Grimwood, B., Hurst, C., Höckert, E., Jæger, K., Kugapi, O., Lemelin, R. H., Lüthje, M., Mazzullo, N., Müller, D., Ren, C., Saari, R., Ugwuegbula, L., & Viken, A. (2019). *Looking at Arctic tourism through the lens of cultural sensitivity: ARCTISEN – A transnational baseline report*. University of Lapland.

Pinheiro, J. L. P. (2009). Transborder cooperation and identities in Galicia and Northern Portugal. *Geopolitics*, *14*(1), 79–107.

Pitelis, C. N., Desyllas, P., & Panagopoulos, A. (2018). Profiting from innovation through cross-border market co-creation and co-opetition: The case of global pharmaceuticals. *European Management Review*, *15*(4), 491–504.

Porfido, E. (2020). Tourism development in the Western Balkans: Towards a common policy. *Annual Review of Territorial Governance in the Western Balkans*, *2*, 24–45.

Şlusarciuc, M., & Tokar, V. (2021). Potential impact of cross-border cooperation on the regional development: Case study Romania-Ukraine border. *Eurolimes*, *30*, 291–342.

Seferaj, K. (2014). Sustainable development aspects in cross-border cooperation programmes: The case of Macedonia and Albania. *EVRODIJALOG Journal for European Issues*, *19*, 337–352.

Shepherd, J., & Ioannides, D. (2020). Useful funds, disappointing framework: Tourism stakeholder experiences of INTERREG. *Scandinavian Journal of Hospitality and Tourism*, *20*(5), 485–502.

Sokolovskyy, O. (2022). Cross-border cooperation within the European neighborhood and partnership instrument "Ukraine-Romania-Moldova". *Copernicus Political and Legal Studies*, *1*, 48–60.

Spiriajevas, E. (2013). The development of international tourism in Lithuania: A comparative analysis of regional aspects. *Baltic Region*, *1*, 82–90.

Stanciu, S. (2022). Romanian-Moldavian tourism analysis and recommendations. *Scientific Papers: Management, Economic Engineering in Agriculture & Rural Development*, *22*(2), 231–238.

Stefko, R., & Nowak, S. (2014). Cooperation shrines of Europe in regional management and development. *Polish Journal of Management Studies*, *10*(2), 209–215.

Stoffelen, A., Ioannides, D., & Vanneste, D. (2017). Obstacles to achieving cross-border tourism governance: A multi-scalar approach focusing on the German-Czech borderlands. *Annals of Tourism Research*, *64*, 126–138.

Tafel, M. C., & Szolnoki, G. (2021). Relevance and challenges of wine tourism in Germany: A winery operators' perspective. *International Journal of Wine Business Research*, *33*(1), 60–79.

Theocharous, A. L., Zopiatis, A., Lambertides, N., Savva, C. S., & Mansfeld, Y. (2020). Tourism, instability and regional interdependency: Evidence from the Eastern-Mediterranean. *Defence and Peace Economics*, *31*(3), 245–268.

Timothy, D. J., Guia, J., & Berthet, N. (2014). Tourism as a catalyst for changing boundaries and territorial sovereignty at an international border. *Current Issues in Tourism, 17*(1), 21–27.

Timothy, D. J., & Saarinen, J. (2013). Cross-border cooperation and tourism in Europe. In C. Costa, E. Panyik, & D. Buhalis (eds), *Trends in European tourism planning and organisation* (pp. 64–76). Channel View.

Timothy, D. J., Saarinen, J., & Viken, A. (2016). Tourism issues and international borders in the Nordic Region. *Scandinavian Journal of Hospitality and Tourism, 16*(Suppl. 1), 1–13.

Uppink Calderwood, L., & Soshkin, M. (2022). *Travel & tourism development index 2021: Rebuilding for a sustainable and resilient future.* World Economic Forum.

Vasanicova, P., Jencova, S., Gavurova, B., & Bacik, R. (2022). Coopetition of European Union countries within destination management. *Journal of Tourism and Services, 13*(24), 71–89.

Vindobona. (2023, July 2). *Austria and Portugal strengthen bilateral cooperation.* https://www.vindobona.org/article/austria-and-portugal-strengthen-bilateral-cooperation

Xie, W., Li, H., & Yin, Y. (2021). Research on the spatial structure of the European union's tourism economy and its effects. *International Journal of Environmental Research and Public Health, 18*(4), 1389.

Zemanová, L. (2022). Comparison of state policy of tourism in V4 countries. *Studia Turistica, 13*(2), 39–51.

Chapter 4

A Taxonomy of Value Creation and Appropriation From Tourism Coopetition

Jako Volschenk[a], Wojciech Czakon[b], Adriana Fumi Chim-Miki[c] and Rui Augusto da Costa[d]

[a]Stellenbosch Business School, South Africa
[b]Jagiellonian University, Poland
[c]Federal University of Campina Grande, Brazil
[d]University of Aveiro, Portugal

Abstract

Coopetition refers to the collaboration or cooperation of competitors with each other with the objective to create value for individuals, firms and society. This chapter provides an overview and taxonomy of different types of value generated by coopetition by considering seven types of capital: financial, manufactured, intellectual, human, social, natural and cultural. It goes beyond the current literature on value creation and appropriation in the tourism industry. It offers a framework for future research on value creation from coopetition and how the interplay of capital in the tourism destination generates a blend of values. These values can be appropriated at common, private, privately captured common or public levels. The results showed that tourism coopetition is an essential strategy for the host society, as it can generate socio-economic, socio-environmental and socio-cultural value.

Keywords: Tourism coopetition; value creation; value appropriation; coopetition taxonomy; coopetition value matrix

Coopetition in Tourism

Coopetition refers to the collaboration or cooperation of competitors with each other (Bengtsson & Kock, 2000), often with the objective to create value for the parties that collaborate (Czakon, Klimas, & Mariani, 2020). In the earliest

Value Proposition to Tourism Coopetition, 41–55
doi:10.1108/978-1-83797-827-420241004

writings about coopetition, Brandenburger and Nalebuff (1996) portrayed a broad definition and referred to a range of stakeholders (i.e. customers, suppliers, competitors and complementors) collectively increasing the "value pie" and sharing in the slices (Dyer et al., 2008; Ritala & Tidström, 2014). Further to the broad definition, some authors have elaborated on multiple types and levels of value addressing various stakeholder constituencies (Chim-Miki et al., 2023; Niesten & Jolink, 2020; Volschenk, 2016, 2018).

Tourism coopetition research is concerned with the context and processes of coopetition in the tourism industry, including drivers of coopetition networks, variables of coopetition, the impact of coopetition as well as the interplay among tourism and other stakeholders or industries (Chim-Miki & Batista-Canino, 2018; Chim-Miki et al., 2023; Czernek & Czakon, 2016; Damayanti et al., 2017).

In line with a broad definition of coopetition, *tourism coopetition* may occur among individuals (interpersonal), inside organisations at a destination (intra-organisational), between competing organisations at a destination (inter-organisational), between different stakeholders (firms, not-for profit entities, communities, public sector, etc.) of a destination (intra-destination coopetition) or destinations (inter-destination or interregional) (Butler & Weidenfeld, 2011; Mariani, 2016; Zemla, 2014).

Tourism coopetition can be defined as the collaboration or cooperation of competitors in the tourism industry with each other and may refer to a range of joint initiatives, such as

- to collectively market a destination to attract more tourists (Gretzel et al., 2006; Wang & Xiang, 2007);
- to offer tourists more complex experiences created jointly (Ritala & Tidström, 2014);
- to collectively provide better customer service (Kylänen & Rusko, 2011);
- to collectively engage with public authorities or other stakeholders to develop tourism (Mariani & Kylänen, 2014).

Coopetition is endemic in tourism (Köseoglu et al., 2021) and is integral to tourism as firms and/or destinations are often interdependent and complementary in what they offer (Carrillo & Barbieri, 2024; Chim-Miki & Batista-Canino, 2018; Czakon, Srivastava, et al., 2020; Nguyen et al., 2022). Integrated tourism experiences often rely on several players to collaborate to create these experiences. Tourists often experience a destination as a coherent entity and seldom interact with only a single firm (Carrillo & Barbieri, 2024; Kylanen & Mariani, 2012). Tourists want *"safety, pleasure, a myriad of shopping alternatives, different activities and so on"* (Pesämaa & Eriksson, 2010). If one of many operators closes, the overall attractiveness also diminishes (Pesämaa & Eriksson, 2010). It is thus in the interest of competitors, for other similar firms to survive. Tourism therefore provides a rich context for coopetition research.

It is critical for policymakers, destination managers, facility owners, facility managers and others to understand the mechanism through which value could be created for local communities but also to understand where one form of benefit could potentially impact future sustainability of touristic destinations. Also, it is essential to understand the dynamics of value creation provided by coopetition in the destinations. For instance, while tourism pays for conservation in some instances (Austin et al., 2022), tourism may also be associated with environmental degradation, habitat encroachment or biodiversity losses. Coopetition under poor incentives is particularly difficult in nature-based tourism destinations (Huybers & Bennett, 2003). Nevertheless, coopetition can be used to balance the creation of positive and negative values.

This chapter investigates the value implications for different stakeholders from tourism coopetition. It goes beyond the current literature about value creation and appropriation in the tourism industry. It provides a framework to further investigate value creation and the interplay of value in the tourism destination.

The Creation Perspective: Value and Capital Creation

Much has been written about the creation of value, the appropriation of value (Volschenk et al., 2016) as well as the dynamics of facilitating value (Chou & Zolkiewski, 2018). In this paper, we use the concept of capital to describe a store of value that *"has a potential capacity to produce profits and to reproduce itself in identical or expanded form"* (Bourdieu, 2018), or can even be destroyed.

Value from coopetition can be described in terms of the type of value. Most literature refers to economic and knowledge value, with more recent authors extending the concept to social and socio-environmental value (Chim-Miki et al., 2023; Niesten & Jolink, 2020).

Extending the concept of value to capital assists in understanding value creation in granular form. Table 4.1 portrays an extension of the six capitals (IIRC, 2013) that incorporates cultural value (Bourdieu, 2019). Cultural capital is of particular importance in this chapter because of the role it plays in the production of tourism, together with other capitals such as natural capital.

Combinations of different forms of value is at the core of understanding how value is created in tourism. A vast number of stakeholders contribute to the network of value elements that includes knowledge (Cortese et al., 2021), cultural, environmental and other forms of value.

Karlsson (2005) explains how a combination of social capital and cultural capital (a sense of heritage around a region called Årjäng) led to tourism-focused entrepreneurship and thus economic value creation, which in turn worked to incentivise the preservation of social and cultural capital. In this way, *"the social and cultural capital of the past stays present in the economic capital of today, as well as in projects of the future"* (Karlsson, 2005).

At the same time, some points regarding the natural capital are under-explored (Volschenk, 2018), also in tourism literature, such as the dilemmas associated with short-term financial objectives of companies vs the long-term survival of the natural source that these first rely on. What manifests in a situation that runs unregulated (Huybers & Bennett, 2003), can be described as a tragedy of the commons (Hardin, 1968) in that the failure to collaborate to preserve nature leads

Table 4.1. Descriptions of Seven Forms of Capitals.

Financial capital	The pool of funds that an organisation has access to, i.e. it would include debt, equity or another source. Financial capital is used to acquire other forms of capital or emanates from the exchange of other forms of capital.
Manufactured capital	Human-created, product-orientated equipment and tools, including buildings. However, manufactured capital can extend outside the firm to also include roads and other public infrastructure. In tourism, this may also refer to heritage buildings.
Intellectual capital	Knowledge-based assets, including R&D competencies, tacit knowledge, processes and intellectual property. Intellectual capital creates shareholder value by combining material, financial and human resources.
Human capital	People's competencies, capabilities and experience, as well as their motivation to innovate. Human capital includes people's ability to lead, manage and collaborate.
Social capital	Institutions and relationships established within and between organisations, communities, stakeholders and other networks to enhance individual and collective well-being. Social and relationship capital includes broader interpretations, such as the ability to exchange information and the organisation's licence to operate, i.e. societal connections that facilitate collaboration.
Natural capital	Natural capital consists of both renewable and non-renewable environmental stocks.
Cultural capital	The symbolic resources embedded within a society's culture, including knowledge, skills, practices, traditions, art, tastes, dispositions and places.

Source: IIRC (2013); Volschenk (2018); Bourdieu (2019).

to a collapse of the resource (Olson, 1971) for all stakeholders. Coopetition is not only beneficial for nature-based tourism destinations but should be considered critical (think for instance of small tropical island tourism). Borrowing from game theory, we know that for one tourism operator to collaborate requires trust that others would do the same (Pesämaa & Eriksson, 2010), illustrating the importance of social capital for the collective governing of natural capital.

Table 4.1 provides a framework that is useful to describe the value that can be created, converted or destroyed. The ability to distinguish forms of value or capital aids in the understanding of how such value come about but also how it could be appropriated.

The Appropriating Perspective: Capturing Value from Coopetition

The value appropriation view concerns who can effectively capture the value created by the coopetition interplay. The term appropriation is often used as synonym to verbs like captured, usurped, allocated or devolved. Extant literature (Volschenk, 2016) has provided more semantic clarity about how the appropriation of value can be described by focussing on the stakeholders who may have claim or access to the value.

Public benefit/value (Orsato, 2009) can take several forms such as socio-economic (for instance jobs), human capital (as in higher well-being), knowledge (public knowledge or awareness), socio-environmental (increased biodiversity or tree-cover) or cultural (preservation or restoration of indigenous heritage). Public benefit may be excludable (rivalrous) in some instances (for example, increased fish populations at a sports-fishing destination) or non-excludable (for example, a rise in fish populations at a scuba-diving destination). In our framework, tourists are considered part of society that benefits from coopetitive initiatives.

Common benefit/value describes the additional value created (and stored as capital) by collaborating players. Such value can come in many forms, for instance, the increasing tourists to a region due to the awareness raised by destination marketing organisations (Wang et al., 2013), sharing competitive information among peers (Cortese et al., 2021) or creating additional value in the tourism products that allow an increase in the willingness to pay (Bowman & Ambrosini, 2000) from tourists.

Privately captured common benefit/value describes the common value captured by any of the parties in the coopetition relationship, as long as the value was created by the collaboration. Destination marketing organisations increase the number of tourists and different hotels would partly capture the increased revenue from accommodation based on their market share or how aggressively they market themselves at the destination.

Private benefit/value occurs in some cases that firms may gain increased revenue outside of the coopetition relationship but because of the relationship. Assume Hotel X is marketing destination A with competitors but also has hotels in another destination B where its competitors are not present. By visiting destination A, tourists recognise the Hotel X when planning to go to the Destination B, so the Hotel X generates value outside of the relationship, but because of the relationship. It follows the economic logic of "spillover effect", that is, gains and benefits that overflow from one area or situation to another.

The Value of Disaggregating Capital Allocation to Different Levels of Stakeholders

It should be noted that value can only be described as created if it was appropriated, regardless of whether is tangible or not. While the two perspectives of value creation and appropriation provides interesting insights, it lacks an integrated view of the value created and appropriated. From an integrated view of the two perspectives, it is possible to understand the dynamic flows and how capital of one kind may *produce profits or reproduce itself in identical or expanded form"* (Bourdieu, 2018).

Table 4.2 provides an extensive typology of value and elaborates on the characteristics and dynamics of each (Ritala & Tidström, 2014). Table 4.2 further extends on the classification of value by including cultural capital. Table 4.3 is

Table 4.2.   A Generic Coopetition value Matrix.

		Value Creation						
		Financial Capital	Manufactured Capital	Intellectual Capital	Human Capital	Social Capital	Natural Capital	Cultural Capital
Value appropriation	Common	Increased funds or access to funds as a result of the coopetition relationship in positive-sum logic (Park et al., 2014; Rai, 2013; Ritala & Tidström, 2014), including increased revenue or lower expenses.	A positive-sum logic (Park et al., 2014; Rai, 2013; Ritala & Tidström, 2014) increase in collective stock of human-created, product-orientated equipment and tools, including buildings.	A positive-sum logic (Park et al., 2014; Rai, 2013; Ritala & Tidström, 2014) increase in the collective knowledge stock of the competitors as a result of the coopetition relationship.	A positive-sum logic (Park et al., 2014; Rai, 2013; Ritala & Tidström, 2014) increase in the collective stock of people's competencies, capabilities and experiences the coopetition partners have access to.	A positive-sum logic (Park et al., 2014; Rai, 2013; Ritala & Tidström, 2014) increase in the collective stock of institutions and relationships that the coopetition partners gain, including goodwill.	A positive-sum logic (Park et al., 2014; Rai, 2013; Ritala & Tidström, 2014) increase in access to natural capital as a result of the coopetitive relationship.	A positive-sum logic (Park et al., 2014; Rai, 2013; Ritala & Tidström, 2014) increase in access to cultural capital as a result of the coopetitive relationship.
	Privately captured common	The component of funds captured by any particular firm from the benefit created within the coopetition initiative. The appropriation can follow either positive or zero-sum logic (Ritala & Tidström, 2014).	A positive-sum logic increases in the manufactured capital of any particular firm (Steinmo & Jakobsen, 2013) that relates to the objectives of the coopetitive initiatives.	A positive-sum logic increases in the knowledge stock of any particular firm (Steinmo & Jakobsen, 2013) that relates to the objectives of the coopetitive initiatives.	A positive-sum logic increases in the human capital of any particular firm (Steinmo & Jakobsen, 2013) that relates to the objectives of the coopetitive initiatives.	A positive-sum logic increases in the social capital of any particular firm (Steinmo & Jakobsen, 2013) that relates to the objectives of the coopetitive initiatives.	The component of natural capital captured by a firm from the benefit created within the coopetition initiative. The appropriation can follow either positive or zero-sum logic (Ritala & Tidström, 2014), depending on whether the resource is a common or public good.	The component of cultural capital captured by a firm from the benefit created within the coopetition initiative. The appropriation can follow either positive or zero-sum logic (Ritala & Tidström, 2014), depending on whether the resource is a common or public good.

Private	Funds generated by a firm outside of the coopetition relationship from skills or resources acquired inside the coopetitive relationship (Dagnino & Padula, 2007, p. 42; Dyer et al., 2008, p. 138; Khanna et al., 1998; Park et al., 2014; Ritala & Tidström, 2014). The appropriation can follow either a positive (Ritala & Tidström, 2014) or zero-sum logic (Rai, 2013).	A positive-sum or zero-sum logic increase in the manufactured capital outside of the coopetitive relationship, but based on knowledge that was acquired inside the coopetitive relationship. Based on different backgrounds and different experiences, firms may learn different things (Steinmo & Jakobsen, 2013, p. 3).	A positive-sum logic increases in the knowledge stock of a firm that has value outside of the coopetitive relationship, but based on knowledge that was acquired inside the coopetitive relationship. Based on different backgrounds and different experiences, firms may learn different things (Steinmo & Jakobsen, 2013, p. 3).	A positive-sum logic increases in the human capital stock of a firm that has value outside of the coopetitive relationship, but based on competencies that was acquired inside the coopetitive relationship.	A positive-sum logic increases in the social capital stock of a firm that has value outside of the coopetitive relationship, but based on the coopetitive relationship.	Natural capital captured by a firm outside of the coopetition initiative, but which can be linked to the initiative. The appropriation can follow either positive or zero-sum logic (Ritala & Tidström, 2014), depending on whether the resource is a common or public good.	Cultural capital captured by a firm outside of the coopetition initiative, but which can be linked to the initiative. The appropriation can follow either positive or zero-sum logic (Ritala & Tidström, 2014), depending on whether the resource is a common or public good.
Public	Socio-economic value: Economic value accruing to society as a result of the coopetitive relationship. The appropriation follows positive-sum logic.	Public infrastructure: In increase in the collective stock of human-created, product-orientated equipment and tools, including buildings and public infrastructure that society has access to. The appropriation follows positive-sum logic.	Public knowledge: An increase in the knowledge stock in society (i.e., public knowledge) as a result of the coopetitive activities or relationship. The appropriation follows positive-sum logic.	A positive-sum increase in the collective stock of society's competencies, capabilities and experiences as a result of the coopetition initiative.	Social cohesion: A positive-sum logic (Park et al., 2014; Ritala Rai, 2013; Ritala & Tidström, 2014) increase in the collective stock of institutions and relationships that society gains as a result of the coopetition initiative.	Socio-environmental value: An increase in environmental value expressed as the utility for society, or as intrinsic value. Such value can, for instance, derive from protecting a species of fauna or flora, reducing resource intensity or reducing waste. The appropriation follows positive-sum logic.	Cultural value: An increase in cultural value expressed as the utility for society, or as intrinsic value. Such value can, for instance, derive from protecting a heritage site or indigenous practices. The appropriation follows positive-sum logic.

similar in structure to Table 4.2 and shows examples from the tourism coopetition literature. It should be noted that the authors could not find examples in the literature for all the cells but provided hypothetical cases where the literature was lacking.

Conclusion

This chapter provides insight into value creation and appropriation of value from tourism coopetition and thus further extends call for understanding of how different manifestations of value interact (Ramkissoon, 2023; Ritala & Tidström, 2014). Of significance is the extension of the six capitals to also consider cultural capital, a major resource to exploit in many destinations.

Apart from representing a taxonomy of value, Table 4.2 provides a diagnostic instrument to analyse cases of tourism coopetition, as well as to identify missed opportunities for value creation and appropriation.

Table 4.3 provides ample evidence that tourism coopetition can create vast amounts of value of different kinds. The table also provides insights into the flow of value, although it requires the reader to form these associations. For instance, destination marketing organisation may market destinations for their environmental or cultural attributes. While the marketing may have a direct impact on tourists to the destination (financial capital), the flow of money could contribute to the protection, maintenance or restoration of natural capital, manufactured capital or cultural capital. It should be clear that almost every sort of capital is connected to other forms of capital. Ultimately, reinforcing loops may confirm the bidirectional impact of different forms of capital on each other.

Limitations and Further Avenues for Research

This chapter did not focus on the drivers of value. Instead, it highlighted the ample opportunity for exploring antecedents and policy mechanisms to create various forms of value. Destination marketing organisations can play a significant role in facilitating almost every type of value creation. The Coopetition Value Matrix does not distinguish between value for all stakeholders. It is a limitation. For instance, customers/clients/tourists are not indicated as a stakeholder to whom value accrues. The economic value captured by consumers – often described in terms of the consumer surplus – may well warrant further investigation and to be separated from public benefit.

The chapter also did not attempt to be exhaustive in the description of capitals or their combinations. Instead, it limited the investigation to the most prominent elements. Spiritual tourism, such as tourists travelling to Mecca, may be sufficiently captured under cultural capital.

We cannot claim that our portrayal of value is exhaustive, but the expanded coopetition value matrix provides an extensive starting point. We could not find evidence of all forms of value in the literature, but we do believe that such value exists and can now be described and documented.

Table 4.3. A Map of Value From Tourism Coopetition.

		Value Creation						
		Financial Capital	Manufactured Capital	Intellectual Capital	Human Capital	Social Capital	Natural Capital	Cultural Capital
Value appropriation	Common	Destination marketing attracts more tourists to a destination (Chim-Miki & Batista-Canino, 2017a, 2017b) Improved tourist experiences may lead to an increase in the willingness to buy, or willingness to pay a premium (Hawkins, 2004) Increased heritage tourism flowing from the Silk Road Heritage initiative (Hawkins, 2004)	Much of destination tourism is seen due to tourists going to see structures, sites or places that were constructed by humans (Ramkissoon, 2023). Interest in these sites lead to higher tourist numbers and potentially further investment in building and preserving such sites.	Hotels create collective competitive intelligence by creating and managing a database to improve competitive advantage (Köseoglu et al., 2021). Sharing information around occupancy, special events (Köseoglu et al., 2021).	With increased tourism, the community gains in capabilities and experience (Ramkissoon, 2023). Companies may benefit from the increased capabilities and experience, either as entrepreneurs, or by employing from the community.	Trust among tour operators and the community of a tourist destination. Trust is critical for facilitating collaboration. Pro-social and pro-environmental behaviours are proposed to influence residents' support for tourism development (Ramkissoon, 2023).	Hotels in Da Nang, Vietnam collaborated to protect the biodiversity of the Son Tra Nature Reserve from encroaching development (Nguyen et al., 2022). The gain in biodiversity is a public non-excludable value. Companies can access the value, but cannot capture it. In cases such as hunting or fishing, companies are able to exploit increased numbers of fauna.	Increased heritage value flowing from the Silk Road Heritage initiative (Hawkins, 2004), meaning more tourists would be attracted to the region. Cultural value is non-excludable.

(Continued)

Table 4.3. (Continued)

| | Value Creation | | | | | | |
	Financial Capital	Manufactured Capital	Intellectual Capital	Human Capital	Social Capital	Natural Capital	Cultural Capital
Privately captured common	Increased tourism from destination marketing. Once tourists arrive at the destination, tour operators, hotels, etc., compete for their business (Chim-Miki & Batista-Canino, 2017a, 2017b)	Owning or establishing buildings of interest creates common value for all stakeholders, but owning the building or site allows revenue to be captured directly from visitors.	The intellectual insights that can be captured by a hotel from the collective intelligence.	Individual companies may benefit from the increased capabilities and experience, either as entrepreneurs, or by employing from the community.	One operator draws on the trust of the community to launch an initiative.	See above. In cases such as hunting or fishing, individual companies are able to exploit increased numbers of fauna.	Cultural value is a public good and cannot be captured by firms directly. They can only capture derived value from cultural value.
Private	A hotel in the partnership gains brand value from the initiative and thus gain tourists in a different geographic maket.	Cultural value is destination specific. We do not see this benefit as transferable to a different geographic region. Entrepreneurs may operate in non-tourism market, but still gain from the increased cultural capital in the region.	Insights that can be applied in other markets that were obtained from intellectual insights in the collaborative initiative	Entrepreneurs may operate in non-tourism market, but gain from the increased human capital in the region. We do not see this benefit as transferable to a different geographic region.	Entrepreneurs may operate in non-tourism market, but gain from the increased social capital in the region. We do not see this benefit as transferable to a different geographic region.	Entrepreneurs may operate in non-tourism market, but gain from the increased natural capital in the region. We do not see this benefit as transferable to a different geographic region.	Cultural value is destination specific. We do not see this benefit as transferable to a different geographic region. Entrepreneurs may operate in non-tourism market, but still gain from the increased cultural capital in the region.

Public	Increased entrepreneurial opportunities for the local communities. Increased per capita income of the region (Ramkissoon, 2023).	Public benefits from maintained or improved infrastructure or heritage sites.	Public awareness increases due to a destination marketing organisations. Such campaigns may focus on environmental or cultural attributes. (Hawkins, 2004)	With increased tourism, the community gains in capabilities, experience, well-being and quality of life (Ramkissoon, 2023).	Interpersonal trust in communities increase with perceived social impact (Kim & Park, 2023; Ramkissoon, 2023). Tourism creates social value if well managed (Oliveira-Ribeiro et al., 2022)	Hotels in Da Nang, Vietnam collaborated to protect the biodiversity of the Son Tra Nature Reserve from encroaching development (Nguyen et al., 2022). The gain in biodiversity is a public non-excludable value. (Volschenk, 2018)	The Silk Road Heritage initiative (Hawkins, 2004) restores a sense of place, an important component of the culture of regions and communities.

When Dmitri Mendeleev created the periodic table of elements, the table provided scientists with descriptions of elements that had never been seen before. These elements were later discovered and scientists could confirm the predicted behaviours of each.

We hope the expanded coopetition value matrix will inspire an investigation of value from tourism coopetition initiatives. Such studies could be in the form of systematic literature reviews, qualitative studies that provide further insight into the rich context of tourism coopetition or quantitative studies that confirm the relationships between different value classifications.

References

Austin, J. E., Wood, M. E., & Leonard, H. B. (2022). Key success factors in environmental entrepreneurship: The case of wilderness safaris. In *World scientific encyclopedia of business sustainability, ethics, and entrepreneurship* (pp. 175–196).

Bengtsson, M., & Kock, S. (2000). "Coopetition" in business networks – To cooperate and compete simultaneously. *Industrial Marketing Management, 29*(5), 411–426.

Bourdieu, P. (2018). The forms of capital. In *The sociology of economic life* (pp. 78–92). Routledge.

Bourdieu, P. (2019). Distinction: A social critique of the judgement of taste. In *Social stratification, class, race, and gender in sociological perspective* (2nd ed., pp. 499–525). Routledge.

Bowman, C., & Ambrosini, V. (2000). Value creation versus value capture: Towards a coherent definition of value in strategy. *British Journal of Management, 11*(1), 1–15.

Brandenburger, A. M., & Nalebuff, B. J. (1996). *Co-opetition.* Doubleday.

Butler, R., & Weidenfeld, A. (2011). *Cooperation competition spatial proximity and stage of development of tourist destinations CAUTHE 2011: Tourism: Creating a brilliant blend.*

Carrillo, B., & Barbieri, C. (2024). Thriving in a world of giants: Craft breweries' workings in a major tourism destination. *Journal of Travel Research,* 00472875231223664.

Chim-Miki, A. F., & Batista-Canino, R. M. (2017). Tourism coopetition: An introduction to the subject and a research agenda. *International Business Review, 26*(6), 1208–1217.

Chim-Miki, A. F., & Batista-Canino, R. M. (2017). The coopetition perspective applied to tourism destinations: A literature review. *Anatolia, 28*(3), 381–393.

Chim-Miki, A. F., & Batista-Canino, R. M. (2018). Development of a tourism coopetition model: A preliminary Delphi study. *Journal of Hospitality and Tourism Management, 37*, 78–88.

Chim-Miki, A. F., da Costa, R. A., & Oliveira-Ribeiro, R. (2023). Tourism coopetition for a better world: A cycle of creation, appropriation, and devolution of social value. *Current Issues in Tourism*, 1–15.

Chou, H. H., & Zolkiewski, J. (2018). Coopetition and value creation and appropriation: The role of interdependencies, tensions and harmony. *Industrial Marketing Management, 70*, 25–33.

Cortese, D., Giacosa, E., & Cantino, V. (2021). Knowledge sharing for coopetition in tourist destinations: The difficult path to the network. *Review of Managerial Science, 15*(2), 275–286.

Czakon, W., Klimas, P., & Mariani, M. (2020). Behavioral antecedents of coopetition: A synthesis and measurement scale. *Long Range Planning, 53*(1), 101875.

Czakon, W., Srivastava, M. K., Le Roy, F., & Gnyawali, D. (2020). Coopetition strategies: Critical issues and research directions. *Long Range Planning, 53*(1), 101948.

Czernek, K., & Czakon, W. (2016). Trust-building processes in tourist coopetition: The case of a Polish region. *Tourism Management, 52*, 380–394.

Dagnino, G. B., & Padula, G. (2007). Untangling the rise of coopetition: The intrusion of competition in a cooperative game structure. *International Studies of Management & Organization, 37*(2), 32–52.

Damayanti, M., Scott, N., & Ruhanen, L. (2017). Coopetitive behaviours in an informal tourism economy. *Annals of Tourism Research, 65*, 25–35.

Dyer, J. H., Singh, H., & Kale, P. (2008). Splitting the pie: Rent distribution in alliances and networks. *Managerial and Decision Economics, 29*(2–3), 137–148.

Gretzel, U., Fesenmaier, D. R., Formica, S., & O'Leary, J. T. (2006). Searching for the future: Challenges faced by destination marketing organizations. *Journal of Travel Research, 45*(2), 116–126.

Hardin, G. (1968). The tragedy of the commons. *Science, 162*(3859), 1243–1248.

Hawkins, D. E. (2004). A protected areas ecotourism competitive cluster approach to catalyse biodiversity conservation and economic growth in Bulgaria. *Journal of Sustainable Tourism, 12*(3), 219–244.

Huybers, T., & Bennett, J. (2003). Inter-firm cooperation at nature-based tourism destinations. *The Journal of Socio-Economics, 32*(5), 571–587.

International Integrated Reporting Council (IIRC). (2013). *Capitals: Background paper for <IR>*. [Online] Available:. http://integratedreporting.org/wp-content/uploads/2013/03/IR-Background-Paper-Capitals.pdf

Karlsson, S. E. (2005). The social and the cultural capital of a place and their influence on the production of tourism–a theoretical reflection based on an illustrative case study. *Scandinavian Journal of Hospitality and Tourism, 5*(2), 102–115.

Khanna, T. R., Gulati, R. & Nohria, N. (1998). The dynamics of learning alliances: Competition, cooperation and relative scope. *Strategic Management Journal, 19*(3), 193–210.

Kim, S., & Park, E. (2023). An integrated model of social impacts and resident's perceptions: From a film tourism destination. *Journal of Hospitality & Tourism Research, 47*(2), 395–421.

Köseoglu, M. A., Yick, M. Y. Y., & Okumus, F. (2021). Coopetition strategies for competitive intelligence practices-evidence from full-service hotels. *International Journal of Hospitality Management, 99*, 103049.

Kylanen, M., & Mariani, M. M. (2012). Unpacking the temporal dimension of coopetition in tourism destinations: Evidence from Finnish and Italian theme parks. *Anatolia, 23*(1), 61–74.

Kylänen, M., & Rusko, R. (2011). Unintentional coopetition in the service industries: The case of Pyhä-Luosto tourism destination in the Finnish Lapland. *European Management Journal, 29*(3), 193–205.

Mariani, M. M. (2016). Coordination in inter-network coopetition: Evidence from the tourism sector. *Industrial Marketing Management, 53*, 103–123. https://doi.org/10. 1016/j.indmarman.2015.11.015

Mariani, M. M., & Kylänen, M. (2014). The relevance of public-private partnerships in coopetition: Empirical evidence from the tourism sector. *International Journal of Business Environment, 6*(1), 106–125.

Nguyen, T. Q. T., Johnson, P., & Young, T. (2022). Networking, coopetition and sustainability of tourism destinations. *Journal of Hospitality and Tourism Management, 50*, 400–411. https://doi.org/10.1016/j.jhtm.2022.01.003

Niesten, E., & Jolink, A. (2020). Motivations for environmental alliances: Generating and internalizing environmental and knowledge value. *International Journal of Management Reviews, 22*(4), 356–377.

Oliveira-Ribeiro, R., Chim-Miki, A. F., & de Araújo Machado, P. (2022). Coopetition at society level: A scale validation. *International Journal of Business Administration, 13*(4).

Olson Jr, M. (1971). *The logic of collective action: Public goods and the theory of groups, with a new preface and appendix* (Vol. 124). Harvard University Press.

Orsato, R. J. (2009). Sustainability strategies and beyond. In R. J. Orsato & R. Orsato (Eds.), *Sustainability strategies: When does it pay to be green?* (pp. 193–208). Palgrave Macmillan UK.

Park, B.-J. R., Srivastava, M. K., & Gnyawali, D. R. (2014). Walking the tight rope of coopetition: Impact of competition and cooperation intensities and balance on firm innovation performance. *Industrial Marketing Management, 43*(2), 210–221.

Pesämaa, O., & Eriksson, P. E. (2010). Coopetition among nature-based tourism firms: Competition at local level and cooperation at destination level. In S. Yami, S. Castaldo, B. Dagnino, & F. Le Roy (eds), *Coopetition: Winning strategies for the 21st century*. Edward Elgar Publishing.

Rai, R. (2013). A co-opetition-based approach to value creation in interfirm alliances: Construction of a measure and examination of its psychometric properties. *Journal of Management, 42*(6), 1663–1699. https://doi.org/10.1177/0149206313515525

Ramkissoon, H. (2023). Perceived social impacts of tourism and quality-of-life: A new conceptual model. *Journal of Sustainable Tourism, 31*(2), 442–459.

Ritala, P., & Tidström, A. (2014). Untangling the value-creation and value-appropriation elements of coopetition strategy: A longitudinal analysis on the firm and relational levels. *Scandinavian Journal of Management, 30*(4), 498–515.

Steinmo, M., & Jakobsen, S. (2013). *Greening an Industry through coopetition: The role of proximity in an R&D alliance to create environmental innovations*. 35th DRUID Celebration Conference, Barcelona, Spain, 17–19 June. http://druid8.sit.aau.dk/ acc_papers/b96ih3sjlnsyeu96apnq04skphpy.pdf. Accessed on April 9, 2024.

Volschenk, J. (2016). *An investigation into environmental coopetition in the South African wine industry*. Stellenbosch University. PhD dissertation.

Volschenk, J. (2018). The value-implications of coopetition. In Fernandez, A.-S., Chiambaretto, P., Czakon, W. & Le Roy, F. (Eds). 2018. *The Routledge companion to coopetition strategy*. Routledge.

Volschenk, J., Ungerer, M., & Smit, E. (2016). Creation and appropriation of socio-environmental value in coopetition. *Industrial Marketing Management, 57*, 109–118.

Wang, Y., Hutchinson, J., Okumus, F., & Naipaul, S. (2013). Collaborative marketing in a regional destination: Evidence from Central Florida. *International Journal of Tourism Research, 15*(3), 285–297.

Wang, Y., & Xiang, Z. (2007). Toward a theoretical framework of collaborative destination marketing. *Journal of Travel Research, 46*(1), 75–85.

Zemla, M. (2014). Inter-destination cooperation: Forms, facilitators and inhibitors – The case of Poland. *Journal of Destination Marketing & Management, 3*(4), 241–252. https://doi.org/10.1016/j.jdmm.2014.07.001

Chapter 5

Coopetition Strategy in the Context of Multilevel Governance: Evidence From UNESCO'S Global Creative Cities Policy

Magnus Emmendoerfer and Elias Mediotte

Universidade Federal de Viçosa, Brazil

Abstract

Emerging debates in public policy emphasise sustainability and the role of the Creative Economy in advancing the UN's Sustainable Development Goals within UNESCO Creative Cities (UCC). However, research on 'coopetition' – a blend of cooperation and competition – remains sparse within these global networks. This study investigates coopetition under Multilevel Governance in UNESCO-designated tourist destinations, offering a comprehensive examination of its dynamics through a multidimensional, jurisdiction-spanning lens. We uncover disparities within Multilevel Governance structures using a qualitative methodology, including documentary and field research with non-participant observation and thematic content analysis. While cooperation strategies are intended to foster reciprocity among social actors and their organisations, competition prevails, resulting in conflicting goals. This study concludes that the UCC label while promoting coopetition, risks reducing these cities to mere 'brands', challenging their legitimacy. This study underscores the complexity of integrating coopetition within UCC governance and its implications for their identity and sustainability objectives.

Keywords: Coopetition; UNESCO creative cities of gastronomy; multilevel governance; social actors; organisational structures; Coopetition in Tourism

Introduction

Governed by unique Organic Laws, Brazilian municipalities enjoy autonomy in political, administrative and financial matters, with responsibilities that include

Value Proposition to Tourism Coopetition, 57–68
Copyright © 2025 Magnus Emmendoerfer and Elias Mediotte
Published under exclusive licence by Emerald Publishing Limited
doi:10.1108/978-1-83797-827-420241005

local legislation, territorial planning, land use and urban development (Brazil, 1988; Art. 30, p. 34). In response to global social, economic, environmental, cultural, political and ethical challenges, these cities increasingly leverage culture and creativity as strategic assets. This shift fosters resilience and adaptability to cultural shifts, improves citizens' quality of life and drives economic growth. Central to this evolution is the concept of Creative Cities, fundamental to the Creative Industries sector, engaging in a wide range of creative, intellectual, artistic and cultural activities (Federação das Indústrias do Estado do Rio de Janeiro - FIRJAN, 2008, p. 24).

Since its establishment in 2004, the UNESCO Creative Cities Network (UCCN) has been operating within dynamic governance frameworks to integrate economic, social and cultural sectors across its network. The UCCN plays a pivotal role in promoting the development of public policies, grassroots projects and best practices through collaboration between the public and private sectors, academia, non-profits and civil society. Built on a multilevel governance approach from local to international scales, the UCCN is committed to making significant contributions to the achievement of the United Nations' Sustainable Development Goals (SDGs) as outlined in the 2030 Agenda.

This study underscores the importance of Multilevel Governance in managing across scales and addressing global trends locally, particularly in the areas of city governance, urban services and social needs. In the competitive environments of Creative Cities, which reflect diverse citizen interests, Multilevel Governance is proposed as a means to encourage political commitments and foster innovation, creativity and policy experimentation (Hall, 2011). We argue that a Multilevel Governance Network should navigate the paradox of cooperation and competition – termed 'coopetition' (Hooghe & Marks, 2020).

Coopetition, blending cooperation and competition based on market logic, entails social actors in organisational settings engaging in both simultaneously (Bengtsson & Kock, 2000). This study aims to explore this duality, that is, the tension between value creation and capture, in the context of UNESCO-designated Creative Cities as tourist destinations, seeking to understand how coopetition functions within Multilevel Governance (Bengtsson & Raza-Ullah, 2016; Bouncken et al., 2015; Roehrich et al., 2024).

Multilevel Governance in the Context of Coopetition

Hooghe and Marks (2020) define Multilevel Governance as managing collective goods across local, national and supranational levels, highlighting the complex interactions across different societal scales. This approach seeks to clarify the intricate policy formulation process involving numerous stakeholders at multiple levels, from local to supranational, emphasising cooperation and the interconnectedness that unites all levels. No single level dominates in this framework, fostering a system of mutual dependence and shared goals (Stephenson, 2013).

The role of local and subnational governments is crucial in Multilevel Governance, as their involvement in collaborative networks underscores their significance in this governance structure (Betsill & Bulkeley, 2006). However, this multilevel interaction can also breed competition, stemming from the tension between collective action and individual or institutional interests.

Exploring Governance, Creative Economy, Culture and Creativity within the UNESCO Creative Cities framework is crucial in shaping public policies and rethinking public spaces. By adopting the Multilevel Governance model, we understand how subnational governments in Brazil engage with creative networks, especially within the UCCN. This approach spans supranational to local levels, emphasising vertical and horizontal integration through a multilevel, jurisdictional strategy.

The main challenge in Multilevel Governance lies in managing the complex interdependence among actors (Touati et al., 2015), balancing the need for cooperation with competitive tendencies. The concept of coopetition, as introduced by Brandenburger and Nalebuff (1996), captures this blend of cooperation and competition among actors, suggesting strategic choices in alliances can lead to diverse outcomes (Bengtsson & Raza-Ullah, 2016; Guo et al., 2023). Coopetition, rooted in Game Theory, illustrates how entities simultaneously collaborate and compete within networks, highlighting the nuanced strategy of navigating governance across various levels and decisions (Mediotte, 2023).

Coopetition presents a paradox, acting both as a strategy to mitigate risk and uncertainty in cooperation and as a source of these challenges in competition, reflecting fundamental human behaviours (Corbo et al., 2023). It embodies an entrepreneurial process that uses causal and effectual logic in decision-making within conflicting governance contexts (Sarasvathy, 2001). In this study, coopetition is explored as a dynamic where cooperation promotes networked governance learning, while competition fuels action, particularly against competitors, fostering an inter-organisational learning platform based on expertise and relational experiences.

We conclude that coopetition operates across various levels and jurisdictions, displaying unique characteristics at each level. According to Brandenburger and Nalebuff (1996), it falls into two main perspectives: Actor-Network Theory, which sees a network of interdependent actors collaborating towards a common goal and competing for outcomes, and Activity Theory, which focuses on coopetitive relationships within activities, highlighting a blend of competitive and cooperative interactions within the same governance structure. This leads to a complex network of paradoxical and tension-filled relationships (Bouncken et al., 2015).

Methodology

This study employs a descriptive qualitative approach for precise analysis and data accuracy, enhanced by case study methodology to deepen our understanding of the subject (Flick, 2018; Yin, 2017). Conducted as field research in July and August 2022 and January 2023, this study uses non-participant observation, enabling researchers to observe the subject community from an external viewpoint (Marconi & Lakatos, 2003, p. 193). The focus is on UNESCO Creative Cities in Florianópolis, Santa Catarina, Brazil.

Florianópolis, the capital of Santa Catarina, is known for its tourism, combining urban attractions with small-town charm and natural beauty, including over 100 distinctive beaches (Floripamanhã, 2013). The selection of Florianópolis for this study is based on several factors: its repeated recognition as Brazil's top tourist destination (Viagem e Turismo, 2020); it is the first Brazilian city to join the UCCN as a Creative City of Gastronomy (UNESCO, 2019); it has the highest per capita GDP (approx. US$ 8620.00) and Human Development Index (0.847) among Brazilian Creative Cities of Gastronomy; top scores in tourism categorisation (Brazil, 2021); it is the first Gastronomy Observatory (Floripamanhã, 2014); and it ranks highly (90th out of 5570) in the Sustainable Development Index of Cities – Brazil (IDSC-BR), indicating its significant position in both gastronomy and other creative sectors. Florianópolis comes in second place in other creative categories, surpassed only by Santos (São Paulo) – Creative City of Cinema, which claims the 16th position.

The Snowball technique was employed to identify relevant social actors and organisations in Florianópolis. Documentary research involved analysing materials from the local government, FloripAmanhã Association, Brazilian Association of Bars and Restaurants (*Associação Brasileira de Bares e Restaurantes* – Abrasel), Union of Hotels, Restaurants, Bars, and Similar establishments in Florianópolis (*Sindicato de Hotéis, Restaurantes, Bares e Similares de Florianópolis* – SHRBS), the Gastronomy Observatory, and UNESCO, mapping 26 organisations linked to respective actors. Additionally, critical content analysis, as outlined by Law et al. (2021) and following Bardin's (2020) methodology, was applied.

Content analysis proceeded in three phases: Pre-analysis (document identification and preliminary selection through initial review), Exploration (in-depth reading and final material selection) and Results Treatment (quantitative and qualitative data analysis). Analysis categories were derived from the Multilevel Governance indicator, focusing on cooperation and its key features. These categories are outlined in Table 5.1.

To enhance result reliability and achieve our goals, we implemented data triangulation using various interactive research methods (Flick, 2018). Data collection began with non-participant observation, followed by documentary research to validate or contest our literature. Then, we applied content analysis to examine the study's relevant data in detail. To triangulate data, we analysed the competition among mapped social actors and the resulting coopetition in Florianópolis. The findings are presented in the following section.

Cooperation, Competition and Coopetition in a UNESCO Creative City of Gastronomy

In our field research in Florianópolis, we adopt a Multilevel Governance approach that encompasses local, regional, national and international levels, focusing on how social actors within a UNESCO-designated Creative City of Gastronomy perceive their roles, as outlined in the Methodology section. We found that local-level cooperation in resource management is challenging.

Table 5.1. Characteristics of the Main Analysis Categories.

	Cooperation	**Competition**	**Coopetition**
Concept	Cooperation involves informal relationships where organisations share information as needed, retain autonomy and authority, and face minimal risk. Resources and rewards remain distinct, with each party granting access to its resources (Mediotte, 2023).	Competition, often horizontal, emerges as organisations vie for shared gains. Nowadays, they frequently form partnerships through social actors to pursue common goals and achieve desired outcomes (Bengtsson & Kock, 2000).	Coopetition blends cooperation and competition among stakeholders, aiming for mutual benefits within a governance structure. It fosters collaborative efforts in a trust-based environment, moving beyond the narrow focus on individual gains (Chim-Miki & Batista-Canino, 2016).
Actor behaviour	Reciprocity	Competition/rivalry	Competition + cooperation
Objectives	Common gains	Individual gains	Common gains

Source: Elaborated by the authors. Adapted from Bengtsson and Kock (2000), Chim-Miki and Batista-Canino (2016), Mediotte (2023), and Winkler and Molinari (2011, p. 10).

Many social actors struggle with allocating time and resources for actions tied to Florianópolis's designation as a Creative City of Gastronomy. Observations indicate that organisations tend to operate on individual demands rather than collectively. Despite mutual goodwill, noted for its positive impact on coopetition (Roehrich et al., 2024; Rusko, 2024; Winkler & Molinari, 2011), organisations act independently, suggesting cooperation is driven by reciprocal demand rather than a shared value for collective urban development. This tendency highlights how competition and the pursuit of individual gains influence this dynamic.

We also noted that collective coopetition actions are hindered by ineffective resource sharing, largely due to resentment among stakeholders towards Florianópolis's municipality for its perceived neglect of the UNESCO designation. Despite the local administration's professed commitment to the Creative City of Gastronomy, past grievances remain unresolved. However, Chim-Miki and Batista-Canino (2016, p. 426) highlight the importance of cooperation: '*The need to cooperate with competitors to market the tourist product more effectively and improve the destination's competitiveness at the regional or global level (...) is also considered intrinsic behaviour to the tourist destination*'. This suggests that cooperative management of shared resources in a governance network should be seen as an opportunity for organisational synergy rather than a constraint (Rusko, 2024).

Public–private partnerships at the local level are ideally envisioned for urban development, yet often considered utopian. Our findings reflect the views of social actors in Florianópolis, noting that while the municipality faces resource limitations, local cooperation shows potential for successful public–private collaboration. However, some actors see this less optimistically, citing concerns similar to those of Rouyre et al. (2024) about governance activities being fragmented within organisational structures.

Rouyre et al. (2024) also point out challenges in accessing detailed data on resources for city development, especially under the Creative City designation, mainly with State organisations. This situation reveals a gap in resource acquisition and use, partly due to State-level actors' limited participation in collaborative efforts despite the potential for co-concession.

The lack of a unified vision among these actors regarding resource sharing and cooperation limits their collective potential, focusing instead on fulfiling individual and organisational demands. Consequently, initiatives tend to occur individually, aimed at the broader development of Florianópolis (FloripAmanhã, 2021) rather than specifically supporting its UNESCO Creative City of Gastronomy label.

There is a notable misalignment in coopetition at the national level, largely due to the distance between national entities and Florianópolis. It is uncertain if this is due to the city's reluctance to collaborate with national organisations or a lack of outreach from these national entities. This issue of limited national cooperation is linked to the international level, specifically with UNESCO 'Paris', affecting higher governance dynamics.

A key issue identified is the inadequate development of partnerships, particularly between Florianópolis and other UNESCO-designated Creative Cities of Gastronomy and UNESCO International. Observations highlight a significant disconnect between the city and UNESCO 'Paris', with a sense of neglect from UNESCO undermining Multilevel Governance (Hooghe & Marks, 2020). The following sections will delve into the Multilevel Governance Framework in the context of coopetition, drawing from field research in Florianópolis during 2022 and 2023 (Fig. 5.1).

This context illustrates that Multilevel Governance within the UNESCO Creative Cities Network (UCCN) is crucial for fostering a social ethos of core governance (Mediotte & Emmendoerfer, 2020). Organisational structures should increasingly collaborate within an inter-organisational framework, leveraging the expertise of social actors in the Multilevel Governance Network to work with Florianópolis's entire gastronomic production chain and cultural vocations.

We propose the creation of mechanisms that recognise the value of the UNESCO Creative City designation, striving for both political and socio-institutional autonomy and enhanced collectivity. This includes promoting inter-municipal cooperation for regional, national and international development, in line with Coopetition Theory. This theory underscores the importance of balancing competition risks and unintended outcomes with cooperation benefits, aiming for collective gains. We observe a need for integrating coopetition more

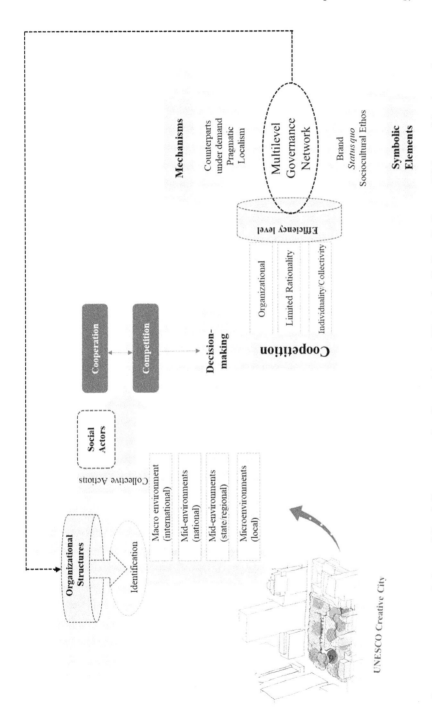

Fig. 5.1.   Framework for Multilevel Governance for Coopetition in Florianópolis Brazil. *Source:* Elaborated by the authors.

effectively as a socio-institutional strategy within the network, requiring multi-dimensional collaboration among social actors and organisational structures.

Tourism Coopetition Research Agenda: Practical Applications and Insights

The findings underscore that cooperation in managing shared resources within a governance network should act as a catalyst for organisational synergy, not a constraint. This emphasises the critical role of coopetition – integrating cooperation and competition among businesses, organisations, governments and communities – in promoting growth and sustainability in the tourism industry. By advancing skill and resource development, these networks facilitate concurrent collaboration and rivalry to attract visitors and business, thereby bolstering tourism marketing and enhancing the competitiveness of destinations from a local to an international scale.

UNESCO Creative Cities are celebrated for leveraging creativity towards sustainable development in tourism; thus, they encompass diverse fields like design, crafts and folk art, gastronomy, literature, cinema, music and digital arts. These cities play a crucial role in enhancing tourism coopetition networks through various practical applications:

- *Marketing Collaboration:* Creative cities can join forces in marketing campaigns to highlight their creative sectors and enhance branding with a creative seal, focusing on products with a Denomination of Origin (DO) or Geographical Indication (GI). An example is the oysters from Florianópolis, which serve as a distinct hallmark of its gastronomic identity and offer a potential starting point.
- *Product Development:* Creative cities can pool knowledge and resources to develop innovative tourism products that blend their creative fields with other sectors. For instance, UNESCO Creative Cities could highlight key products from other cities in the UCCN, encouraging visits to other creative cities.
- *Sharing Best Practices:* Creative cities can exchange insights and technologies for cultural heritage preservation and sustainable development, aiding others to learn from UNESCO Creative Cities' successes and challenges. For example, networked innovation labs in tourism (Emmendoerfer et al., 2023) offer an efficient means to achieve this.
- *Training and Development:* Creative cities can jointly develop programs for tourism professionals, artists, creative economy producers and students to enhance service quality and foster cultural and economic sustainability. For instance, a shared creative cultural agenda within the UCCN can boost study and creative tourism (Emmendoerfer & Ashton, 2014) at various territorial levels.
- *Cultural Vocation Events:* Creative cities can work together to host events and festivals that showcase their creative specialities, attracting a broad audience and enhancing their profile as creative tourist destinations (Richards, 2014).

A prime example is the National Oyster Festival (FENAOSTRA) in Florianópolis, which effectively promotes local coopetitive tourism.

- *Strengthening Local Development Organisations:* The practical applications mentioned can be managed by local productive arrangements (LPAs) or tourism-focused social organisations serving as Creative Hubs (Hill et al., 2021).

Coopetition in tourist destinations seeks to optimise benefits and intertwines with tourism and creativity. Echoing Emmendoerfer (2019), tourism coopetition fosters synergies that enhance regions while competition spurs innovation and improvement. UNESCO Creative Cities could be pivotal in tourism coopetition networks, serving as hubs for experimentation, entrepreneurship and innovation.

The study also identifies limitations and opportunities in coopetition across governance levels – local, national and international. It highlights a misalignment at the national level, possibly due to the gap between national entities and specific cities, and points out the challenges in forming international partnerships, especially between UNESCO and Creative Cities of Gastronomy, underlining the complexities of global coopetition.

In the context of UNESCO Creative Cities as tourist destinations, coopetition is viewed not just as interaction within a single creative industry but as participation in a broader tourism ecosystem. This encompasses diverse ideas, industries, creative classes and stakeholder relations, significantly enhancing competitiveness and uniqueness for those committed to the UNESCO Creative City title. Being part of this global network fosters a creative complex where tourism coopetition functions as a business ecosystem, with organisations and stakeholders striving for network consistency across various spatial scales and activities. It emphasises the connectivity of values, traditions and modernity and the creation of distinctive products through collaborative efforts and competitive promotion, as the Coopetition Theory suggests.

Moreover, this study enriches the concept of tourism coopetition within UNESCO Creative Cities, highlighting the importance of inter-municipal cooperation for development across scales, in line with the Coopetition Theory. It notes the potential for successful local public–private partnerships and the difficulty of compartmentalising resources and activities. Thus, these discussions could form the basis for future research on tourism coopetition networks.

Final Considerations

This study reveals disparities in the Multilevel Governance of a UNESCO Creative City, particularly in how social actors and organisational structures interact, highlighting a blend of cooperative strategies with competitive elements aiming for reciprocity. It shows that the UNESCO Creative City title creates an environment where goals conflict, pushing it towards being seen more as a 'brand', raising questions about the title's (de)legitimisation.

Coopetition Theory suggests that failing to articulate the social, economic, cultural and environmental significance of the UNESCO Creative City designation leads to a disconnect between the title's intended purpose and its actual relevance. This issue is compounded by the unclear impacts of social actors' activities within a Multilevel Governance Network.

Our study also notes a shift towards understanding coopetition in tourism, with Florianópolis seeking a competitive advantage through its Gastronomy brand and its inclusion as UCCN. However, this effort is concentrated within a core governance group that lacks complete oversight of creative activities.

We point out the nascent state of Multilevel Governance theory, with an emerging governance subculture that lacks a clear, jurisdictional and multidimensional framework extending from local to international levels. This leads to a theoretical gap in understanding sociability (cooperation), scale diversity in offering collective goods (coordination) and politicisation (collaboration). This gap is particularly notable in the socio-institutionalisation between cooperation and competition (coopetition).

This study advances the concept of tourist coopetition in UNESCO Creative Cities, underscoring inter-municipal cooperation's role in fostering development across levels, consistent with Coopetition Theory. It highlights the potential of local public–private partnerships and addresses the challenges of segregating resources and activities in organisational structures. These insights pave the way for promising research agendas on tourism coopetition networks.

Acknowledgements

We thank the National Council for Scientific and Technological Development of Brazil (CNPq) and Minas Gerais State Research Support Foundation (FAPEMIG), Brazil.

References

Bardin, L. (2020). *Analise de conteúdo* (p. 70). Edições.
Bengtsson, M., & Kock, S. (2000). "Coopetition" in business Networks—To cooperate and compete simultaneously. *Industrial Marketing Management, 29*(5), 411–426.
Bengtsson, M., & Raza-Ullah (2016). A systematic review of research on competition: Toward a multilevel understanding. *Industrial Marketing Management, 57,* 23–39.
Betsill, M., & Bulkeley, H. (2006). Cities and the multilevel governance of global change. *Global Governance, 12*(2), 141–159.
Bouncken, R. B., Gast, J., Kraus, S., & Bogers, M. (2015). Coopetition: A systematic review, synthesis, and future research directions. *Review of Managerial Science, 9,* 577–601.
Brandenburger, A., & Nalebuff, B. (1996). *Co-opetition.* Doubleday Publishing.
Brazil. (1988). *Constituição da República Federativa do Brasil.* Presidência da República. https://www.planalto.gov.br/ccivil_03/constituicao/constituicao.htm
Brazil. (2021). *Mapa do Turismo 2019-2021.* shorturl.at/dnpB2.

Chim-Miki, A. F., & Batista-Canino, R. M. (2016). A pesquisa sobre Coopetição: Em direção a uma melhor compreensão do construto e sua aplicação no turismo. *Revista Turismo Visão e Ação, 18*(3), 424–447.

Corbo, L., Kraus, S., Vlačić, B., Dabić, M., Caputo, A., & Pellegrini, M. M. (2023). Coopetition and innovation: A review and research agenda. *Technovation, 122*, 1–14.

Emmendoerfer, M. L. (2019). Creative tourist regions as a basis for public policy. In N. Duxbury & G. Richards (eds), *A research agenda for creative tourism* (pp. 151–166). Edward Elgar.

Emmendoerfer, M. L., & Ashton, M. S. G. (2014). Territórios Criativos e suas Relações com o Turismo. *Journal of Tourism and Development, 4*(21/22), 459–468.

Emmendoerfer, M., Richards, G., Silva-Junior, A. C., & Mediotte, E. J. (2023). Creative tourism and innovation laboratories for tourism development in the post-pandemic context: Evidence and reflections. *Brazilian Annals of Tourism Studies, 13*(1).

Federação das Indústrias do Estado do Rio de Janeiro [FIRJAN]. (2008). *A cadeia da indústria criativa no Brasil.* https://www.firjan.com.br/firjan/empresas/competi tividade-empresarial/industria-criativa/default.htm

Flick, U. (2018). *Introduction to qualitative research* (6nd ed.). Sage.

Floripamanhã. (2013). *Florianópolis: Cidade Unesco da Gastronomia.* shorturl.at/ fpwEQ.

Floripamanhã. (2014). *Unesco city of gastronomy.* shorturl.at/uILT3.

FloripAmanhã. (2021). *Relatório Anual de Indicadores de Florianópolis.* https:// materiais.floripamanha.org/rapi-indicadores-da-rede-de-monitoramento-cidadao-2021

Guo, R., Yin, H., & Liu, X. (2023). Coopetition, organizational agility, and Innovation performance in digital new ventures. *Industrial Marketing Management, 111*, 143–157.

Hall, C. M. (2011). A typology of governance and its implications for tourism policy analysis. *Journal of Sustainable Tourism, 19*(4–5), 437–457.

Hill, I., Manning, L., & Frost, R. (2021). Rural arts entrepreneurs' placemaking – How 'entrepreneurial placemaking' explains rural creative hub evolution during COVID-19 lockdown. *Local Economy, 36*(7–8), 627–649.

Hooghe, L., & Marks, G. (2020). A postfunctionalist theory of multilevel governance. *The British Journal of Politics & International Relations, 22*(4), 820–826.

Law, R., Ye, H., & Chan, I. C. C. (2021). A critical review of smart hospitality and tourism research. *International Journal of Contemporary Hospitality Management, 34*(2), 623–641.

Marconi, M. A., & Lakatos, E. M. (2003). *Fundamentos de metodologia científica* (5nd ed.). São Paulo.

Mediotte, E. J. (2023). *Governança Multinível em Cidades Criativas da UNESCO: Atores Sociais e Estruturas Organizacionais no contexto da Sustentabilidade em Florianópolis Brasil.* [Tese de Doutorado, Universidade Federal de Viçosa, Viçosa, Brasil].

Mediotte, E. J., & Emmendoerfer, M. L. (2020). *Core governance.* Zenodo. https:// zenodo.org/doi/10.5281/zenodo.6946431

Richards, G. (2014). Creativity and tourism in the city. *Current Issues in Tourism, 17*(2), 119–144.

Roehrich, J. K., Davies, A., Tyler, B. B., Mishra, A., & Bendoly, E. (2024). Large interorganizational projects (LIPs): Toward an integrative perspective and research agenda on interorganizational governance. *Journal of Operations Management*, *70*(1), 4–21.

Rouyre, A., Fernandez, A. S., & Estrada, I. (2024). Co-evolution of governance mechanisms and coopetition in public-private projects. *Journal of Operations Management*, *70*(1), 50–79.

Rusko, R. (2024). Coopetition networks in tourism destinations: A literature review. In M. A. Camilleri (Ed.), *Tourism planning and destination marketing* (2nd ed., pp. 79–92). Emerald.Camilleri.

Sarasvathy, S. D. (2001). Causation and effectuation: Toward a theoretical shift from economic inevitability to entrepreneurial contingency. *Academy of Management Review*, *26*(2), 243–263.

Stephenson, P. (2013). Twenty years of multi-level governance: 'Where Does It Come From? What Is It? Where Is It Going?'. *Journal of European Public Policy*, *20*(6), 817–837.

Touati, N., Maillet, L., Paquette, M.-A., Denis, J.-L., & Rodríguez, C. (2015). *Understanding multilevel governance processes: The case of the Québec Healthcare System*. Annals of II International Conference on Public Policy, Catholic University of Milan. [Paper presented].

United Nations Educational Scientific and Cultural Organization (Unesco). (2019). *Creative cities network*. shorturl.at/nqQT8.

Viagem e Turismo (2014). *O que é o prêmio o melhor de viagem e turismo?*. Editora Abril. shorturl.at/sHINT.

Winkler, N. C., & Molinari, G. T. (2011). Competição, Colaboração, Cooperação e Coopetição: Revendo os conceitos em estratégias interorganizacionais. *Revista ADMpg Gestão Estratégica*, *4*(1), 1–12.

Yin, R. K. (2017). *Case study research and applications: Design and methods* (6th ed.). Sage.

Chapter 6

Coopetitive Action of Small-Scale Accommodations

Maya Damayanti[a], Mohd Alif Mohd Puzi[b], Sari Lenggogeni[c] and Hairul Nizam Ismail[a]

[a]Universitas Diponegoro, Indonesia
[b]Universiti Teknologi Malaysia, Malaysia
[c]Universitas Andalas, Indonesia

Abstract

Most industry players in the tourism sector are small-scale businesses that are prone to failure, especially within five years of establishment. Coopetition can be an innovative alternative strategy that enables small-scale business owners to compete and cooperate in a destination. The qualitative method comprises interviewing business owners and adopting the institutional analysis and development framework for small-scale accommodation in Indonesia and Malaysia. Findings highlight those geographical settings, values and norms as the main contributions of human practices shaping the culture. Moreover, the collectivist attitude provides more opportunities for coopetition, as unity is the main priority of society. The case in Indonesia reveals that local institutions regulate the behaviour, whereas the case in Malaysia shows family kinship in business activities. In general, coopetitive behaviour starts from product marketing to the customer service stage by competing personally but sharing resources if the demand is higher than capability. Accommodation owners can gain guests individually, and if during service, the number of customers exceeds the capacity of the accommodation, the owner will share the guests with other accommodation owners. The symbiosis relationship is where a win-win situation is preferable to ensure that a tourism destination can cater to more demand with limited resources. Although both cases practice coopetition based on the suitability of the cultural and local rules, the interpretation and approach differ.

Value Proposition to Tourism Coopetition, 69–81
doi:10.1108/978-1-83797-827-420241006

Keywords: Coopetition; family-owned hotels; homestays; IAD framework; Indonesia; Malaysia

Introduction

Accommodation is a crucial part of tourism activities. This sector provides much-needed facilities for tourists who want to stay at a particular destination. Accommodation typologies vary from large-scale companies with chains in various regions, executive resorts, apartments, Airbnb, bed and breakfast and homestays to camping parks, giving different options for visitors to a destination (McKercher et al., 2023).

Currently, the government and researchers are concerned mainly with the development of small and medium accommodations to provide special attention or policies to support this business. This is related to the significant contribution of small- and medium-sized enterprises in general, which has opened up job opportunities for the community, as recorded in Europe, where this group absorbs 80% of the workforce (EUROSTAT, 2020); in Indonesia, approximately 89% (Sasongko, 2020); and in Malaysia, approximately 47.8% (SMEinfo, 2024). In terms of defining this type of accommodation, in general, the criteria employed are the number of workers, as applied by Europe with a maximum of 49 workers (EUROSTAT, 2020), Indonesian micro and small industries with 1–19 workers (BPS Indonesia, 2023) and the Malaysian service sector with not more than 30 workers (SMEinfo, 2024). Small-scale accommodations encounter significant challenges in business operations, particularly regarding finance, market access, entrepreneurship and competition with similar businesses (Sabel et al., 2024; Thomas et al., 2011).

Hence, scholars recognise coopetition as an alternative approach to acknowledging specific firms' behaviours, particularly small- and medium-sized enterprises, in overcoming their challenges. Coopetition allows two or more firms to cooperate and compete in a particular situation or activity. In the context of small-scale accommodation, coopetition not only provides economic benefits by reducing the cost of production through cooperation but also stimulates firms' innovations by learning the success story of the competitor (Kallmuenzer et al., 2021) and specialising their products (Lindström & Polsa, 2016).

The discourse of coopetition mostly uses the concept of game theory as the basis for developing this concept. In game theory, competition with others is considered a zero-sum game, and cooperation is a positive-sum game that emphasises mutual benefits (Brandenburger & Nalebuff, 1995). The concept of coopetition is also discussed on the basis of the relationship between 'cooperation' and 'competition' activities that occur simultaneously between different groups of economic actors in the creation of value products (Brandenburger & Nalebuff, 1996). The same actors might also perform coopetition in their simultaneous competition and cooperation at the same time (Bengtsson & Kock, 2000; Galvagno & Garraffo, 2010). Moreover, coopetition might arise simultaneously in the same actor when sharing several resources or sequentially on the same resources (Damayanti et al., 2017).

In the context of small-scale accommodations, coopetition is expected to run successfully in a network where small firms are located in geographical proximity (Granata et al., 2018; Sabel et al., 2024). Small firms can easily access resources to cooperate and compete, such as accessing local services and infrastructures, as well as market/tourists in a destination (Lindström & Polsa, 2016). Thus, this study aims to explore the coopetition behaviours of small-scale accommodations located in geographical proximity. Two cases are selected in this study, that is, homestays in Samiran Village, Boyolali, Indonesia, which represented small-scale accommodation in a rural area, and family-owned hotels in Langkawi Island, Malaysia, which represented small-scale accommodation on a small island.

Method

This research uses a qualitative and multiple case studies approach to clarify the actual conditions (Creswell & Creswell, 2017; Yin, 2009), such as small-scale accommodation in Samiran Tourism Village, Indonesia, and Langkawi Island, Malaysia. Data were collected using semi-structured interviews with key players in managing the accommodation. Next, the analysis used content analysis through a systematic process, namely, coding and identifying themes/categories that would describe the substance or message (Krippendorff, 2013).

The research adopts the institutional analysis and developed (IAD) framework introduced by Ostrom to examine individual behaviours (action situations) as interactions among actors influenced by external factors, that is, attributes of the community, biophysical condition and rules in use (Nyaupane et al., 2022; Ostrom, 2013). Attributes of the community relate to the location of each action and the situation in which the actors are embedded in their daily business activities. Biophysical conditions refer to the nature of goods or shared resources among the actors. Rules in use discuss the common understandings among actors that describe what actions, behaviours or outcomes are required, prohibited or permitted. By analysing these external factors, this research explores how and why tourism actors engage in coopetition. Thus, in the analysis process, this research will first discuss coopetitive actions, followed by discussions of external factors.

Samiran Tourism Village, Indonesia, as the First Case Study

Samiran Tourism Village is located in Selo District, Boyolali Regency, Central Java Province. In 2007, this tourism village was developed in response to Mount Merapi climbers' arrivals that pass this village and spend several hours before and after climbing the mountain. During their visits, the visitors can explore and experience the beauty of the village. The tourists' activities include picking vegetables and fruit, soft tracking, learning gamelan, learning dance, milking cows, learning to make cheese and biogas and outbound. Tourists can also see local arts, such as cultural carnivals, dance performances and Mount Merapi alms ceremonies. While visiting Samiran

Tourism Village, tourists can stay in homestays provided by the residents, where they live together with community members and enjoy local dishes provided by the homeowner. There are 25 homestays located in two hamlets assigned as the centre of accommodation in this village. The house owner provides at least two bedrooms and a bathroom for visitors. The guests can interact with the host as they share the house and enjoy local cuisine in their breakfast as a compulsory service. The homestay owners are members of a community organisation called Pokdarwis (*Kelompok Sadar Wisata*/tourism awareness group) *Guyub Rukun*. This informal institution can be found in every village in Indonesia that implements community-based tourism to empower the community as the main actors at a tourist destination.

Langkawi Island, Malaysia, as a Second Case Study

Langkawi Island is the primary island destination for Malaysian tourism. Tourism development is initiated by the former prime minister to accelerate the local community's economic growth. Consequently, the island was awarded a duty-free title in 1987 and Geopark by UNESCO in 2007. One of the government agencies, Majlis Amanah Rakyat, which emphasises local community empowerment, introduced a tourism business assistance programme. The agency provided free chalets and soft loans to create new ventures. Interestingly, the local community participating in the development programme has become a significant player in the Langkawi tourism industry after more than 30 years. The destination can even attract government investment of more than USD 200 million.

Consequently, 18 families have become significant players in Langkawi Island's tourism industry, which includes accommodation, restaurants, travel agencies, duty-free shops and souvenir producers. These families have a good reputation among local entrepreneurs, and their brand represents Langkawi Island. One family has been doing the same business and has owned the company since 1837. These families have a kinship attitude to each other because island communities tend to have distant blood relationships. Consequently, every family has family ties and cooperates to develop the destination as a community rather than an individual company.

Results and Discussion

Coopetition as an Action Situation

The First Case

The first cooperation action of a homestay in Samiran Village was illustrated at the beginning of its establishment. In this situation, owners have limited financial resources and must provide standard-compliant facilities to customers.

Second, the homestays manage the water supply collectively. The location of the village in a mountainous area and the limited facilities connecting water sources to residents' homes have an impact on the availability of water for homestays in this village, especially during the dry season and when the need for clean water is very high along with the number of homestay guests. Therefore, the homestay decided to use these facilities collectively. Because they implemented a gravity water system, they used water alternately. When homestays in higher areas have met their water needs, the water supply will be turned off, allowing homestays in lower areas (far from water sources) to have a clean water supply. In certain situations, when the water supply is insufficient, some homestay owners collectively purchase clean water from water providers to reduce their budget.

The third and main cooperation action between homestay owners can be observed in managing large numbers of guests (groups). Usually, these guests take tour packages at Samiran Tourism Village. Visitors will enjoy several tourist attractions and stay at least one night in this Tourist Village. This type of tourist will be managed by Pokdarwis, who will organise all tourist activities while visiting this village. Cooperation among homestays is conducted by serving tourists together. Pokdarwis will allocate homestays according to capacity, room availability and considerations of fairness (efforts are made so that all homestays will have the opportunity to have guests, even if not on one occasion). This cooperation between homestay managers continues by providing services based on standards to satisfy guests, who will visit again on another occasion, either in a group or individually, by staying in the same homestay. In terms of profit, the Pokdarwis manage it from the price of the package chosen by the visitors. The homestay owner will benefit in accordance with the agreement between the Pokdarwis and homestay owners and the number of nights the guest(s) spent.

In terms of competition, the homestays in Samiran Village compete to gain customers. In the previous discussion, homestay owners usually have guests managed by Pokdarwis; however, they have the right to find their guests. The owners will market their homestays through digital platforms and social media with the target potential visitors. Meanwhile, for visitors who are already in this destination but have not yet received accommodation, homestay owners attempt to attract them by putting up attractive and eye-catching signboards.

Next, the owners also compete to provide the best service for guests, which includes hospitality, cleanliness, the taste of the dishes (breakfast) and the facilities' completeness. Through these efforts, guests are expected to have a memorable experience, and on the next occasion, they will return to stay at this homestay or recommend it to their friends or family. This good service will also be noted by the Pokdarwis management, who will evaluate the performance of each homestay based on visitor satisfaction assessments. To provide the best service for visitors, Pokdarwis will consider the reputation of each homestay in addition to equal opportunities to serve visitors.

The Second Case

Cooperation in the Malaysian case begins with inheriting the most paramount asset, the land. The government agency provided the landowner with financial assistance and chalet construction during the founder's generation.

Interestingly, the land is the cumulative profit as the business grows, and the profit sharing grows accordingly, even to the new generation in the family. The family will utilise the asset either for rental or as collateral for the new business. To reduce dependency on financial institutions, families can also create their own bank for future business expansion.

Furthermore, the second most valuable asset for the family business is the network established by several generations. These business networks are created over a long period of time, and the family reputation in the local business setting assists the new generation in building new networks. The use of networks is essential for business survival as the trust between all stakeholders is high for the family business.

Thus, utilising the family capital reflects the family's teamwork to achieve the union's objective. In addition, to ensure that the family can run and determine the business direction, the family member must acknowledge other's weaknesses and strengths. The family applied the constitutional monarchy as the family leader would decide the best course for the business with the advice and assistance of other family members. Tolerance and collective objective pursuit simultaneously create a sense of union and rivalry as every family member gives their best performance towards the business.

Competition in Malaysia emphasises the individual (family member) and the families to grab opportunities. The tourism industry provides the best opportunity as family members are free to create new ventures. Sharing resources such as finances and networks creates opportunities for family members, especially for dissatisfied family members. The primary business is an opportunity platform for family members to test different approaches or be independent of the main family. One of the reasons for this is family expansion, considering that the new nuclear family requires more profit to sustain the lifestyle.

In addition, the family will create new ventures due to the collective behaviour of the family. This action is the test bed for the new generation of the family to learn business management while the family has the control to ensure profit. The family leader will control the progress and monitor the performance to ensure a high success rate. Consequently, every individual (family member) and family within the case study live in symbiosis and compete simultaneously.

Hence, the family business in Langkawi has a business diversification mindset and even has to compete with other families. This mindset is to diversify capital and increase profit for the growing family. Preventing all eggs from being in one basket is the motto to ensure financial security. Interestingly, the new business is also an opportunity for the family to explore new businesses. The family can pull the brake if there is no future profit by having small investment losses.

The presence of actors within close geographical distance, that is, Samiran Village and Langkawi Island, plays significant roles in the coopetition among actors (Lindström & Polsa, 2016). They build cooperation activities on the basis of their relationship and knowledge of the actor's characters and capacities. The two cases above show coopetition behaviour between small-scale accommodation providers in a tourist destination. Limited resources, such as finance and facilities, are the main factors behind cooperation between actors. In contrast, limited demand, namely, tourists visiting a destination, is the main factor behind competition between actors (Della Corte & Aria, 2016; Lindström & Polsa, 2016).

External Factors of Coopetition

Attributes of the Community

In the first case, the homestay owners play two roles in this village's tourism development. They are individual players with property to be rented as accommodation for visitors. Their actions mainly gain profits from tourism activities in this village. Conversely, they are also members of the Pokdarwis who must follow all agreements among the members. Here, the main objective of the Pokdarwis is to ensure the welfare of all villagers by maintaining the sustainability of tourism activities in this village.

Meanwhile, in the second case, accommodation concentrates on accommodation, duty-free products and local medicine (the famous sea cucumber oil). Due to the high number of tourists coming to the island, the family owners utilise the profits to generate new ventures, diversify the business and provide opportunities to the younger generations. However, all business owners will collaborate as inseparability is the key to the destination's success rather than relying on a single business performance. They will exchange experience, knowledge and skills with each other to strengthen the quality of the services.

The involvement of actors in the coopetition actions also indicates the existence of trust among them. Trust is a prerequisite for cooperation among actors (Czernek & Czakon, 2016; Kallmuenzer et al., 2021; Ostrom & Walker, 2003). In the first case, the actors build their trust not instantly through intensive meetings in the Pokdarwis but also through cooperation actions in coping with their challenges and their closeness as neighbours. In the second case, family-owned businesses learn from each other by sharing resources such as networks, knowledge, skills and rooms based on trust as neighbours.

The presence and role of social networks in both cases illustrate the existence of social capital in the coopetition between the actors. Intensive interactions between the actors in both economic and social activities create bonding and leverage trust among them (Arregle et al., 2007; Crick & Crick, 2021). Vice versa, such coopetitive actions are generated through the social capital that each actor has, namely social networks (Teixeira et al., 2019), such as being a member of an extended family and/or a member of a community group.

Biophysical Conditions

In the first case, the main biophysical conditions or shared resources of the homestay owners are visitors to the destination. In a cooperation situation, each homestay can serve visitors based on the allocation from the Pokdarwis. In contrast, each homestay tries to gain a market (visitors) through individual marketing and services in a competitive situation. Occasionally, the homestays share clean water during the dry season. The homestay owners also share the beautiful scenery of this village, which is located in the valleys of Mount Merapi and Mount Merbabu. This strategic location provides an advantage in attracting more guests.

In the second case, accommodation relies on natural resources such as beaches where all the businesses cluster along the famous Chenang Beach, sharing the tourism activities along the beach so that guests can choose freely and even stay in different accommodations. Each company is independent, but due to distant blood relationships, they cooperate by sharing knowledge, skills, networks and rooms to cater to the high volume of group tourists. Every business emphasises the individual brand by establishing relationships with guests (to create repeat customers) for long-term profit orientation.

The two cases in this study are located in tourist destinations that have natural beauty in the form of mountains and beaches, so tourism actors in this area share natural beauty as an attraction for potential consumers. In this context, nature can be classified as a public good that is free for everyone to access (Ostrom, 2013). However, of course, the homestay or hotel owners have to buy land and/or buildings for their business, particularly the property in a strategic location with the best view of the beach or mountain. In this case, land and buildings are included as private goods where the use of the goods is attached to the owner, who has the property rights (Ostrom et al., 2010). It is also illustrated that the homestay owners compete and cooperate in accessing spring water as a source of clean water. These resources can be classified as common pool resources where everyone is free to access them, but consumption of these resources will affect the benefits of other people who also consume them (Ostrom, 2013).

Rules in Use

In the first case, most of the rules of coopetition are defined by Pokdarwis as the leading actor in this tourism village. These rules apply not only to homestay owners but also to all tourism actors in this tourism village, including transportation service providers, traditional dancers and music players, vegetable farmers, cattle breeders and small industries processing agricultural products, which are tourist attractions in this village.

The main rule among members is that the Pokdarwis will regulate the distribution of visitors/guests for each tourist attraction. This rule is applied to ensure that all tourism actors have the same opportunity to serve tourists or gain benefits from tourism activities. This distribution is carried out based on the number of tourists who come, the readiness of tourism actors and the evaluation of previous performance. If the number of tourists who come is sufficiently large, more tourism actors will be involved in this tourism activity. If the tourism actors at that time are not ready to receive guests because of other agendas or particular situations, then the guests will be transferred to other tourism actors. If the results of the previous performance evaluation are unsatisfactory, then the tourist actor will not have the opportunity to serve tourists before improving themselves according to the evaluation results.

Another rule related to homestays is that each homestay has the right to find its own guests. This rule avoids homestay dependence on group guests managed by Pokdarwis. The characteristics of visitors to this area vary, not only in large groups, which Pokdarwis usually manage but also in small groups (such as families) or individuals who can stay at homestays without going through Pokdarwis.

In addition, related to cooperation between homestay owners in providing clean water collectively, each homestay must take water under the joint agreement. Water can be divided equally between homestays, or homestay owners who want to take more water must be willing to pay more than others. These provisions have been agreed upon and implemented to avoid conflicts.

In the second case, the norm and attitude practice are to ensure the family's survivability through the business' resilience. Hence, every family will try to be more innovative, and this healthy competition will create more opportunities for the future generation. Business failure will lead the family towards crisis as the family members' lives highly depend on the business' profit. The family lifestyle is already embedded in the tourism business, and it has become the new generation's responsibility to protect it. The business also provides job security and bread for the family. Retired family members monitor business performance to ensure that family interest is always prioritised.

Family businesses in Langkawi prefer small profit continuity because of long-term profit orientation. Tourism products such as rooms per night are perishable, and families decide to ensure that every room has high occupancy. Flexible prices to attract tourists are the preferred method. This method is the bargaining session between tourists and owners to create a win-win situation. There is also an unspoken consensus among the families to follow the peak season price, which will generate profit in the case study. All these approaches create regular customers who can bring a more stable income to the family.

However, depending on their management capability, the family will only expand the business. Slow and steady is how a family conducts business, relying on family members as the primary human resources. The family also requires ample time to familiarise themselves with the business environment and stabilise their income. This action will reduce losses and focus on long-term profit orientation. Accordingly, the new generation is trusted to grab future opportunities based on the family's accruing capital.

In addition, the family has debt phobia as the family is capable of fully utilising the asset without any loan if they must. The negative impression of the loans is to avoid burdening the new generation. Every profit will be half, and the financial institution will take that as interest. A loan is unavoidable if the situation pressures the family, but this is the least preferable method. The family insists on growing their capital for future business expansion or new venture creations.

In both cases, coopetitive behaviour does not occur spontaneously but is structured in a pattern of relationships between actors. In the first case, this coopetitive behaviour is regulated by a local organisation, Pokdarwis, which includes all tourism actors in this village. Hence, the rules used in competition among the actors result from their consensus or agreement to ensure equal benefits for all (Biel et al., 2008), particularly in sharing resources. Meanwhile, in the second case, coopetitive behaviour is structured in the family, which for generations regulates relationships between family members to ensure the welfare of family members and their family's legacy.

The existence of this group or social network also influences the decision-making of each actor in the coopetition. In this case, each actor must consider the group gain (Mitchell et al., 2012) from all members of his social network. Each accommodation owner must follow the Pokdarwis decision, which regulates the distribution of visitors to each homestay, considering the equal distribution of benefits. This phenomenon also occurred in the second case; these families protected their ownership in the community from external influence by creating a business association. In terms of decision-making, these family hotels might pursue non-financial and family-related goals (Kallmuenzer et al., 2021) to ensure the sustainability of their family business. The commitment of these actors in implementing collective decisions is a critical factor for the success of coopetition between actors (Chin et al., 2008).

Conclusion

A tourism destination is an arena with cooperation and competition behaviour for survivability and profit orientation. Coopetition is intense among small-scale enterprises, especially accommodation in peripheral areas such as islands and villages, as illustrated in Fig. 6.1. This arena is the medium of interaction with complex and dynamic relationships between actors. The IAD framework provides

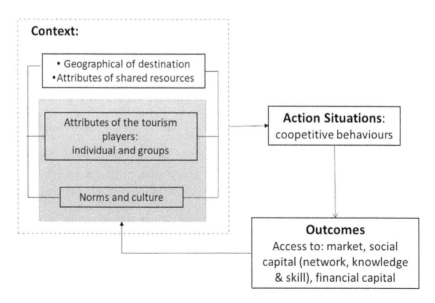

Fig. 6.1.   Coopetitive Behaviours of Small-Scale Accommodation.

a better understanding that small-scale accommodation's cooperative behaviour is strongly influenced by attributes such as family or village community members. A community's existence is a means for actors in geographical proximity to be economically and socially interdependent. This connection also encourages consensus agreements in the form of norms, which become rules for business management, namely coopetition.

The existence and role of social networks in coopetitive behaviour can be an input for policymakers in developing a tourism destination. Policymakers should first approach existing social networks as cooperation or family businesses before initiating tourism development. This approach is to obtain feedback to design a programme that suits the needs and dynamics of the group. Moreover, regulated norms and culture within families and community groups can prevent conflict between actors through capital (social and financial) management and motivate actors to participate in coopetition. This framework can be refined by including longitudinal studies on the dynamics of groups/social networks that influence the sustainability of coopetition behaviour between actors.

References

Arregle, J.-L., Hitt, M. A., Sirmon, D. G., & Very, P. (2007). The development of organizational social capital: Attributes of family firms. *Journal of Management Studies, 44*(1), 73–95. https://doi.org/10.1111/j.1467-6486.2007.00665.x

Bengtsson, M., & Kock, S. (2000). "Coopetition" in business networks–To cooperate and compete simultaneously. *Industrial Marketing Management, 29*(5), 411–426. https://doi.org/10.1016/S0019-8501(99)00067-X

Biel, A., Eek, D., & Gärling, T. (eds). (2008). *New issues and paradigms in research on social dilemmas.* Springer US.

BPS Indonesia. (2023). *Profil Industri Mikro dan Kecil 2022 (Profile of micro and small industries 2022).* BPS Indonesia (Indonesian Statistic Bureau).

Brandenburger, A. M., & Nalebuff, B. J. (1995). *The right game: Use game theory to shape strategy* (Vol. Vol. 73). Harvard Business Review.

Brandenburger, A. M., & Nalebuff, B. J. (1996). *Co-opetition.* HarperCollinsBusiness.

Chin, K. S., Chan, B. L., & Lam, P. K. (2008). Identifying and prioritizing critical success factors for coopetition strategy. *Industrial Management & Data Systems, 108*(4), 437–454.

Creswell, J. W., & Creswell, J. D. (2017). *Research design: Qualitative, quantitative, and mixed methods approaches* (5th ed.). Sage publications.

Crick, J. M., & Crick, D. (2021). Coopetition and family-owned wine producers. *Journal of Business Research, 135*, 319–336. https://doi.org/10.1016/j.jbusres.2021.06.046

Czernek, K., & Czakon, W. (2016). Trust-building processes in tourist coopetition: The case of a Polish region. *Tourism Management, 52*, 380–394. https://doi.org/10.1016/j.tourman.2015.07.009

Damayanti, M., Scott, N., & Ruhanen, L. (2017). Coopetitive behaviours in an informal tourism economy. *Annals of Tourism Research, 65*, 25–35. https://doi.org/10.1016/j.annals.2017.04.007

Della Corte, V., & Aria, M. (2016). Coopetition and sustainable competitive advantage. The case of tourist destinations. *Tourism Management, 54*, 524–540. https://doi.org/10.1016/j.tourman.2015.12.009

EUROSTAT. (2020). *Small and medium-sized enterprises: An overview.* https://ec.europa.eu/eurostat/web/products-eurostat-news/-/DDN-20200514-1

Galvagno, M., & Garraffo, F. (2010). The promise of coopetition as a new theoretical perspective in strategic management. In S. Yami, S. Castaldo, G. B. Dagnino, & F. L. Roy (eds), *Coopetition: Winning strategies for the 21st century* (pp. 40–57). Edward Elgar Publiching Limited.

Granata, J., Lasch, F., Le Roy, F., & Dana, L.-P. (2018). How do micro-firms manage coopetition? A study of the wine sector in France. *International Small Business Journal, 36*(3), 331–355. doi:10.1177/0266242617740412

Kallmuenzer, A., Zach, F. J., Wachter, T., Kraus, S., & Salner, P. (2021). Antecedents of coopetition in small and medium-sized hospitality firms. *International Journal of Hospitality Management, 99*, 103076. https://doi.org/10.1016/j.ijhm.2021.103076

Krippendorff, K. (2013). *Content analysis: An introduction to its methodology* (3rd ed.). SAGE Publications.

Lindström, T., & Polsa, P. (2016). Coopetition close to the customer — A case study of a small business network. *Industrial Marketing Management, 53*, 207–215. https://doi.org/10.1016/j.indmarman.2015.06.005

McKercher, B., Prideaux, B., & Thompson, M. (2023). The relationship between accommodation type and tourists' in-destination behaviour. *Tourism Recreation Research*, 1–10. doi:10.1080/02508281.2023.2221070

Mitchell, M. S., Cropanzano, R. S., & Quisenberry, D. M. (2012). Social exchange theory, exchange resources, and interpersonal relationships: A modest resolution of theoretical difficulties. In K. Törnblom & A. Kazemi (eds), *Handbook of social resource theory: theoretical rxtensions, empirical insights, and social applications* (pp. 99–118). Springer New York.

Nyaupane, G. P., Poudel, S., & York, A. (2022). Governance of protected areas: An institutional analysis of conservation, community livelihood, and tourism outcomes. *Journal of Sustainable Tourism, 30*(11), 2686–2705. doi:10.1080/09669582.2020.1858089

Ostrom, E. (2013). Do institutions for collective action evolve?. *Journal of Bio-economics*, 1–28. doi:10.1007/s10818-013-9154-8

Ostrom, E., Hess, C., & De Geest, G. (2010). Chapter 4: Private and common property rights. In G. D. Geest (Ed.), *Encyclopedia of law and economics*. Edward Elgar Publishing Limited.

Ostrom, E., & Walker, J. (eds). (2003). *Trust and reciprocity: Interdisclipinary lessons from experimental research.* Russell Sage Foundation.

Sabel, K., Dalborg, C., von Friedrichs, Y., & Kallmuenzer, A. (2024). The importance of network coopetition for the robustness of micro-enterprises in times of crisis. *International Small Business Journal, 0*(0), 02662426241228283. doi:10.1177/02662426241228283

Sasongko, D. (2020). *UMKM Bangkit, Ekonomi Indonesia Terungkit (SMEs rise, Indonesia's economy leverages).* https://www.djkn.kemenkeu.go.id/artikel/baca/13317/UMKM-Bangkit-Ekonomi-Indonesia-Terungkit.html

SMEinfo. (2024). *Official National SME Definition.* https://www.smeinfo.com.my/official-definition-of-sme/

Teixeira, R. M., Andreassi, T., Köseoglu, M. A., & Okumus, F. (2019). How do hospitality entrepreneurs use their social networks to access resources? Evidence from the lifecycle of small hospitality enterprises. *International Journal of Hospitality Management, 79*, 158–167. https://doi.org/10.1016/j.ijhm.2019.01.006

Thomas, R., Shaw, G., & Page, S. J. (2011). Understanding small firms in tourism: A perspective on research trends and challenges. *Tourism Management, 32*(5), 963–976.

Yin, R. K. (2009). *Case study research: Design and methods* (4th ed.). SAGE Publications.

Part Two

Co-create Tourism Business and Products: Co-entrepreneurs Using Coopetition Strategies

Chapter 7

Co-location and Coopetition as the Sources of Slow (City) Tourism: Case Rovaniemi

Anna-Emilia Haapakoski, Juulia Tikkanen and Rauno Rusko

University of Lapland, Finland

Abstract

This chapter considers the role and features of co-location and coopetition in the framework of slow (city) tourism using the city of Rovaniemi as a case study example. Rovaniemi, as a tourism destination, contains three main service agglomerations: Santa Claus Village near the Arctic Circle and the Official Airport of Santa Claus, the City centre with three shopping centres and Ounasvaara sports centre, which together constitute, based on co-location, and intentional and unintentional coopetition, one attractive destination providing possibilities for tourism due to several services and activities of the area. Slow tourism is an important emerging tendency to enable the possibility of diminishing overtourism and rethinking the value(s) of local development. Through applying the concepts of slow into tourism city planning, the empowerment and well-being of local communities in increasingly popular global destinations like Rovaniemi are emphasiscd. Rovaniemi, the city now known as the hometown of Santa Claus, has multilevel coopetitive activities to create year-round locally engaging tourism in order to restrain the development of seasonal overtourism.

Keywords: Tourism planning; slow tourism; coopetition; co-location; local resilience

Introduction

In this chapter, concepts of slow tourism and slow cities are explored in the city of Rovaniemi in Finland, related to the perspectives of co-location and coopetition. Rovaniemi, also known as the capital city of Lapland, is a rapidly growing tourism destination. What started from a local folklore narrative of Santa Claus

Value Proposition to Tourism Coopetition, 85–102

Copyright © 2025 Anna-Emilia Haapakoski, Juulia Tikkanen and Rauno Rusko

Published under exclusive licence by Emerald Publishing Limited

doi:10.1108/978-1-83797-827-420241007

residing in the area currently attracts millions of visitors from all over the world to this small city. Rovaniemi is officially known as The Official Hometown of Santa Claus under a community trademark granted by the EU (Ilola et al., 2014). Santa Claus Village, located on the marking point of the Arctic Circle, is one of the most popular attractions in Rovaniemi. It is also the centre of Christmas tourism, a typically highly seasonal form of tourism that attracts visitors to experience the seasonal festivities around December. Rovaniemi, however, stretches the time-bonds of Christmas, as Santa Claus Village is open year-round.

Although tourism brings economic and social benefits to the city in terms of money and employment, it is now, with consideration for pressing tourism-related issues like overtourism, transportation emissions and global pandemics, critical to discuss viable alternatives to a fast-paced life and travelling that we consider normal (Klarin et al., 2023). Slow City, the Cittáslow movement, has its focus on building capacity by valuing the specialness of localities and bringing together existing strengths in a city. While the Cittáslow movement has often been ana-lysed as resistance to the forces of globalisation, it can also be framed through the concept of resilience (Pink & Lewis, 2014). Slow tourism has been explored by various authors as a concept of rescaling tourism to more sustainable proportions regarding the global impacts of tourism mobility and the effects on the localities. Combining these concepts of slow, the potential of 'slow (city) tourism' is dis-cussed as a planning framework for the city of Rovaniemi.

Successful regional slow tourism needs networks, which are based on coop-eration between several firms and organisations. Many of these firms provide competitive products and services. Furthermore, often, a couple of destinations compete practically for the same visitors, thus engaging in simultaneous coop-eration and competition (Farelnik, 2020). Co-location, that is, the proximity of many services and service agglomerations, is the foundation of slow city tourism (Sørensen & Bærenholdt, 2020). This nearness enables proximity tourism, trav-elling slowly and staycationing, for which Rovaniemi is an evident example of a potential slow tourism destination. Contemporary literature on slow tourism nearly neglects the concepts of co-location and coopetition, though their impor-tance is evident as sources for this kind of tourism.

This chapter focuses on co-location and coopetition (Brandenburger & Nalebuff, 1996) and discusses the framework of slow (city) tourism for plan-ning, using the city of Rovaniemi as the case study example. This case study analysis leans on public materials on tourism planning in Rovaniemi (initially 156 official and unofficial online publications and finally, after careful qualification, 31 analysed media texts) and experiences of authors about the development projects in the area of Rovaniemi.

Slow (City) Tourism as a Framework for Planning

'Slow tourism' or 'slow travel', like other concepts of slow, has received increasing academic interest in the last two decades, mainly due to their inherent relevance to sustainability (Klarin et al., 2022, 2023). The concept of slow tourism follows the philosophy of previous slow movements and develops ideas in the context of tourism practices. The first of slow movements, slow food, dates back to 1986 in Italy, when a group of activists protested against fast-food changing the local food culture, as the fast-food chain McDonald's was opening a restaurant by the cultural heritage site of the Spanish Steps in Rome (van Bommel & Spicer, 2011). Since then, different slow movements, such as slow travel (Dickinson & Lumsdon, 2010), slow city (Pink, 2008) and slow fashion (Pookulangara & Shephard, 2013) have emerged with the aim of countering fast-paced, globalised lifestyles born out of industrial revolution. In a time of ecological distress and expanding high-speed infrastructure, ideas have entered the public debate on transport (Møller Jess, 2023). Slow movements have developed first-hand as bottom-up movements by locals and consumers. The role of media has been significant in disseminating ideas (Germann Molz, 2009; Klarin et al., 2022). Central to all of these applications of 'slow' is addressing the issue of time poverty and quick solutions for society by encouraging more thorough connections between people, place and life in general (Heitmann et al., 2011).

Slow cities, formally known as Cittáslow, were first established in 1999 by mayors of three Italian towns in response to what they perceived as the 'fast' and globally homogenising influence of globalisation (Pink, 2008). Slow cities as a planning framework for cities and towns emphasises local distinctiveness and seeks to improve the quality of life for its residents. According to Pink and Servon's (2013) ethnographic research in Spanish and UK slow cities, local leaders were less concerned with the actual speed of life than what comes with this acceleration, that is, the threat of losing the quality and uniqueness of their home city's specific, existing ways of living and practising livelihoods. Slow movements' main efforts thus include maintaining forms of face-to-face sociality and local ties, including the relationship to the land and its produce (Pink & Lewis, 2014).

Slow cities engage (slow)city planning by disseminating a model for local governance (Pink, 2008, p. 331). Through an analysis of two German Slow Cities, Hersbruck and Waldkirch, Mayer and Knox (A) conclude that the town's ability to provide and engage in alternative development agendas is derived from their cross-sector collaborations across the public, voluntary and business sectors. They suggest that 'congruency is achieved through the multiple ways in which the Slow City status can be interpreted and applied by the various supporters for urban development processes' (2006, p. 331). Pink and Lewis (2014) suggest that slow can act as a form of resilience, which enables local values and policies to co-exist with forces that are not consistent with their principles. Cittaslow's principles and criteria for the member cities outline a framework for sustainable urban development and quality of life that focuses on everyday sensory pleasure.

By combining the concepts of slow cities and slow tourism, we explore the concept of slow (city) tourism as an alternative framework for tourism development. Unlike Slow Food and Cittáslow, there are not yet established criteria or actor networks for slow tourism. Slow tourism has been considered from multiple perspectives. One of the first central elements of developing tourism has been and prevails to be the necessity of transport. In the ideology of slow tourism, however, moving away from carbon-heavy airline-focused travelling is central, mainly due to environmental-ethical reasons (Dickinson & Lumsdon, 2010; Klarin et al., 2023). Tourism, therefore, is suggested to take on new forms and consumer perspectives in more proximate environments (Salmela et al., 2021). Travelling to farther destinations on land, moving slowly enough to experience the changing place, and planning for longer stays in destinations are encouraged (Fullagar et al., 2012). Slow-travelling consumers endorse mindfulness in travelling and discovering destinations in a responsible manner, promoting tourists' consumption-oriented enjoyment of experience through slow-paced and low carbon emission travel patterns (Klarin et al., 2023). Although the slow movement shies away from mass consumption, it is not anti-consumerist because it values the experiences of learning about the traditions through engaging in performative activities of art and purchasing locally grown food, for instance.

Conway and Timms (2010, p. 74) suggest that slow travel might very well be a suitable form of tourism development undertaken, especially in advanced 'capitalist countries with nationally integrated and well-developed infrastructures, comprehensive transportation networks and relatively small distances between amenity-rich and environmentally attractive rural and urban destination'. This is the case regarding Rovaniemi, which would indeed allow tourism planning to include more options for arriving by land, proximity tourism, day-tripping, staycations and other forms of slow tourism.

Co-location and Coopetition in Tourism Planning

Coopetition can be simply understood as simultaneous cooperation and competition of actors (Rusko, 2024). This approach is both promising and challenging in understanding cooperation between different competing actors, such as firms, organisations, networks and individuals (Rusko et al., 2013). Coopetition is becoming more popular in business and tourism, especially regarding the relationships between firms and other actors, and has been acknowledged as an important feature in the context of tourism and tourism destinations (Chim-Miki et al., 2020; Rusko, 2024).

Tourism destinations contain several levels and relationships between actors. Thus, this starting point provides various possibilities and perspectives for cooperation and coopetition, that is, multifaceted forms of coopetition (Chim-Miki & Batista-Canino, 2017). One of the drivers for coopetition is the geographical proximity or co-location of the competing firms in the tourism destinations (Grauslund & Hammershøy, 2021). Kylänen and Rusko (2011) emphasise the linkage between co-location and especially unintentional coopetition, which means intentional cooperation to have unintentional competitive features and vice versa (see also Rusko, 2018).

In Rovaniemi, coopetition has been studied in relation to Christmas tourism, which has made Rovaniemi one of the most famous Christmas destinations in the world (Rusko et al., 2013). The theme of Christmas is seen to be one of the main reasons why firms, public authorities, organisations and associations cooperate with each other (Rusko et al., 2013). 'Santa Claus Village' as well as 'Santa Park' and 'The Official Airport of Santa Claus' are located relatively close to each other at the heart of the Arctic Circle (Fig. 7.1).

However, studies on cooperation remain limited to the perspective of firms and other co-located actors and their interaction. Therefore, one aim of this chapter is to extend the conceptual approach of coopetition to include local residents as tourism planners who are a crucial part of a tourism destination as it is their home. This approach becomes apparent, for instance, in the definition of responsible tourism, as it is defined as 'making better places for people to live in and better places for people to visit' (Cape Town Declaration, 2002). The emphasis of this definition is particularly in this order: locals live in the destinations, while tourists are only visitors. Responsible tourism planning, therefore, critically calls for more local engagement, which we also emphasise in this study.

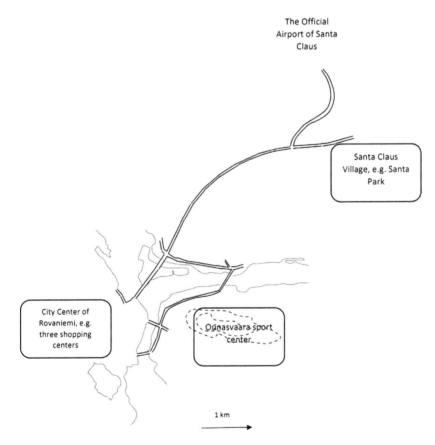

Fig. 7.1.   Three Main Destinations of the City of Rovaniemi. *Source: Elaborated by the authors.*

Research Design

Methodology

This chapter makes an initiative for tourism development discussions to meet complex perspectives related to tourism growth and to consider planning visions. Methodologically, this chapter leans on a case study strategy (Yin, 2014). The case study is focused on studying tourism planning in the context of Rovaniemi, Finland. For this purpose, 156 media texts written in Finnish were first collected. The media texts were chosen to be analysed due to the lack of studies regarding coopetition, co-location and slow (city) tourism as a framework for tourism planning. The aim of the analysis was to look for expressions related to coopetition and co-location in the texts. Furthermore, the analysis revealed some criticism in the form of seasonal overtourism, which is analysed in this study. The data cover all relevant media texts found with the search words 'Rovaniemi' and 'tourism planning', excluding advertisements (62), large (strategic) project or programme reports (22), educational thesis (4) and practices (1), official announcements (8), zoning documents (20), and the documents with duplicate content from the final analysis. Furthermore, two texts were impossible to open, and six texts had duplicate content. After careful content evaluation, only 31 media texts were analysed by applying content analysis to form a current state image of tourism planning in Rovaniemi.

After forming a descriptive image of the current, we continued to discuss the potential of a slow (city) tourism framework for the case of Rovaniemi. Table 7.1 shows the other basic features of the analysed media texts. Most of the texts were

Table 7.1. Features of the Analysed Finnish Media Texts.

Total number of media texts	*156*
Excluding:	*−125*
Advertisements	62
Reports, strategic programs	22
Educational thesis, practice	5
Do not open or paywall	2
Official announcement (municipality, project)	8
Zoning documents	20
Duplicate	6
Media texts in the final analysis	*31*
Including:	
News	13
Blogs	6
Announcements	5
Posts	4
Articles (short)	3

online newspaper articles or blog posts on the websites of associations or other non-governmental organisations (NGOs). 13 out of 31 media texts were news published by newspapers or YLE (Finnish Broadcasting Company), and three out of 13 news were published by association or public organisation. Furthermore, the analysis covered six blogs, five announcements, four posts (on Facebook, LinkedIn or YouTube) and three short articles, mostly provided by the City of Rovaniemi.

Rovaniemi

The city of Rovaniemi, located at 66° North, is the capital of Lapland County in Finland and, by total land area, the largest city in Finland and Europe. In 2022, 64,535 inhabitants lived in the city (Statistics Finland, 2022). The surrounding environment of Rovaniemi is shaped by forested hills, such as Ounasvaara, where urban nature can be accessed all year round through four seasons. Ounasvaara specialises as a centre for sports, especially downhill skiing, and cross-country skiing. This is one of the main service agglomerations of Rovaniemi and an important place for locals' free time. People who live in Rovaniemi appreciate the small-town identity and closeness to nature.

In the city centre, Rovaniemi has several small shops, restaurants and a few shopping centres surrounding the main square. The main square is named after the Finnish Eurovision winner of 2006, Lordi, who has origins in Rovaniemi. The distance between shopping centres and Ounasvaara is only a couple of kilometres, and the distance from centre of Rovaniemi to Santa Claus Village is approximately eight kilometres (Fig. 7.1). Santa Claus Village consists of dozens of competing gift shops and experienced producers, but they also have intentional cooperation activities in addition to unintentional or tacit cooperation and coopetition. These three centres are the main three service agglomerations in Rovaniemi, shared by local residents and visiting tourists.

Rovaniemi is the second biggest city as a tourist destination after Helsinki, the capital of Finland (The City of Rovaniemi, n.d.). In Rovaniemi, tourism has been growing rapidly in the last decades. The development path of tourism in the city has been strongly growth-oriented, which can be seen, for example, in increased number of flights and visitor numbers. This growth is mostly based on the city's image as a Christmas tourism destination in which the needs and wants of Christmas tourists have been highlighted.

Outcomes

A media text search by Google with the words 'Rovaniemi' and 'tourism planning' yielded a total of 156 media texts, but mostly, they were useless to the analysis due to strong advertisement or official zoning and/or project information content. The final analysis covers 31 media texts (Table 7.2). Table 7.2 emphasises the theme of slow tourism, which takes care of the threat of overtourism, for instance. Perhaps due to strong tourism seasonality, many media texts (nine out of 31) also consider the

Table 7.2. Finally Analysed Media Texts.

No.	Type of Media Text	Some Details	Focus (Growth of Tourism Versus Overtourism)	Rate of Competition 1: Cooperation 2: Cooperation-Based Coopetition 3: Coopetition 4: Competition-Based Coopetition 5: Competition	Year
1	Blog	Individual (on the local cloth industry project)	Neutral	3	?
2	Blog	Individual	Neutral	1	?
3	News	Newspaper (*Kaleva*) about the zoning of Ounasvaara.	Overtourism	4, 5	2004
4	Announcement/ News	Angrybirds – park opening (STTInfo & Lappset)	Neutral	2	2012
5	News	About the safety plan of tourism for Rovaniemi (YLE)	Overtourism (partly)	1	2013
6	Blog, institute	Lapinkampus blog	Growth	2, 3	2019
7	Announcement	Event about the rush in tourism	Overtourism	4	2019
8	Youtube post	Video, about the event focused on overtourism	Overtourism	5	2019

9	Blog, event	Lapland University of Applied Sciences	Neutral	1	2019/2020?
10	Article/News	Article of the City to public about the numeric (growth) aims.	Growth	1, 2	2020
11	News	MTVuutiset.fi about the effects of Covid-19 in tourism	Neutral	1	2020
12	News (organisation)	Introduction about tourism investments in Rovaniemi by Lapland Above Ordinary	Growth	3	2020/2021
13	News	*Iltalehti* newspaper: Tips to avoid rush in Lapland tourism	Overtourism (partly)	4	2021
14	News	Centre for Economic Development, Transport and the Environment. News with interview.	Neutral	1	2021
15	News (comment)	Individual comment in *Lapin Kansa* newspaper about missing possibilities of inhabitants and tourism firms to affect tourism planning.	Overtourism (partly)	5	2022
16	News	*HS* newspaper	Growth	1	2022
17	Blog	Blog about snow construction	Neutral	4	2022
18	News	*Iltalehti* newspaper	Neutral	2	2022
19	Announcement	Tourism statistics provided by Visit Rovaniemi	Neutral	-	2023

(Continued)

Table 7.2. (*Continued*)

No.	Type of Media Text	Some Details	Focus (Growth of Tourism Versus Overtourism)	Rate of Competition 1: Cooperation 2: Cooperation-Based Coopetition 3: Coopetition 4: Competition-Based Coopetition 5: Competition	Year
20	Announcement (University)	Announcement of new book about the responsible tourism planning, University of Lapland	Overtourism	4, 5	2023
21	News	Growth records of tourism in Lapland (YLE) – for example, traffic jam in airport.	Growth (mostly)	4	2023
22	Post in LinkedIn	Responsible tourism (University of Lapland)	Overtourism	4, 5	2023
23	Article	Wikipedia: Tourism in Lapland	Neutral	–	2023
24	Blog, Association	Association Rovaniemen elävä kaupunkikeskusta ry	Neutral	1, 2	2023
25	Post in LinkedIn	LinkedIn, individual about a tourism event and investments	Growth	2	2023
26	Announcement/ News	Investment project of Lapland Hotels (ePressi)	Growth	2	2023

27	Facebook post	Event (Business Rovaniemi)	Neutral	1	2023
28	News	*Koillis-Sanomat* newspaper about tourism investments	Growth	2	2023
29	Article	City of Rovaniemi about new hotel project	Growth	1	2023
30	News	Travel organisation about off-seasons and the responsibility of tourism	Overtourism	2	2023
31	Blog	Blog of individual in the pages of travel organisation	Neutral	2	2023?

problems of tourism, such as missing possibilities of inhabitants, researchers and tourism firms to affect tourism planning (media texts 15, 20, 22 and 3), safety (5) and rush (13, 7, 8, 30). Similarly, the growth of tourism, especially in the form of planned investments, was a usual theme of media texts (12, 10, 6, 21, 16, 25, 26, 28, 29).

Even the most critical media texts express the importance of coopetition and co-location. These are based on the thought and need for cooperation between different tourism stakeholders: inhabitants, official actors, firms and researchers of the city, which partly seem to have contradictory aims in tourism development. Media texts consider either the shortage of cooperation (and coopetition) or functional cooperation and coopetition in the forms of new investments, for instance. Table 7.2 also shows the 'Rate of competition', that is, the various alternative roles of cooperation, coopetition and competition for each media text using a scale of 1-5, where 1 is cooperation (media texts 5,10, 9, 24, 2, 16, 14, 29 and 11), 2 is cooperation-based coopetition, 3 is coopetition, 4 is competition-based coopetition and 5 is competition (media texts 15, 20, 22, 3, 8). Elements of coopetition were addressed in media texts 12, 6, 21, 1, 13, 25, 7, 26, 27, 4, 17, 18, 28, 30 and 31, the strongest emphasis being in media texts 12, 6 and 1. On average, this analysis yielded a value of 2.55, which means that media texts emphasise more cooperation than competition in the tourism sector of Rovaniemi. Alternatively, this outcome reveals the importance of cooperation-based coopetition in this material.

Furthermore, the content of media texts related to cooperation versus competition is relatively stable. The correlation between the 'Rate of competition' and years is -0.1244, which implies, due to low absolute value, that the annual development of the rate of competition is relatively stable but slightly decreasing. A negative sign cautiously indicates that the content of media texts has gradually developed more towards cooperation than competition in the long term. A more thorough textual analysis follows in the discussion part.

Discussion

Planning Tourism for Rovaniemi or Planning Rovaniemi for Tourism?

> In the case of Rovaniemi, the needs of tourists should also be taken into account. With their help, we are able to maintain a better service offering all year round. But can tourism be the starting point for all planning? (24)

Rovaniemi is already known to be a globally attractive tourism destination, as the media has also entitled it to be 'a growing international tourism city' (19). Indeed, approximately half a million tourists visit Rovaniemi every year (The City of Visit Rovaniemi, n.d.), and the number is estimated to keep growing. For the winter season of 2023–2024, the amount of international direct flights increased by 24 % (Visit Rovaniemi, n.d.). In the media, Rovaniemi is often envisioned as this ever-growing 'international tourism city', which the slogan of the city of Rovaniemi also explicates (The City of Visit Rovaniemi, n.d.). Still, the main pulling factors of tourism are seen to be a clean, calm and quiet environment. This is controversial to the envisioned and expected tourism growth as the growing numbers of tourists mean tourism construction and increased land and amenity use, which the environment, including its quietness and calmness, needs to side-step from.

Signs of mass tourism are starting to be noticeable and also discussed by the media and locals. Among these are ignorant behaviour, as in tourists' lack of knowledge regarding the environment, irritated locals, disturbing sounds of snowmobiles, exhaust fumes of tourist buses in the city centre and crowding of locals' favourite recreational spaces, such as forest/wilderness huts, which have become increasingly used by tourism companies (15). Signs of mass tourism can also be seen through examples of increasing construction and contradicting local values. For instance, the local forested hill and one of the service agglomerations in the city, Ounasvaara, is seen to have become dismembered due to tourism construction. One of the media texts addressed that 'new construction is being planned there [Ounasvaara] in the name of increasing tourism jobs' (3). This article's heading entails the question, 'Do we sacrifice Ounasvaara to the altar of tourism?' An increase in tourism numbers also means an increase in services provided for tourists. In Rovaniemi, animals, such as huskies and reindeer, are widely engaged in tourism production in terms of creating monetary value. Industrialisation reduces costs in that economies of scale can be gained from mass production. This is often, unfortunately, accompanied by a loss of quality and the introduction of inhumane treatment of the environment and animals involved (Heitmann et al., 2011).

It is a dangerous misconception that tourism can keep growing without sub-stantial impacts on the locality. To be able to control tourism, planning ahead is required. Tourism strategies are seen to act as a common guideline for tourism stakeholders in tourism development (Finland's Tourism Strategy, 2019). How-ever, there is no current tourism strategy for the city of Rovaniemi. The last strategy is made for the years 2007–2010 (Rovaniemi's Tourism Strategy, 2006). Similarly, the media texts that speak about tourism planning call out the lack of and need for collaborative tourism planning in Rovaniemi.

Sourcing Slow (City) Tourism through Co-location

> First of all, it would be good to find out what we residents and entrepreneurs want from our own hometown. What is the cityscape where we want to live and be, or where we want to invite friends and visitors? The construction of the city must start from the perspective of our residents because we walk these city streets and use the services of the city centre every day. (24)

According to Honoré (2005), who was among the first public advocates for slow philosophy, the main idea of the slow philosophy is balance. This is a good ground to propose slow (city) tourism as a potential concept for planning in a city where tourism is starting to strongly affect the living environment and the experiences of locals. By this, the aim is to highlight alternative options for what is considered development. With offering slow (city) tourism as a theoretical framework, we want to emphasise the balance between preserving a 'hometown' and developing a 'tourism destination'. In the media texts, the need for this approach is not visible but rather is implicated by the acceleration of fast-paced tourism construction and investments with short-sighted visions regarding Rovaniemi as an everyday living environment. The accommodation construction projects (12, 25, 26), including luxury accommodations, such as glass igloo villages (6), remain unevaluated regarding the long-term effect. City planning should start with the locals' needs and wants in their hometown, where tourists are the only visitors. However, it becomes apparent in the media texts that locals can influence decision-making, that is, tourism planning, by either voting in elections or making a complaint about a certain project (15). Thus, a common vision for the locality seems to be lacking.

Although the ideology of slow tourism has not yet developed into any institutionalised network, such as its precedents slow food and slow cities have, it seems fruitful to apply it in an actual planning context. Adopting a slow tourism framework calls for a re-evaluation of the city's priorities and revisiting the value of developing tourism in the first place (Heitmann et al., 2011). In the context of practical development, (new) priorities would include focusing on the natural and cultural uniqueness of the place as a starting point, developing low-impact tourism, and maximising local linkages through tourism (Serdane, 2020). Additionally, slow tourism proposes a market mechanism that is local and self-supporting (Heitmann et al., 2011). Local engagement in tourism, both as consumers and as practitioners of it, is emphasised to increase empowerment and decrease path-dependencies of international operators and customer flows.

Serdane (2020) suggests that the development of tourism using a slow philosophy is directly related to the capability of the tourism industry to form partnerships and cooperation between various local service providers for two main reasons: first, since slow tourism implies staying at a destination for longer, there is a need for complex tourism offerings that often can be developed among several service providers. Second, partnerships and cooperation in the tourism industry are linked with the willingness of tourists to look for and enjoy different experiences during the same trip.

Propositions for Coopetition in Slow Tourism Planning

> All the most typical businesses related to the tourism industry can be found nearby. Cooperation between companies benefits and complements each other, even if mutual competition is fierce. (6)

Currently, the coopetition benefits are recognised to some extent in Rovaniemi as the tourism destination builds between multiple typical service and product offerings related to tourism. Nowadays, a large part of the coopetition is unintentional, where an increasing number of tourism service providers increasingly attract tourists to the same area. In addition, the complexity of a multi-stakeholder and intersectoral operational environment calls for specialised competencies in foresight, the identification of strategic shifts and the creativity of partnerships (Kylänen & Rusko, 2011). As the high volumes of tourists and operators are starting to receive attention, getting together to organise practices for the desired way forward seems to be in place.

Especially related to shifting the perspective of tourism development towards the slow tourism framework, the value of coopetition deserves more recognition and also requires more openness to diverse local actors. This is important not just for sharing a vision but also in order to create interesting opportunities to explore the life of Rovaniemi from new angles. At this stage of work, partners, such as universities, are important to help recognise convergences and envision operating models. In one of the media texts, a good example of this was found:

> The VillaInno project improves the growth and innovation capabilities of small and medium-sized companies in Lapland on sheep farms and in the contexts of handicrafts and cultural tourism, continuing and renewing the cultural heritage of handicrafts [...] the project supports renewing business and the ideation of new products and services by bringing together craftsmanship and expertise from different design fields in such a way that new services and products emerge from tradition, strengthen Lapland's regional identity, and continue and renew cultural traditions. (1)

Rethinking and re-branding an alternative vision of tourism requires joint effort within the city and the companies involved in coopetition to create the destination market. Early signs of shifting the focus of tourism planning towards more traditional experiences were found in the media data. Similarly to Conway and Timms (2010), who observed the growth of Caribbean tourism into a mass market with a high level of foreign dependency, we propose it is time to start envisioning slow tourism networks to rethink the tourism market. This is important for securing local livelihoods and decentralising the tourist industry from foreign control to local empowerment.

Conclusion

In this study, we have used the concepts of coopetition and co-location to make a case for a slow (city) tourism model for destination planning. In both slow tourism and coopetition literature, this conceptual setting is new, yet a current one, especially due to the urgent need and demands to consider the sustainability of development. The City of Rovaniemi is a heavily growing tourism destination, and the media reports precipitous growth in foreign visitor numbers. However, this path of development can be questioned considering the city's social and environmental capacity. Within the chapter, we have highlighted the threat of short-sighted and fragmented tourism development visions and the importance of supporting informed local coopetition in achieving destination resilience.

The case study was built using media texts as evidence to demonstrate the planning environment and to develop an analysis of co-location and coopetition as sources of slow (city) tourism. By applying the concepts of slow cities and slow tourism to the context of a growing tourism destination, we have discussed the importance of maintaining local roots and the sense of place in tourism planning. Foresight, local control and democracy are crucial in order to empower local businesses. Slow (city) tourism offers a novel approach to coopetition networks considering sustainability (see Klarin et al., 2023). Previous studies on coopetition remain limited to the perspective of firms, other co-located actors and their interaction. Therefore, this study offers a valuable contribution to the coopetition paradigm by extending the conceptual approach, especially in tourism studies. This study works as an opening for future research into the topic. The media texts as data are limited in evaluating this point of view further, and therefore, the future steps would be to include locals by conducting interviews and mapping its managerial and governmental implications.

References

Brandenburger, A. M., & Nalebuff, B. J. (1996). *Co-opetition: A revolution mindset that combines competition and cooperation.* Crown Business.

Cape Town Declaration. (2002). Retrieved January 16, 2024, from http://responsibletourismpartnership.org/cape-town-declaration-on-responsible-tourism/

Chim-Miki, A. F., & Batista-Canino, R. M. (2017). The coopetition perspective applied to tourism destinations: A literature review. *Anatolia, 28*(3), 381–393. https://doi.org/10.1080/13032917.2017.1322524

Chim-Miki, A. F., Medina-Brito, P., & Batista-Canino, R. M. (2020). Integrated management in tourism: The role of coopetition. *Tourism Planning & Development, 17*(2), 127–146. https://doi.org/10.1080/21568316.2019.1574888

Conway, D., & Timms, B. F. (2010). Re-branding alternative tourism in the Caribbean: The case for 'slow tourism. *Tourism and Hospitality Research, 10*(4), 329–344. https://doi.org/10.1057/thr.2010.12

Dickinson, J., & Lumsdon, L. (2010). *Slow travel and tourism.* Routledge. https://doi.org/10.4324/9781849776493

Farelnik, E. (2020). Cooperation of slow cities as an opportunity for the development: An example of Polish National Cittaslow Network. *Oeconomia Copernicana, 11*(2), 267–287. https://doi.org/10.24136/oc.2020.011

Finland's Tourism Strategy. (2019). *Yhdessä enemmän – kestävää kasvua ja uudistumista Suomen matkailuun: Suomen matkailustrategia 2019–2028 ja toimenpiteet 2019–2023.* Retrieved January 16, 2024, from http://urn.fi/URN:ISBN:978-952-327-772-4

Fullagar, S., Wilson, E., & Markwell, K. (2012). *Slow tourism: Experiences and mobilities.* Channel View Publications.

Germann Molz, J. (2009). Representing pace in tourism mobilities: Staycations, slow travel and the amazing race. *Journal of Tourism and Cultural Change, 7*(4), 270–286. https://doi.org/10.1080/14766820903464242

Grauslund, D., & Hammershøy, A. (2021). Patterns of network coopetition in a merged tourism destination. *Scandinavian Journal of Hospitality and Tourism*, *21*(2), 192–211. https://doi.org/10.1080/15022250.2021.1877192

Heitmann, S., Robinson, P., & Povey, G. (2011). Slow food, slow cities and slow tourism. In P. Robinson, S. Heitmann, & P. Dieke (eds), *Research themes for tourism* (pp. 114–127). CABI. https://doi.org/10.1079/9781845936846.0114

Honoré, C. (2005). In *In Praise of slow: How a worldwide movement is challenging the cult of speed*. Orion Books Ltd.

Ilola, H., Hakkarainen, M., & García-Rosell, J. (2014). *Joulu ainainen?: Näkökulmia Rovaniemen joulumatkailuun. Matkailualan tutkimus- ja koulutusinstituutti.* Retrieved January 16, 2024, from https://urn.fi/URN:ISBN:978-952-6620-28-2

Klarin, A., Park, E., & Kim, S. (2022). The slow movements: Informetric mapping of the scholarship and implications for tourism and hospitality. *Journal of Hospitality & Tourism Research*. 109634802211160. https://doi.org/10.1177/1096348 0221116049

Klarin, A., Park, E., Xiao, Q., & Kim, S. (2023). Time to transform the way we travel?: A conceptual framework for slow tourism and travel research. *Tourism Management Perspectives*, *46*, 101100. https://doi.org/10.1016/j.tmp.2023.101100

Kylänen, M., & Rusko, R. (2011). Unintentional coopetition in the service industries: The case of Pyhä-Luosto tourism destination in the Finnish Lapland. *European Management Journal*, *29*(3), 193–205. https://doi.org/10.1016/j.emj.2010.10.006

Mayer, H., & Knox, P. L. (2006). Slow cities: Sustainable places in a fast world. *Journal of Urban Affairs*, *28*(4), 321–334. https://doi.org/10.1111/j.1467-9906.2006. 00298

Møller Jess, L. (2023). Degrowth and the slow travel movement: Opportunity for engagement or a consumer fad?. *Debates in post-development and degrowth*, vol. 2. Tvergastein.

Pink, S. (2008). Sense and sustainability: The case of the Slow City movement. *Local Environment*, *13*(2), 95–106. https://doi.org/10.1080/13549830701581895

Pink, S., & Lewis, T. (2014). Making resilience: Everyday affect and global affiliation in Australian Slow Cities. *Cultural Geographies*, *21*(4), 695–710. https://doi.org/10. 1177/1474474014520761

Pink, S., & Servon, L. J. (2013). Sensory global towns: An experiential approach to the growth of the Slow City movement. *Environment & Planning A: Economy and Space*, *45*(2), 451–466. https://doi.org/10.1068/a45133

Pookulangara, S., & Shephard, A. (2013). Slow fashion movement: Understanding consumer perceptions—An exploratory study. *Journal of Retailing and Consumer Services*, *20*(2), 200–206. https://doi.org/10.1016/j.jretconser.2012.12.002

Rovaniemi's Tourism Strategy. (2006). *Rovaniemi: Lapin sykkivä sydän - Matkailus-trategia 2007–2010*. Retrieved January 15, 2024, from https://www.rovaniemi.fi/ loader.aspx?id=db00aa34-f4f0-40f6-8691-877f26ff0373

Rusko, R. (2018). Coopetition for destination marketing: The scope of forging relationships with competitors. In *Tourism planning and destination marketing* (pp. 75–98). Emerald Publishing Limited.

Rusko, R. (2024). Coopetition networks in tourism destinations: A literature review. In M. A. Camilleri (Ed.), *Tourism planning and destination marketing* (2nd ed., pp. 79–92). Emerald Publishing Limited. https://doi.org/10.1108/978-1-80455-888-120241004

Rusko, R., Merenheimo, P., & Haanpää, M. (2013). Coopetition, resource-based view and legend: Cases of Christmas tourism and city of Rovaniemi. *International Journal of Marketing Studies*, *5*(6), 37. https://doi.org/10.5539/IJMS.V5N6P37

Salmela, T., Nevala, H., Nousiainen, M., & Rantala, O. (2021). Proximity tourism: A thematic literature review. *Matkailututkimus (Verkkoaineisto)*, *17*(1), 46–63. https://doi.org/10.33351/mt.107997

Serdane, Z. (2020). Slow philosophy in tourism development in Latvia: The supply side perspective. *Tourism Planning & Development*, *17*(3), 295–312. https://doi.org/10.1080/21568316.2019.1650103

Sørensen, F., & Bærenholdt, J. O. (2020). Tourist practices in the circular economy. *Annals of Tourism Research*, *85*, 103027. https://doi.org/10.1016/j.annals.2020.103027

Statistics Finland. (2022). *Väestönmuutokset ja väkiluku alueittain, 1990–2022, Rovaniemi*. Retrieved January 22, 2024, from https://www.stat.fi/tup/alue/index.html

The City of Rovaniemi. (n.d.). *Kasvava kansainvälinen kaupunki*. Retrieved January 23, 2024, from https://www.businessrovaniemi.fi/fi/Miksi-Rovaniemi/Kasvava-kansainvalinen-matkailukaupunki

van Bommel, K., & Spicer, A. (2011). Hail the snail: Hegemonic struggles in the slow food movement. *Organization Studies*, *32*(12), 1717–1744. https://doi.org/10.1177/0170840611425722

Visit Rovaniemi. (n.d.). *Visit Rovaniemi – matkailutilastoja ja taustatietoja. Mitä Rovaniemen matkailun aluemarkkinointi tuo yrityksille?* Retrieved January 23, 2024, from. https://www.visitrovaniemi.fi/fi/ammattilaisille/media/matkailutilastoja/

Yin, R. K. (2014). *Case study research: Design and methods* (5th ed.). SAGE.

Chapter 8

Leveraging Co-entrepreneurship Through Coopetition: The Role of Governance Mechanisms in Tourism Destinations

Joice Denise Schäfer and Rogério João Lunkes

Federal University of Santa Catarina, Brazil

Abstract

This study examines the role of destination management organisations (DMOs) in fostering coopetition – the coexistence of cooperation and competition – within tourism destinations. Focussing on the governance exerted by these organisations, we analyse how formal and informal control mechanisms contribute to the development of tourism destinations as integrated products (coentrepreneurship). Utilising a multicase study approach and content analysis supported by MAXQDA software, we found that formal governance mechanisms, when supporting and developing informal mechanisms, enhance levels of coopetition at the tourism destination. This approach strengthens the vision of shared objectives among local businesses, creating an ideal context for coentreprencurship. The findings highlight the significance of DMOs and both formal and informal mechanisms in the governance of network coopetition and its implications for coentrepreneurship, offering new insights into destination management.

Keywords: Coopetition; governance; tourism destinations; coentrepreneurship; destination management organisations

Introduction

Recent literature has highlighted the increasing adoption of a hybrid approach of competition and cooperation, termed coopetition (Nalebuff & Brandenburger, 1996). Coopetition involves a paradoxical relationship between two or more actors simultaneously engaged in both cooperative and competitive interactions,

Value Proposition to Tourism Coopetition, 103–114

Copyright © 2025 Joice Denise Schäfer and Rogério João Lunkes

Published under exclusive licence by Emerald Publishing Limited

doi:10.1108/978-1-83797-827-420241008

regardless of whether their relationship is horizontal or vertical (Bengtsson & Kock, 2014; Rosa et al., 2023). Coopetition has been employed to develop competitive advantages, foster innovation, promote the creation and sharing of knowledge, and, as a result, improve the performance of the actors involved (Damayanti et al., 2021; Mariani, 2016). Tourism destinations offer an ideal empirical setting for studying coopetitive interactions because adjacent competing businesses in a specific geographical area must cooperate to enhance the competitiveness of the destination (Chim-Miki & Batista-Canino, 2017a; Schuhbert, 2023). In this regard, a tourism destination functions as a natural centre of coopetition, balancing competition and collaboration, which enhances outcomes for stakeholders and the tourism destination as a whole (Chim-Miki & Batista-Canino, 2017a, 2018). This strategy allows destination businesses to achieve common goals while maintaining their individual competitiveness (Damayanti et al., 2021).

Tourists consume the 'tourism destination' as an integral product formed by various organisations (Chim-Miki & Batista-Canino, 2018). Thus, the tourism destination can be understood as a unit of analysis that forms a strategic network with a shared objective (i.e., to improve the destination's competitiveness) that represents a collective enterprise (Chim-Miki & Batista-Canino, 2017b). The actions taken by a tourism destination as an integral product are defined by Chim-Miki and Batista-Canino (2018) as coentrepreneurship. Scholars have suggested that a governance system is necessary to achieve a vision of collective efficiency and to drive a network through collective entrepreneurship (Chim-Miki & Batista-Canino, 2018; Tuohino & Konu, 2014) because the different nature of competitive strategies (conflicting interests) and cooperative strategies (common interests) in coopetition can cause potential conflicts (Bengtsson & Kock, 2014; Damayanti et al., 2019). The inherent contradictions in coopetition reflect these struggles between value creation (which arises from cooperation-dominated interactions) and value sharing and appropriation (which arises from competition-dominated interactions) (Chim-Miki & Batista-Canino, 2018; Mariani, 2016). To engage in successful coentrepreneurship, businesses in tourism destinations must learn to handle the tensions that result from coopetition (Mariani, 2016). To improve holistic management, create synergy among multiple agents, and avoid the side effects of coopetition, tourism destinations can create representative organisations called destination management organisations (DMOs) (Chim-Miki & Batista-Canino, 2017a). These organisations function as centres for interorganisational networks, which include complementary companies, competing companies, and suppliers.

The governance of destinations through DMOs is a complex and multidimensional process that involves coordinating various actors and resources to ensure the sustainable and effective development of a tourism destination (Farsari, 2023). DMOs play a crucial role in the planning, coordination, and management of the capacities and resources of various stakeholders, and they contribute to the effective sustainable management of tourism destinations (D'Angella et al., 2010; Chim-Miki & Batista-Canino, 2017b; Farsari, 2023). For this purpose, DMOs rely on two main governance mechanisms: formal or contractual governance mechanisms, which include the implementation of rules, regulations, standardised operational procedures, and formal decision-making structures; and informal or relational governance mechanisms, which encompass mutual trust, social ties, and positive expectations of partner companies (Mariani, 2016; Ness et al., 2021; Roehrich et al., 2020). While the former is based on formal structures and legal contracts, the latter is based on informal social relationships (Errichiello & Micera, 2021; Huang et al., 2023). Recent research has highlighted the complementarity of these two mechanisms in the governance of tourism destinations (Bichler & Lösch, 2019; Ness et al., 2021; Roehrich et al., 2020).

There are two gaps in the literature on coopetition and tourism and on coopetition and governance (Chim-Miki et al., 2020). Although previous discussions have identified the main formal and informal governance mechanisms applicable to interorganisational coopetition (e.g., Bichler & Lösch, 2019; Mariani, 2016; Ness et al., 2021; Rahman et al., 2022; Schuhbert, 2023), such as the Destination Management Organisation (DMOs), they have not clarified how these mechanisms become more or less critical for developing a unified vision of the destination. To address these gaps, we conducted a qualitative analysis of two tourism destinations, coordinated by different DMOs, in the mountain region of the Brazilian state of Rio Grande do Sul (Brazil), known as the 'Serra Gaúcha', to better understand the formal and informal structures and governance mechanisms that are applied in the context of interorganisational coopetition to manage tourism destinations. The results of this study provide valuable insights into how these mechanisms can be critical in forming a unified vision of the destination and achieving successful coentrepreneurship in tourism based on their effects on the destination's coopetition.

Research Methods

Sample and Data Collection

In terms of data collection, two DMOs located on different tourist routes in the Serra region of Rio Grande do Sul (Brazil) were selected. The first, known as 'Caminhos de Pedra' and located in the municipality of Bento Gonçalves, began to be formed in 1992, when an entrepreneur and a local architect decided to invest in tourism development based on Italian traditions and architecture. For this purpose, they identified the activities traditionally developed by Italian families who settled in the area beginning in the 1850s and restored the houses built at that time. The local DMO was structured in 1997 and currently has 77 members. The second tourism circuit is known as the 'Vale dos Vinhedos'. The 'Vale dos Vinhedos' circuit was initiated by six winegrowers to jointly face a crisis that was affecting wine producers in the mid-1990s. To survive the crisis, the entrepreneurs decided to organise a local DMO (founded in 1995) for tourism development and to obtain recognition as a geographical entity. Currently, Vale dos Vinhedos has 90 entrepreneurs participating in the DMO. These cases are interesting because they involve consolidated tourism destinations with DMOs that have been active for more than 20 years.

To understand the object of study, triangulate the obtained data, and lend a stronger foundation for the study's results, we used semistructured interviews, nonparticipant observations, and document analysis. The main goal of the semistructured interviews was to understand the meanings that the interviewees attached to the questions or situations related to the topic of interest. Accordingly, we developed a base script with nine questions derived from the literature, aiming to understand the context and the interviewees' perspectives regarding their businesses, the DMO, and the tourism destination.

The interviews were conducted in January 2024. To define the theoretical sample (the number of interviewees) for the study, we employed Glaser and Strauss's principle of theoretical saturation (2017), which adds rigour to the qualitative sampling process. Therefore, the criterion for concluding the interviews was the theoretical saturation of the analysed categories. Thus, 24 individuals were interviewed, 11 of whom were linked to Caminhos de Pedra (5 members, 5 board members, 1 member of the technical team of the DMO) and 13 of whom were linked to Vale dos Vinhedos (8 members, 4 board members, 1 member of the technical team of the DMO). The interviews lasted for a total of 26 hours and 26 minutes. After conducting the interviews, we transcribed them using the Reshape software programme, which enables the researcher to become familiar with the content.

We also employed nonparticipant observation, which included reconnaissance visits to the research site and an analysis of the expressions and various intonations used by the interviewees, as well as the working context of the DMOs. Finally, we performed document analysis. The basis for this analysis consisted of websites, social media, and the DMOs' creation statutes, internal statutes, and terms of responsibility. The documents were made available by these institutions for analysis during the data collection phase.

Data Analysis

To analyse the data, we conducted narrative analysis, as well as compared theoretical and empirical patterns derived from the theoretical framework and the research field, a method also known as the pattern matching technique of data analysis (Trochim, 1989). While narrative analysis enabled us to interpret the in-depth interviews, the pattern matching technique made it possible to compare existing theory and the data collected. Table 8.1 displays the constitutive elements of analysis (CEs), the descriptions of the elements (DEs), the constitutive definitions (CDs) related to the analysed theoretical principles, and the operational definitions (ODs), which refer to the operationalisation of concepts in empirical practice.

To facilitate the organisation, categorisation, and interpretation of the data obtained from these businesses, we used MAXQDA Version 24 software for qualitative data analysis. The results of the coding procedure were compared,

Table 8.1. Data Categorisation.

Constitutive Elements (CEs)	Descriptions of the Elements (DEs)	Constitutive Definitions (CDs)	Operational Definitions (ODs)
CE1	Formal Governance Mechanisms	Formal organisational structures and principles employed in the management and coordination of inter-company relationships (Mariani, 2016; Ness et al., 2021; Roehrich et al., 2020).	Rules, regulations, standardised operational procedures, and formal decision-making structures established by the DMOs.
CE2	Informal Governance Mechanisms	Behavioural guidelines that impose social obligations on the relationship (Roehrich et al., 2020).	Social ties, trust relationships, and positive expectations.
CE3	Co-Entrepreneurship	Tourist destination as an integral product (Chim-Miki & Batista-Canino, 2018).	Vision of the destination as an integral product promoted by the collective.

Source: Research Data (2024).

and the relevant findings for each code were examined across the various interviews and highlighted by selected quotations. Finally, the codes were evaluated in terms of their impact and relevance to the current study.

Results

Case 1: Caminhos de Pedra

Regarding the formal governance mechanisms used by the DMO of Caminhos de Pedra, the interviewees noted the existence of a statute in which rules to be followed by the businesses are defined and a term of responsibility and commitment to this statute that must be signed by participating businesses (a2, a10, a11). Importantly, the DMO uses the survey of activities traditionally developed by

Italian families who settled in the tourism destination to guide entrepreneurs seeking to open new businesses along this tourist circuit (a1, a3, a8). The DMO follows a principle of inhibiting direct competition, meaning that at least 70% of the products sold by each business must show some differentiation from those of other member businesses (a1, a3, a10).

In addition to the mentioned aspects, the interviewees emphasised the focus of local governance on preserving the history and culture of Italian immigrants, which includes language and typical dances, but primarily involves the preservation of local architecture, namely, stone houses (a1, a2, a5, a8). The rules related to the preservation of architecture proved somewhat contradictory to those of the interviewees. While some underscored the relevance of stone houses as important cultural and historical factors that contribute to local tourism, others believed that the association should not interfere 'internally' in these businesses in this manner and should focus instead on promoting the destination (a7, a9, a11).

New entrepreneurs who wish to start a local business and become part of the DMO must submit a project, either in written or oral form, to the local board of governance, which assesses the proposal's adherence to the statute and the local master plan in considering its approval (a1, a2, a4, a5, a10). The board of the DMO is elected and is composed of business owners located along the tourist circuit (a2). The board makes decisions at its monthly meetings and holds an annual assembly (open to the public) to ensure accountability. All matters discussed in the meetings are recorded in the meeting minutes. This document is considered the formal record of the organisation's goals and plans (a3).

Notably, although there is a formal decision-making structure, interviewees a1, a4, a5, and a6 often referred to the final decision-making power as being held by the entrepreneur who conceived of the DMO and originally invested in the tourist circuit. This individual exerts a strong informal influence on local decisions. The more established entrepreneurs who participated in the construction of the tourist circuit had strong social ties, continuously took part in the DMO's board, and perceived the collective work and achievements of the DMO as having greater value. At various times, they highlighted Caminhos de Pedra as a collective and integral product rather than merely a cluster of individual businesses (a1, a3, a5, a8, and a10).

The founders of Caminhos de Pedra share the objective of developing a tourist circuit based on the preservation of Italian historical and cultural heritage. However, this purpose does not seem to be very clear to the more recent entrepreneurs – those who founded their businesses after 2010 (a6, a7, and a11). Therefore, many of them perceive the DMO as a space that should focus on promoting the marketing of the tourism destination and reduce its involvement in historical aspects or in architectural and cultural preservation. Some interviewees stressed that there are many divergent opinions in this regard, 'with one thinking one way and another thinking another' (a4 and a11). The lack of a shared vision regarding the objectives of the tourism destination among the circuit's founders and new entrepreneurs undermines the development of Caminhos de Pedra as a collective enterprise.

Case 2: Vale dos Vinhedos

Vale dos Vinhedos exhibits several similarities with Caminhos de Pedra regarding formal governance mechanisms, particularly the statute, term of responsibility, and financial contribution. However, unlike Caminhos de Pedra, Vale dos Vinhedos does not seek to inhibit competition among local entrepreneurs. In contrast, its governance restricts the set of activities that can be developed in the area (those linked to wine tourism), which leads to a high concentration of wineries, restaurants, and hotels in this circuit (b1, b5, b7, b8, b11). Interviewees b5, b10, and b13 mentioned that it is common for competing entrepreneurs to share knowledge and try each other's products and services. According to the interviewees, when they leave a competing establishment that offers a good product, they feel motivated to make something even better (b1, b10, and b13). Although Vale dos Vinhedos does not impose restrictions related to the architecture of the businesses, it does enforce restrictions in terms of preserving the local landscape. For a new project to be approved by local governments, at least 70% of its area must be devoted to grape cultivation (b1, b7, and b11).

To become a member, an entrepreneur must submit a project for the board's consideration and secure the endorsement of two active entrepreneurs in the DMO. This rule is known to all interviewees. There are also some distinctive features of the formal decision-making structure, compared to those of the Caminhos de Pedra. In Vale dos Vinhedos, although the statute provides an electoral mechanism, in practice, a more cooperative approach has been established. According to interviewee b13, who has previously held the position of president of the DMO, the president proposes the members of the board. The presidential candidate and the proposed board are presented at an assembly, where the associate votes for or against their approval and may suggest a replacement for any nominee. At the end of the term, it is common for the vice president of the previous board to propose a new board and to present it for approval at an assembly. This procedure ensures the continuity of the DMO's plans and goals and prevents the division of the tourist circuit into groups due to elections (b12 and b13). In addition, the DMO works with small groups that coordinate activities and maintains a 'Supreme Council', which acts as a group of advisors to the current president (b5, b11). The Supreme Council comprises the former presidents of the association.

Interviewees who were ex-presidents stated that it is common for the president and other board members to make informal visits to businesses. However, in situations requiring DMO intervention, requests are usually formalised through the organisation's WhatsApp account (b12 and b13). In addition to frequent interactions due to the proximity of businesses, interviewees stated that they have informal meetings following the association meetings, visit competing businesses, and even undertake benchmarking trips with entrepreneurs from the same sector, aiming to continually improve the products offered by the destination (b2, b3, b4, b7, b8, b9, b10, b12, and b13).

The interviews also demonstrated that the members of Vale dos Vinhedos share common goals: to promote Brazilian wine and Vale dos Vinhedos as a reference region in wine to attract more tourists to the circuit (wine tourists). The organisations understand that to achieve this goal, it is important to promote the destination as an integral product resulting from collective entrepreneurship. Evidence of this vision is present in the statements of interviewees b10 and b13, who affirm that when participating in events and fairs, all of the entrepreneurs share the same vision for Vale dos Vinhedos, promoting the tourism destination as a whole. In addition, wineries are coproducing a wine to cover the DMO's costs and funding other joint activities to further develop the wine circuit (b13).

Discussion of the Results

Our analysis of the results revealed two noteworthy findings. The first concerns the role of the DMO in the studied tourist circuits. According to previous studies, DMOs play a crucial role in planning, coordinating, and managing various stakeholders and resources, contributing to the effective, sustainable management of tourism destinations (e.g., D'Angella et al., 2010; Chim-Miki & Batista-Canino, 2017b; Farsari, 2023). According to the results of this study, there seems to be a consensus on the role of the DMO in the promotion, governance, regional development, and preservation of tourism destinations in Vale dos Vinhedos. In Caminhos de Pedra, however, there are some divergences of opinion, especially regarding preservation.

Caminhos de Pedra is focussed on preserving its cultural and historical heritage, with an emphasis on local architecture. By contrast, Vale dos Vinhedos is concerned with maintaining the current landscape, which should not be altered by new investments. Interviewees from Vale dos Vinhedos unanimously agreed that preserving the local landscape was and should be a governance objective. This perspective was evident when interviewee b13 reported a case of a project that was deemed unfeasible by the DMO due to its impact on the local landscape. According to him, the members agreed to reject this project. Conversely, some entrepreneurs from Caminhos de Pedra expressed discomfort with the preservation of architectural standards required by the DMO. In their view, the DMO should focus on promoting the destination to tourists rather than on internal aspects of the circuit.

Second, although tourism destinations are a natural context for coopetition (Chim-Miki & Batista-Canino, 2017a; Schuhbert, 2023), different combinations of formal and informal governance mechanisms seem to influence levels of competition and cooperation. From the studied cases, it may be inferred that coentrepreneurship tends to manifest more in environments that employ formal governance mechanisms as a complement to informal mechanisms. Notably, however, the use of governance mechanisms seems to be related to the levels of competition and/or cooperation expected by DMOs. In the first case studied, the DMO of Caminhos de Pedra aims to stimulate noncompetition and cooperation among enterprises, employing mainly formal governance mechanisms. However, the findings of this study indicate that, in the long term, this approach could lead to a more individualistic perspective among entrepreneurs. Informal governance mechanisms, such as trust, tend to lead to longer periods of coexistence, information sharing and objectives among DMO participants. In some cases, informal mechanisms can be more effective than formalised contracts (Mariani, 2016) and are determinant factors for efficient collaborative governance (Bichler & Lösch, 2019; Rahman et al., 2022). Without these mechanisms, or with underdeveloped ones, the objectives of the tourist circuit, the roles of the DMO, and the motivation for developing formal governance mechanisms tend not to be fully understood by new entrepreneurs. This gap in understanding leads them to question these mechanisms and see their business not as an integral part of the tourist circuit but rather as an individual business within it.

On the other hand, Vale dos Vinhedos naturally stimulates competition and cooperation (coopetition) simultaneously. The DMO encourages the opening of businesses in the same niche, the sharing of knowledge and practices among them, and distinctive businesses within the tourist circuit. Healthy competition among companies seems to lead to the continuous improvement of local products and services, making the tourist circuit increasingly attractive. The sharing of knowledge and information among entrepreneurs is established not through formal governance mechanisms but through informal mechanisms that arise as a result of them. In other words, the formal mechanisms employed by the DMO seem to promote informal mechanisms, such as trust: formal meetings are followed by informal social gatherings; proposals for new ventures must secure the endorsement of local businesses; and the formal decision-making structure is based on trust rather than elections. Moreover, none of the interviewees expressed opposition to this power structure. Thus, in the second case studied, it is evident that formal governance mechanisms promote or reinforce informal mechanisms, which affect coentrepreneurship.

Our results corroborate the findings of previous studies in three aspects. The first two are (1) differences in the effectiveness of joint interactions among stakeholders when they employ different combinations of governance mechanisms in tourism destinations (Baggio et al., 2010) and (2) the complementarity of formal and informal governance mechanisms in tourism destinations (Bichler & Lösch, 2019; Ness et al., 2021; Roehrich et al., 2020). The impact of these findings is evident in how destinations perceive the new generation of entrepreneurs. In Caminhos de Pedra, more recent entrepreneurs are apparently the least involved and least active in the DMO and have a different mindset, which is very focussed on financial returns to the detriment of the historical and cultural aspects that gave rise to the circuit (a1 and a3). By contrast, in Vale dos Vinhedos, the new generation is seen as even more engaged with the cause and exhibits greater ease in relating to competitors and developing the destination as a whole (a11 and a13). Bichler and Lösch (2019) noted that the social integration of new entrepreneurs is a key aspect of tourism governance.

Finally, the third aspect is that this study corroborates is the work of Tuohino and Konu (2014) and Chim-Miki and Batista-Canino (2018), namely, in confirming the relevance of governance to developing a shared vision and guiding the tourism destination as a collective enterprise. However, these results must be interpreted cautiously, as they may be influenced by other variables not considered in this study. Aspects such as cultural, functional, and organisational similarities can trigger less formal coordination mechanisms (Mariani, 2016), which may or may not be directly related to actions promoted by the DMO. Another aspect identified by Taylor et al. (2007) is that certain segments seem more inclined towards forming cooperative networks, such as wine tourism.

Conclusion

This study aimed to analyse how formal and informal control mechanisms contribute to the development of tourism destinations as integrated products (coentrepreneurship). Through a multicase study of Brazilian destination management organisations (DMOs), we discovered that formal mechanisms should support and reinforce the development of informal mechanisms to promote balanced levels of cooperation and competition. This balance of coopetition leads to greater sharing of knowledge and information and alignment among stakeholders and fosters the development of the destination as an integral product resulting from a collective enterprise.

This chapter contributes to the literature by highlighting how formal and informal governance mechanisms employed by DMOs affect the levels of coopetition and coentrepreneurship in tourist circuits. The findings of this study indicate that governance that is too focussed on formal mechanisms can, in the medium and long term, compromise a shared vision of the destination's objectives and its governance. This approach can increase internal competition and individualistic behaviour and raise questions about the role of the DMO. Within this context, there is hardly any scope for facilitating coentrepreneurship as an integral product arising from collective entrepreneurship. On the other hand, employing formal mechanisms as tools for the development and reinforcement of informal mechanisms tends to increase levels of competition and cooperation in the tourism destination and strengthen the vision of shared objectives among businesses, creating an ideal context for coentrepreneurship.

The results of this study have several implications for the management of tourism destinations. First, the findings highlight the importance of DMOs being responsible not only for managing the financial resources and marketing of a destination but also for regional development based on local characteristics and the preservation of its historical and cultural heritage. Second, they demonstrate that within a tourism context, the quality of products and services tend to be improved more quickly as a collective undertaking. These improvements are even better when the involved parties consider the quality of the whole and are significantly motivated by high-level competition. To develop a tourist circuit as a coenterprise, championing a common objective is essential. When this objective clearly demonstrates that the focus is on competing in terms of the external aspects of the tourism destination (such as Italian heritage or wine tourism), the governance of the coopetitive relationship among businesses tends to be less complex. Finally, in the medium and long term, formal and informal governance mechanisms can affect the tourist circuit's level of coopetition. Therefore, it is important for DMOs to understand how to combine formal and informal governance mechanisms to achieve the desired levels of competition and cooperation to ensure coentrepreneurship throughout the tourist circuit.

The research has two main limitations. First, the context of this investigation is restricted to two Brazilian tourist circuits. Scholars should be cautious when generalising the results to other tourism destinations, as the studied locations have unique cultural, historical, and organisational characteristics, which may not be applicable to other settings. Second, this investigation focusses mainly on interactions among local entrepreneurs mediated by DMOs, neglecting other variables and the perspectives of other relevant stakeholders such as the local community (non-entrepreneurs), tourists, and public agents. Thus, future research could explore in greater depth how the involvement of these other actors may influence formal and informal governance mechanisms and their effects on coopetition and coentrepreneurship. Future research could benefit from including additional variables that may impede or facilitate the development of coentrepreneurship within tourist circuits.

References

Baggio, R., Scott, N., & Cooper, C. (2010). Improving tourism destination governance: A complexity science approach. *Tourism Review, 65*(4), 51–60.

Bengtsson, M., & Kock, S. (2014). Coopetition—Quo vadis? Past accomplishments and future challenges. *Industrial Marketing Management, 43*(2), 180–188.

Bichler, B. F., & Lösch, M. (2019). Collaborative governance in tourism: Empirical insights into a community-oriented destination. *Sustainability, 11*(23), 6673.

Chim-Miki, A. F., & Batista-Canino, R. M. (2017a). The coopetition perspective applied to tourism destinations: A literature review. *Anatolia, 28*(3), 381–393.

Chim-Miki, A. F., & Batista-Canino, R. M. (2017b). Tourism coopetition: An introduction to the subject and a research agenda. *International Business Review, 26*(6), 1208–1217.

Chim-Miki, A. F., & Batista-Canino, R. M. (2018). Development of a tourism coopetition model: A preliminary Delphi study. *Journal of Hospitality and Tourism Management, 37*, 78–88.

Chim-Miki, A. F., Medina-Brito, P., & Batista-Canino, R. M. (2020). Integrated management in tourism: The role of coopetition. *Tourism Planning & Development, 17*(2), 127–146.

D'Angella, F., De Carlo, M., & Sainaghi, R. (2010). Archetypes of destination governance: A comparison of international destinations. *Tourism Review, 65*(4), 61–73.

Damayanti, M., Scott, N., & Ruhanen, L. (2019). Coopetition for tourism destination policy and governance: The century of local power?. In *The Future of Tourism: Innovation and Sustainability* (pp. 285–299).

Damayanti, M., Tyas, W. P., & Aswad, W. O. S. J. (2021). Conceptualizing multi actors' collaboration in smart tourism destination. *IOP Conference Series: Earth and Environmental Science, 673*(1), 1–14.

Errichiello, L., & Micera, R. (2021). A process-based perspective of smart tourism destination governance. *European Journal of Tourism Research, 29*, 2909.

Farsari, I. (2023). Exploring the nexus between sustainable tourism governance, resilience and complexity research. *Tourism Recreation Research*, *48*(3), 352–367.

Glaser, B., & Strauss, A. (2017). *Discovery of grounded theory: Strategies for qualitative research*. Routledge.

Huang, G. I., Karl, M., Wong, I. A., & Law, R. (2023). Tourism destination research from 2000 to 2020: A systematic narrative review in conjunction with bibliographic mapping analysis. *Tourism Management*, *95*(1), 1–19.

Mariani, M. M. (2016). Coordination in inter-network co-opetitition: Evidence from the tourism sector. *Industrial Marketing Management*, *53*, 103–123.

Nalebuff, B., & Brandenburger, A. (1996). *Coopetition*.

Ness, H., Haugland, S. A., & Aarstad, J. (2021). Interfirm resource integration in destination contexts. *Current Issues in Tourism*, *24*(1), 66–81.

Rahman, M. S. U., Simmons, D., Shone, M. C., & Ratna, N. N. (2022). Social and cultural capitals in tourism resource governance: The essential lenses for community focussed co-management. *Journal of Sustainable Tourism*, *30*(11), 2665–2685.

Roehrich, J. K., Selviaridis, K., Kalra, J., Van der Valk, W., & Fang, F. (2020). Inter-organizational governance: A review, conceptualisation and extension. *Production Planning & Control*, *31*(6), 453–469.

Rosa, F. S., Compagnucci, L., Lunkes, R. J., & Monteiro, J. J. (2023). Green innovation ecosystem and water performance in the food service industry: The effects of environmental management controls and digitalization. *Business Strategy and the Environment*, *32*(8), 5459–5476.

Schuhbert, A. (2023). Specifying destination-based networks by governance-mode: A social capital approach to innovative capacity in a rural destination of Azerbaijan. *Tourism Planning & Development*, *20*(5), 832–854.

Taylor, P., McRae-Williams, P., & Lowe, J. (2007). The determinants of cluster activities in the Australian wine and tourism industries. *Tourism Economics*, *13*(4), 639–656.

Trochim, W. M. (1989). Outcome pattern matching and program theory. *Evaluation and Program Planning*, *12*(4), 355–366.

Tuohino, A., & Konu, H. (2014). Local stakeholders' views about destination management: Who are leading tourism development?. *Tourism Review*, *69*(3), 202–215.

Chapter 9

Coopetition Local Index (i-COOL): A Tool to Measure Coopetition Level at Tourism Destinations

Adriana Fumi Chim-Miki[a] *and Rosa M. Batista-Canino*[b]

[a]Federal University of Campina Grande, Brazil
[b]Universidad de Las Palmas de Gran Canaria, Spain

Abstract

This chapter aims to present an aggregate index to measure the coopetition level of tourism destinations, a tool named the Local Coopetition Index (i-COOL). The index comprises 30 variables based on soft and hard data distributed in 7 factors: Co-location, Competition, Associationism, Cooperation, Strategic Management, Co-Entrepreneurship and Tourism Co-Production. The i-COOL has a math formulation that allows comparison of the coopetition levels among different destinations, cities, or countries. In this chapter, we present the results of an empirical application of the i-COOL in the context of two Brazilian cities, namely, Curitiba and Foz do Iguaçu. Findings showed the level of coopetition in the destinations and indicated the variables that destination managers should prioritise to improve tourism development. The i-COOL framework can be used as a monitor of tourism coopetition to support destination managers in improving competitiveness from the coopetition strategy.

Keywords: Tourism coopetition; coopetition local index (i-COOL); tourism destination; strategic management; coopetitiveness

Introduction

Resource mobilisations and joint action to achieve shared goals among value chain participants represent the coopetition strategy (Brandenburger & Nalebuff, 1996). Coopetition is a coupled system in which the participants maintain some

Value Proposition to Tourism Coopetition, 115–134

Copyright © 2025 Adriana Fumi Chim-Miki and Rosa M Batista-Canino
Published under exclusive licence by Emerald Publishing Limited
doi:10.1108/978-1-83797-827-420241009

interdependence without losing organisational separateness (Luo, 2007); a constructive tension between companies or networks to generate collaboration among firms that compete in the same markets (Czernek & Czakon, 2016; Della Corte & Sciarelli, 2012); a co-adaptation system among firms in which coopetition represents the formation of subsystems that allow the participants' self-organisation (Dagnino, 2012).

Coopetition is a hybrid behaviour resulting from competition and cooperation that occurs among networks and organisations or within organisations, including relations among competitors, suppliers, complementary businesses, government agencies, local people, and customers to achieve a common goal despite the existence of individual interests (Chim-Miki & Batista-Canino, 2017a). The strategy of coopetition tends to generate value co-creation (Volschenk et al., 2016); therefore, it is a sectoral development driver. Thus, monitoring the degree of coopetition is essential to tourism destination managers.

This chapter aims to present a tool to monitor tourism coopetition: the Local Coopetition Index (i-COOL). We used the theoretical coopetition model of Chim-Miki and Batista-Canino (2018) and associated it with a math formulation adapted from the World Economic Forum techniques to global monitors. In the sequence, we tested i-COOL in two Brazilian cities, considering the tourism industry a suitable context for testing the tool. Tourism destinations have characteristics that promote the formation of coopetition networks, such as high atomisation of the supply, an integrated management approach, interdependence, and complementarity of the offer (Della Corte & Sciarelli, 2012; Kylänen & Rusko, 2011).

From the Coopetition Model to a Coopetition Index: The Tool i-COOL

The literature presents two main approaches to analysing indicators related to coopetition. On the one hand, studies show some variables as inductors of coopetition and, on the other hand, variables as results of coopetition strategies. The high number of variables produced a dispersion of knowledge, hindering the consolidation of findings towards coopetition indicators (Bouncken et al., 2015; Chim-Miki & Batista-Canino, 2017a). Coopetition suffers from the same problems as other multidimensional constructs. Due to its complexity, multidimensionality, and relativity, many ways exist to measure it. So, studies have focussed more on the analysis of inductors of coopetition behaviour than its measuring. For example, Bengtsson and Kock (2000) analysed the driving factors for this behaviour, such as heterogeneity of resources, customer proximity, and the degree of conflict in the organisational goals; Chin et al. (2008) studied the success factors, identifying 7 critical factors and 17 sub-factors grouped into three dimensions: management commitment, development of relationships, and communication management; Peng et al. (2012) examined a series of 31 indicators verifying whether the use of coopetition creates advantages for the firms involved.

Chim-Miki and Batista-Canino (2018) published a theoretical coopetition tourism model based on scholars' consensus to help practitioners identify the destination performance towards coopetition. The expert panel validated 30 indicators to verify the coopetition level, creating a model with the most important indicators of coopetition related to tourism destinations distributed in seven factors: co-location, associationism, competition, cooperation, strategic management, entrepreneurship, and co-production.

Co-Location factor – Based on Industrial District approaches (Hjalager, 2000) and Cluster Theory (Porter, 1980), some scholars highlight geographical proximity as a driver of coopetition. Co-location represents the density of tourism companies in the shared space that potentially cooperate to develop a common purpose, even if they have particular goals. Tourism scholars have researched the advantages of coopetition networks due to shared resources such as frontier destinations (Della Corte & Sciarelli, 2012; Kylänen & Rusko, 2011) and tourism clusters (Taylor et al., 2007). Two forces interact in this factor. On the one hand, the partners' physical, social, and economic similarities capture the shared values previously identified by Morgan and Hunt (1994). On the other hand, the complementarity and interdependence of tourism involve working with others to achieve individual and collective goals (Parra et al., 2011).

Competition factor – Porter's five competitive forces (Porter, 1979) are an important part of the coopetition model. Studies on coopetition performed in tourism destinations by Della Corte and Sciarelli (2012) demonstrated that in contexts with higher competition than cooperation, the coopetition network generates better advantages than in contexts where cooperation is higher than competition. Another approach was given by Ritala (2012), which considers the destination's position in the marketplace as a motivator of coopetition alliances since they help to co-opt the main rivals and defend the destination's competitive position. This viewpoint is also supported by several scholars inside and outside of the tourism sector.

Associationism factor – The development of tourism destinations is increasingly focussed on community and collaborative approaches, as demonstrated by Wang and Krakover (2008). The combination of knowledge, skills, capital resources, and collaborative strategy leads to a synergy that opens opportunities and creates innovative solutions, making it possible to achieve better levels than each partner would obtain individually (Chin et al., 2008; Luo, 2007). In this sense, the propensity to actively participate in collaborative relationships can be seen in tourism business associations (Chim-Miki Costa & Okumus, 2024).

Cooperation factor – The degree of cooperation among companies and between the public and private sectors at the destination is the cornerstone of coopetition (Wang & Krakover, 2008). Cooperation depends on entrepreneurial trust and has been extensively studied due to the importance of enhancing work systems that require interdependence, such as teamwork and participatory management (Parra et al., 2011). Mutual trust reduces stress and improves resilience, leading to an increased exchange of information, a search for joint solutions to common problems, and better results (Bouncken & Fredrich, 2012; Cheng et al., 2000).

Strategic management factor – The ability to generate assets through joint processes is an essential driver to generate competitive advantages and successful partnerships (Chin et al., 2008). In the tourism destination, strategic management has the role of developing participatory planning in order to contribute to the fair distribution of tourism benefits among the stakeholders, minimising situations that could be detrimental to the achievement of common objectives (Della Corte & Sciarelli, 2012). Strategic management reduces the negative aspects of competition and tends to promote a suitable context for coopetition relations (Kylänen & Rusko, 2011).

Co-Entrepreneurship factor – Tourism destinations are related to co-preneurs' behaviour and the governance system (Chim-Miki et al., 2016). Co-entrepreneurship is an action resulting from tourism governance that conducts the destination as an integral product as if it were a single project (Chim-Miki & Batista-Canino, 2017b; Kylänen & Mariani, 2012; Kylänen & Rusko, 2011). The entrepreneur's perception of integrative management provides recognition and support towards Destination Organisation Management (DMO). A governance system with the effective participation of various social and economic spheres works as a coopetition hub (Chim-Miki Costa & Okumus, 2024).

Co-Production factor – Management of the destination as an integral product and using a coopetition strategy in a continuous process can increase tourism production, raising the destination's market position. Therefore, co-production is a result and a process of coopetition. Tourism destinations usually consider the tourism density, productivity, and employment rates in the sector as tourism production and performance (Della Corte & Aria, 2016; Della Corte & Sciarelli, 2012; Kylänen & Mariani, 2012).

Coopetition is managerial thinking and strategy that can optimise systems (Quintana-Garcia & Benavides-Velasco, 2004). Therefore, integrative models should be developed to measure a system, network, or sector's coopetition capacity. Considering that, we proposed a method to become the coopetition model in an index of coopetition (i-COOL), based on the variables suggested by Chim-Miki and Batista-Canino (2018) to establish a way to measure each factor. Thus, the i-COOL comprised 30 variables, and the final result is an unweighted average of objective and subjective variables (Fig. 9.1).

In the i-COOL, the objective variables are key measures collected from a survey with tourism associations and ratios calculated from official secondary quantitative data (hard data). On the other hand, the subjective measures capture the contextual conditions of coopetition behaviour, so these data were obtained through an entrepreneurial perception survey (soft data). According to Cheng et al. (2000), subjective variables are evaluated individually through appropriate indicators, generally using more than one item and perception scales such as the Likert scale (Hair et al., 1998).

However, using this mix of hard and soft data in the same math model to provide a result as a classificatory and comparative index for tourism destinations (i-COOL) demands a data normalisation to convert all the variables to the same scale. We adopted the data normalisation method used on the standard validated by the World Economic Forum (WEF) in the Tourism & Travel Competitiveness

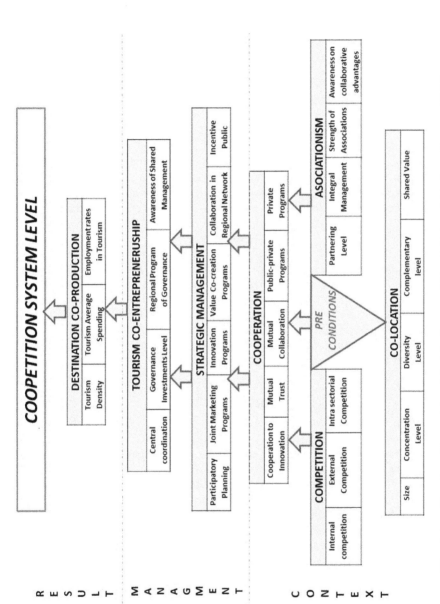

Fig. 9.1.   Tourism Coopetition Model. *Source:* Chim-Miki and Batista-Canino (2018).

Index and the Global Competitiveness Report. Since this conversion, the measure isolated of coopetition is transformed into an index of coopetition related to a circumscribed region (i-COOL). The standard formula for converting each hard data indicator to the 1-to-7 scale is

$$\frac{6 \times (SVD - SVBRJ) + 1}{(SVARJ - SVBRJ)}$$

SVD = Score of the variable in the destination analysed
SVBRJ = Score of the variable in the smaller destination of the region analysed
SVARJ = Score of the variable in the biggest destination of the region analysed

The sample minimum and sample maximum are the lowest and highest scores of the overall sample, respectively. For those hard data indicators for which a higher value indicates a worse outcome, we rely on a normalisation formula that, in addition to converting the series to a 1-to-7 scale, reverses it, so that is

$$\frac{-6 \times (SVD - SVBRJ) + 7}{(SVARJ–SVBRJ)}$$

This normalisation considers the region's smallest and largest destination (or city), converting the hard data (objective variables) into a regional comparative index based on a scale of 1–7. The subjective variables do not need normalisation because a perception survey collects the data on a 7-point Likert scale. Consequently, the coopetition Index (i-COOL) ranking ranges from 1 to 7 points, where 7 is the highest rating of coopetition capacity in a tourism destination, and 1 is the lowest rating.

An Empirical Test of i-COOL

Context of Analysis

An empirical test of i-COOL was performed in two Brazilian tourism cities, which were selected according to two criteria: (1) to be in the same province and (2) to be one of the 10 most competitive Brazilian tourism cities. Thus, the cities of Curitiba and Foz do Iguaçu attended these criteria. Curitiba is the capital of the Parana Province, Brazil's eighth most populous city with a diversified range of leisure and cultural tourism. It is considered one of the best Brazilian cities to live.

Foz do Iguaçu is a border city where the Parana River and the Iguaçu River join. It is a triple border area between Brazil (city of Foz do Iguaçu), Argentina (city Puerto Iguazu), and Paraguay (Ciudad del Este). The city has great importance in international tourism due to a huge natural attraction – the Iguazu falls – which receives about 1,8 million visitors a year (https://www.destino.foz.br/observatorio).

An entrepreneurs' perception survey was performed to respond the subjective variables. A structured self-administered questionnaire with 44 perception questions on a 7-point Likert scale and 13 questions of classificatory data was used.

Face-to-face surveys were conducted. The questions were unordered to improve the overall reliability of the instrument. The objective variables were obtained through personal surveys with top managers of the destinations' tourism associations and official statistical data.

i-COOL Results

As previously explained, the i-COOL was proposed as an index to verify coopetition in a region or group of destinations. It follows the standard system for normalisation of hard data validated by the WEF, which uses the highest and lowest value in the analysed region to represent the index's extremes points. This research considered the group of cities of Paraná Province in Brazil. Therefore, the data set of the smallest and largest destinations of Paraná province were used to normalise the hard data. The largest tourism destination is one of the sample cities, Foz do Iguacu; and, the smallest is Curiúva city. However, the largest destination regarding geographical area and number of companies is Curitiba. Thus, the hard data were normalised based on the classification provides by the Report of Paraná Turismo Agency.

Next paragraphs and figures present the results of each factor and detail the questions used as the scale to measure both objective and subjective variables of coopetition model. We used validated scales to subjective variables (entrepreneurial perception survey) extracted from previous research on inter-organizational networks. However, we did adaptation to tourism network context, thus we verified the values of Alfa de Cronbach. Results were adequate to social sciences analysis.

In the Co-Location factor (L), Foz do Iguaçu has a smaller and lesser dense entrepreneurial tourism network (L1, L2, L4). Due to results of these variables, the city presented a lower position on this factor. Nevertheless, it should be noted that there is a more entrepreneurial perception about interdependence and complementarity (L5) among the firms in Foz do Iguaçu. Also, Foz do Iguaçu showed a high score on the variable 'shared values' (L4). These results indicate that although the business network is smallest and most geographically dispersed, the entrepreneurs in Foz do Iguaçu are more united (Fig. 9.2).

Results of Competition factor (CP) confirm the uniqueness of the Iguassu destination which has an inimitable natural resource (the Iguassu Falls). This situation produces a low entrepreneurial perception about external competition (CP2). Nevertheless, the intra-sectorial competition (CP3) and internal competition (CP1) in Foz do Iguaçu is higher than Curitiba because the informal economy and the offer of substitute products or services are characteristics of border areas in Latin America. By contrast, Curitiba is a big city, a typical urban destination. The firms perceive high external competition (CP1), but low inter-sectorial competition (CP3), because the offer is more differentiated (Fig. 9.3).

The analysis of the Associationism factor (A) indicates a keen awareness of Coopetition's benefits at Iguassu destination (Fig. 9.4). Foz do Iguaçu firms are associated with more than one tourism organisation generating a dense network

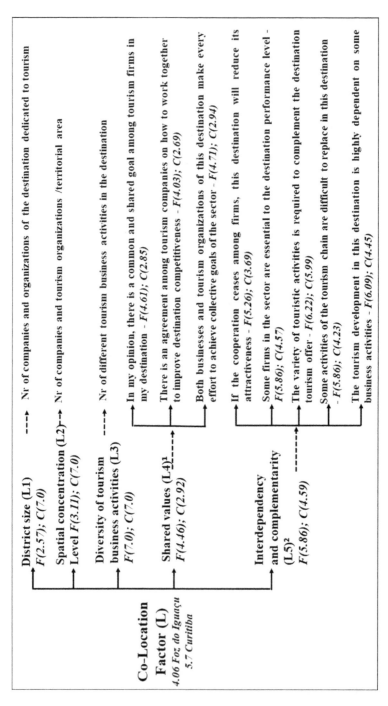

Fig. 9.2.   Scales and Results of Co-location Factor of Foz do Iguaçu and Curitiba. F: Foz do Iguacy city; C: Curituba City.

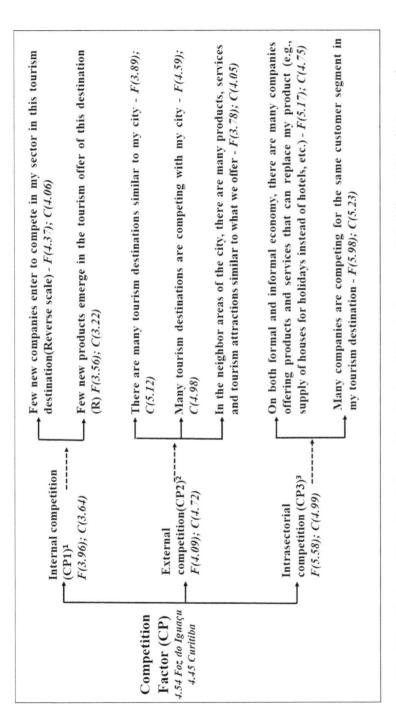

Fig. 9.3. Scales and Results of Competition Factor of Foz do Iguaçu and Curitiba. F: Foz do Iguacy city; C: Curituba City.

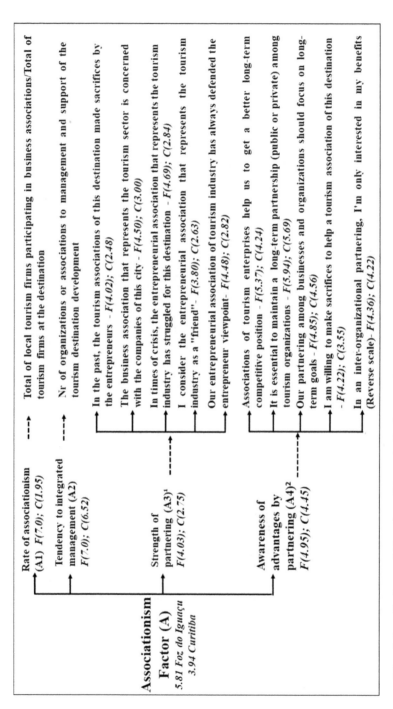

Fig. 9.4.   Scales and Results of Associationism Factor of Foz do Iguaçu and Curitiba. F: Foz do Iguacy city;
C: Curituba City.

(A1) providing strong business associations (A3) and, it tends to integrate management to the sector (A2). Although that the cities have a similar awareness of partnering advantages (A4), in Curitiba, there is a low participation of firms in business associations according to these results.

Variables of Cooperation factor (C) had presented great variations. Foz do Iguaçu show a higher number of joint programmes in both public and private spheres (C1, C2, C3). That is, there are more collaborative networks focussed on collective development. Meanwhile, the entrepreneurial perception shows that mutual trust (C4) and mutual collaboration (C5) still needs to improve in both cities. Although that, in Foz do Iguaçu was higher than in Curitiba. Field observations support these results. Tourism enterprises in the Iguassu destination are older than Curitiba firms; this can produce a more stable and maturity business network facilitating mutual trust and the cooperation. In turn, Curitiba, as a capital city, has a business tissue that frequently changes, hence the mutual trust and mature relations among enterprises tend to decrease (Fig. 9.5).

Results of Strategic Management (SM) factor show that entrepreneurs in Foz do Iguaçu perceive much more the integrated management in the tourism industry (SM6). Also, they performed more co-marketing actions (SM1) and co-innovation programmes (SM2) than Curitiba's entrepreneurs. However, programmes of value co-creation (SM3) were rare in Foz do Iguaçu, whereas they were a common strategy Curitiba city. On the other side, both cities had a medium level of public programmes covering the whole tourism chain (SM4). Collaboration with other networks outside the tourism industry (SM5) in Foz do Iguaçu it is slightly higher. In the end, Strategic Management factor was 15% higher in Foz do Iguacu city than in Curitiba due to the more participation of private sector both in joint programmes and tourism planning (Fig. 9.6).

In the Co-Entrepreneurship factor (E), the variable that indicates the level of joint investment in the sector (E1) reaches the highest score in Foz do Iguacu. Indeed, this city is a national example as regards creating a common fund for tourism management, composed of public and private contributions, tourist fees, and part of the tourist attraction tickets (Fig. 9.7). By contrast, Curitiba had a low level of co-investment in tourism although it had a biggest firm's agglomeration. Both cities have an essential role as inductors of regional tourism defined by Brazilian public policies of tourism, especially Curitiba that is the capital of the province. They are part of a list of 65 tourism destinations considered drivers to tourism development by Ministry of Tourism (MTur). However, results indicated that Foz do Iguaçu had a better action on the regional development (E2).

The two subjective variables of the Co-Entrepreneurship factor (E3 and E4) presented low scores in both cities although slightly higher in Foz do Iguacu. Results indicate entrepreneur's perception is weak in both towns regarding support to co-management (E3), but even weaker was the judgement on its participation in the integrated management (E4). In the end, the Co-Entrepreneurship factor (E) was 50% higher in Foz do Iguaçu than Curitiba. This result is consistent with the strategy observed in the city, which had created an organisation for 'Integrated Management' to plan and develop the Iguassu Destination, including the three border areas of Brazil-Argentina-Paraguay, and it produces a large

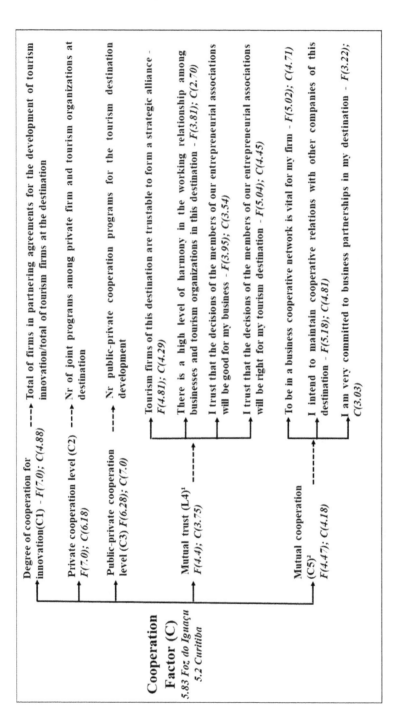

Fig. 9.5.   Scales and Results of Cooperation Factor of Foz do Iguaçu and Curitiba. F: Foz do Iguacy city; C: Curituba City.

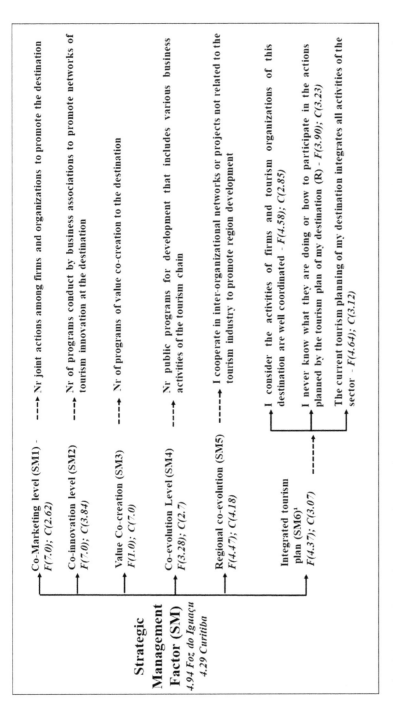

Fig. 9.6.   Scales and Results of Strategic Management Factor of Foz do Iguaçu and Curitiba. F: Foz do Iguaçu city; C: Curituba City.

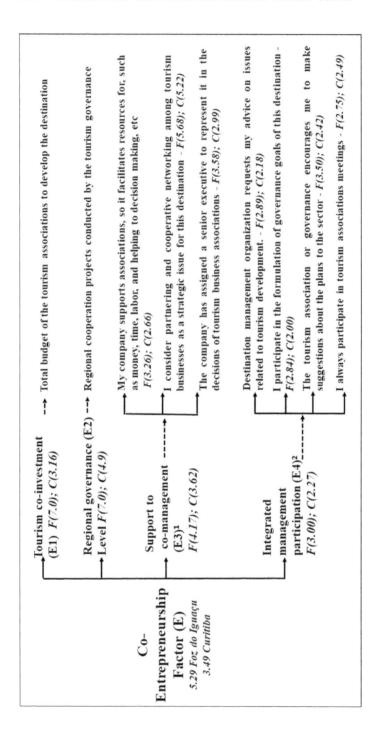

Fig. 9.7.   Scales and Results of Co-entrepreneurship Factor of Foz do Iguaçu and Curitiba. F: Foz do Iguacy city; C: Curituba City.

number of programmes to interorganisational networks. In turn, in Curitiba each tourism business association performs its actions in isolation, and, although there is a friendly atmosphere among the various business associations, neither the integrated management nor the combined funds for investment in the development of the destination were consolidated.

The last factor measures the results that can impact the industry. It is Co-production (P) because it is a result of joint efforts of all stakeholders in the destination. The variables indicated that Foz do Iguaçu had a higher tourism density than Curitiba (P1). Indeed, Foz do Iguaçu rate reported 10 tourists by person (local population), while Curitiba rate is 2 visitors by person. Also, in Foz do Iguaçu the main tourism flow is international and for leisure, which generates higher daily spending in this city (P2) than in Curitiba, an urban and business destination. Similarly, the impact on the employment level (P3) was higher in Foz do Iguaçu than in Curitiba because tourism is one of main activities in this city. Rates show 23.11% of jobs are in the tourism industry in Foz do Iguaçu, while in Curitiba only 5.51% are tourism jobs. (Fig. 9.8).

These results were supported by economic data which indicated the elevated dependence of Foz do Iguaçu city of the tourism sector. By contrast, Curitiba is a crowded city, so the low tourist density hinders the stakeholder's perception of the tourism character of the town. Although these variables are not exclusive result of coopetition, its outgrowth also is a product of joint actions among the interorganisational networks. Curitiba had a business density of 5.8 tourism firms per square kilometre. It is an urban destination that receives approximately 3.6 million of tourists per year; however, its tourist density was low, around 1.96 tourists per inhabitant. The average expenditure daily in the destination was US$ 98.6, and the average length of stay was 3.6 days (Tourism Observatory of Curitiba). In turn, Foz do Iguaçu is a distinct tourism agglomeration. It had low business density, corresponding to two tourism firms per square kilometre, but high tourism density, 9.76 tourists per inhabitants (Tourism Observatory of Foz do Iguaçu).

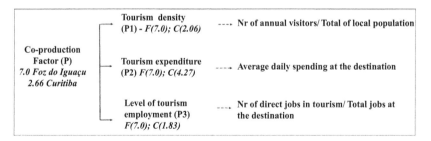

Fig. 9.8.   Scales and Results of Co-production Factor of Foz do Iguaçu and Curitiba. F: Foz do Iguacy city; C: Curituba City.

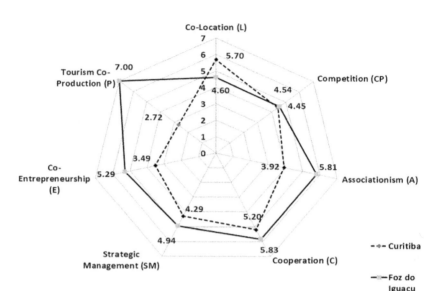

Fig. 9.9.   Results of the Coopetition Factors (i-COOL) in Foz do Iguaçu and Curitiba. Brazil.

Fig. 9.9 shows the coopetition ranking for the destinations. Final results indicate that Foz do guaçu city has more coopetition capacity (i-COOL) than Curitiba city (5.23 versus 4.27 in the city of Curitiba).

Conclusion

This study aimed to present a structured model and method to measure the level of coopetition providing an index to regions or countries, the i-COOL. It is a strategic management tool that considers the competitiveness advantages obtained from the relational component, i.e., through joint actions among the network partnering.

The i-COOL results for Foz do Iguaçu and Curitiba were consistent with previous data collected in interviews, field observations, and the economic data for these cities (see Chim-Miki et al., 2016). Foz do Iguaçu is a case of successful tourism destination in Brazil, due to its international tourism development, even though it is not a sun and beach destination neither a city located in the Brazilian most accessible areas. Variables of i-COOL showed that part of this success comes from its business tissue, which established a broad coopetition network composed by many sectorial sub-networks including by extending to border cities. Foz do Iguaçu performs many joint programmes and has an Integrative Management Institution created to be a hub of interorganisational efforts (Chim-Miki et al., 2016).

Studies of Bengtsson and Kock (2014) showed coopetition allows small and medium enterprises (SMEs) to create business opportunities in industries. Usually, the tourism industry has a lot of SMEs, but the sector needs management of coopetition networks (Della Corte & Sciarelli, 2012). When firms understand the independence, they search for a balance between cooperative and competitive forces (Della Corte & Aria, 2016; Wang & Krakover, 2008). The governance structure in Foz do Iguaçu legitimacy improved agility and flexibility by balancing different coopetitive relationships, creating and maintaining opportunities for all stakeholders.

Besides that, entrepreneurial perception in both cities has indicated recognition on partnering advantages. The entrepreneurs also recognised its low actuation regarding supporting and participating in the business associations. It seems a contradiction between thinking and practices entrepreneurial. Face that, most important is the business associations since findings of Bengtsson and Kock (2000) showed that individuals within the company usually act following one logic of interaction (cooperation or competition), therefore, for a hybrid behaviour of Coopetition is necessary an intermediate actor, such as a collective association. In this way, the inherent tensions of coopetition are managed (Czernek & Czakon, 2016), as well as regulation and control of relationship is established (Bengtsson & Kock, 2000). Association density of Foz do Iguaçu confirms these theoretical assumptions.

On the other hand, Curitiba is a competitive destination in Brazil. The city has a high flow of urban and businesses tourism, good connections, and accessibility, being a cosmopolitan city with the highest quality of life in Brazil according to national statistics. In the Brazilian ranking of tourism competitiveness, Curitiba is above Foz de Iguaçu; however, i-COOL results show that regarding coopetition it remains below – see Fig. 9.9. An analysis of i-COOL variables shows better co-production, co-marketing, and more actions for regional co-evolution of the tourism industry in Foz do Iguaçu and, these efforts are generating better sectorial co-production to the city. Thus, maybe tourism destinations should search to establish higher coopetition level than concentrated its efforts to develop competitiveness level. Since, coopetition provides more inclusion, opportunities, and union (Luo, 2007). It represents the co-optation among organisations without losing the frontiers of individuality and its own goals (Dagnino, 2012). Indeed, management of coopetition networks develops collective thinking while competitiveness focusses on individual thought (Cygler et al., 2014).

The i-COOL better performance in Foz do Iguaçu indicates that the joint effort to plan, promote, and manage the destination as an integral product generates a consolidated coopetition network, a tourism co-entrepreneurship. Previous studies on coopetition and inter-organisational networks indicated the mutual trust and awareness on coopetitive advantages induce the entrepreneurs to act together, reducing uncertainty and sharing the risk in the sector (Luo, 2007).

Our results showed physical proximity and size of the network are not the primary source of relational closeness and shared values that lead to mutual trust and cooperation (Cheng et al., 2000; Luo, 2007). Other factors, such as social ties may be more relevant to entrepreneurial perception on interdependence and shared values. In this sense, Foz do Iguaçu is a smaller city than the large capital of the province (Curitiba), a context that favoured the formation of social ties among participants of associations or business.

The results supported previous findings on coopetition levels. For instance, Wang and Krakover (2008) indicated that cooperation, competition, and coopetition coexist among the tourism stakeholders with different levels of formalisation, integration, and structure. These levels were found in Foz do Iguaçu and Curitiba although both cities are part of the same tourism programme developed by Brazilian Ministry of Tourism, that is, both are point out as regional tourism drivers. In this sense, i-COOL contributes to the policy public due to provide extra information on cities to promote the regional development, based not only on its tourism attractiveness but also in the power and maturity of entrepreneurial tissue towards to collectivism. It is the *coopetitiveness* paradigm (Chim-Miki & Batista-Canino, 2017a).

In summary, the i-COOL result showed the coopetition capacity, the maturity of the entrepreneurial network and the governance level in the cities analysed towards a shared vision, common goals, and collectivism. Foz do Iguaçu results reinforce the background of coopetition, as a joint effort among competitors, complementary enterprises, suppliers, and both public and private organisations, generating an interorganisational network that was the foundations of the tourism coopetition.

The analysis of each factor and variable measured by i-COOL identifies the weaknesses of an interorganisational network. It allows establishing strategies to act on them to improve the relational capacity of the partners to promote a real tourism co-entrepreneurship. We concluded that the proposed model and its formulation as a Coopetition Local Index fulfil its function, i.e., it is a tool to analysis regions, cities, tourism destinations or business networks beyond the traditional resource's capacity analysis. It is a potential new monitor to regional development analysis since the current monitors don't include the relational perspective. Another possibility is the i-COOL to be another dimension to add to competitiveness monitors as an updated approach, that is, from competitiveness to *coopetitiveness* perspective (Chim-Miki & Batista-Canino, 2017a).

The main limitation of our research was the number of cities used for the empirical test. More cities would allow us to perform factorial analysis to check the importance of each factor in the model. Thus, a future line of research would be to replicate this method using samples that cover an entire country or province and perform a correlation analysis of the factors and variables contained in this model. Moreover, we recommend further research related to contextual factors that can impact the development of business networks and collective efforts. These results will allow acting on the destination's weaknesses, leading to improvements in coopetition strategy.

References

Bengtsson, M., & Kock, S. (2000). "Coopetition" in business Networks—To cooperate and compete simultaneously. *Industrial Marketing Management, 29*(5), 411–426.

Bengtsson, M., & Kock, S. (2014). Coopetition—Quo vadis? Past accomplishments and future challenges. *Industrial Marketing Management, 43*(2), 180–188. https://doi.org/10.1016/j.indmarman.2014.02.015

Bouncken, R. B., & Fredrich, V. (2012). Coopetition: Performance implications and management antecedents. *International Journal of Innovation Management, 16*(05), 1250028. https://doi.org/10.1142/S1363919612500284

Bouncken, R. B., Gast, J., Kraus, S., & Bogers, M. (2015). Coopetition: A systematic review, synthesis, and future research directions. *Review of Managerial Science, 9*, 577–601. https://doi.org/10.1007/s11846-015-0168-6

Brandenburger, A. M., & Nalebuff, B. J. (1996). *Co-opetition: A revolutionary mindset that combines competition and cooperation in the marketplace.* Harvard Business School Press.

Cheng, E. W., Li, H., & Love, P. E. D. (2000). Establishment of critical success factors for construction partnering. *Journal of Management in Engineering, 16*(2), 84–92.

Chim-Miki, A. F., & Batista-Canino, R. M. (2017a). The coopetition perspective applied to tourism destinations: A literature review. *Anatolia, 28*(3), 381–393. https://doi.org/10.1080/13032917.2017.1322524

Chim-Miki, A. F., & Batista-Canino, R. M. (2017b). Tourism coopetition: An introduction to the subject and a research agenda. *International Business Review, 26*(6), 1208–1217. https://doi.org/10.1016/j.ibusrev.2017.05.003

Chim-Miki, A. F., & Batista-Canino, R. M. (2018). Development of a tourism coopetition model: A preliminary Delphi study. *Journal of Hospitality and Tourism Management, 37*, 78–88. https://doi.org/10.1016/j.jhtm.2018.10.004

Chim-Miki, A. F., Batista-Canino, R. M., & Medina-Brito, P. (2016). Coopetición en un destino turístico de frontera entre Argentina, Brasil y Paraguay: El caso Poloiguassu. *Semestre Económico, 19*(40), 145–174. https://doi.org/10.22395/seec.v19n40a6

Chim-Miki Costa, R. A., & Okumus, F. (2024). Investigating the strategic role of business sssociations in willingness toward tourism coopetition. *Current Issues in Tourism.* https://doi.org/10.1080/13683500.2024.2333910. (in press).

Chin, K., Chan, B. L., & Lam, P. (2008). Identifying and prioritizing critical success factors for coopetition strategy. *Industrial Management & Data Systems, 108*(4), 437–454.

Cygler, J., Gajdzik, B., & Sroka, W. (2014). Coopetition as a development stimulator of enterprises in the networked steel sector. *Metalurgija, 53*(3), 383–386.

Czernek, K., & Czakon, W. (2016). Trust-building processes in tourist coopetition: The case of a Polish region. *Tourism Management, 52*, 380–394. https://doi.org/10.1016/j.tourman.2015.07.009

Dagnino, G. B. (2012). *Handbook of research on competitive strategy.* Edward Elgar Publishing.

Della Corte, V., & Aria, M. (2016). Coopetition and sustainable competitive advantage. The case of tourist destinations. *Tourism Management, 54*, 524–540.

Della Corte, V., & Sciarelli, M. (2012). Can coopetition be source of competitive advantage for strategic networks?. *Corporate Ownership and Control, 10*(1), 363–379.

Hair, J. F., Anderson, R. E., Tatham, R. L., & Black, W. C. (1998). *Multivariate data analysis* (5th ed.). Prentice-Hall.

Hjalager, A. (2000). Tourism destinations and the concept of industrial districts. *Tourism and Hospitality Research, 2*(3), 199–213.

Kylänen, M., & Mariani, M. M. (2012). Unpacking the temporal dimension of coopetition in tourism destinations: Evidence from Finnish and Italian theme parks. *Anatolia, 23*(1), 61–74.

Kylänen, M., & Rusko, R. (2011). Unintentional coopetition in the service industries: The case of pyhä-luosto tourism destination in the finnish lapland. *European Management Journal, 29*(3), 193–205.

Luo, Y. (2007). A coopetition perspective of global competition. *Journal of World Business, 42*(2), 129–144.

Morgan, R. M., & Hunt, S. D. (1994). The commitment-trust theory of relationship marketing. *Journal of Marketing*, 20–38.

Parra, M. G., De Nalda, A. L., & Perles, G. S. M. (2011). Repensando la confianza como factor crítico en la gestión organizativa/Rethinking trust as a critic factor in the organizational behaviour. *Cuadernos de Gestión, 11*, 33.

Peng, T. A., Pike, S., Yang, J. C., & Roos, G. (2012). Is cooperation with competitors a good idea? An example in practice. *British Journal of Management, 23*(4), 532–560.

Porter, M. E. (1979). How competitive forces shape strategy. *Harvard Business Review, 57*(2), 137–145.

Porter, M. (1980). *Corporate strategy: Techniques for analyzing industries and competitors*. The Free Press.

Quintana-Garcia, C., & Benavides-Velasco, C. A. (2004). Cooperation, competition, and innovative capability: A panel data of European dedicated biotechnology firms. *Technovation, 24*(12), 927–938.

Ritala, P. (2012). Coopetition strategy ? when is it successful? empirical evidence on innovation and market performance. *British Journal of Management, 23*(3), 307–324.

Taylor, P., McRae-Williams, P., & Lowe, J. (2007). The determinants of cluster activities in the Australian wine and tourism industries. *Tourism Economics, 13*(4), 639–656. https://doi.org/10.5367/000000007782696050

Volschenk, J., Ungerer, M., & Smit, E. (2016). Creation and appropriation of socio-environmental value in coopetition. *Industrial Marketing Management, 57*, 109–118. https://doi.org/10.1016/j.indmarman.2016.05.026

Wang, Y., & Krakover, S. (2008). Destination marketing: Competition, cooperation or coopetition?. *International Journal of Contemporary Hospitality Management, 20*(2), 126–141.

Part Three

Co-consolidate the Tourism Destination: Endogenous Resources and the Coopetition Behaviour at the Host Society

Chapter 10

The Coopetition Model in the Tourism Sector: The Proliferation of Reusable Cup-Sharing Schemes

Nadine Leder[a], Maria Saju Abraham[a] and Jin Hooi Chan[b]

[a]Cardiff University, UK
[b]University of Greenwich, UK

Abstract

The tourism sector has realised an increasing need to transition towards sustainability. As the sector comprises a high number of entrepreneurs and small- and medium-sized enterprises, it faces specific limitations, which include, amongst others, knowledge transfer, skills and technology, financial and policy support, customer acceptance, and cultural taboos. To overcome these limitations, the sector thrives on encouraging interaction between ecosystem participants. One of the strategies to encourage interaction between ecosystem participants is the application of coopetition strategies. Coopetition strategies combine the advantages of cooperation and competition to generate value and achieve fruitful collaboration. However, their implementation is still limited. The purpose of this chapter is to examine the potential and practice of coopetition strategies among SMEs in addressing sustainability issues. Therefore, the study explored 10 European reusable cup-sharing schemes based on their level of applying coopetition. In doing that, the study aims to understand the supporting characteristics of existing cup schemes. It seeks to develop a framework for different levels of coopetition in achieving sustainability in the tourism and hospitality sector.

Keywords: Single-use plastics; circular economy; organisational innovation; reusable cup schemes; coopetition; tourism and hospitality sector

Value Proposition to Tourism Coopetition, 137–153
Copyright © 2025 Nadine Leder, Maria Saju Abraham and Jin Hooi Chan
Published under exclusive licence by Emerald Publishing Limited
doi:10.1108/978-1-83797-827-420241010

Introduction

The tourism sector has been identified as a resource-intensive sector, with an ongoing debate on its accountability for sustainable development. Despite efforts to implement sustainable solutions and practices in the sector, specific challenges are encountered. With the high number of small and medium enterprises (SMEs) worldwide, knowledge transfer, skills, and access to technology can be as challenging as consumer acceptance and cultural taboos faced when implementing and streamlining sustainable solutions. In fact, many sustainable or circular economy solutions require a good level of economies of scale and market power to be financially viable and to ensure social acceptance (Pan et al., 2018).

This is particularly true for challenges involving common goods. Organisational innovation is required to avoid the 'tragedy of the commons' paradox in which individuals with access to a common resource tend to act in their own interest, ultimately leading to resource exploitation and depletion (Hardin, 1968). Therefore, tourism enterprises need to have the willingness to adopt a system-level collaborative approach and to move away from traditional business models and strategies to ultimately gain the flexibility and ability to engage and respond to complex and sometimes paradoxical business activities which generate significant environmental and societal impacts (Christ et al., 2017; Lewis, 2000; Manzhynski & Biedenbach, 2023).

There has been increasing interest in experimenting with innovative organisations to tackle challenging sustainability problems in the tourism sector. One of the notable forms is a coopetitive approach, known as collaboration amongst competitors, to reduce costs, avoid duplicated efforts, and enhance economies of scale (Brandenburger & Nalebuff, 2021). However, by forming coopetitive business models and schemes, there is a need to understand their formation processes and characteristics (Weijs et al., 2022), which ultimately leads to a significant positive impact on sustainability. Despite the literature focussing on a diverse range of industry sectors, there is a gap in the literature investigating coopetition and sustainability, particularly coopetition schemes for sustainability in the tourism and hospitality sector (Chan et al., 2020). To address this gap, this chapter presents desk-based secondary data research on European reusable cup schemes.

A reusable cup scheme aims to reduce environmental impact, e.g., single-use plastic waste and embedded energy and emission, by providing beverages in reusable cups for a small deposit. Customers regain their deposit upon the successful return of their cup. To ensure the success and uptake of a cup scheme, an ecosystem is to be constructed, building on the principle of coopetition, and comprising, amongst others, a platform operator, many cafes and restaurants, bio-based cup suppliers, logistics companies, cup-washing operators, local authorities, and residents and visitors in a geographically defined catchment.

This chapter examines the potential and practice of coopetition strategies among SMEs in the tourism sector. Ten European cup schemes were selected, and their coopetition strategies were explored based on publicly available data. This allowed us to understand the supporting characteristics of existing cup schemes and develop a framework for different levels of coopetition in achieving sustainability in the tourism and hospitality sector.

This chapter continues with a short literature review on sustainability and coopetition, followed by the methods section. Then, the schemes are introduced, with detailed categorisation, analysis, and discussion. This chapter closes with a concise conclusion section and some recommendations.

Literature Review

Sustainable Tourism and Single-Used Plastics

The World Tourism Organisation defines sustainable tourism as 'tourism that takes full account of its current and future economic, social, and environmental impacts, addressing the needs of visitors, the industry, the environment, and host communities' (UN Tourism, 2024). Scholarly debates argue similarly, foregrounding that sustainable tourism can only be successfully implemented when contributing to the sustainable growth of the economy and society at a local and global scale whilst equally demonstrating an understanding of sustainable use of resources and the environment (Liu, 2003; Lu & Nepal, 2009). However, unmanaged and uncontrolled tourism development can contribute to global climate change, ecosystem degradation, consumerism, and loss of natural habitat (Ozturk et al., 2016).

A notable concern alongside these challenges is the growing issue of plastic pollution originating from tourism activities (Zhang et al., 2022, pp. 1–17). Although plastics are indispensable today, they can pose a considerable threat to the environment. Hence, there is an urgent need for change and innovative solutions. The UN sustainability goals, with their commitment towards, amongst others, clean water (SDG 6), sustainable cities (SDG 11), and responsible consumption and production (SDG 12), have emphasised the urgency and opened the way for policymakers to act. A variety of policymakers around the world have followed this call. In Europe, the European Commission launched a plastics strategy intending to reach '100% reusable or recyclable plastic packaging by 2030' (Tsai et al., 2022).

Coopetition in Reusable Cup Schemes

Reducing plastic packaging in the tourism sector requires close collaboration among different partners along the value chain (Munten et al., 2021). Recent debates have shown a growing interest in coopetition strategies. The concept of coopetition has existed for many years, with a specific rise in research and publications over the last two decades (Della Corte, 2018; Gernsheimer et al., 2021).

Coopetition is generally seen as a combination of cooperation and competition (Dorn et al., 2016; Chin et al., 2008). It encompasses the idea that organisations, normally interacting in rivalry due to conflicting interests, are now collaborating to safeguard mutual interest (Christ et al., 2017; Chin et al., 2018). Although the concept combines the element of cooperation with competition, there is still scholarly discourse, leading to various definitions and a diverse understanding and implementation of coopetition (Yadav et al., 2022). Despite the variety of definitions evolving over time (Bengtsson & Kock, 2014; Yadav et al., 2022), the perspectives of these definitions are broadly structured into either a value network of stakeholders comprising of suppliers, customers and competitors, and complementors; or a more narrowed perspective of coopetition between two directly competing organisations (Bengtsson & Kock, 2000, 2014; Brandenburger & Nalebuff, 2021). For this study, we follow Bouncken et al. (2015) definition, which sees coopetition as 'a strategic and dynamic process in which economic actors jointly create value through cooperative interaction, while they simultaneously compete to capture part of that value' (p. 591).

Coopetition is often applied in the field of strategic management by investigating strategic performance indicators of business entities and their partners (Dorn et al., 2016; Estrada et al., 2016), with a further focus on identifying economic benefits and success factors achieved through coopetition (Christ et al., 2017; Chin et al., 2018). In doing so, the literature identified management leadership, development of trust, long-term commitment, conflict management systems, knowledge and risk sharing, organisational learning, and information systems support as predominant success factors (Chin et al., 2018). However, due to the concept's vulnerable and possibly damaging nature, coopetition is considered mutually as a complex and challenging organisational phenomenon. Challenges have been observed alongside triggering tensions amongst participating partners, knowledge leakages, or opportunistic behaviour. Despite these hurdles, businesses demonstrate an increasing interest in unlocking the synergistic benefits of this concept (Gernsheimer et al., 2021).

Coopetition has developed a variety of dimensions and levels. The literature has classified the paradox across six dimensions: firm relation level, firm type level, organisational unit level, value chain level, geographic position level, and theoretical lens level (Gernsheimer et al., 2021). For the value chain perspective, coopetition is classified as horizontal coopetition, which includes the coopetition of direct competitors; and vertical coopetition, which consists of the coopetition of organisations in the same industry but operating at different stages of the supply chain (Tidström & Rajala, 2016). Narrowing this to a firm-relation level perspective, research has been conducted on inter-firm, intra-firm, network, and platform level (Dorn et al., 2016; Gernsheimer et al., 2021). Despite the dominance of research in the inter-firm domain, the network level has gained further attention within the specific sector of tourism and hospitality (Gernsheimer et al., 2021). The networking level allows organisations to connect competitively, as well as strategically (Gernsheimer et al., 2021). For example, the co-marketing of activities among different tourist destinations while competing for tourist money (Chim-Miki & Batista-Canino, 2017; Gernsheimer et al., 2021). However, criticism includes that these different dimensions contribute to the divergence in the field (Devece et al., 2019; Gernsheimer et al., 2021).

In the era of sustainability, coopetition thrives on encouraging interaction between ecosystem participants as a collective effort to counter weaknesses in some sustainable solutions, such as low market power, high capital costs, and lack of economies of scale. Due to the nature of the cup schemes, this research focusses on inter-firm level coopetition, which refers to the coopetition and generation of value between organisations in the same industry or market (Gernsheimer et al., 2021).

Methodology

To examine the phenomena around reusable cup schemes and explore their different coopetition levels, the study follows an abductive case study design. Abductive reasoning fosters the creation of learning loops, ultimately allowing for the combination of real-life observation and the matching of theoretical insights (Danermark, 2002; Spens & Kovács, 2006). As a first step, this study draws on the experience and insights from implementing a reusable cup scheme (Chan et al., 2022) before 10 European reusable cup schemes are explored. The data was analysed based on thematic coding to allow the identification of patterns and occurrences related to business models, as well as the nature and characteristics of coopetition.

In the second step, the level of competition that these unique schemes demonstrate has been identified and discussed. To be able to identify the level of coopetition, the reusable cup schemes were analysed based on six activities:

- Usage of technological applications;
- Promotion activities for the scheme;
- Financial logistics involving the deposit return scheme;
- Logistics involving the return and cleaning of cups;
- Logistics involved in relocating cups amongst participating business entities;
- Logistics involved in the replacement and handling of broken cups.

This allowed the development of a framework for coopetition levels, depicted in Fig. 10.1.

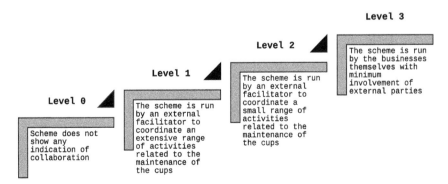

Fig. 10.1.   Levels of Coopetition. *Source:* Elaborated by the authors.

Comparing and Contrasting Reusable Cup Schemes

Introduction of Cup-Schemes

Aware of the vast number of cup schemes, we have selected 10 schemes catering for a geographical area within Europe. All 10 cup schemes were founded between 2012 and 2022. They are equipped with a profound background and experience in their set-up and operational actions undertaken. In the following, we explore the different schemes based on five characteristics (business model, catchment area, ownership/source of finance, technology application and usage, and operational view) to highlight their unique contributions and efforts towards a sustainable tourism sector; and to conclude the level of coopetition demonstrated by each scheme.

The Characteristics of the Cup Schemes

The first characteristic is the type of *business model* adopted by the scheme. Two B2C business models, *direct sales* and *subscription-based*, are adopted across the schemes. A subscription-based scheme adopts an approach where customers can buy and return their cups at any participating business entity. Advantages for such subscription-based schemes include reduced exposure to customer loyalty, eventually leading to a higher level of scalability for the cup scheme (EMF, 2023). However, subscription-based schemes often rely on a facilitator or mediator in the form of an NGO, council, ad-hoc consultancy team, or private for-profit entity, handling necessary admin-related tasks. In direct sales models, participating schemes can purchase a set number of cups for their own discretion and usage. This model seems to be advantageous for areas with a confined catchment area, such as sporting events in stadiums.

The second characteristic is the type of *catchment area* design for a scheme. The schemes exhibit varying degrees of different catchment areas, ranging from local initiatives focussed on specific cities or towns to nationwide programmes operating across multiple locations in a country. For instance, some schemes primarily target specific cities and pre-defined areas within the communities, such as University campuses, local communities, or beachside destinations. Schemes operating on a national scale were often more wide spreading, covering multiple regions within their respective country. Noticeable was the variety of operational activities that schemes can be involved with. For instance, some, highly community-driven, schemes concentrate their activities in specific regions or catchments of high population density and footfall. In contrast, others focussed on events where huge crowds gathered for a short period of time.

The third characteristic is the *ownership and sources of finance*, where the schemes adopt a rather wide variety of models, reflecting diverse strategies for financing sustainability initiatives. Several schemes are initiated and funded by local councils and/or governmental bodies. This indicates a commitment from public authorities to support sustainability efforts and promote environmentally friendly practices at the community level. Other schemes attracted their funding from corporations and long-term sustainable investors. These investors likely see the potential for financial returns alongside positive environmental impacts, aligning with their corporate social responsibility goals.

Crowdfunding is another fundraising method utilised by schemes. This approach not only provides funding but also fosters community involvement and awareness. Community-driven schemes rely on support from local businesses, organisations, and community groups. Another form seems to be funding by from private investors, demonstrating the role of venture capital and private equity in supporting innovative solutions to environmental challenges.

While some schemes prioritise community impact and environmental stewardship through non-profit, grant-based models, others adopt profit-driven strategies to sustain their operations. This duality in focus highlights the nuanced motivations driving sustainability initiatives, with some prioritising social responsibility, while others seek financial viability. It is a notable observation that small schemes demonstrate a slight tendency towards grant-based sources of financing.

Technological applications and usage is the third characteristic to compare the schemes. In doing so, some schemes leverage mobile applications to streamline cup transactions and enhance user experience. Some schemes employ dedicated apps that facilitate the borrowing and return of reusable cups, ensuring seamless transactions and automated payment processing, whereas others do not utilise any specific app for their operations, relying instead on traditional methods for cup management and customer engagement.

The absence of dedicated apps in some schemes may limit their ability to streamline transactions and engage users effectively. However, this simplicity may reduce barriers to participation for businesses and customers, as they do not need to navigate unfamiliar digital platforms. The applications used by the schemes themselves may differ greatly. For instance, the apps used different approaches to functionality and user-experience to ultimately foster the adoption of reusable cups with potential clients. One app seemed to emphasise customer convenience and engagement, offering features such as seamless cup borrowing and return processes, integrated payment processing and location-based services to help users find participating coffee shops easily. In contrast, another app prioritised business operations and logistics, providing functionalities tailored to packaging ordering, drop-off point management and transaction tracking for participating businesses. Whist one app focussed on promoting individual behaviour change and community engagement through user interface, the other app targeted businesses' needs for efficient inventory management and waste reduction strategies. But despite their differences, both apps play important roles in promoting sustainability and reducing single-use waste in their respective communities.

Lastly, we look at the *operational view* in managing the schemes. When in contact with the end-consumer, the schemes are either based on a multiple or single deposit return point. A single-point deposit return scheme is set up so that customers can only return their cups to the business entity from which they purchased them. This appears to be an advantageous modus operandi for confident catchment areas, such as sporting events or music festivals. It is not uncommon that, with this operational viewpoint, cup schemes provide an entire 'hospitality package' for their business clients. Doing so can include providing any return facilities, such as vending machines or digital return applications. On the other hand, multipoint deposit return schemes are advantageous for catchment areas with a more open layout, for instance, cities or seaside areas. The consumer who has bought the cup is provided with a return option at any participating business without a time limit in the return process.

Table 10.1 provides an overview of the characteristics and schemes investigated.

Levels of Coopetition

In the previous section, we outlined the different approaches to reusable cup schemes. In this section, we aim to cluster them based on their level of coopetition. In doing so, we use the following key activities applied in operating a cup scheme: usage of technological applications; promotional activities for the scheme; financial logistics involving the deposit return scheme; logistics involving the return and cleaning of the cup, as well as the relocation of cups amongst participating business entities; and the handling and replacement of broken cups as criteria. Table 10.2 provides an overview of the schemes and the main responsible operating party for this activity. Differentiating between activities managed by the coffee shop (X) or by the external facilitator (ν) allows the categorisation of a scheme based on three coopetition levels. Schemes with three or more of the above activities facilitated externally are classified as Level 1, while schemes with three or fewer activities facilitated by an external agent are classified as Level 2. Schemes consisting of competing firms which jointly come together to work on a coopetition project without a facilitator are classified with the highest level of coopetition: Level 3. No Level 0 scheme, i.e., scheme is being initiated and operated primarily by a single company, is included.

A detailed summary is provided below in Table 10.2.

Findings suggest that the presence of facilitators, whether private entities, community groups, or governmental bodies, is evident across most schemes. Furthermore, distinct patterns in the role of facilitators across different levels of coopetition within cup schemes have been identified. Schemes operating at Level 1, characterised by extensive external facilitation, typically involve third-party facilitators coordinating various activities such as cup cleaning, logistical service provision alongside relocation of cups or the replacement of defective cups. It is observed that schemes operating at Level 1 exhibit a high degree of centralisation and coordination. In contrast to schemes operating at Levels 2 and 3, coopetition at Level 1 requires a strong need for external facilitation to ensure smooth operation and meaningful value generation ultimately. In comparison, schemes operating at Level 2 and Level 3, with less (or none) external facilitation, demonstrate greater involvement of participating businesses in their operational execution. However, external support is not neglected and can be seen as an

Table 10.1. Cup Schemes Overview.

Cup Scheme	Business Model	Catchment Area	Ownership/Sources of Finance	Technology Application and Usage	Operational View
Scheme 1	Subscription-based model	Community focussed	Non-profit/grant based	Uses technological applications	Multipoint deposit return scheme
Scheme 2	Direct sales model to targeted events	Undefined catchment area	Privately owned – privately funded (P&L)	Does not use technological applications	Single point deposit return
Scheme 3	Subscription-based model	Undefined catchment area	Privately owned – privately funded (P&L)	Uses technological applications	Multipoint deposit return scheme
Scheme 4	Direct sales model	Undefined catchment area	Privately owned – privately funded (P&L)	Does not use technological applications	Single point deposit return scheme
Scheme 5	Direct sales model	Undefined catchment area	Privately owned – privately funded (P&L)	Uses technological applications	Multipoint deposit return scheme
Scheme 6	Direct sales mode	Community-focussed, with partially national out roll	Privately owned – privately funded (P&L)	Does not use technological applications	Multipoint deposit return scheme

(Continued)

Table 10.1. (*Continued*)

Cup Scheme	Business Model	Catchment Area	Ownership/Sources of Finance	Technology Application and Usage	Operational View
Scheme 7	Subscription-based model	Community-focussed	Non-profit – grant based	Does not use technological applications	Multipoint deposit return scheme
Scheme 8	Direct sales model – coordination-based model	Community-focussed	Non-profit, run by council – grant based	Does not use technological applications	Multipoint deposit return scheme
Scheme 9	Direct sales model	Community-focussed	Non-profit, run by council – grant based	Does not use technological applications	Multipoint deposit return scheme
Scheme 10	Joint-purchase model	Community-focussed	No formal entity, self-run/ collectively operated, grant based	Does not use technological applications	Multipoint deposit return scheme

Source: Elaborated by the authors.

additional supporting mechanism. Outsourcing of key logistical or promotional activities is frequently observed.

Facilitated schemes on Levels 1 and 2 exhibit a high level of operational efficiency and effectiveness in operating their reusable cup schemes. Schemes with facilitators demonstrate a broader geographical coverage. For instance, some nationwide schemes operate with thousands of dispensing points. This is often enabled by substantial financial backing from investors or received funding grants. However, operating on such a large scale requires the streamlining of operational processes. This is often given by the usage of app-based systems. Additional external facilitators can be entry points for coopetitive partnerships at this operational level, as they foster relationships amongst participating business entities. These indicators further underscore the role of facilitators in driving the success of the schemes and fostering a sustainable initiative among business entities. In doing so, these facilitators catalyse environmental impact through enhanced outreach, a streamlined usage of resources, and an increase in operational effectiveness.

There is an observation towards schemes on Levels 2 and 3 forming strong bonds and partnerships with NGOs and local communities. Some schemes experienced strong support by local councils and governments, exemplifying collaborative approaches that involve a variety of stakeholders to advance sustainability goals.

Based on the analysis in Table 10.2, the following coopetition levels can be attributed to explored cup schemes:

- Level 1: Scheme 1; Scheme 2; Scheme 4; Scheme 5; Scheme 6.
- Level 2: Scheme 3; Scheme 7; Scheme 9.
- Level 3: Scheme 8; Scheme 10.

It must be emphasised that neither of the coopetition levels should represent a favourable outcome or level. On the contrary, the coopetition levels aim to provide a situational overview of the different forms of coopetition, ultimately aiding organisations in understanding what activities are involved in collaborating and which considerations need to be made when deciding on the form of competition in the realisation of the cup scheme.

As each coopetition level scenario follows a slightly different reusable cup scheme approach, there are distinct challenges and barriers to overcome when aiming to roll out such a scheme. For instance, on Level 1, some schemes offer businesses the opportunity to engage from the pilot stage onwards, fostering a sense of ownership and collaboration. In addition, an applied centralised information system ensures transparency and problem resolution to enhance operational efficiency. However, pure reliance on app-based transactions could limit inclusivity amongst different ranges of customers and, in the worst outcome, hinder accessibility for some customers. On the other hand, some schemes provide alternatives without app dependencies. Their emphasis on external cleaning reduces operational and technological burdens on businesses, promoting ease of

Table 10.2. Activities Provided by the Scheme's Management and Coffee Shop/Events.

	Technology Usage	Promotional Activities	Deposit Collection	Washing Cups	Service Provision	
					Relocating Cups	Replacing Cups
Scheme 1	✔	✔	✔	X	✔	✔
Scheme 2	X	✔	X	✔	✔	✔
Scheme 3	X	✔	X	X	✔	✔
Scheme 4	X	✔	X	✔		✔
Scheme 5	✔	✔	✔	✔	✔	✔
Scheme 6	X	N/A	X	✔	✔	✔
Scheme 7	X	✔	X	X	✔	✔
Scheme 8	X	N/A	X	X	X	N/A
Scheme 9	X	✔	X	X	✔	✔
Scheme 10	X	X	X	X	X	X

Source: Elaborated by the authors.

Agenda: X = activity is managed by the coffee shop; ✔ = activity is managed by the external facilitator.

adoption. However, the absence of a dedicated technological app might hinder transactional tracking and customer engagement, process optimisation, and potentially impacting scalability. Hence, it is important for organisations planning to implement a cup scheme to understand the values of their customers, as well as their needs.

Another observed advantage of Level 2 coopetition models is the subscription-based approach. This model actively fosters sustainable practices while accommodating business flexibility. For example, by decentralised cup cleaning responsibilities, these schemes empower community/competing firm involvement and reduce logistical complexities. However, the reliance on cafés for cup management may introduce inconsistencies in service quality and cup availability. Meanwhile, schemes supported by a government-backed initiative, leveraging public-private partnerships to drive the scheme's adoption. This can support a scheme's inclusivity and allow for city-wide support to facilitate widespread acceptance, but scalability might be constrained by reliance on municipal resources and infrastructure.

The Level 3 coopetition model highlights a clear tendency to business (competing) community-driven initiatives, prioritising local engagement in the drive to reduce environmental impact. These schemes might be initiated with the help of an external moderator (such as ad-hoc project teams like FACET Project) who are only active during the initiation stage (Chan et al., 2022). The circular deposit system encourages customer participation and behaviour change, aligning with sustainability goals. Moreover, the absence of subscription fees makes these schemes financially accessible for businesses, fostering widespread adoption and reducing admin to a minimum. However, operational challenges like cup circulation management and hygiene standards may arise without centralised oversight. Despite these challenges, the community-centric approach fosters a sense of collective responsibility and ownership, driving long-term sustainability objectives.

The analysis of the various schemes' business models and operational views revealed a diverse landscape of approaches towards cup provision and management. Models such as subscription-based, direct sales, and coordination-based operations are employed across the schemes, each tailored to fit specific contexts and objectives. Subscription-based models ensure continuous revenue streams, fostering long-term partnerships and facilitating ongoing support for cup services. Meanwhile, direct sales models offer flexibility, catering to targeted events or one-off purchases. Operational views, such as multiple-point deposit return schemes, promote widespread cup reuse and customer engagement.

One of the primary difficulties a scheme can face is the adoption barrier presented by the requirement for customers to download an app, sign up, and enter payment details. This process can slow down service, impacting the seamless flow of transactions within businesses, particularly those with high traffic volumes like cafes and eateries. The need to prepare users for this process before their visit is highlighted as a strategy to mitigate this challenge, emphasising the importance of proactive customer education and seamless integration into the service workflow.

Future schemes should investigate integration with existing payment systems – credit/debit card or other payment apps.

Additionally, the schemes identify a range of operational and management challenges. For instance, schemes responsible for cleaning and maintaining their own cups and ensuring consistent engagement and adherence to scheme protocols among staff can be challenging. Moreover, issues such as refund charging discrepancies and the inconvenience of customers having to queue twice, once to purchase and again to return the cups, demonstrate the importance of refining operational processes and enhancing user experience to encourage participation and streamlined operations.

Moreover, schemes that involve relocation of cups, whether through rental or deposit systems, face logistical complexities and challenges for optimisation. Coordination between scheme operators and participating businesses is crucial to ensure the smooth circulation of cups, minimise loss rates, and maintain an adequate supply to meet demand. Challenges such as cup shortages, loss rates, and the need for ongoing marketing efforts to re-engage users highlight the dynamic nature of managing reusable cup schemes within diverse community contexts.

Furthermore, the financial sustainability of these initiatives presents a persistent challenge. Concerns over the viability of deposit systems, budget constraints for supporting unreturned cups, and the need for continuous marketing to sustain user engagement underscore the importance of long-term strategies for scaling and maintaining these schemes.

Conclusion

The tourism sector is currently experiencing a shift towards more innovative and sustainable solutions (Chan et al., 2023). With the sector being identified as resource-intensive and the growing issues around plastic and other single-use packaging waste, this study investigated the potential and practice of coopetition strategies among SMEs in the tourism sector by examining reusable cup schemes. In doing so, 10 reusable cup schemes were compared, and a framework for the different levels of coopetition was developed to discuss and highlight challenges and barriers in achieving sustainability within the sector. As many cup schemes and other coopetitive schemes bring meaningful positive impacts on the environment and community, this study provides insights that are useful for future proliferation and successes in implementing these schemes, which is encouraged.

One of the key findings is that different business models were adopted with various key roles of the scheme facilitators. A facilitator or mediator allows for centralised management of the scheme, reducing possible administration and management tasks, which can be especially supportive for smaller business entities with restricted knowledge, human, and financial resources. Contrary, there are different barriers and challenges to small community-based scheme in which competing small cafes and restaurants require to come to mutual agreement when actively establishing a cup scheme. This enhances localness and sense of place attachment, as well as encourage local innovation (Chan et al., 2020, 2021). While acknowledging the advantages of a small community-based scheme, one of the major challenges for these schemes includes the processes of deposit collection and other logistics challenges related to the redistribution of cups. The long-term sustainability of these schemes might be challenging because of the fluidity of the management team. Especially in smaller, more community-based cup schemes, the advantages of centralised facilitators are more obvious, including technology, experience, and a clear focal point for strategy and operational matters.

The conceptual framework on coopetitive levels can provide practical guidance for organisations aiming to contribute to the design of cup schemes. Based on the framework, Level 1 is for business entities that want fewer management and administrative burdens, ideally in a confined area or for events. Level 3 cooperation suits smaller, more community-based cup schemes, but they might face various logistics and longevity challenges in managing them.

The study has some limitations. It needs to be acknowledged that the schemes are not representative and have been restricted to the geographical area of Europe. This is also secondary data research based on publicly available information that has not been validated via interviews. It needs to be emphasised that all cup schemes are current business entities that are constantly changing and developing. The research replicates the standing from the beginning of 2023.

Based on the study, future research in coopetitive schemes can further examine various aspects in more detail: the formation processes of these schemes, the contractual arrangements of parties at all levels of coopetition, the motivations of businesses and consumers in engaging directly with these schemes, and the issues affecting the longevity of these schemes.

Acknowledgements

This work is partly funded by the FACET Project – Interreg 2Seas Programme under the European Regional Development Fund [2S07-034] and the On-campus Internships scheme by the Learning and Teaching Academy of Cardiff University.

References

Bengtsson, M., & Kock, S. (2000). Coopetition' in business networks—To cooperate and compete simultaneously. *Industrial Marketing Management, 29*(5), 411–426. https://doi.org/10.1016/S0019-8501(99)00067-X

Bengtsson, M., & Kock, S. (2014). Coopetition—Quo vadis? Past accomplishments and future challenges. *Industrial Marketing Management, 43*(2), 180–188. https://doi.org/10.1016/j.indmarman.2014.02.015

Bouncken, R. B., Gast, J., Kraus, S., Bogers, M. (2015). Coopetition: A systematic review, synthesis, and future research directions. *Review of Management Science, 9*, 577–601. https://doi.org/10.1007/s11846-015-0168-6

Brandenburger, A., & Nalebuff, B. (2021). The rules of co-opetition: Rivals are working together more than ever before. Here's how to think through the risks and rewards. *Harvard Business Review*. Magazine January-February.

Chan, J. H., Chen, S.-Y., Piterou, A., Khoo, S. L., Lean, H. H., & Hashim, I. (2021). An innovative social enterprise: Roles and challenges faced by an arts hub in a World Heritage Site in Malaysia. *City, Culture and Society, 25*(June 2021), 100396.

Chan, J. H., Hashim, I. H. M., Khoo, S. L., Lean, H. H., & Piterou, A. (2020). Entrepreneurial orientation of traditional and modern cultural organisations: Cases in George Town UNESCO World Heritage Site. *Cogent Social Science, 6*(1), 1810889.

Chan, J. H., Roskam, H., van Maldegem, A., Ieromonachou, P., Sciacca, A., Von Schomberg, L., Coles, A. M., Witt, S., Zavala, J., Métreau, E., Debruyne, D., & Brinkman, M. (2023). *Whitepaper: Accelerating the adoption of the Circular Economy in the tourism and leisure sector: the 3-M Framework as the Foundation of Circular Entrepreneurship*. Interreg 2 Seas project FACET.

Chan, J. H., Zavala, J., & Leder, N., (2022). *Reusable cup scheme in Norfolk's seaside town of Hemsby*. Available at: https://www.circularonline.co.uk/insight/case-study-reusable-cup-scheme-in-norfolks-seaside-town-of-hemsby/. Accessed: 10/02/2024.

Chim-Miki, A. F., & Batista-Canino, R. M. (2017). Tourism coopetition: An introduction to the subject and a research agenda. *International Business Review, 26*(6), 1208–1217. https://doi.org/10.1016/j.ibusrev.2017.05.003

Chin, K., Chan, B. L., & Lam, P. (2008). Identifying and prioritizing critical success factors for coopetition strategy. *Industrial Management & Data Systems, 108*(4), 437–454. https://doi.org/10.1108/02635570810868326

Christ, K. L., Burritt, R. L., & Varsei, M. (2017). Coopetition as a potential strategy for corporate sustainability. *Business Strategy and the Environment, 26*, 1029–1040. https://doi.org/10.1002/bse.1967

Danermark, B. (2002). *Explaining society: Critical realism in the social sciences*. Routledge.

Della Corte, V. (2018). Innovation through coopetition: Future directions and new challenges. *Journal of Open Innovation: Technology, Market, and Complexity, 4*(4), 47. https://doi.org/10.3390/joitmc4040047

Devece, C., Ribeiro-Soriano, D. E., & Palacios-Marques, D. (2019). Coopetition as the new trend in inter-firm alliances: Literature review and research patterns. *Review of Managerial Science, 13*(2), 207.

Dorn, S., Schweiger, B., & Albers, S. (2016). Levels, phases and themes of coopetition: A systematic literature review and research agenda. *European Management Journal, 34*(5), 484–500. https://doi.org/10.1016/j.emj.2016.02.009

Estrada, I., Faems, D., & de Faria, P. (2016). Coopetition and product innovation performance: The role of internal knowledge sharing mechanisms and formal knowledge protection mechanisms. *Industrial Marketing Management, 53*, 56–65. https://doi.org/10.1016/j.indmarman.2016.05.013

Gernsheimer, O., Kanbach, D. K., & Gast, J. (2021). Coopetition research - A systematic literature review on recent accomplishments and trajectories. *Industrial Marketing Management, 96*, 113–134. https://doi.org/10.1016/j.indmarman.2021.05.013

Hardin, G. (1968). The tragedy of the commons. *Science, 162*(3859), 1243–1248.

Lewis, M. W. (2000). Exploring paradox: Toward a more comprehensive guide. *Academy of Management Review, 25*(4), 760–776. Available at: https://doi.org/10.2307/259204

Liu, Z. (2003). Sustainable tourism development: A critique. *Journal of Sustainable Tourism, 11*(6), 459–475. https://doi.org/10.1080/0966958030866721

Lu, J., & Nepal, S. K. (2009). Sustainable tourism research: An analysis of papers published in the Journal of Sustainable Tourism. *Journal of Sustainable Tourism, 17*(1), 5–16. https://doi.org/10.1080/09669580802582480

Manzhynski, S., & Biedenbach, G. (2023). The knotted paradox of coopetition for sustainability: Investigating the interplay between core paradox properties. *Industrial Marketing Management, 110*, 31–45. https://doi.org/10.1016/j.indmarman.2023.02.013

Munten, P., Vanhamme, J., Maon, F., Swaen, V., & Lindgreen, A. (2021). Addressing tensions in coopetition for sustainable innovation: Insights from the automotive industry. *Journal of Business Research, 136*, 10–20. https://doi.org/10.1016/j.jbusres.2021.07.020

Ozturk, I., Al-Mulali, U., & Saboori, B. (2016). Investigating the environmental Kuznets curve hypothesis: The role of tourism and ecological footprint. *Environmental Science and Pollution Research, 23*, 1916–1928.

Pan, S.-Y., Gao, M., Kim, H., Shah, K. J., Pei, S.-L., & Chiang, P.-C. (2018). Advances and challenges in sustainable tourism toward a green economy. *Science of the Total Environment, 635*, 452–469. https://doi.org/10.1016/j.scitotenv.2018.04.134

Tidström, A., & Rajala, A. (2016). Coopetition strategy as interrelated praxis and practices on multiple levels. *Industrial Marketing Management, 58*, 35–44. https://doi.org/10.1016/j.indmarman.2016.05.013

Tsai, C.-H. (K.), Su, C.-H. (J.), Lin, L.-C., & Brown, E. A. (2022). Keep CUP the good work! Is sustainable consumption a promise or all talk?. *Journal of Teaching in Travel & Tourism, 22*(4), 415–424. https://doi.org/10.1080/15313220.2022.2056562

UN Tourism. (2024). *Sustainable development.* Available: https://www.unwto.org/sustainable-development. Accessed: 01 15, 2024.

Weijs, R. H., Coles, A. M., & Chan, J. H. (2022). *Joint purchase in a circular economy.* EU Interreg 2 Seas project FACET.

Yadav, N., Kumar, R., & Malik, A. (2022). Research: A bibliometric analysis of research articles published between 2010 and 2020. *Journal of Business Research, 145*, 495–508. https://doi.org/10.1016/j.jbusres.2022.03.005

Zhang, J., Quoquab, F., & Mohammad, J. (2022). *What do we know about plastic pollution in coastal/marine tourism? Documenting its present research status from 1999 to 2022.* October-December 2023. https://doi.org/10.1177/21582440231211706

Chapter 11

Analysing Coopetition in the Wine Business Ecosystem: A Literature Review

Marcia Mariluz Amaral, Luiz Carlos Da Silva Flores and Sara Joana Gadotti Dos Anjos

UNIVALI, Brazil

Abstract

This research delves into the intricate dynamics of coopetition within the intersection of the wine industry and tourism. By bridging vitiviniculture and wine tourism, the study investigates both intentional and unintentional cooperation, associationism, and cluster effects. Employing bibliometric analysis provides insights that contribute to interdisciplinary understanding, laying the groundwork for future research. The study evaluates the impact of business ecosystems and competitive advantages on coopetition from a territorial perspective. It emphasises the strategic importance of coopetition as a dynamic interplay between collaboration and competition, fostering innovation and growth in vitiviniculture and wine tourism. By synthesising a diverse range of literature, the research unveils historical collaborative efforts and explores key concepts such as clusters and ecosystems. It concludes with a proposed model capturing coopetition layers, serving as a valuable tool for business and regional governance. This research enhances comprehension of the complexities within the wine business ecosystem, providing actionable insights for stakeholders and suggesting avenues for future studies, including the exploration of coopetition in shared wine territories.

Keywords: Wine tourism; wine industry; wine business; coopetition; wine business ecosystem

Value Proposition to Tourism Coopetition, 155–170
Copyright © 2025 Marcia Mariluz Amaral, Luiz Carlos Da Silva Flores and Sara Joana Gadotti Dos Anjos
Published under exclusive licence by Emerald Publishing Limited
doi:10.1108/978-1-83797-827-420241011

Introduction

In contemporary tourism trends, wine tourism holds remarkable importance, aligning with new consumer patterns emphasising experiential aspects and a higher frequency of visits within a shorter time frame. Wine tourism is the harmonious integration of wine territory and visitor engagement, with the wine industry (vitiviniculture) forming the foundation and tourism acting as a support channel for direct sales at wineries. The increasing recognition of wine tourism's potential to boost winery sales and contribute to territory development has attracted interest from scholars across disciplines such as geography, economics, sociology, and business management (Marco-Lajara et al., 2023).

Considering the interdisciplinary nature of investigation on wine tourism and its inherent connection with the wine industry, this study employs a comprehensive approach, utilising both literature review and content analysis methodologies. Its primary objective is to pinpoint and consolidate crucial aspects of coopetition within the wine business ecosystem. Starting from the core domain of vitiviniculture, which comprehends grape growing (viticulture) and wine production (viniculture), it extends to the realm of wine tourism (Sigala, 2019; Telfer, 2001).

This research provides a general theoretical background, a bibliographical survey, and a comparative analysis in several stages. Firstly, it delves into the dynamics of cooperation and competition among businesses, particularly within the wine industry. Next, it delves into tourism as an extension of vitivinicultural ventures. Following that, the study investigates coopetition within the wine tourism ecosystem. Additionally, a bibliometric analysis is employed to explore publications related to coopetition in the wine industry and wine tourism. Ultimately, this study concludes with insightful discussions and a proposed research agenda aimed at further enriching understanding in this domain.

Navigating Cooperative Paths Among the Wine Industry Competition

Collaborative arrangements within the enterprise setting have a rich historical background and manifest in diverse ways. In the 1980s, the industrial district concept involved businesses in a specific activity clustering together to promote economies of scale. This model distributes tasks and value chain activities to local small- and medium-sized enterprises (SMEs) influenced by nearby industries, offering either economic or social advantages. Participation in an industrial district extends beyond knowledge sharing; it entails an active interplay of collaboration and competition (Scaringella & Radziwon, 2018). Innovative initiatives and institutional arrangements facilitated by this approach significantly contribute to the development of wine industries, notably observed in regions like Italy (Pomarici et al., 2021).

An alternative manifestation of cooperation is associationism or cooperativism, which is shaped by social mechanisms and fundamental rules of interaction, as observed in relationships within wine cooperatives. In the management of these alliances, it is essential to ensure a fair and equitable distribution of profits in the number of all participants, as they collectively own the association (Salvagni et al., 2020). These networks prove effective in addressing the challenges posed by the modest average size of businesses (Pomarici et al., 2021), as well as becoming a cultural merit (Fensterseifer, 2007) and a leverage for innovation. Although cooperativism emphasises cooperation, competition is typically absent within this environment (Salvagni et al., 2020).

A different viewpoint on the dynamic relationship among networks was presented by Moore (1993) as a business ecosystem concept, inspired by digital and biological ecosystems. In this model, companies function as integral components across industries, evolving capabilities through collaboration and competition. Additionally, Moore proposed initiating a business ecosystem with a core set of synergistic relationships and then expanding its scale and scope. Effective ecosystems manage space by meeting demand or regulating supply, potentially leading to conflicts (Moore, 1996). The integration of the ecosystem concept into tourism showcases a long-standing collaboration among industry stakeholders and government bodies. The goal is to maximise individual benefits, accomplish mutual objectives, and secure the sustainability of the system (Salvado, 2023b).

Further, Porter (1998) introduced the theory of clusters, which are closely interconnected networks of companies and associated institutions within a specific activity. These clusters foster both competition and cooperation amidst their members, exhibiting shared traits and complementary strengths. They are linked to related clusters, as seen in the relationship between the wine industry and the wine tourism clusters (Porter, 1998). These interconnections generate synergies, extending beyond economies of agglomeration. Moreover, clusters are influenced by historical, social, cultural, and environmental factors, as observed in industries like wine and tourism. The cooperative structure in global clusters leads to coopetition, representing a transitional model towards deeper partnerships within emerging clusters worldwide (Dana et al., 2013; Fensterseifer, 2007).

Various types of strategic alliances can be instrumental in building core competencies. These coalitions can enhance research and technology capabilities, address skill imbalances among firms, accelerate the development of new products, reduce barriers to entry into new markets, and promote increased capacity utilization and economies of scale (Telfer, 2001). Collaborative initiatives, such as the development of new service offerings in wine firms, like wine tourism, strategically enhance negotiation dynamics and boost the industry (Prokeš, 2013). Additionally, collaborative promotional initiatives among wineries involved in wine tourism, along with idea sharing, cultivate camaraderie and a feeling of belonging (Alonso, 2011).

Cooperation and competition intertwine in business through various intentional or unintentional, formal or informal, and regional or global interactions. Coopetition can be a deliberate, structured strategy, carefully planned, or arise spontaneously (Chim-Miki & Batista-Canino, 2017). These interactions can also be formalised or not, as commonly seen in informal collaborations between wineries for distribution and promotional campaigns (Crick & Crick, 2021;

Pomarici et al., 2021). Wine producers often engage in coopetition in market-oriented activities to access new opportunities and resources, which benefits SMEs in their market (Crick & Crick, 2021). Besides, these enterprises often recognise that their production volumes are insufficient for venturing into mass markets, such as export, prompting them to strategically shift focus towards the tourism sector (Senkiv et al., 2022).

A perspective on the evolution of competition, contending that it encompasses elements of cooperation and conflict, leads to coevolution. Nevertheless, although the compelling interplay of cooperative and competitive forces in coopetition is an important element in business ecosystems (Moore, 1996), it is understood that coopetition does not necessarily require an ideal balance between competitive and cooperative elements with all partners (Sigala, 2019). Moreover, some level of rivalry will persist despite collaboration in businesses (Crick & Crick, 2021) as noted earlier.

Tourism as an Extension of the Wine Industry

Wine tourism integrates aspects of the wine industry, wine territories, and tourism. It facilitates direct sales and marketing with a vertical integration strategy. This approach involves combining vitivinicultural ventures with associated tourism services, collectively referred to as 'wine businesses' in this study. The service provided by these businesses can vary from primary attractions such as cellar door tastings and winery visits to a diversity of offerings like restaurant meals, shop purchases, gallery and museum visits, event attendance, overnight stays, and even outdoor occupations like vineyard tours (Pomarici et al., 2021; Senkiv et al., 2022; Sigala, 2019).

Recognising the benefits of wine tourism is crucial for either wine producers or tourism stakeholders. This form of tourism not only functions as a targeted marketing tactic but also represents an avenue for the advancement of destinations by drawing in visitors. Beyond merely winery visits, tourists often engage in various activities like dining, shopping, exploring cultural venues, attending events, and staying overnight (Senkiv et al., 2022). Given that many visitors seek diverse experiences rather than focussing solely on one activity or attraction, there is an opportunity to enhance their overall travel experience in a captivating wine destination (Alonso, 2011).

Tourism success in the wine industry and region relies on visitors recognising the merit of hybrid schemes and the integration of goods and services. The combination of wine-associated products, hospitality, gastronomy, and tourist amenities creates a distinctive and unique experience (Maracaja et al., 2023). These various complementarities play a vital role in enhancing the overall tourism experience (Porter, 1998). Furthermore, the landscapes in wine territories are key attractions for tourists, providing picturesque viewpoints, with vineyards and rural scenery easily seen due to greater exposure, which hold important appeal (Rachão et al., 2019; Senkiv et al., 2022).

SMEs in the wine field can greatly benefit by adopting wine tourism as a vertical company strategy. These wineries often face challenges when competing with larger counterparts, leading them to compromise on wine quality to cut costs. This compromise affects the value of wine, impacting numerous SMEs in the wine industry (Senkiv et al., 2022). Therefore, their competitive advantage should not only emphasise economies of scale and scope but also flexible systems that contribute to a continuous innovation trajectory, such as vertical integration (Moore, 1996).

Coopetition in the Wine Tourism Ecosystem

Wine establishments, facing unique challenges, can benefit from partnerships to maximise vertical opportunities, enhancing tourism and territorial identity (Pomarici et al., 2021; Rachão et al., 2019; Senkiv et al., 2022). Close collaboration among diverse stakeholders is essential for achieving success in this endeavour. This collaborative approach in a setting favourable to coopetition involves a mutual agreement, a shared purpose, and alignment of practices to achieve communal complex goals (Moore, 1996; Rachão et al., 2019; Telfer, 2001).

Crick and Crick (2021) highlight coopetition as a prevalent strategy in the global wine activity, aiding in overcoming limitations and boosting wine tourism. This multifaceted approach not only functions as a potent marketing strategy but also offers value to wine tourists, potentially fostering long-term consumer relationships. Additionally, Sigala (2019) notes that tourism destinations operate as platforms, fostering coopetition ecosystems where organisations balance competition and collaboration for mutual benefit. This perspective resonates with Moore's (1996) assertion that business environments transcend traditional industry boundaries, thriving within or across these lines in an ecosystem.

The business ecosystems' conceptualisation has been significantly shaped by various aspects of the territorial approach, notably industrial districts. However, industrial and service ecosystems exhibit distinctions, with the latter emphasising firms' direct supplier–customer networks and giving lower priority to other stakeholders (Scaringella & Radziwon, 2018). Also, the service ecosystem is described as an energetic structure that evolves over time, involving various interconnected social and economic entities. These bodies interact through institutions and technology to collaboratively produce and trade service offerings and resources, ultimately aiming to generate value together (Gretzel et al., 2015).

Tourism functions within a service ecosystem, linking the wine industry to this network through wine tourism, which plays a crucial role in regional development. By integrating primary, secondary, and tertiary sectors within a cultural tourism ecosystem, wine tourism creates a comprehensive business environment. This habitat thrives when cooperative strategies are implemented within the activity (Salvado, 2023b).

Coopetition in the tourism sector is notable for its significant internal and external competitive forces within destinations, creating a conducive environment for the emergence of coopetition. Unique factors in tourism, including intense inner competition, high complementarity and interdependence among tourism services, and the fragmentation of the tourism supply, contribute to establishing coopetitive ecosystems within destinations. This operational approach allows them to collectively address common threats and collaboratively enhance the overall value of the destination (Sigala, 2019).

This study investigates coopetition within the domain of wine tourism, highlighting the ecosystem where the wine industry acts as the central establishment. To enhance understanding of the segment and its subset, wine tourism, a comprehensive literature review was conducted. Within this review, particular attention was given to examining the cooperative and competitive dynamics uniting wine businesses, with a specific emphasis on those involved in wine tourism, as detailed in the subsequent section in which the methodology applied is presented.

Methodology

Aiming to understand the scenario of the wine business ecosystems and how they evolve into coopetition and accomplish the aim of this study, a quantitative approach utilising citation data and advanced statistical tools via a bibliometric analysis was used to uncover knowledge structures (Díaz et al., 2023) and explore publications related to coopetition in the wine industry and tourism, to identify connections between concepts in these domains.

Aria and Cuccurullo (2017) describe the process of employing bibliometric methods in research, involving formulating questions, selecting approaches, and categorising inquiries. The three main question types include understanding knowledge bases, exploring research fronts, and establishing social network structures. Notable decisions in study design include timeframe and data collection methods. Analysis is done using bibliometric or statistical software tools, and results are visually presented using mapping software. The authors stress the importance of interpretation in the concluding phase, noting that while bibliometric methods offer insights, they cannot replace comprehensive reading.

The following process (Aria & Cuccurullo, 2017; Díaz et al., 2023; Donthu et al., 2021; Kotur, 2023; Marco-Lajara et al., 2023; Page et al., 2022) were used in this research:

a. Data was collected on Web of Science (WoS) and Scopus repositories in November 2023.
b. Search strategy included key words [coopetit* OR co-opetit* OR competit* AND cooperat* (Topic) AND wine (Topic)], and no restrictions imposed with respect to the research field, the publication date or the language, resulting in 258 studies (WoS $n = 118$, Scopus $n = 140$), dating from 1991 to 2023.
c. Data was uploaded to the open-source tool Zotero where duplicates were merged, and studies not related to main purpose (technology, food science, etc.)

were excluded ($n = 28$), resulting in 129 studies (journals' articles, proceedings, books, etc.).

d. Using the R Studio package, data were uploaded to the software tool Bibliometrix to proceed with the analysis.

e. Terms were merged, such as 'wine cooperatives' into 'cooperatives'; 'sustainable development' into 'sustainability' and 'co-opetition' into 'coopetition', for example.

f. Analysis of this entire record was performed on Bibliometrix, such as 'Annual Production'; 'Author Impact'; 'Authors Production Over Time'; 'Most Relevant Authors'; 'Co-occurrence Network'.

g. A sub-database was created after selecting only those in which 'tourism' was mentioned in the 'abstract' ($n = 21$).

h. Steps 'd' and 'e' were executed again to run 'Co-occurrence Network' analysis.

i. Data from the step 'g' (title, authors, abstract, main purpose, relation to coopetition, relation to wine tourism, locus) was summarised in an Excel spreadsheet.

j. Seven papers were excluded from the record, because they have restricted access, or the language was not familiar (English, Spanish and Portuguese) to the authors of the present study.

k. Results were critically analysed, and the 14 studies (step 'i') were fully read.

l. Other six studies associated with coopetition in the wine tourism segment, cited in the database were also included in the spreadsheet (step 'i'), and were fully read. Resulting in 20 studies in this sub-database.

After data extraction from the two main bibliographic repositories, namely Clarivate Analytics WoS and Scopus, we used the Bibliometrix software because it offers a suite of tools specifically designed for quantitative research in bibliometrics. Bibliometrix is coded in the R language, known for its open-source environment. The notable strengths that make R preferable for scientific computation include its robust statistical algorithms, access to high-quality numerical routines, and integrated data visualisation tools (Aria & Cuccurullo, 2017).

Findings

The analysis began by examining the complete record, which involved tracking the evolution of research paradigms and conducting a comprehensive thematic assessment to deepen understanding of the investigation domain (Donthu et al., 2021). Although the initial paper in the database (Freeman, 1991) did not directly address wine matters, it referenced wine in a figurative context. Freeman (1991) noted the presence of cooperative research in competitive industries before it was formally recognized as an innovation by firms, akin to 'new wine in old bottles', a concept further explored by Scaringella and Radziwon (2018). The earliest paper related to the present research objective was centred around cooperation and competition in the winemaking segment of New Zealand, by Harfield (1999).

Telfer's (2001) study examines strategic alliances in Canadian wine tourism, albeit without explicitly using the term, hence it was included in the previously mentioned step 'l'. The author delineates two main strategies for these alliances: horizontal, aimed at safeguarding the wine industry's core competencies, and vertical, involving multi-sector partnerships. While Telfer advises caution in the latter due to potential conflicts of interest, such as competition with partner establishments like restaurants, he underscores the considerable benefits of collective efforts among predominantly small-scale wineries. Strengthening ties, be they formal or informal, with various industries amplifies tourism's multiplier effect and fosters rural development.

Considering the complete information, the author with the highest impact was Jon Hanf, whose papers were focussed on the cooperative wine business model in Germany. He co-authored a study related to wine tourism (step 'g' above) written in German (Ruediger & Hanf, 2017), or this, we can't wholly include it in the analysis. However, from the article abstract, we understood that wine activity in Germany is pursuing new alternatives, with one option being wine tourism, due to rising national and international competition. Its findings conclude that cooperatives in that country integrate wine tourism events into their structure as a marketing tool rather than for value addition.

As mentioned earlier, this current study employed keyword co-occurrence as the primary analysis in the sub-database, in which tourism was an important subject of the field. This matrix was used to map and cluster terms extracted from abstracts within the bibliographic collection on Bibliometrix (Aria & Cuccurullo, 2017). It was found that while some studies focussed on cooperation, the competitive aspect was associated with the competitiveness of wine regions (Flores et al., 2016; García Revilla & Martínez Moure, 2021; Maracaja et al., 2023; Maumon & Bédé, 2023; Mazurkiewicz-Pizlo, 2016; Pomarici et al., 2021; Prokeš, 2013) rather than competition within the wine industry or tourism. Most of the analysed literature about coopetition within wine enterprises comprises case studies that delve into specific regions or countries.

Case in point, cooperation levels among wineries in a specific United States wine region are examined by Alonso (2011). Although not explicitly termed 'coopetition', this study was incorporated into step 'l' of the information set. Alonso finds that winery partners prioritise a collective approach, emphasising group efforts over individual initiatives to pursue shared goals collectively. While the study covers various aspects of the wine industry, its focus on collaboration is significant for promoting local wine trails or wine tourism. Additionally, it highlights a common interest among wineries in attracting visitors and increasing wine sales for mutual prosperity.

It is noted that wine regions in which progress is attributed to the primary efforts invested in associationism have gained regional significance by effectively balancing cooperation and competition. One such example is southern Brazil, as Salvagni et al. (2020) emphasised. The authors mention that incorporating cultural and territorial elements, along with the identification as a wine region, has played a vital role in devising tourism strategies to generate income for grape growers. The significant advantages stemming from cooperation, as self-managed enterprises empower workers to achieve greater independence and improve their living standards, are also emphasised.

Furthermore, the profound impact of territorial and venture factors on producers' collaborative and proactive strategies is presented by da Rocha Oliveira Teixeira et al. (2023), particularly in networks of organic and biodynamic producers in Italy. According to them, this creates a supportive habitat for sustainable practices and cooperation among wineries rooted in shared environmental and societal principles. Additionally, some scenarios showcase leadership patterns tied to specific locations, winemaking traditions, and wine tourism, acting as innovation drivers. From these authors' perspectives, this strategic approach diverges from conventional competitive postures associated with geographical origin.

Besides, the connections between the wine industry and tourism clusters in Australia are identified by Taylor et al. (2007) as a primary focus on the significance of the industry, rather than location, in influencing cooperative pursuits. The authors observe that participants in wine tourism were more actively involved in these affairs than those in tourism or hospitality within the same region. Additionally, they note that there was no evidence indicating that the size of the cluster influenced cooperative affairs, highlighting the crucial role of sunk costs in shaping cluster ventures. Sunk costs, covering tangible and intangible assets, are generally lower in tourism than in wine production, leading the authors to conclude that cooperative pursuits are more sustainable in wine production than in tourism.

Focussing on the wine tourism business model, in a study conducted by Sigala (2019), also in Australia, the importance of various organisational forms, such as associations and entrepreneurial endeavours, is highlighted for effectively managing coopetitive arrangements and achieving collective benefits. The study underscores the critical need for a governance mechanism to develop, manage, and monitor the implementation of co-creation conditions and practices within the coopetition network. It emphasises the necessity of establishing an efficient system with an external entity overseeing inter-organisational connections, as coopetition demands adept management of tensions among partners in collective entrepreneurial endeavours.

The research mainly focussed on Dressler and Paunovic (2019), who suggested creating a collaborative wine bar and shop in a German wine region to enhance wine-related experiences by uniting wineries and stakeholders. According to the authors, integrating hospitality, wine-associated goods, and tourism services can create unique offerings tailored to meet emerging needs and explore less competitive markets. The authors believe this approach offers an ideal framework to address wine producers' challenges, such as a limited understanding of wine tourism, inadequate brand loyalty and marketing skills, and a need for partnerships with tourism stakeholders.

A study in New Zealand (Crick et al., 2022), coauthored by the most relevant author in the entire database, James M. Crick, identifies four coopetition styles of the wine industry's players in the tourism sector. Firstly, 'goods focus' wineries, as smaller and focussed on wine production, prefer individualistic networking with minimal coopetition. Secondly, 'community service approach' wineries are smaller but offer augmented services and actively engage in coopetition to enhance benefits. Thirdly, 'service focus' companies, more significant with resources, that operate individually without coopetition. Finally, 'team players' as larger entities actively embrace coopetition, leveraging diverse assets for an expanded product portfolio.

In line with examining the effects of coopetition in wine production on tourism, Crick and Crick (2021) present a literature review and conclude that engaging in market-oriented campaigns can empower wineries to host communal wine events. In this study, coopetition is presented as advantageous for smaller wine producers facing resource constraints, as it enhances appeal to wine tourists and creates positive associations with their locals with a customer-focussed approach. These authors suggest companies should be vigilant for opportunistic behaviour from competitors and be prepared to terminate coopetition relationships if the downsides outweigh the benefits. Furthermore, they highlight that mismanagement of coopetition can lead to difficulties and negative performance outcomes for either small or large wine producers.

Josefina Salvado collaborates on several studies concerned with the topic of the current research. In the earliest (Salvado & Kastenholz, 2017), wine tourism is highlighted as a complex context, in which participants are urged to form intricate connections within a fragmented ecosystem that includes supply, demand, processes, activities, and resources. According to this study, these connections should reflect varied perspectives on space development, incorporating a diverse range of unique resources and skills. Salvado and Joukes (2021) state that the competitiveness of wine tourism is intricately connected to the sustainability of the territory. Moreover, this connection leads to a unique enrichment logic where natural, cultural, and personal assets, along with partner relationships, are valued and enhanced rather than manipulated or exploited.

Wine tourism as a systemic occurrence that holds potential for regional development is underscored by Salvado (2023a). The author introduces the 'Enotourism Coopetition Model', outlining the components of the 'wine tourism core business', including wine businesses, distribution channels (tour operators, travel agencies, etc.), and direct suppliers (wine, gastronomy, hospitality, and clusters). The subsequent layer, termed 'wine tourism extended business', encompasses regional complementary (products and services suppliers). Further the 'Wine Tourism Ecosystem' is presented comprising influential players, often perceived as external entities (trade associations, regulatory bodies, government, local communities, and other stakeholders).

Discussion

The literature examination suggests (Freeman, 1991; Scaringella & Radziwon, 2018) that collaborative efforts among competitors have existed long before being formally recognised and studied under the term coopetition. Moreover, key concepts relevant to such relationships and business contexts, namely business ecosystems (Moore, 1996), clusters (Porter, 1998), industrial districts (Scaringella & Radziwon, 2018), and associativism (Salvagni et al., 2020) have been utilised in the exploration of competition among businesses alliances-related studies.

This research explored the intricate dynamics of coopetition within the wine businesses, drawing insights from various studies across different regions. We found that the distinction between horizontal and vertical alliances (Pomarici et al., 2021; Senkiv et al., 2022; Telfer, 2001) underscores the strategic choices wineries face, balancing the protection of core competencies and engaging in multi-sector collaborations, such as tourism (Alonso, 2011; Crick & Crick, 2021; Crick et al., 2022; Dressler & Paunovic, 2019; Salvado, 2023a; Taylor et al., 2007).

Its findings indicate that tourism services offer appealing opportunities and tap into markets with less competition, unlike the traditional product-centric approaches seen in the wine industry. Producers who adopt a strategic approach departing from conventional competitive stances tied to geographical origin are actively involved in collaborative strategies (da Rocha Oliveira Teixeira et al., 2023; Dressler & Paunovic, 2019). Significantly, there are observable differences in coopetition dynamics between the industry and tourism business segments. However, wine tourism remains intricately linked to ventures in vitiviniculture, and the fusion of these sectors forms an ecosystem where coopetition dynamics are inseparable.

Moreover, the benefits and challenges of coopetition in wine tourism can vary depending on factors such as region, costs, business focus, approach, and winery size (Crick & Crick, 2021; Crick et al., 2022; Telfer, 2001). Nevertheless, there is a consensus that coopetition serves as a vital sales and marketing strategy for both individual wineries and the broader wine region (Crick & Crick, 2021; Dressler, 2016; Marco-Lajara et al., 2023; Senkiv et al., 2022). Consequently, successful coopetitive arrangements require collaborative endeavours, though these efforts may sometimes be uneven (Crick & Crick, 2021; Sigala, 2019). While local tourism governance mechanisms can facilitate these ecosystems (Mazurkiewicz-Pizlo, 2016; Sigala, 2019), this is not a prevailing trend.

Considering the uncovered complexity of the wine businesses coopetition ecosystem, and the multiple sectors involved, another perspective for the model proposed by Salvado (2023a) is recommended. The suggested in this study (Fig. 11.1) specifically captures the intricate dynamics of potential coopetition within wine tourism, emphasizing its central activity: vitiviniculture. While it does not encompass the entire wine tourism ecosystem of a region, it sheds light on the essence of wine tourism. This perspective allows for the easy identification of layers of cooperation and competition, providing a clear understanding to business management, particularly for SMEs, and regional governance in the development of effective strategies.

To illustrate, various wine businesses can be viewed as potential coopetitors across all levels of this ecosystem, given the similarity in their offered products and services. However, while hospitality and commercial enterprises within the same region might serve as direct clients for winery products, they become potential coopetitors in the realm of tourism. Consequently, a meticulous

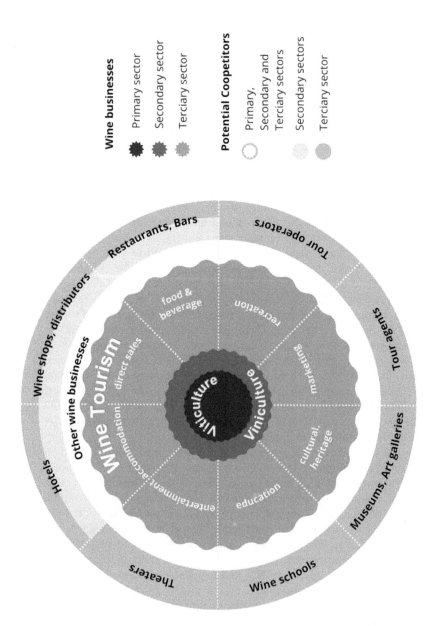

Fig. 11.1.   Potential Coopetition in the Wine Business Ecosystem. *Source:* Own Production Based on Moore (1996) and Salvado (2023a).

approach to product pricing for direct sales to visitors at the winery is crucial to avoid negatively impacting existing commercial relationships.

Conclusion

Overall, this study significantly advanced the theoretical understanding of coopetition dynamics in the wine industry and its implications for tourism. By synthesising considerations from various sources and examining fundamental concepts, the research provided a nuanced understanding of the strategic challenges faced by the wine industry and tourism, offering valuable insights for wine businesses, regional authorities, and scholars.

The results illuminated the inherent mixture of competition and cooperation among wine companies operating in the same geographical and industrial context. This synthesis, intentional or circumstantial, underscored the complex interplay of forces shaping the wine business environment. Additionally, the investigation highlighted differences in coopetition dynamics between the wine industry and the tourism sector, showcasing some strategic adaptations made by producers to leverage tourism offerings.

However, a significant gap in the existing literature was the need for a comprehensive examination of the specific strategies employed by wine enterprises to navigate coopetition within the tourism sector. Furthermore, it is imperative to acknowledge the limitations of this research. Despite adhering to standard procedures, these constraints may arise from differing interpretations of the search criteria. Consequently, certain articles may have been unintentionally excluded from this analysis, in addition to those omitted due to restricted access or the authors' unfamiliarity with the languages.

Despite these limitations, the findings on coopetition within the wine business ecosystem and the proposed model for identifying coopetition layers provide valuable insights for researchers and practitioners alike. This research underscores the close connection between coopetition in wine tourism and the wine industry, highlighting the significance of investigating existing or potential coopetition across the layers of this ecosystem in empirical studies. These insights deepen our understanding of the complexities of coopetition within this environment, which have been overlooked in previous literature, and provide practical guidance for stakeholders.

It is crucial to recognise that while the study shed light on the historical context of cooperation among competitors, it also acknowledged limitations in fully exploring all aspects and theories of cooperative and competitive relationships within its scope. Additionally, while the research offered valuable insights into coopetition dynamics within the wine sector, it did not thoroughly address the nuances of coopetitive interactions between wineries and other tourism-related businesses like hospitality establishments and commercial ventures. Therefore, future research should understand the strategies wine businesses employ to navigate coopetition within the broader tourism ecosystem, considering interactions with various stakeholders.

References

Alonso, A. D. (2011). "Standing alone you can't win anything": The importance of collaborative relationships for wineries producing muscadine wines. *Journal of Wine Research*, *22*(1), 43–55. https://doi.org/10.1080/09571264.2011.550761

Aria, M., & Cuccurullo, C. (2017). bibliometrix: An R-tool for comprehensive science mapping analysis. *Journal of Informetrics*, *11*(4), 959–975. https://doi.org/10.1016/j.joi.2017.08.007

Chim-Miki, A. F., & Batista-Canino, R. M. (2017). Tourism coopetition: An introduction to the subject and a research agenda. *International Business Review*, *26*(6), 1208–1217. https://doi.org/10.1016/j.ibusrev.2017.05.003

Crick, J. M., & Crick, D. (2021). Market-oriented activities and communal wine consumption events: Does coopetition make a difference?. *Journal of Wine Research*, *32*(3), 161–187. https://doi.org/10.1080/09571264.2021.1971642

Crick, J. M., Crick, D., Chaudhry, S., & Park, M. (2022). *The dark-side of coopetition: It's not what you say, but the way that you do it*. 2-4 PARK SQUAREABINGDON OX14 4RN, OXON, ENGLAND. Routledge Journals, Taylor & Francis Ltd. https://doi.org/10.1080/0965254X.2019.1642936

da Rocha Oliveira Teixeira, R., Arcuri, S., Cavicchi, A., Galli, F., Brunori, G., & Vergamini, D. (2023). *Can alternative wine networks foster sustainable business model innovation and value creation? The case of organic and biodynamic wine in Tuscany*. Frontiers Media SA. https://doi.org/10.3389/fsufs.2023.1241062

Dana, L.-P., Granata, J., Lasch, F., & Carnaby, A. (2013). *The evolution of co-opetition in the Waipara wine cluster of New Zealand*. UniCeSV - Universita degli Studi di Firenze. https://doi.org/10.1016/j.wep.2013.05.001

Díaz, E., Esteban, Á., Koutra, C., Almeida, S., & Carranza, R. (2023). Co-creation of value in smart ecosystems: Past trends and future directions in tourism literature. *Journal of Hospitality and Tourism Technology*, *14*(3), 365–383. https://doi.org/10.1108/JHTT-04-2021-0122

Donthu, N., Kumar, S., Mukherjee, D., Pandey, N., & Lim, W. M. (2021). How to conduct a bibliometric analysis: An overview and guidelines. *Journal of Business Research*, *133*, 285–296. https://doi.org/10.1016/j.jbusres.2021.04.070

Dressler, M. (2016). *Strategic winery reputation management – Exploring German wine guides*. Emerald Group Publishing Ltd. https://doi.org/10.1108/IJWBR-10-2014-0046

Dressler, M., & Paunovic, I. (2019). *Customer-centric offer design: Meeting expectations for a wine bar and shop and the relevance of hybrid offering components*. Emerald Group Holdings Ltd. https://doi.org/10.1108/IJWBR-07-2018-0036

Fensterseifer, J. E. (2007). *The emerging Brazilian wine industry: Challenges and prospects for the Serra Gaúcha wine cluster*. Emerald Group Publishing Ltd. https://doi.org/10.1108/17511060710817221

Flores, S. S., Farias, C., Andrade, G., & Russi, M. T. (2016). Competitive and innovation factors in wine tourism clusters: A comparative study between consolidated and emerging regions in Brazil and Uruguay. In J. Aurand (Ed.), 17 AVE DU HOGGAR PARC D ACTIVITES COUTABOEUF BP 112, F-91944 CEDEX A, FRANCE: E D P Sciences. https://doi.org/10.1051/bioconf/20160703024

Freeman, C. (1991). Networks of innovators: A synthesis of research issues. *Research Policy*, *20*(5), 499–514. https://doi.org/10.1016/0048-7333(91)90072-x

García Revilla, M. R., & Martínez Moure, O. (2021). Wine as a tourist resource: New manifestations and consequences of a quality product from the perspective of sustainability. Case analysis of the province of Málaga. *Sustainability*, *13*(23), 13003. https://doi.org/10.3390/su132313003

Gretzel, U., Sigala, M., Xiang, Z., & Koo, C. (2015). Smart tourism: Foundations and developments. *Electronic Markets*, *25*(3), 179–188. https://doi.org/10.1007/s12525-015-0196-8

Harfield, T. (1999). *Competition and cooperation in an emerging industry*. John Wiley and Sons Inc. https://doi.org/10.1002/(SICI)1099-1697(199906/07)8:4<227::AID-JSC438>3.0.CO;2-E

Kotur, A. S. (2023). A bibliometric review of research in wine tourism experiences: Insights and future research directions. *International Journal of Wine Business Research*, *35*(2), 278–297. https://doi.org/10.1108/IJWBR-07-2022-0024

Maracaja, K. F. B., Schramm, V. B., Schramm, F., Valduga, V., & Trindade, J. R. (2023). *Application of MCDM using PROMETHEE II for evaluation of wine tourism services* HOWARD HOUSE, WAGON LANE, BINGLEY BD16 1WA, W YORKSHIRE, ENGLAND. Emerald Group Publishing Ltd. https://doi.org/10.1108/IJWBR-07-2022-0025

Marco-Lajara, B., Martínez-Falcó, J., Millan-Tudela, L. A., & Sánchez-García, E. (2023). Analysis of the structure of scientific knowledge on wine tourism: A bibliometric analysis. *Heliyon*, *9*(2). https://doi.org/10.1016/j.heliyon.2023.e13363

Maumon, N., & Bédé, D. (2023). Wine tourism next-gen: A case study of a virtual reality implementation in a wine cooperative in France. In M. Sigala & C. Haller (eds), *Technology advances and innovation in wine tourism* (pp. 95–113). Springer Nature Singapore. https://doi.org/10.1007/978-981-19-8277-4_7

Mazurkiewicz-Pizlo, A. (2016). The importance of non-profit organisations in developing wine tourism in Poland. *Journal of Tourism and Cultural Change*, *14*(4), 339–349. https://doi.org/10.1080/14766825.2015.1102922

Moore, J. F. (1993, May). Predators and prey: A new ecology of competition. *Harvard Business Review*. https://hbr.org/1993/05/predators-and-prey-a-new-ecology-of-competition

Moore, J. F. (1996). *The death of competition: Leadership and strategy in the age of business ecosystems* (1st ed.). HarperBusiness.

Page, M. J., McKenzie, J. E., Bossuyt, P. M., Boutron, I., Hoffmann, T. C., Mulrow, C. D., Shamseer, L., Tetzlaff, J. M., Akl, E. A., Brennan, S. E., Chou, R., Glanville, J., Grimshaw, J. M., Hróbjartsson, A., Lalu, M. M., Li, T., Loder, E. W., Mayo-Wilson, E., McDonald, S., McGuinness, L. A., Stewart, L. A., Thomas, J., Tricco, A. C., Welch, V. A., Whiting, P., Moher, D. (2022). A declaração PRISMA 2020: Diretriz atualizada para relatar revisões sistemáticas. *Revista Panamericana de Salud Pública*, *46*, 1. https://doi.org/10.26633/RPSP.2022.112

Pomarici, E., Corsi, A., Mazzarino, S., & Sardone, R. (2021). *The Italian wine sector: Evolution, structure, competitiveness and future challenges of an enduring leader*. Springer Science and Business Media Deutschland GmbH. https://doi.org/10.1007/s40797-021-00144-5

Porter, M. E. (1998, November). Clusters and the new economics of competition. *Harvard Business Review*. https://hbr.org/1998/11/clusters-and-the-new-economics-of-competition

Prokeš, M. (2013). *Development of wine tourism in south Moravia.* https://doi.org/10. 11118/actaun201361072669

Rachão, S., Breda, Z., Fernandes, C., & Joukes, V. (2019). Enogastronomy in Northern Portugal: Destination cooperation and regional identity. *Advances in Hospitality and Tourism Research*, 216–237. https://doi.org/10.30519/ahtr.573163

Ruediger, J., & Hanf, J. H. (2017). In J. Aurand (Ed.), *The use of wine tourism as a possibility of the marketing with wine cooperatives.* 17 AVE DU HOGGAR PARC D ACTIVITES COUTABOEUF BP 112, F-91944 CEDEX A, FRANCE: E D P Sciences. https://doi.org/10.1051/bioconf/20170903023

Salvado, J. (2023a). Ecossistema de Enoturismo: Proposta de modelo de coopetição entre as partes interessadas. *Tourism and Hospitality International Journal*, 6(2), 77–93. Páginas. https://doi.org/10.57883/THIJ6(2)2016.30308

Salvado, J. (2023b). *O ECOSSISTEMA DE ENOTURISMO: COCRIAÇÃO DE VALOR ATRAVÉS DE REDES DE COOPETIÇÃO ENTRE STAKEHOLDERS E VALORIZAÇÃO DOS PATRIMÓNIOS ALIMENTARES.* https://doi.org/10. 13140/RG.2.2.35315.60968

Salvado, J., & Joukes, V. (2021). *Build sustainable stakeholders' interactions around wine & food heritage: The douro wine tourism case.* Universidade de Aveiro. https:// doi.org/10.34624/rtd.v1i36.7877

Salvado, J., & Kastenholz, E. (2017). Sustainable wine tourism eco-systems through co-opetition. *Revista Turismo & Desenvolvimento*, (27/28), 1917–1931.

Salvagni, J., Valduga, V., & Nodari, C. H. (2020). *Cooperation, innovation and tourism in the grape and wine region, Brazil*; [Cooperación, innovación y turismo en la región vitícola y vinícola de Brasil]. Pontificia Universidad Javeriana. https://doi. org/10.11144/Javeriana.cdr17.citg

Scaringella, L., & Radziwon, A. (2018). Innovation, entrepreneurial, knowledge, and business ecosystems: Old wine in new bottles?. *Technological Forecasting and Social Change*, *136*, 59–87. https://doi.org/10.1016/j.techfore.2017.09.023

Senkiv, M., Schultheiß, J., Tafel, M., Reiss, M., & Jedicke, E. (2022). Are wine-growers tourism promoters?. *Sustainability*, *14*(13), 7899. https://doi.org/10.3390/su14137899

Sigala, M. (2019). Building a wine tourism destination through coopetition: The business model of ultimate winery experiences Australia. In M. Sigala & R. N. S. Robinson (eds), *Wine tourism destination management and marketing* (pp. 99–112). Springer International Publishing. https://doi.org/10.1007/978-3-030-00437-8_8

Taylor, P., McRae-Williams, P., & Lowe, J. (2007). *The determinants of cluster activities in the Australian wine and tourism industries.* IP Publishing Ltd. https:// doi.org/10.5367/000000007782696050

Telfer, D. J. (2001). Strategic alliances along the Niagara Wine Route. *Tourism Management*, *22*(1), 21–30. https://doi.org/10.1016/S0261-5177(00)00033-9

Chapter 12

Exploring Barriers Arising from Coopetition: A Case Study in the Brazilian Wine Tourism Industry

Jefferson Marlon Monticelli[a], Tatiane Pellin Cislaghi[b] and Kettrin Farias Bem Maracajá[c]

[a]Unisinos, Brazil
[b]Federal Institute of Education, Science and Technology of Rio Grande do Sul, Brazil
[c]Federal University of Rio Grande do Norte, Brazil

Abstract

Our research aims to understand how coopetition can create barriers to tourism by focussing on the collective interests that seek to preserve the identity of a geographical indication (GI). We conducted a qualitative longitudinal study that analyses a Brazilian wine industry, specifically the Vale dos Vinhedos (a GI region in Southern Brazil), because it provides examples of leveraging coopetition to develop the area. The study was conducted over 10 years (2012–2022), collecting primary data from representatives of the Brazilian wine industry in 36 semi-structured interviews. Interviewees emphasised how the Vale dos Vinhedos vocation is founded on natural beauty and tranquillity, aiming to preserve aspects that value wine culture. The study found that wineries and formal institution agents established a coopetition strategy to stop uncontrolled expansion in real-estate development, blocking the entry of new ventures such as hotels and timeshares that could distort the region's character. Consequently, coopetition does not merely hinder the progression of tourism to real estate ventures; instead, it functions as an informal, and occasionally a formal, regulatory mechanism. While initially perceived as a drawback, upon examining the social, cultural, and economic advantages, this phenomenon emerges as a market control strategy that enhances the region.

Value Proposition to Tourism Coopetition, 171–185
doi:10.1108/978-1-83797-827-420241012

Keywords: Tourism coopetition; barriers to tourism; formal institution agents; geographical indication; Brazilian wine industry

Introduction

In today's intricate business environment, firms often employ coopetition – a strategy of concurrently pursuing cooperation and competition – to navigate uncertainties stemming from emerging markets, rapid technological changes, and intensified global competition (Czakon et al., 2020). As a well-developed theory, coopetition attracts attention from researchers and practitioners exploring its role in value creation and capture and in competitive strategies influenced by institutions (Gnyawali & Ryan Charleton, 2018; Hidalgo et al., 2022).

Coopetitive relationships can offer insights into the development of tourism destinations amidst complexity (Fong et al., 2018). Local products, crucial in tourism, gain greater significance with Geographical Indications (GIs), such as Champagne in France or Port in Portugal, emphasising the geographical essence of coopetition manifesting in varying degrees of competition and collaboration (Chiambaretto et al., 2025). A prime example of this is the Vale dos Vinhedos (literally, the Valley of the Vineyards) in Brazil. Situated in Southern Brazil, in the state of Rio Grande do Sul, it stands as the premier wine-producing region in the country, known for its picturesque landscapes, vineyards, and wineries.

By 2023, Brazil had seen a significant increase in GI registrations, boasting 109, which equated to a 60% increase over 2019, with potential growth in accredited regions (Forbes, 2024). The Vale dos Vinhedos was the first Geographical Indication in Brazil, marking a turning point in wine tourism and impacting job creation, tourist attraction, local product consumption, and socio-territorial revitalisation (Dolci et al., 2023). The Brazilian wine industry in Vale dos Vinhedos is known for its extensive production, displaying a dynamic interplay of competition and cooperation among regional producers and managers (Maracajá et al., 2022).

Managed by the Serra Tourism Association (Atuaserra), the wine region aims for balanced development across its 37 municipal districts, supported by the Ministry of Tourism (Aprovale, 2024). Coopetitive strategies have evolved in this emerging market subject to considerable government influence (Monticelli et al., 2022). These strategies have extended beyond financial performance and strategic positioning to address new entrants in the tourism industry (Fong et al., 2018). Notwithstanding, coopetition has a dark side, with potential negative outcomes for firms and tourism development, inviting researchers to explore how coopetition can create barriers through a focus on the collective interest in preserving the identity of a geographical indication (GI) (Crick et al., 2020). This study sought to understand the dynamics of coopetition and its implications for tourism when focussed on preserving the identity of a geographical indication.

The Institutional Dynamics of Coopetition in Wine Tourism Destinations

In contemporary business environments, coopetition, the simultaneous pursuit of cooperation and competition, has been recognised as context-dependent (Czakon et al., 2020). Firms leverage coopetition to offer learning opportunities to stakeholders, fostering tourism destinations by competing for resources while engaging in collaborative efforts (Nguyen et al., 2022). Despite its potential, only some studies have explored coopetition in tourism destinations from an institutional perspective. Notable exceptions include research studying Italian opera houses and an analysis of theme parks in Finland and Italy (Kylänen & Mariani, 2012; Mariani, 2007).

Researchers often adopt one of two distinct institutional approaches to coopetition. Some explore it through an informal lens, delving into the impact of rules, culture, and ethics (Klimas, 2016). Others scrutinise the use of formal institutions, safeguarding intellectual property and comprehending regulatory influences (Telg et al., 2023). However, these approaches are often employed in studies conducted in developed nations with efficient institutions (Galkina & Lundgren-Henriksson, 2017).

Coopetition involves exogenous variables influenced by the external context and endogenous variables arising from knowledge structures (Czakon et al., 2020). Environmental changes and knowledge structures shape coopetitive relationships, requiring strategic finesse to prevent adverse outcomes. Coopetition's dynamic nature, influenced by the institutional environment, necessitates a processual approach highlighting interactions and tensions (Rafi-Ul-Shan et al., 2022; Sánchez-García et al., 2024).

The underexplored dark side of coopetition is marked by value destruction, fostering of hostile behaviours, suspicion, and geographical overlap risks (Albert-Cromarias et al., 2022). In tourism, where power relationships and physical presence play crucial roles, coopetition's negative outcomes can hinder development.

Coopetition in the Vale dos Vinhedos Wine Tourism Destination

Coopetition, blending cooperation and competition, is a strategic concept that extends into many different industries, including the dynamic realm of wine tourism (Luongo et al., 2023). In wine tourism destinations, coopetition involves wineries and tourism entities simultaneously collaborating and competing to enhance the overall visitor experience (Crick et al., 2020). This intricate dance maximises benefits for the stakeholders involved.

Wine tourism destinations feature competing wineries recognising the mutual benefit of creating a compelling destination (Kozak & Baloglu, 2010). Collaborative efforts such as joint marketing and events elevate the region's collective appeal. Coopetition fosters innovation by sharing research, sustainable practices, and wine-growing techniques (Cantino et al., 2019; Granata et al., 2018).

Beyond the wineries, wine tourism coopetition involves various other stakeholders, creating comprehensive packages for a seamless visitor experience (Ammirato et al., 2015). These tourism products encourage more extended visitor stays, benefiting the entire destination. However, maintaining a delicate balance is crucial, as too much competition without collaboration can result in a fragmented tourist experience (Dressler & Paunovic, 2019).

Vale dos Vinhedos is a prominent wine tourism region in Brazil that exemplifies the positive impact of coopetition. The region's winemakers' association, Aprovale, was established in 1995 and drives sustainable wine tourism development, enhancing products and services through collaboration (Aprovale, 2024). Coopetition in the region has increased employment opportunities, cultural preservation, and a significant rise in tourism (Freire et al., 2023).

Despite coopetition's success, it has a dark side that should not be overlooked. Tensions between firms can lead to hostile behaviours, negatively impacting the stakeholders involved (Albert-Cromarias et al., 2022). Maintaining a strategic balance between cooperation and competition is vital for long-term prosperity in the evolving wine tourism industry (Karagiannis & Metaxas, 2020).

Method

We registered in detail and analysed the evolution of a geographical location over time, exploring its response to new opportunities and conflicts, mainly focussed on the dilemma of steering between the promotion and development of tourism in the region and protecting and preserving the identity of the Vale dos Vinhedos GI (Fig. 12.1).

For data collection, our study employed a meticulous combination of semi-structured interviews, observation, and document analysis. This comprehensive approach, including the examination of formal institutions and firms' websites, annuals, magazines, and books, was crucial for the triangulation of data, as recommended for qualitative research objectives (Langley & Abdallah, 2011). This rigorous process not only ensured the reliability of our findings but also helped to delimit events that unfolded along the entire process.

A longitudinal study was conducted over 10 years (2012–2022), collecting primary data from representatives of the Brazilian wine industry in 36 semi-structured interviews with representatives from 16 wineries and 20 formal institution agents. The representatives interviewed included executives, managers, consultants from these wineries and formal institution agents who actively developed the region through the concession of Geographical Indication (GI) status. In the initial phase, we gathered data in 2012 and 2013 in 18 semi-structured interviews with representatives from wineries and formal institutional agents. We also conducted three follow-up interviews with the initial participants. The second phase occurred in 2017. This phase comprised six semi-structured interviews with four participants from the previous phase and two new participants. The third phase in 2022 involved nine interviews with representatives from formal institutional agents who had yet to be part of the earlier stages. Before constructing the narrative, we meticulously reconstructed the process as a map, identifying key events and establishing a temporal sequence that effectively captured the discourse surrounding tourism and the GI in the Vale dos Vinhedos. All interviews were conducted in Portuguese, recorded, and transcribed. We adopted procedures to guarantee the reliability of the transcriptions and to guarantee the rigour of the study.

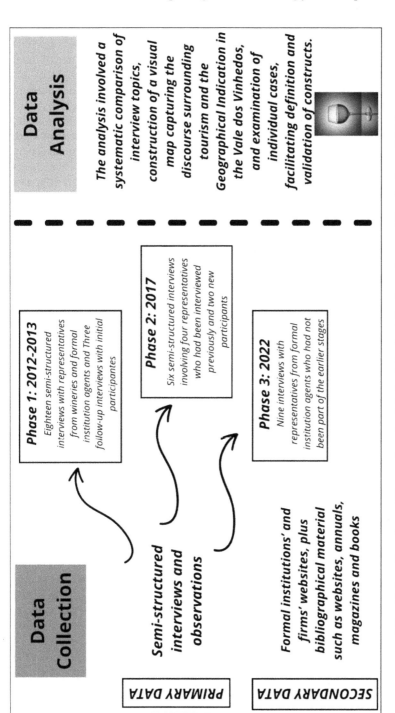

Fig. 12.1.   Roadmap Illustrating the Methodological Design. *Source:* The Authors (2024).

We conducted a selective coding process to integrate and refine the categories underpinning the periods and events shaping the Geographical Indication (GI) process. In the realm of research, interviews served as the primary source of data, contributing to the identification of cross-case patterns and exploration of differences and similarities within the narratives. We thus used the main quotes to present the case analysis. The analysis involved a systematic comparison of interview topics, a visual map, and individual cases, facilitating the definition and validation of constructs. Throughout this process, 'in vivo' codes were employed, aligning with the language and terms used by key informants, as recommended by Langley and Abdallah (2011). We juxtaposed fieldwork data with categories derived from existing theory and conducted an analysis. This approach helped us understand the relationships between the theoretical framework and the empirical findings.

Analysis and Discussion of Results

Coopetition and Establishment of the Vale dos Vinhedos

Coopetition, a unique blend of cooperation and competition, plays a pivotal role in shaping the strategies, collaborations, and overall success of wineries in Vale dos Vinhedos. These wineries have united their efforts to achieve common goals, such as establishing Geographical Indications (GIs) or regional branding. These collaborations involve shared resources, knowledge exchange, and joint marketing efforts, showcasing the cooperative side of coopetition (Crick & Crick, 2021).

While competition is a part of the picture, coopetition in the wine industry is about much more. It's a catalyst for innovation and knowledge sharing among wineries that collaborate on research and development, technology adoption, and sustainable practices. This demonstrates how coopetition can drive positive advancements within an industry, beyond the realm of competition (Sánchez-García et al., 2024).

The establishment of Vale dos Vinhedos is intricately linked to Brazil's relaxation of protectionism in the 1990s, when the frontiers were opened, and the country integrated with the global market. This process was marked by changes in international trade policies enacted in bilateral and multilateral agreements. During this period, a group of six wineries initiated informal discussions on implementing a Geographical Indication (GI) in the Vale dos Vinhedos, concurrently considering creation of a formal institutional agent to aid in this process and in the region's development. Embrapa Uva e Vinho, the Brazilian Agricultural Research Corporation's grape and wine department, played a crucial role as the formal institution agent supporting the Geographical Indication project, providing technical expertise and guidance (Tonietto et al., 2022).

In 2002, wines that meticulously adhered to the stringent standards established by the Vale dos Vinhedos Association of Fine Wine Producers (Aprovale) and Embrapa Uva and Vinho received the prestigious Indication of Origin seal. This achievement not only established the Vale dos Vinhedos Indication of Origin but also provided a strong assurance of quality. In 2012, the level of recognition was raised to Geographical Indication status, a distinction granted only to wines meeting specific technical specifications. This further contributed to a higher value-added product, increased consumer confidence, and media promotion for Vale dos Vinhedos. In the same year, the Geographical Indication progressed to a Denomination of Origin (DO), an exclusive classification in the Brazilian wine sector, denoting wines expressing the excellence of the Vale dos Vinhedos terroir.

There are around 1000 wineries in Brazil, the majority of which are small family properties, with a mean area of 2 hectares per property, concentrating on craft wines or table wines. Only 150 firms produce fine wines (Aprovale, 2024). The Brazilian wine industry is influenced by a large number of formal institution agents (e.g., Ibravin, Aprovale, Embrapa, etc.) that have consolidated over the years and were created to foster growth in the industry and to fill large gaps in knowledge, techniques, regulations, legislation, markets, and other elements.

Brazilian wineries cooperate to achieve common strategic goals, especially when they have well-defined strategies. However, they compete when they do not trust each other and have cultural motivations, incurring risk of opportunistic behaviours. Competition is fierce in the region, discouraging cooperation and favouring individualistic actions based on pride, tradition, and upholding the family names represented by the wines. These two contrasting phenomena are illustrated in the interview excerpts presented below:

> I think that when they have a common goal, that's the main route, motivation, for coopetition. And particularly when resources are scarce, or depending on the market of course, in the internationalisation process. (Professor and academic researcher)

> At the winery, there is interest (in coopeting), but I am more interested in promoting my product, my brand, my name. And there is another powerful factor - that the wineries are all family businesses. So, because it is a family firm, there is also tradition, pride in bearing the name of my family. Moreover, usually those who work there, those who are in the highest positions, the board directors, management, are part of the family. So, it's like this, I'm [Valduga family X], I'm [Salton family Y], I'm Miolo. I am better than you, you are better than me. I see that there is this clash of forces, let's say. (Exportation Supervisor at Winery I)

Strategies of cooperation among competitors facilitated exchanges of experience and learning and expansion of networks through interactions with wineries, formal institutions agents, and traditional events. This cooperative approach strengthened the concept of coopetition, where wineries collaborated and competed simultaneously in various areas, generating value and creating a national wine identity through the GI system. Sharing resources and knowledge resulted in shared benefits, particularly in increased domestic and international market shares. Consumer recognition and appreciation of national wines, bolstered by international awards, further stimulated tourism in the region.

Consequences of Coopetition: Expansion of Tourism, Triggering a Real Estate Boom

At the start of the century, the winemaking region in South Brazil obtained GI accreditation, which triggered many critical events in the region, particularly acceleration of the urbanisation process. The Vale dos Vinhedos DO has a total area of 72 km². It is distributed across three towns, Bento Gonçalves, accounting for 61% of the area; Garibaldi, equating to 34%, and Monte Belo do Sul, with 5% of the DO area (Tonietto et al., 2022).

Recognition of the Vale dos Vinhedos as a Geographical Indication was an important step with repercussions in several areas, particularly regarding the region's sustainable economic development. The GI adds value not only to the products but also to the winemakers, to their working environment, and the rural properties; it increases winemakers' involvement in the cycle of national and international sales; it encourages investment in production, including new vineyards, technological improvements in the field and agricultural industry; it even helps to convince young people not to leave the area, making family succession more likely; it contributes to maintenance of the products' typical characteristics and the regional cultural heritage; it increases the added value of the wines and supports quality control, supporting customer confidence; and, finally, it also enables expansion of wine tourism activities (Aprovale, 2024). In these terms, wine tourism provided a reason for pooling resources and encouraged the wineries to cooperate. Thus, while the wineries still compete intensely for markets, they also cooperate in other areas to access new resources and capabilities, improving the tourism destination.

Specifically about expansion of wine tourism in the Vale dos Vinhedos, construction of hotel developments began to heat up in the region in 1999 (Architect, Complan, interviewed in 2022). Our results indicate that real estate speculation (with substantial increases in the value of properties and of land, by up to 500% over recent years), directly attributable to the Vale dos Vinhedos GI creation, constitutes a threat to the regional wine landscape. The need for planning and controlling land use soon became clear, with formal regulation by Law number 10.257, the Cities Statute, on 10 July 2001. This law obliged towns with more than 20,000 inhabitants to draw up a Town Plan, identifying areas of special interest for tourism and areas with significant environmental impact (Tonini et al., 2011).

This process ended up generating conflict, since the definitions set out in the Bento Gonçalves Town Plan tended to dominate, even though, as mentioned above, the Vale dos Vinhedos is contained within the area of three different municipal districts (Architect, Complan). As a result of the increasing popularity of the area, the increasing value afforded to development and infrastructure, with the growth of wine tourism in the form of new developments such as restaurants, bed and breakfasts, and retail outlets, the Vale dos Vinhedos began to receive substantial visitor volumes, becoming Brazil's number one wine tourism destination.

The year of 2010 was notable for conflicts linked to real estate developments. As the value of buildings and land increased in the region, landowners and winemakers began to sell their properties to build residential developments within the certified area, which should have been used to expand vineyards, threatening the landscape and even putting the Vale dos Vinhedos' GI status at risk (Architect, Complan). The pressure and tensions linked to real estate speculation were exacerbated from 2010 onwards, particularly after DO status was granted in 2012. From 2006 to 2013, many developments were approved without due technical justifications, for essentially financial ends, without regard for community interests. The representative from Aprovale emphasises this phenomenon: 'The Vale is easy to sell, because it is the best wine tourism route in Brazil' (Aprovale Executive Director, interviewed in 2022). Meanwhile, in 2012 a participatory action headed by Aprovale with the involvement of other formal and informal actors in the chain, including the community, seeking to protect heritage, achieved recognition of the Vale dos Vinhedos as Historic and Cultural Heritage of Rio Grande do Sul state. In parallel, the Rio Grande do Sul Public Prosecutor intervened in many decisions to prevent destruction of the character of the landscape and halt the uncontrolled growth of housing estates, timeshares, and industrial parks in the area demarcated as a DO (Architect, Complan). The interviewee from Aprovale also pointed out:

> [...] here in this region, you can see that they have an entity that tried to join forces. If on the one hand there is fierce competitiveness, when I started twelve or thirteen years ago, people would say to visitors, 'look, his wine (from a different vineyard) is no good.' Or you would ask 'what's your neighbour's wine like?,' and they'd say, 'well... it's...' Nowadays that's changed. Now they don't say that anymore because they've understood the power of the group. But they still argue, they'll go to the restaurants and fight over their position on the wine list and go to the shops and claim their space. (President of Aprovale, interviewed in 2013)

More than 10 years later, the Aprovale representative's words still resonate with sense about the evolution of the Vale dos Vinhedos, not just as a region known for grape and wine production or as a wine tourist destination but also as a community that organised through coopetition to expand its strategic options.

Despite the efforts to coordinate a cooperation strategy among elements of organised civil society to block new real estate developments, the association reverberated with internal conflicts from 2014 onwards. These conflicts accentuated the existing differences between association members, such as, for example, differences in firm size, the lack of common objectives, investments to publicise and add value to the GI in Brazil and abroad, and, logically, by the movement triggered by the rising land prices. As a result, many association members stopped participating in the formal institution agent. They began to invest in other business interests, unrelated to grape growing or production of grape juice and still and sparkling wines (Vice-president of the Senior Board and Financial Board,

Aprovale, interviewed in 2022). This created competition mainly between actors attempting to purchase land.

Coopetition as a Barrier to Tourism

More recently, new conflicts arose about construction and real-estate developments in the Vale dos Vinhedos. In 2021 and 2022, mega development projects, such as resorts, began to take over the winemaking lands certified with DO status. Political interests, acting through electoral campaigns and value adding, triggered the critical events marking this phase. The problem of the three different Town Plans of the cities that make up the DO region (Bento Gonçalves, Garibaldi and Monte Belo do Sul) remained, despite the passage of years. 'This lack of coordinated planning left loopholes for continuous approval of inappropriate constructions by the towns of Garibaldi and Monte Belo do Sul' (President of the Vale dos Vinhedos District Planning Council/President of the Vale dos Vinhedos Residents and Community, interviewed in 2022).

At that juncture, Aprovale published an open letter to the Vale do Vinhedos community. In the letter, Aprovale warned that the region's sustainable development was under threat, both in the sense that increasing the supply of hospitality capacity in the Vale dos Vinhedos is not a reasonable justification for new real estate developments, and regarding the vineyard landscape and to the impact on wine tourism itself. The association is adamant that the Vale dos Vinhedos' vocation for tourism is founded on its natural beauty and tranquility, free from overcrowding, and on preservation of aspects that value wine culture (Aprovale, 2022).

Intellectual property and the Denomination of Origin is one of the most worrying issues, according to their open letter, because '*the GIs are recognized by the Brazilian State to the extent that their wines are imbued with qualities or characteristics that are exclusively or essentially due to their geographical context, including both natural and human factors*' (article 178 of Law 9.279) (Brazil, 1996). As such, a DO cannot survive if none of these factors are present. It is therefore necessary to commit to a reevaluation and planning process, so that entrepreneurs, producers, public administrators, and the community in general understand the negative impacts that real-estate developments in the region could trigger, leading not only to loss of its DO status but also, within the scope of the sustainable development of the Vale dos Vinhedos, to loss of its vocation for wine tourism, which is currently recognised both nationally and internationally (Aprovale, 2022).

This understanding is shared by the representative from the Vale dos Vinhedos District Planning Council: '*Points that must be considered with relation to these mega developments include problems with mobility, public transport, sanitation, water, daycare, and health care. All of this growth does not fit in the Valley*' (President of the Vale dos Vinhedos District Planning Council/President of the Vale dos Vinhedos Residents and Community). Along these lines, for example, it was estimated that the influx of the workers needed for construction of the buildings planned for just two urban development projects submitted in 2021 and 2022 would result in 2,500 workers travelling to work in the Vale dos Vinhedos every day for an estimated 6 years of construction. Considering that the Vale dos Vinhedos only has around 2,300 residents, the population would double in volume, without the infrastructure to deal with the repercussions, including water and electricity supplies, public roads, sewage, and refuse collection. Moreover, these workers would constitute a labour force that does not exist in the region. It can thus be inferred that that they would bring their families with them, with the consequent demand for infrastructure to provide health care, education, and housing, which the town is unable to offer (President of the Vale dos Vinhedos District Planning Council/President of the Vale dos Vinhedos Residents and Community).

In response to the movement, a public meeting was held, and as a result of cooperation between different formal institution agents, the project to change the Town Plan of Bento Gonçalves to permit construction of the mega developments within the DO area was taken off the Bento Gonçalves City Hall agenda. In addition to removing the project, City Hall also announced the launch of a Vale dos Vinhedos Landscape Management and Development Plan, involving the municipal districts that make up the Vale dos Vinhedos Geographical Indication area – Bento Gonçalves, Garibaldi, and Monte Belo do Sul (Aprovale, 2024). The owner of the Winery K explained:

> We (the entrepreneurs from Vale dos Vinhedos) are not against progress, we're not against development. We're not against having more hotels, more restaurants, more bed and breakfasts; But all in context. (...) The Vale began, and the Vale became what it is today because of what? Because of the vineyards and the wine. Added to this, fine dining and tourism. You cannot strip the region of its character.

As the years passed, the GI was consolidated as a central point in the economic, social, and environmental development of the Vale dos Vinhedos region (Fig. 12.2). On the one hand, this is manifest in increased wine production linked to wine tourism, fine dining, and hospitality and to production of a wide variety of inputs and the cultural heritage. Representatives of both public and private organisations still stress the need for investment in the region's infrastructure and the importance of fostering the feeling of belonging to the GI territory, pointing to the increase in the value of both tangible and intangible assets to illustrate the point. On the other hand, this mobilisation blocks the entry of new real estate developments that could lead to further development of the region and expand its potential for wine tourism with condominiums, resorts, and construction of thematic hotels.

At the same time, coopetition has been an effective approach to institutional threats and challenges, especially those resulting from the different perspectives related to the benefits of the Vale dos Vinhedos' Geographical Indication (GI) (Monticelli et al., 2022). As such, coopetition has played a relevant role while, at the same time, impeding development of tourism through the real estate projects.

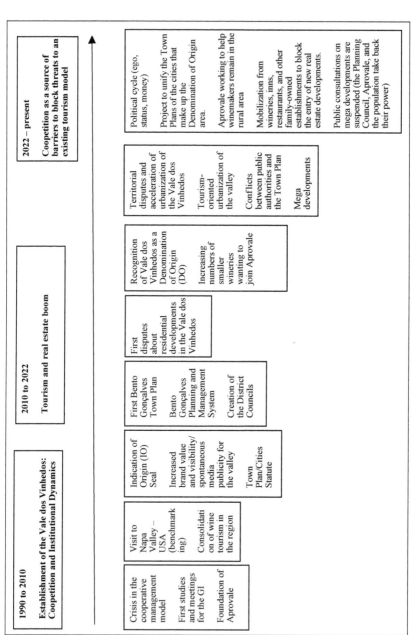

Fig. 12.2.   Timeline of the Recent Development of the Vale dos Vinhedos. *Source:* The Authors (2024).

To stop this uncontrolled expansion, wineries and formal institution agents established a coopetition strategy to block the entry of new ventures such as hotels and timeshare resorts that could distort the region's character.

Final Comments

This study aimed to understand how coopetition can create barriers to tourism through coopetition focussed on collective interests that seek to preserve the identity of a geographical indication. We focus our research on the Vale dos Vinhedos region when it is at a crossroads, choosing between maintaining what has been achieved to date in terms of recognition of the winemaking region and its tourism; or allowing even more development, also focussed on exploiting tourism, but tied to real estate developments.

From a theoretical perspective, coopetition does not merely hinder the progress of tourism via real estate ventures; rather, it functions as an informal and occasionally formal regulatory mechanism. While initially perceived as a drawback, upon examining the social, cultural, and economic advantages, this phenomenon emerges as a market control strategy that enhances the region.

From a managerial perspective, we found that the GI constitutes a central driver of development in the Vale dos Vinhedos, whether economic, social, or environmental, by increasing winemaking activity in conjunction with fine wine dining, hospitality, with production of winemaking equipment and supplies, and with the Vale's cultural heritage. However, this movement is also creating a need for increased public and private infrastructure, increasing the feeling of community belonging, and appreciating the value of the material and immaterial heritage of the territories of the geographical indications.

Despite its contributions, this study does have limitations. First, the investigation took place in a single destination. Still, as this is Brazil's most important wine-producing region, the research could be easily expanded to encompass other such regions. Second, it is necessary to collect more perspectives from representatives of real estate developers, hotels, and other tourism businesses to evaluate different perceptions about the challenge of steering between promoting the region's development and preserving its characteristics. Consequently, we suggest investigating coopetition and institutions within an integrated analytical framework.

References

Albert-Cromarias, A., Asselineau, A., & Blanchard, G. (2022). Value creation, appropriation and destruction in coopetitive relationships among micro-firms. *Industrial Marketing Management, 104*, 366–375.

Ammirato, S., Felicetti, A. M., Della Gala, M., Aramo-Immonen, H., & Jussila, J. (2015, September). Knowledge management and emerging collaborative networks in tourism business ecosystems. In *European conference on knowledge management* (p. 19). Academic Conferences International Limited.

Associação de Produtores do Vale dos Vinhedos (Aprovale). (2022). *Open letter to the community, public bodies and the press.* Aprovale - Associação dos Produtores de Vinhos Finos do Vale dos Vinhedos. Available at: https://www.valedosvinhedos.com.br/blog/carta-aberta-a-comunidade-orgaos-publicos-e-imprensa

Associação de Produtores do Vale dos Vinhedos (Aprovale). (2024). *Associação de Produtores do Vale dos Vinhedos. A Aprovale.* Retrieved 10 Jan. 2023 from https://https://www.valedosvinhedos.com.br/sobre

Brazil. (1996). *Lei no. 9.279, de 14 de maio de 1996.* Brazil, 1996.

Cantino, V., Giacosa, E., & Cortese, D. (2019). A sustainable perspective in wine production for common-good management: The case of Fontanafredda biological "reserve". *British Food Journal, 121*(2), 259–274.

Chiambaretto, P., Fernandez, A. S., & Le Roy, F. (2025). What coopetition is and what it is not: Defining the "hard core" and the "protective belt" of coopetition. *Strategi c Management Review, 6*(1), forthcoming.

Crick, J. M., & Crick, D. (2021). The dark-side of coopetition: Influences on the paradoxical forces of cooperativeness and competitiveness across product-market strategies. *Journal of Business Research, 122,* 226–240.

Crick, J. M., Crick, D., & Tebbett, N. (2020). Competitor orientation and value co-creation in sustaining rural New Zealand wine producers. *Journal of Rural Studies, 73,* 122–134.

Czakon, W., Klimas, P., & Mariani, M. (2020). Behavioral antecedents of coopetition: A synthesis and measurement scale. *Long Range Planning, 53*(1), 101875.

Dolci, T., Silva, L., Cristóvão, A., & Souza, M. (2023). Instituições e o desenvolvimento do enoturismo: Reflexões sobre o Alto Douro Vinhateiro (Portugal) e o Vale Dos Vinhedos (Brasil). *Revista Turismo & Desenvolvimento, 43,* 133–148. https://doi.org/10.34624/rtd.v43i0.33061

Dressler, M., & Paunovic, I. (2019). Customer-centric offer design: Meeting expectations for a wine bar and shop and the relevance of hybrid offering components. *International Journal of Wine Business Research, 31*(1), 109–127. https://doi.org/10.1108/IJWBR-07-2018-0036

Fong, V. H. I., Wong, I. A., & Hong, J. F. L. (2018). Developing institutional logics in the tourism industry through coopetition. *Tourism Management, 66,* 244–262. https://doi.org/10.1016/j.tourman.2017.12.005

Forbes. (2024). *Indicação Geográfica no Brasil cresce 60% em quatro anos.* Retrieved 10 January 2023 from https://forbes.com.br/forbesagro/2024/01/indicacao-geografica-no-brasil-cresce-60-em-quatro-anos

Freire, R. M. L., Maracajá, K. F. B., Valduga, V., & Nascimento, A. B. F. M. D. (2023). Análise da Imagem Afetiva dos Turistas no Destino Vale dos Vinhedos-RS. *Turismo: Visão e Ação, 25,* 114–133.

Galkina, T., & Lundgren-Henriksson, E. L. (2017). Coopetition as an entrepreneurial process: Interplay of causation and effectuation. *Industrial Marketing Management, 67,* 158–173.

Gnyawali, D. R., & Ryan Charleton, T. (2018). Nuances in the interplay of competition and cooperation: Towards a theory of coopetition. *Journal of Management, 44*(7), 2511–2534.

Granata, J., Lasch, F., Le Roy, F., & Dana, L. P. (2018). How do micro-firms manage coopetition? A study of the wine sector in France. *International Small Business Journal, 36*(3), 331–355.

Hidalgo, G., Monticelli, J. M., Pedroso, J., Verschoore, J. R., & de Matos, C. A. (2022). The influence of formal institution agents on coopetition in the organic food industry. *Journal of Agricultural & Food Industrial Organization, 20*(2), 61–74.

Karagiannis, D., & Metaxas, T. (2020). Sustainable wine tourism development: Case studies from the Greek region of Peloponnese. *Sustainability, 12*(12), 5223.

Klimas, P. (2016). Organizational culture and coopetition: An exploratory study of the features, models and role in the Polish Aviation Industry. *Industrial Marketing Management, 53*, 91–102.

Kozak, M., & Baloglu, S. (2010). *Managing and marketing tourist destinations: Strategies to gain a competitive edge* (Vol. Vol. 21). Routledge.

Kylänen, M., & Mariani, M. M. (2012). Unpacking the temporal dimension of coopetition in tourism destinations: Evidence from Finnish and Italian theme parks. *Anatolia, 23*(1), 61–74.

Langley, A., & Abdallah, C. (2011). Templates and turns in qualitative studies of strategy and management. In D. D. Bergh & D. J. Ketchen (Eds.), *Building methodological bridges (Research Methodology in Strategy and Management*, Vol. 6, pp. 201–235). Emerald Group Publishing Limited. https://doi.org/10.1108/S1479-8387(2011)0000006007

Luongo, S., Sepe, F., & Del Gaudio, G. (2023). Regional innovation systems in tourism: The role of collaboration and competition. *Journal of Open Innovation: Technology, Market, and Complexity, 9*(4), 100148.

Maracajá, K. F. B., Batista Schramm, V., Schramm, F., & Valduga, V. (2022). A multicriteria model for evaluation of Brazilian wineries from a tourism destination perspective. *International Journal of Wine Business Research, 34*(1), 52–68.

Mariani, M. M. (2007). Coopetition as an emergent strategy: Empirical evidence from an Italian consortium of opera houses. *International Studies of Management & Organization, 37*(2), 97–126.

Monticelli, J. M., Garrido, I. L., Vieira, L. M., Chim-Miki, A. F., & Carneiro, J. (2022). Can competitors cooperate? The impact of formal institution agents in promoting coopetition among emerging market exporters. *Journal of Business & Industrial Marketing, 37*(9), 1915–1932.

Nguyen, T. Q. T., Johnson, P., & Young, T. (2022). Networking, coopetition and sustainability of tourism destinations. *Journal of Hospitality and Tourism Management, 50*, 400–411.

Rafi-Ul-Shan, P. M., Grant, D. B., & Perry, P. (2022). Are fashion supply chains capable of coopetition? An exploratory study in the UK. *International Journal of Logistics Research and Applications, 25*(3), 278–295.

Sánchez-García, E., Martínez-Falcó, J., Marco-Lajara, B., & Georgantzis, N. (2024). Value creation in the wine industry—A bibliometric analysis. *European Food Research and Technology*, 1–14.

Telg, N., Lokshin, B., & Letterie, W. (2023). How formal and informal intellectual property protection matters for firms' decision to engage in coopetition: The role of environmental dynamism and competition intensity. *Technovation, 124*, 102751.

Tonietto, J., Falcade, I., Guerra, C. C., & Zanus, M. C. (2022). As Indicações Geográficas de vinhos do Rio Grande do Sul (Capítulo V). In E. M. O. (Org.) Ferronato (Ed.), *Indicações Geográficas do Rio Grande do Sul registradas até março de 2021* (pp. 71–94). MAPA/AECS.

Tonini, H., Lavandoski, J., & Barretto, M. (2011). Políticas públicas e enoturismo: O plano diretor do vale dos vinhedos, sul do Brasil. *Tourism & Management Studies*, (1), 829–838.

Chapter 13

Enhancing Business Strategies in Tourism Through Coopetition: An Essay

Sofia Almeida and João Domingues

CETRAD-Europeia, Universidade Europeia and Universidade de Trás os Montes e Alto Douro, Portugal

Abstract

This research explores the paradigm of coopetition and the different theories that contribute to its evolution. The variation of cooperation and competition in a relationship depends on the resource flows identified in the literature. However, this research focusses on coopetition behaviours in the business world. Coopetition, simultaneous collaboration, and competition between firms, has emerged as a pivotal factor influencing organisational success in today's dynamic business environment. Based on game theory, the different types of competitive relationships between adversaries will also be presented in this chapter, where the interdependencies between the players and their choices to co-operate or compete are explored. Another perspective presented is how companies use game theory to achieve gains in both zero-sum and non-zero-sum games by changing the players, the perceptions of risk, the associated returns, and the rules and scope of the game. This chapter also will show the prisoner's dilemma applied to business practices. Finally, we present the 'tit-for-tat' theory of strategy. The conclusion underscores the need for organisations to navigate a delicate balance between collaboration and competition to thrive in a complex and interconnected tourism global marketplace.

Keywords: Coopetition; game theory; prisoner's dilemma; tit-for-tat; zero-sum game; tourism management

Value Proposition to Tourism Coopetition, 187–200
Copyright © 2025 Sofia Almeida and João Domingues
Published under exclusive licence by Emerald Publishing Limited
doi:10.1108/978-1-83797-827-420241013

188 Sofia Almeida and João Domingues

Introduction

> Michael Corleone: Keep your friends close, but your enemies closer. – The Godfather, Part III, In: Brandenburger and Nalebuff (1998, p. 36).

The concept of coopetition has been broadly discussed for several decades, first being debated in the corporate world and later a more scientific basis. Coopetition is studied in this research in line with the need to find and measure coopetition behaviours and evidence for them within companies. The majority of companies both cooperate to achieve a common goal and also compete to reach individual objectives. This research explores the coopetition archetype and the different theories contributing to its evolution. The difference between cooperation and competition in a relationship relies on the resources identified in the literature; notwithstanding, this exploratory research focusses on coopetition behaviours and an analysis of them in different types of competitive relationships between adversaries.

Furthermore, this chapter aims to analyse and present different types of competitive relations between competitors, based on game theory, where the interdependence between agents and their choices between cooperation and competition are explored. Another relationship analysed is how companies use game theory to achieve gains in zero-sum and non-zero-sum games by changing players, risk perception, associated returns, and the rules and purpose of the game. The prisoner's dilemma (Axelrod, 1981) and 'tit-for-tat' will also be applied to company practices.

Throughout this research, whenever possible, corporate-related examples will be applied to the models mentioned above, more specifically to the tourism sector. We hope this research will contribute to broadening the spectrum of coopetition literature as applied to the tourism sector. As for management contributions, we hope that the presentation of the different coopetition strategies can inspire managers. All the examples of different companies and coopetition behaviours in this research can help the decision-making process.

Coopetition

Coopetition is 'a dyadic and paradoxical relationship that arises when two companies are cooperating in some activities, while competing with each other in activities' (Bengtsson & Kock, 2000, p. 412). Although it has already been studied in both the corporate and scientific fields for several decades, the term 'coopetition' is still generally understood as a fusion of the concepts of 'competition' and 'cooperation'. Coopetition has its roots in the corporate and strategic management domains. It was introduced by Von Neumann and Morgenstern in 1944 and is intrinsically linked to game theory (Bonel & Rocco, 2007). The concept was later popularised by Brandenburger and Nalebuff (1996), who applied this concept to a market scenario where two or more corporations simultaneously compete and cooperate, consequently creating added value and competitive advantages to help differentiate themselves in highly competitive industries.

In 1998, Doz and Hamel proposed an approach more connected to the competition aspect of the concept, by mentioning that coopetition involves firms collaborating with competitors to find new solutions to market challenges, while maintaining their rivalry and increasing competitive advantage (Doz & Hamel, 1998). Focussed on small corporations, Nooteboom (1994) research explores the dynamics of coopetition among small firms, mainly how they promote innovation while facing constraints related to scarce resources and network relationships, typical of these types of organisations. More focussed on inter-organisational relationships, Oliver (1990) research indicates that trust, dependence, market power, and environmental uncertainty are the main factors influencing organisational coopetition dynamics. With a broader view of the concept, Ref. (Kostis et al., 2024), work indicates that coopetition and interfirm rivalry are among the biggest factors shaping industry dynamics and empowering innovation. Coopetitive behaviours are a must for modern companies, according to Ref. (Almeida, 2023, p. 76): 'It is strategically important for modern companies to adopt coopetitive behaviours which do not arise simply from the combination of competition with cooperation, but instead from the creation of a new form of strategic independence among companies'.

In past research, two main types of coopetition are described and that must be distinguished: horizontal and vertical coopetition. On one hand, horizontal coopetition is 'A relationship in which two companies collaborate at the same stage of the value chain to create, produce, and launch a new product on a market that will compete with other products of coopetitors' (Le Roy et al., 2022, p. 8). On the other hand, the same authors mention that 'Vertical coopetition is a relationship in which two companies cooperate at different stages of the value chain and simultaneously horizontally compete on the final market with their products' (Le Roy et al., 2022, p. 9).

Due to its high complexity, vertical coopetition can be understood from multiple perspectives, such as a (i) permanent exchange of goods/services between companies that actively compete and cooperate; (ii) relationship management with suppliers throughout the value chain, where there are tensions between value creation and appropriation; and (iii) a market-based relationship in which two competitors are involved in a supplier–retailer relationship concerning specific products or services (Rajala & Tidström, 2021). Because coopetition is a multidisciplinary field, it can also be studied from a company performance point of view (Crick et al., 2024). These authors further indicate that coopetition effectiveness is heavily influenced by factors such as the level of competition, market dynamism, and disruptive technology. From a marketing point of view, during the COVID-19 pandemic, Crick and Crick (2020) indicate that coopetition became an effective business-to-business marketing strategy as decision makers can further extend coopetition efforts to a post-pandemic world. Among small- and medium-sized firms, Ref. (Thomason et al., 2013) further state that coopetition networks are highly influenced by social relations and resource-based determinants. In the finance industry, Ref. (Dong et al., 2023) suggest that,

Table 13.1. Coopetition Applied to the Business Management.

Authors	Main Results	Object of Study
Crick et al. (2024)	The authors suggest that coopetition has strong and positive contributions to company and organisational performance. Moreover, coopetition efforts are found to be moderated by competitive intensity, market dynamism, and technological turbulence.	Company performance
Crick and Crick (2020)	During the COVID-19 pandemic, the authors indicate that coopetition can be an effective business-to-business marketing strategy, decision makers should be careful with whom they collaborate with and, if after the end of the pandemic, the existing coopetition relationships will cease to exist.	Marketing management
Dong et al. (2023)	The authors suggest that both high- and low-cost firms should proactively cooperate with competitors to maintain competitiveness and simultaneously focus on differentiation based on their competitive market positioning.	Finance and strategy
Thomason et al. (2013)	Among small firms, the authors indicate several socially complex, relational and resource-based determinants that foster coopetition.	Broader field of management

Source: Authors own.

between high- and low-cost firms, both competitors cooperate to maintain market competitiveness and positioning. A synthesis of coopetition applied to the business management is presented in Table 13.1.

Competitive Behaviour in a Cooperative Environment

According to Azevedo and Matos (2006), the intensity of competition between rivals is a critical determinant in the development of new products and new technologies. The competitive environment favours continuous innovation in companies, which is crucial for a prominent position and superior gains over opponents. Thus, it is possible to infer that an industry's high degree of innovation indicates a high level of competition and, consequently, a great competitive dynamic. Hitt et al. (2002) concur that competitive dynamics result from a series of competitive actions and responses between companies competing within a particular industry. As a result of these dynamics, the main characteristic of competition is based on maximising individual gains. Hunt and Morgan (1995) analyse competitive rivalry at an intermediate level, between the industry and company levels, making it possible to understand the differences within an industry. At this level, the networks and relationships between competitors can be observed and analysed, as the theory on strategic groups provides tools that distinguish the groups of rivals where there is a greater propensity to develop relationships. To analyse competitive behaviours and extrapolate them to a business reality, game theory concepts or scenarios will be analysed to help understand and categorise the world around us. In the context of game theory and decision-making, concepts like the zero-sum game, the prisoner's dilemma, and tit-for-tat describe specific scenarios or strategies that arise in various situations.

The Contribution of Game Theory

In today's corporate and academic scope, coopetition is 'the simultaneous pursuit of cooperation and competition among firms to leverage strategically important resources for superior value creation purposes' (Kostis et al., 2024, p. 158). The concept of coopetition was first introduced in academic research by Brandenburger and Nalebuff (1996) and was based on game theory, developed by John von Neumann and Oskar Morgenstern. This idea refers to the mathematical study of situations where possible conflicts of interest can emerge (Owen, 2012, pp. 391–398). Currently, game theory focusses on positive sum games in which the added value increases when applied to relationships of competition and cooperation. Brandenburger and Nalebuff (1996, p. 7) stated, 'Game theory focuses directly on the most pressing issue of all: finding the right strategies and making the right decisions'. Moreover, economists believe that markets cannot only be analysed through classic theories as these exclude cooperative and strategic partnerships between corporations. Furthermore, some authors believe that coopetition is as old as human beings' desire to co-operate and compete.

Game theory, often associated with the concept of 'business-as-usual', has a rich historical context. It emerged during the Second World War, a time when British naval forces engaged in a strategic game with German submarines, aiming to understand their rivals' strategic thinking to gain an edge (Waddington, 1973). The British realised that the optimal moves were not intuitive and applied concepts and theories, later known as game theory, which enabled them to outmanoeuvre their competitors (Brandenburger & Nalebuff, 1996). Today, this theory employs positive-sum games, where the value increases when applied to competitive and co-operative relationships.

First Scenario: Zero-Sum Game

Brandenburger and Nalebuff (1996) illustrate how companies use game theory to achieve gains in both zero-sum and non-zero-sum games by changing the players, the perceptions of risk, the associated returns, and the rules and scope of the game. The authors suggest that the logic of game theory encourages managers to (i) embrace competitive imitation to gain an advantage and (ii) focus on the strategic moves of other players, rather than their strategic positions. However, game theory is also criticised for being too Machiavellian, as it emphasises that opportunism is vital to understanding the structure and management of strategic relationships between companies.

According to Costa (1996), the functioning of the market should not be analysed exclusively from the perspective of classical economic theory, since classical theories include acts such as cooperation between organisations and strategic alliances, which are responsible for introducing distortions into the market. Despite this, some economists claim that creating interconnections (e.g., networks) adds value to the market. The arguments used to support this claim are grouped into three theories: 'the zero-sum and non-zero-sum game', 'the prisoner's dilemma', and the 'tit-for-tat strategy'.

In the first theory, the difference between cooperation and competition can be seen as the difference between a zero-sum game and a non-zero-sum game (Jarillo, cited in Costa, 1996, pp. 129–130) and using the following situation in a zero-sum game: in a game, the amount of money gained by the winners is equal to the amount of money lost by the losers. But there are situations in which all the players can win, since the money won can come from someone else or another source. The money won by everyone could be the money given by the spectators willing to pay to watch the game. In this situation, nobody loses: all the players win money from people who have not lost it but are willing to exchange it for some entertainment (Costa, 1996).

The zero-sum game strategy is extensively developed in Costa (1996). A practical example of a zero-sum game scenario in the tourism sector can be found in the island of Cyprus in the Mediterranean Sea. Being heavily influenced by political conflicts between Greece and Turkey throughout its history, tourism professionals from both countries have different perspectives on managing the tourism industry on the island (Jacobson et al., 2015). The authors research suggests that three-fourths of Turkish Cypriots tourism professionals view that the current status quo of the tourism industry on the island is a win for Greek Cypriots and a loss to the Turkish side (zero-sum game). Moreover, the same research indicates that most Greek and Turkish Cypriots believe that a joint tourism sector is not possible, and it would cause a win–loss scenario.

Second Scenario: The Prisoner's Dilemma

The second theory, the 'the prisoner's dilemma', is based on a situation where the police catch two thieves (Peter and Paul). Realising that there is no evidence, the police want the two thieves to confess to their acts. Costa (1996) reports four possible scenarios in the prisoner's dilemma scenario. Scenario i) illustrates the situation where the two thieves are placed in direct competition, i.e., if both prisoners speak, both are sentenced to five years in prison. In imperfect competition, i.e., where only one speaks (scenarios ii. and iii.), one is acquitted, and the other is sentenced to 10 years. However, it is unlikely that such a situation will happen, since both prisoners want to go free or, if convicted, want a short prison sentence and from this aspiration, it emerges that the best strategy to be followed by both is a situation in which the thieves co-operate with each other by deciding not to speak. In doing so, both prisoners are sentenced to two years (scenario iv.). For a more detailed analysis of this theory, see Axelrod (1981) and Costa (1996).

Third Scenario: 'Tit-for-Tat'

The third theory is the tit-for-tat strategy, an expression meaning 'equivalent retaliation'. Some assumptions that support the co-operation strategy can also be found in the prisoner's dilemma theory, as it is argued that by co-operating, companies tend to be more successful than if they engage in predatory forms of competition (Costa, 1996). The tit-for-tat strategy specifies the following rule (Jarillo, cited in Costa, 1996, pp. 139–140): 'a company begins to co-operate and at any stage, it must do exactly what its coopetitor did in the previous move. In other words, everything!' According to Jarillo, the strategy has been validated by empirical evidence and proves that by imitating and co-operating with each other, the winning strategies, i.e., the best solutions to problems, are reproduced and improve the type of solutions chosen to tackle them. The tit-for-tat strategy is particularly well developed by Axelrod (1981) in The Evolution of Cooperation.

According to Axelrod (1981), the tit-for-tat strategy has some rules and advantages as it emphasises the norms of kindness (in the sense of initiating cooperation with other players), clarity in communicating the 'rules of the game' and the consequence of a player's moves, retaliation against an 'unnecessary' defection by a player and forgiveness for occasional acts of opportunism. While kindness and forgiveness challenge trust between players, retaliation and clarity guarantee against the risks of opportunism that a non-cooperative player can provoke in another co-operative player. An important assumption supporting the three theories is that cooperation is identified with intra-company behaviour and competition with inter-company relations. As such, it is difficult to define the company's boundaries, i.e., the area within which co-operation dominates and outside which competition controls. The boundary between co-operation and competition does not necessarily have to coincide with the legal limits of a company. There can be co-operation between companies and competition within them (Jarillo, quoted in Costa, 1996, p. 130). In this game strategy, called 'tit-for-tat', players obtain higher economic benefits through mutual co-operation, either through unilateral defection or mutual competition (Axelrod, 1981). In this game, a player begins to co-operate with his counterpart and then responds symmetrically to the other player's strategic moves, co-operatively for a co-operative move and competitively for a competitive move.

Coopetition in the Tourism Sector

In the tourism sector, coopetition-related literature is still in its early stages and is still scarce; however, its potential impacts on the industry are noteworthy. Among tourism agents and stakeholders, coopetition networks with high levels of integration and participation can contribute to co-marketing efforts, where the destination is jointly promoted, as well as its competitive advantages (Wang & Krakover, 2008). Coopetition dynamics in tourism can enable stakeholders to promote knowledge and know-how, risk, and cost-sharing (Chim-Miki & Batista-Canino, 2017). At a destination level, co-location, associationism, competition, cooperation, and co-production are the five factors Chim-Miki and Batista-Canino (2018) suggest for developing a coopetition model. Furthermore, coopetition relations between tourism destinations are further noted as creating social value for local communities through social awareness (Chim-Miki et al., 2023). The same authors indicate that investments in technology and innovation at a destination level significantly predict social value creation. Wu and He (2022) researched a study about Finnish and Italian theme parks. They found that competing companies tended to cooperate during peak seasons, sharing knowledge and resources to achieve competitive advantage. Tourism companies in the Santa Claus Village in Rovaniemi, Finland, started coopetitive relationships to promote the destination's image and attract more tourists (Kylänen & Mariani, 2012). Coopetition can benefit all parties involved, such as improving service quality, strengthening innovation, and increasing market share, while also contributing to the sustainable development of tourism destinations.

In the highly competitive travel agencies and tour operators' sector, Guo et al. (2014) indicate that companies tend to form coopetitive relationships with hotels to increase market share. Moreover, according to the same authors, online travel agencies promote strategic partnerships with competitors to leverage distribution channels while maintaining their competitive edge in other areas. Czernek and Czakon (2016) interviewed representatives from Polish tourism firms who said they participate in coopetitive relationships because of their relationships with the competitive firm, make personal contacts and even friends, or develop the community.

Within the hotel industry, current literature regarding the coopetition topic is still scarce; however, hotels can simultaneously compete and cooperate with a wide range of tourism agents that help drive business and potentiate competitive advantages (Almeida et al., 2021). For example, hotels can simultaneously connect with vast audiences via booking platforms such as Booking.com or Expedia and compete with direct bookings on their websites (Bahar et al., 2022). Moreover, being mostly managed by families with scant industry and business knowledge, family influence, short-term economic gains, and tourism destination networks are found to be the greatest predictors of coopetition within small hotels (Kallmuenzer et al., 2021). Another study focusses on six hotels in Cape Town, South Africa, found that coopetition was affected by external factors, such as geographic proximity, economic climate, and the role of a third party, as well as internal factors, such as management and ownership, clear organisational goals, communication skills among leadership, and management structure (Wu & He, 2022). Table 13.2 presents some examples of coopetition applied into the Tourism sector.

Coopetition has been widely developed in research related to the goods industry. Still, it lacks critical consistency for companies providing services, despite tourism being one of the areas that has attracted the most attention from researchers. The duality of coopetition in tourism is represented by Grängsjö (2003) showing a duck and a rabbit in the same image, common know by: 'duck and rabbit illusion'. The duck represents the situation in which a tourism company serves the interests of the destination, and the rabbit represents the situation in which the destination serves the interests of tourism companies. According to the author, the choice of situation changes depending on the perspective, as does the analogy with tourist destinations.

Table 13.2. Coopetition Applied Into the Tourism Sector.

Authors	Main Results	Sector
Chim-Miki et al. (2023)	The study explains how coopetition relationships in a tourism destination create social value through social awareness, technological, and innovation levels of society and social commitment. Moreover, the authors indicate that investments in technology and innovation in the tourism industry are the biggest predictors of social value creation for local population.	Tourism destinations
Bahar et al. (2022)	Using grounded theory, the research suggests that Hotels are encouraged to implement multidisciplinary approaches to coopetition based on contextual factors. Furthermore, it identifies spaces where cooperation and competition can be separated, namely distribution channels and hotel space.	Hotels and travel agencies
Quynh Trang Nguyen et al. (2022)	The paper highlights the complexity of tourism stakeholders' relationship as a key ingredient to foster coopetition.	Tourism destinations
Wu and He (2022)	Coopetition between hotels in Cape Town, South Africa.	Hotels
Almeida et al. (2021)	Coopetition strategy applied to a Hotel marketing Consortium.	Hotels

(Continued)

Table 13.2. *(Continued)*

Authors	Main Results	Sector
Kallmuenzer et al. (2021)	Mostly managed by families or small-scale businesses, family influence, economic benefits and destination networks has antecedents of coopetition among hospitality enterprises.	Hotel (SME)
Veronica et al. (2021)	In their Macau based research, the authors suggest that, among tour operators, the emergence of coopetition has significant implications for the overall structure of the local tourism supply chain.	Tour operators
Chim-Miki and Batista-Canino (2018)	The paper aims to develop an explanatory coopetition model for tourism destinations. It identifies co-location, associationism, competition, cooperation, strategic management, co-entrepreneurship, and co-production, has the seven factors required to develop a coopetition model.	Tourism destinations
Romero et al. (2018)	Through surveys conducted in Spanish enterprises in the restaurant business, findings from this paper suggest that coopeting restaurant chains introduce and stimulate process innovation in the market in a greater scale.	Restaurants
Czernek and Czakon (2016)	Authors interviewed representatives from Polish tourism firms.	Tourism companies
Grängsjö and Gummesson (2006)	The paper provides insights into destination marketing and the conditions and outcome of competitor co-operation in a local, horizontal hotel network.	Hotel networks
Grängsjö (2003)	Results of the study show that there are two different sets of values in the destination, and these determine and distinguish the way firms are involved in networking.	Tourism destinations

Source: Authors own.

Conclusion

In conclusion, this research delves into the complex realm of coopetition with a focus on business, particularly the tourism sector. The study sheds light on the nuanced behaviours and interactions of companies within this corporate network, where cooperation and competition coexist in pursuit of individual and collective objectives. The exploration of coopetition archetypes and relevant theories, coupled with a specific focus on the hotel industry, enriches the understanding of the dynamics at play. The analysis incorporates insights from game theory, unveiling the intricacies of competitive relations among tourism stakeholders. By applying concepts such as the prisoner's dilemma and tit-for-tat strategies, the research provides a comprehensive examination of decision-making and strategic moves within the competitive landscape of businesses. The crucial challenge is applying it to the tourism sector.

Those concepts can contribute to academic research in tourism in several ways. As a first contribution in tourism, stakeholders often engage in strategic decision-making regarding resource allocation, pricing, marketing strategies, and collaborations. Understanding the principles of game theory, including concepts like zero-sum game and the prisoner's dilemma, can provide insights into how these stakeholders make decisions in competitive environments. A second contribution to the tourism sector involves various stakeholders such as hotels, tour operators, transportation providers, and destination management organisations, among others. These actors may engage in both cooperative and competitive interactions. The prisoner's dilemma illustrates the tension between individual and collective interests, helping researchers analyse situations where cooperation may be beneficial but not guaranteed due to self-interest. Tit-for-tat, a strategy emphasising reciprocity and cooperation followed by retaliation in response to defection, can inform research on collaborative strategies in tourism. For example, tour operators and hotels may engage in partnerships or alliances and an understanding of how reciprocity influences these relationships can provide insights into the dynamics of cooperation in the industry. Zero-sum game concepts can be applied to resource management in tourism destinations. For instance, limited resources such as beachfront space or cultural heritage sites may lead to conflicts among stakeholders competing for access. Analysing these conflicts through the lens of zero-sum games can help identify strategies for more equitable resource allocation. Overall, these concepts from game theory provide analytical tools for understanding the complexities of decision-making, cooperation, and competition in the tourism industry. By applying them to various aspects of tourism research, scholars can gain deeper insights into the behaviour of stakeholders and develop strategies for sustainable and mutually beneficial outcomes.

One of the paths for future research is to research the dynamics of coopetition models in the tourism sector over time, considering factors such as technological advancements, market trends, and evolving consumer preferences. This could involve longitudinal studies to understand how coopetition strategies adapt and evolve in response to changing industry landscapes. Another path is researching the formation and dynamics of coopetition networks among tourism destinations, including factors that facilitate or hinder collaboration among competing destinations. Understanding how destinations cooperate and compete to attract visitors could inform destination management strategies. The third and last path should explore the relationship between coopetition and innovation within the tourism sector, including how collaborative competition drives product development, service enhancements, and business model innovations.

References

Almeida, S. (2023) Coopetition in tourism. In: Jafari, J. and Xiao, H. (eds) *Encyclopedia of tourism*, Springer Nature Switzerland AG 2023, pp. 76–77. https://doi.org/10.1007/978-3-319-01669-6_706-1

Almeida, S., Campos, A. C., Costa, C., & Simões, J. M. (2021). Competing through coopetition: A strategy for success in hotel marketing consortia. *Journal of Mediterranean Tourism Research*, *1*(1), 39–52. https://doi.org/10.5038/2770-7555.1.1.1004

Axelrod, R. (1981). The evolution of cooperation. *American Association for the Advancement of Science*, *211*(4489), 1390–1396.

Azevedo, J. R., & Matos, F. R. N. (2006). *Cooperacão e competicão simultanea em uma rede de negócios: A coopeticão na Valexport*. XII SIMPEP.

Bahar, V. S., Nenonen, S., & Starr Jr, R. G. (2022). On the same boat but singing a different tune: Coopetition between hotels and platforms close to customers. *Industrial Marketing Management*, *107*, 52–69. https://doi.org/10.1016/j.indmarman.2022.09.020

Bengtsson, M., & Kock, S. (2000). "Coopetition" in business Networks: To cooperate and compete simultaneously. *Industrial Marketing Management*, *29*(5), 411–426.

Bonel, E., & Rocco, E. (2007). Coopeting to survive; surviving coopetition. *International Studies of Management & Organization*, *37*(2), 70–96.

Brandenburger, A. M., & Nalebuff, B. J. (1996).*Co-opetition: A revolution mindset that combines competition and cooperation: the game theory strategy that's changing the game of business*. Doubleday.

Chim-Miki, A. F., & Batista-Canino, R. M. (2017). The coopetition perspective applied to tourism destinations: A literature review. *Anatolia*, *28*(3), 381–393. doi/abs/10.1080/13032917.2017.1322524

Chim-Miki, A. F., & Batista-Canino, R. A. (2018). Development of a tourism coopetition model: A preliminary Delphi study. *Journal of Hospitality and Tourism Management*, *37*, 78–88. https://doi.org/10.1016/j.jhtm.2018.10.004

Chim-Miki, A. F., Costa, R. A. da, & Oliveira-Ribeiro, R. (2023). Dimensions of tourism coopetition for social value creation. *Anatolia*. https://doi.org/10.1080/13032917.2023.2247800

Costa, C. (1996). *Towards the improvement of the efficiency and effectiveness of tourism planning and development at the regional level: Planning and networks: The Case of Portugal*. University of Surrey. PhD Thesis.

Crick, J. M., & Crick, D. (2020). Coopetition and COVID-19: Collaborative business-to-business marketing strategies in a pandemic crisis. *Industrial Marketing Management*, *88*, 206–213. https://doi.org/10.1016/j.indmarman.2020.05.016

Crick, J., Friske, W., & Morgan, T. A. (2024). The relationship between coopetition strategies and company performance under different levels of competitive intensity, market dynamism, and technological turbulence. *Industrial Marketing Management, 118,* 56–77. https://doi.org/10.1016/j.indmarman.2024.02.005

Czernek, K., & Czakon, W. (2016). Trust-building processes in tourist coopetition: The case of a Polish region. *Tourism Management, 52,* 380–394. https://doi.org/10.1016/j.tourman.2015.07.009

Dong, R., Guan, X., Liu, B., & Chen, S. (2023). Coopetition strategy in an imbalanced competitive environment. *International Journal of Production Research.* https://doi.org/10.1080/00207543.2021.2020928

Doz, Y. L., & Hamel, G. (1998). *Alliance advantage: The art of creating value through partnering.* Harvard Business Press. ISBN 0-87585.616.5.

Grängsjö, F. Y. (2003). Destination networking: Co-opetition in peripheral surroundings. *International Journal of Physical Distribution & Logistics Management, 33*(5), 427–448. https://doi.org/10.1108/09600030310481997

Grängsjö, F. Y., & Gummesson, E. (2006). Hotel networks and social capital in destination marketing. *International Journal of Service Industry Management, 17*(1), 58–75.

Guo, X., Zheng, X., Ling, L., & Yang, C. (2014). Online coopetition between hotels and online travel agencies: From the perspective of cash back after stay. *Tourism Management Perspectives, 12,* 104–112. https://doi.org/10.1016/j.tmp.2014.09.005

Hitt, M. A., Ireland, R. D., & Hoskisson, R. E. (2002). *Administracão estratégica.* Pioneira CengageLearning Edicões Ltda.

Hunt, S. D., & Morgan, R. M. (1995). The comparative advantage theory of competition. *Journal of Marketing,* 1–15.

Jacobson, D., Webster, C., Shapiro, K., Musyck, B., & Orphanides, S. (2015). Cyprus settlement: A zero sum game for tourism?. *European Journal of Tourism Research, 11,* 21–34. https://doi.org/10.54055/ejtr.v11i.192

Kallmuenzer, A., Zach, F., Wachter, T., Kraus, S., & Salner, P. (2021). Antecedents of coopetition in small and medium-sized hospitality firms. *International Journal of Hospitality Management, 99,* 103076. https://doi.org/10.1016/j.ijhm.2021.103076

Kostis, A., Albers, S., Vanderstraeten, J., Chinchanikar, S., & Bengtsson, M. (2024). Coopetitive dynamics, really? Towards an interaction perspective on coopetition. *Industrial Marketing Management, 116,* 158–169. https://doi.org/10.1016/j.indmarman.2023.12.005

Kylänen, M., & Mariani, M. M. (2012). Unpacking the temporal dimension of coopetition in tourism destinations: Evidence from Finnish and Italian theme parks. *Anatolia, 23*(1), 61–74. https://doi.org/10.1080/13032917.2011.653632

Le Roy, F., Robert, F., & Rhizlane, H. (2022). Vertical vs horizontal coopetition and the market performance of product innovation: An empirical study of the video game industry. *Technovation, 112,* 102411. https://doi.org/10.1016/j.technovation.2021.102411

Nooteboom, B. (1994). Innovation and diffusion in small firms: Theory and evidence. *Small Business Economics, 6*(5), 327–347. https://doi.org/10.1007/BF01065137

Oliver, C. (1990). Determinants of interorganizational relationships: Integration and future directions. *Academy of Management Review.* https://doi.org/10.5465/amr.1990.4308156

Owen, G. (2012). *Game theory* (pp. 391–398). https://doi.org/10.1016/B978-0-12-373932-2.00178-2

Quynh Trang Nguyen, T., Johnson, P., & Young, T. (2022). Networking, coopetition and sustainability of tourism destinations. *Journal of Hospitality and Tourism Management, 50*, 400–411. https://doi.org/10.1016/j.jhtm.2022.01.003

Rajala, A., & Tidström, A. (2021). Unmasking conflict in vertical coopetition. *Journal of Business & Industrial Marketing, 36*(13), 78–90. https://doi.org/10.1108/JBIM-08-2019-0381

Romero, I., Gómez, I. P., & Zabala-Iturriagagoitia, J. M. (2018). 'Cookpetition': Do restaurants coopete to innovate?. *Tourism Economics*. https://doi.org/10.1177/1354816618811551

Thomason, S. J., Simendinger, E., & Kiernan, D. (2013). Several determinants of successful coopetitionin small business. *Journal of Small Business and Entrepreneurship*. https://www.tandfonline.com/doi/abs/10.1080/08276331.2012.761800

Veronica, H. I. F., Fok Loi Hong, J., & Kin Anthony Wong, I. (2021). The evolution of triadic relationships in a tourism supply chain through coopetition. *Tourism Management, 84*, 104274. https://doi.org/10.1016/j.tourman.2020.104274

Waddington, C. K. (1973). *II World War: Operational research against the U-Boat.* Eleck Science.

Wang, Y., & Krakover, S. (2008). Destination marketing: Competition, cooperation or coopetition?. *International Journal of Contemporary Hospitality Management, 20*(2), 126–141. https://doi.org/10.1108/09596110810852122

Wu, M., & He, J. (2022). Horizontal tourism coopetition strategy for marketing performance evidence from theme parks. *Frontiers in Psychology, 13*, 917435.

Part Four

Co-promote the Tourism Sector: Including the Visitors in the Coopetition Process to Co-produce the Destination

Chapter 14

The Impact of the Local Residents' Voice and Social Media Brand Engagement on Coopetition in Tourism Destinations: The Mediating Role of Knowledge Sharing

Elahe Hosseini[a]*, Milad Ebrahimi*[a] *and Aidin Salamzadeh*[b]

[a]Yazd University, Iran
[b]University of Tehran, Iran

Abstract

This study explores the impact of the residents' voice and social media brand engagement on coopetition in tourism destinations with the mediating role of knowledge sharing. The study's statistical population includes tourists who visited Iran. The sample was 243 tourists who visited Iranian tourist different villages in the spring of 2023. This empirical study adopted a descriptive correlational method and used PLS3 for data analysis. The effects of residents' voices, knowledge sharing, and engagement with social media improve cooperation between tourism destinations, help create platforms for creativity and innovation in this industry, and ensure the promotion of sustainability and attractiveness of tourism. Therefore, the mutual analysis of the effects of different factors in rural tourism in Iran is valuable in providing a new method to improve the tourism experience in this field.

Keywords: Coopetition; knowledge sharing; residents' voice; social media brand engagement; sustainability

Introduction

Tourism is referred to as an efficient catalyst for economic and social reconstruction and development and is applied as a successful solution to solve challenges in many developing countries (Madanaguli et al., 2022). Rural tourism is

Value Proposition to Tourism Coopetition, 203–218

Copyright © 2025 Elahe Hosseini, Milad Ebrahimi and Aidin Salamzadeh

Published under exclusive licence by Emerald Publishing Limited

doi:10.1108/978-1-83797-827-420241014

one of the most significant types of tourism that can improve domestic tourism and was introduced from the 1950s onwards. Rural tourism is a strategy that serves the function of developing and diversifying the regional economy by planning and identifying the advantages and restrictions of villages (Rosalina et al., 2021). A large population of low-income and indigent people live in rural areas, and the development of tourism leads to improved employment and income, the provision of infrastructure services, etc. (Pan et al., 2021). Therefore, the principal role of the voice of local residents in achieving the expansion and success of the tourism destination should not be underrated (Chong, 2020). Researchers claim that tourism is based on service marketing and interaction (Morgan & Ranchhod, 2010). Coopetition is a behaviour representing the essential organisational methods of tourism destinations, especially when considering the interdependence and complementarity of this sector (Chim-Miki & Batista-Canino, 2017). Thus, residents, as active beneficiaries, must get involved in achieving coopetition in tourism destinations' potential (Stone & Nyaupane, 2020).

Theoretically, residents should only behave against brand promises if they consider them compatible with their anticipations, ideas, etc. Accordingly, the community should be included in brand promises by stating their ideas and recommendations and establishing mutual internal communication (Hakala, 2021). Destination marketing organisations are crucial in promoting destinations, attracting visitors, and enhancing visitor experiences (Camilleri, 2018). Residents can share their experiences and engage with destination marketing organisations by providing feedback, sharing their experiences on social media platforms, surveys and feedback forms, participating in events, and contributing to the overall narrative of the destination as they communicate directly with guests or tourists. By actively communicating with destination marketing organisations, residents can help shape the perception of their destination and contribute to its success in attracting visitors and boosting the local economy (Gowreesunkar et al., 2018).

Consequently, highlighting dyadic internal communication will assist residents in behaving in ways that reflect the ethnic specifications of the tourism destination (Xiong & King, 2019). By engaging in direct communication with tourists, residents can share authentic insights, traditions, and customs that align with the ethnic identity of the destination. This direct interaction allows residents to showcase their cultural heritage, provide personalised recommendations, and create meaningful connections with visitors (Roberts et al., 2017). Such communication inspires local residents to connect to the tourism destination. Due to market fluctuations, firms strive to enhance their performance to expand or endure. As a result, innovation becomes crucial since it can potentially leverage the firm's performance (Tidd & Bessant, 2020). To the degree that limited resources, knowledge, and information are shared or transferred, networks and cooperation are also seen as sources of competitive advantage through innovation (Zeng et al., 2010). In particular, coopetition – defined as competitors working together – occurs when businesses collaborate and compete at the same time (Resende et al., 2018).

In sum, rigorous literature assessments on coopetition in tourism demonstrated that studies rarely focus on the results of coopetition in society, tourism, or any other sector (Chim-Miki et al., 2023). Tourism destination's unique features – such as the high concentration of SMEs, interdependent businesses, governance that unites firms to develop and promote the destination, co-location, cultural proximity, and inter-connection – make it an appropriate setting for creating coopetition networks. SMEs in the tourism industry work together to maximise the use of public goods, such as the sea and landscapes (Chim-Miki & Batista-Canino, 2017; Zeng et al., 2010). From there, they compete to provide different services, such as lodging, food, entertainment, and transportation (Mariani, 2016).

Tourism industry investigations in Italy (Della Corte & Aria, 2016), Poland (Czakon & Czernek-Marszałek, 2021), and Brazil (Chim-Miki & Batista-Canino, 2017), investigations of coopetition in tourism encompassed various sectors and regions, such as event sports in New Zealand (Werner et al., 2015) and gastronomy in Spain (Romero-Cortes et al., 2019). Della Corte and Aria (2016) study examined two Italian tourism competitive networks (Naples & Sorrento) and found notable variations in the cooperation and competition composite scores and the overall coopetition index. They argue that greater levels of competition in a network of tourism destinations lead to greater cooperation.

Most coopetition models are built on the premise of participant behaviour about their respective dispositions towards cooperation or competition. Other models address the different places and circumstances in the productive chain that can lead to coopetition (Chim-Miki & Batista-Canino, 2017). It is crucial to recognise that the diversity of resources among participating organisations is the driving force behind coopetition interactions. This dynamic can offer competitive advantages when leveraged individually, but it may also necessitate collaboration to access resources that are not universally shared. Therefore, scholars have delved into the key success factors in coopetition-based management strategies and the impact of coopetition on a destination's or region's competitiveness (Leite et al., 2023), highlighting the potential benefits of this concept.

From the literature review, it is evident that the topic of tourism coopetition is in need of further research and attention. The current number of papers is relatively low, and there is a lack of a specific model for tourism coopetition. Moreover, the nature of the coopetition relationship, particularly in comparison to other constructs, requires clarification (Chim-Miki & Batista-Canino, 2017). Also, no direct study to the impact of the local residents' voice and social media brand engagement on coopetition in tourism destinations has been conducted so far.

Theoretical Foundations and Hypotheses Development

Rural tourism is considered an essential development strategy in many economies, especially in developing countries, where tourism is a crucial tool for poverty reduction and local economic development (Ma et al., 2020). However, tourism development requires cooperating with different companies and factors (Chim-Miki & Batista-Canino, 2017). Also, tourism coopetition can effectively

develop sustainable tourism (Nguyen et al., 2022). Besides, coopetition can promote information and strengthen the connections between tourist attractions,
leading to tourists' satisfaction and the economic success of tourist attractions
(Yang, 2018). Innovation usually results from combining knowledge, which often
implies exchanging knowledge between different sources. Therefore, coopetition
can help gather knowledge resources and lead to innovation (Estrada et al., 2016).
Thus, residents are considered one of the main stakeholders in tourism development. In tourism destinations, coopetition serves to convey information and
generate adequate knowledge (Scott et al., 2008). As a result, it can be argued that
knowledge is more valuable when shared between stakeholders, and the tourism
industry does not achieve full development without coopetition between different
players (Zehrer & Hallmann, 2015). However, people may be more likely to
hoard knowledge rather than share it with others because they fear it will diminish
their power and competitive advantage (Rastegar & Ruhanen, 2023). The authors
present the research hypothesis:

> *Hypothesis 0 (H0).* The Local residents' voice, and Social media brand
> engagement with the mediating role of Knowledge sharing have a significant
> impact on the Coopetition in tourism destinations.

Voice is an optional extra-role behaviour focussing on enhancing the organisational environment by sharing thoughts or concerns about issues in the
workplace (Hosseini & Ferreira, 2023). Voice fosters creativity and innovation by
strengthening collective decision-making and organisational learning (Kremer
et al., 2019). Voice behaviour is significant in the tourist sector because it facilitates locals sharing the knowledge they have received from visitors, as the industry
is more participatory and involves constant engagement between locals and guests
(Braun et al., 2013). As one of the most critical stakeholders in tourism, residents
influence tourism as much as they are affected by tourism (Nadalipour et al.,
2019). Residents are not just hosts, they also have the power to influence tourism
(Stone & Nyaupane, 2020). Local residents can be active problem solvers and
value creators (Zhang et al., 2022). So voice behaviour helps local residents share
what they've gained from visitors (Braun et al., 2013). As a result, they cause
Coopetition in tourism destinations. Residents' voices are a source of information, especially in tourism, so several studies have tried to fill in the knowledge gap
by examining voice behaviour in the tourism sector (Amani, 2022). For this
reason, the mediating role of knowledge sharing and interaction with the local
residents' voice is addressed to create a more comprehensive picture of Coopetition in tourism destinations. The first hypothesis of the research is as follows:

> *Hypothesis 1a (H1a).* The Local residents' voice has a significant impact on
> Coopetition in tourism destinations.
> *Hypothesis 1b (H1b).* The Local residents' voice has a significant impact on the
> Coopetition in tourism destinations with the mediating role of Knowledge
> sharing.

Social media is a powerful tool that facilitates interaction and shapes the perception of customers towards their favourite brands (Wang et al., 2021) as well as determines and creates positive attitudes and behaviours of residents towards the destination (Nunkoo et al., 2023). Also, social media is an essential tool for increasing the participation of residents in developing tourism (Senyao & Ha, 2022). Thus, it can lead to coopetition in tourism destinations. While researchers are increasingly interested in social media, insufficient studies still examine the relationship between knowledge sharing and social media (Edwards et al., 2017). This lack of research on whether and how tourism businesses share their knowledge with other businesses through social network participation needs to be addressed (McLeod et al., 2024). Based on existing reasoning about social media engagement, second hypotheses are presented to test the main and interactive effects of independent variables on dependent variables.

> *Hypothesis 2a (H2a)*. Social media brand engagement has a significant impact on the Coopetition in tourism destinations.
>
> *Hypothesis 2b (H2b)*. Social media brand engagement has a significant impact on the Coopetition in tourism destinations with the mediating role of knowledge sharing.

Knowledge sharing is the voluntary exchange of opinions, ideas, and theories between individuals and organisations (Obrenovic et al., 2022). It is a popular research topic (Edwards et al., 2017). Knowledge sharing through stakeholders has played an important role in a tourism destination in an increasingly competitive environment that can lead to innovation (Liu & Yan, 2022). In addition, knowledge sharing can also enhance problem-solving skills (Azeem et al., 2021), and even cause creativity (Yao et al., 2023). Knowledge sharing can lead to coopetition, a combination of cooperation and competition (Ritala & Hurmelinna-Laukkanen, 2013). When organisations and stakeholders share knowledge, they may cooperate in certain aspects while simultaneously competing in other areas. Knowledge sharing may also help with learning and potentially help companies and stakeholders understand and pursue coopetition activities simultaneously (Seepana et al., 2020). The concept of knowledge sharing and coopetition has been noticed in recent years (Bacon et al., 2020). However, coopetition research is sparse and limited, and some areas of research are deeply explored, while others are ignored (Ritala et al., 2016). Hence, despite the decisive role of coopetition, which is a fundamental issue in tourism research (Nguyen et al., 2022). So far, the impact of knowledge sharing has not been studied in coopetition with tourism destinations (Vasanicova et al., 2022). The third hypothesis of the research is as follows:

> *Hypothesis 3 (H3)*. Knowledge sharing has a significant impact on the Coopetition in tourism destinations.

Materials and Methods

This research is practical and quantitative. The statistical population includes the tourist villages of Iran. According to the information provided by the Tourism Deputy of Cultural Heritage, Handicrafts and Tourism Organization, currently,

465 target villages for tourism have been identified and registered in Iran. The study's statistical population includes tourists who visited in different villages of Iran in the spring of 2023. The researcher created a twenty-item questionnaire and graded it on a five-point Likert scale to collect the data in person. Local residents' voice and social media brand engagement are regarded as the independent variable, and information sharing acts as a mediator between the dependent variable – coopetition in tourism destinations – and the mediator in this study. The suggested paradigm can be used in different markets and environments, but it might produce different results depending on those markets' specifics. Because the society's standard deviation was unavailable, a sample of 30 participants was selected for this study and given a questionnaire to calculate the sample size. Based on Cochran's formula and the presumption that the statistical population is small, we determined the number of samples needed at the 95% confidence level, 0.1 accuracy, and 0.62 variance as 243 tourists. Moreover, the analysis of the findings has been conducted in the quantitative part using structural equation modelling with PLS3 software; it does not necessarily require normal distribution of the data (See Formula 14.1)

$$n = \frac{N Z_{\frac{q}{2}\sigma_X^2}^2}{\varepsilon^2 (N-1) + Z_{\frac{q}{2}\sigma_X^2}^2} \tag{14.1}$$

Results

Descriptive Statistics

The data analysis showed that 67% of the respondents were men and 33% were women; 17% held a Ph.D., 47% held a master's degree, and 36% had a bachelor's degree or lower; 27% were single and 73% were married; and 11% had five, 51% had 5–10, and 38% had more than 10 years of experience.

The Fit of the Measurement Model

We verified the validity and reliability using a wide variety of criteria. Convergent and divergent validity were used to evaluate the construct. In addition, the instrument's reliability was estimated using Cronbach's Alpha coefficient and composite reliability. An AVE value greater than 0.5 confirms the model's validity. The acceptable constructs showed composite reliability values and the derived Cronbach's Alpha coefficient greater than 0.7, as shown in Table 14.1.

The square root of variance was used to calculate the divergent validity, and the average variance was used to assess the convergent validity. Consequently, the model's validity and reliability were deemed satisfactory by the SmartPLS 3.0 software, as demonstrated by the results in Tables 14.1 and 14.2.

We used the ordinary least squares (OLS) to assess the structural goodness of fit, which follows the t-distribution. The result is significant and trustworthy because it is more than 1.96 (Thomas, 2003). According to the results, the

Table 14.1. Questions, Variables, Cronbach's Alpha, Composite Reliability, and Convergent Validity.

Variables	Questions	Cronbach's Alpha	Combined Reliability (CR)	Communality	AVE	R²	Q²	Loadings Factor
Local residents' voice		0.964	0.972	0.965	0.874	—	—	
	I communicate my opinions about work issues to the even if my opinion is different and the disagrees with me.							0.930
	I speak to about new project ideas or procedure changes.							0.954
	I speak to eliminate redundant or unnecessary procedures.							0.954
	I try to persuade to change organisational rules or policies that are nonproductive or counterproductive.							0.911
	Sharing ideas and thoughts is for the benefit of the organisation and beyond the responsibility of individuals.							0.924
Social media brand engagement		0.936	0.952	0.937	0.798	—	—	
	Social media is effective in the coopetition in tourism destinations.							0.855
	Social networks are effective for conducting research in the coopetition in tourism destinations.							0.892
	Social media is effective for participatory learning in the coopetition in tourism destinations.							0.903
	Social networks are effective for coopetition in tourism destinations.							0.894
	Social media is effective for knowledge sharing.							0.920
Knowledge sharing		0.934	0.950	0.936	0.794	0.730	0.743	
	Experiences and knowledge contribute to coopetition in tourism destinations.							0.872
	Knowledge sharing affects coopetition in tourism destinations.							0.886
	Managers use knowledge sharing in companies for high performance and coopetition in tourism destinations.							0.942
	Managers exchange research ideas in coopetition in tourism destinations.							0.923
	Knowledge sharing through social media contributes to coopetition in tourism destinations.							0.827

(Continued)

Table 14.1. (*Continued*)

Variables	Questions	Cronbach's Alpha	Combined Reliability (CR)	Communality	AVE	R²	Q²	Loadings Factor
Coopetition in tourism destinations		0.912	0.935	0.914	0.741	0.777	0.677	
	Coopetition can spread information and strengthen communication.							0.820
	Increasing coopetition in tourism destinations can reduce the residents' negative perception of the presence of tourism.							0.828
	I am very pleased with the inclusion and influence of residents in the planning and development of tourism.							0.914
	When planning tourism, the quality of life of residents is taken into account.							0.914
	Active participation can lead to creating a creative environment and innovation in tourism destinations.							0.823

Table 14.2. Divergent Validity.

Variables	1	2	3	4
Coopetition in tourism destinations	0861			
Knowledge sharing	0.820	0.891		
Local residents' voice	0.847	0.812	0.935	
Social media brand engagement	0.830	0.840	0.878	0.893

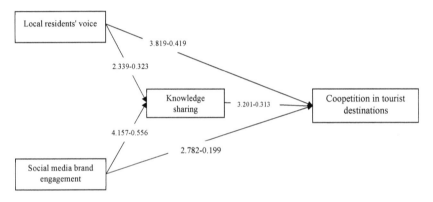

Fig. 14.1.   T value and Standard Factor Loadings.

acquired values of the five pathways are higher than the critical value (1.96) at the 95% reliability level (See Fig. 14.1). It shows that five research hypotheses are supported, the path efficiency is shown, and the structural model fit is demonstrated.

Three values of 0.19, 0.33, and 0.67 are considered for weak, medium, and strong values of the coefficient of determination (R2). This criterion shows the impact of exogenous variables on an endogenous variable (Hair Jr et al., 2021). This criterion was calculated for Knowledge Sharing, and its value is 0.730; for Coopetition in tourism destinations, it is 0.777; thus, the structural model requires a suitable goodness of fit. It computes the Q2 criterion for every dependent construct – the associated coefficient of determination results from the research constructs' total values. According to Kline (2023), all endogenous constructs with low, medium, and strong predictive power should be 0.2, 0.15, and 0.35. An appropriate rate is indicated by the Q2 estimates, which are 0.743 for knowledge sharing and 0.677 for competition in tourism areas.

The path coefficient of the structural model between −1 and +1 was determined using the PLS-SEM algorithm. The stronger the association, the closer the value is to 0, the less strong the correlation, and the positive and strongly correlated value is closer to +1. Fig. 14.1 shows that the greatest impact factor was connected to knowledge sharing acting as a mediator, social media brand engagement has a big impact on competition in tourist areas.

The Goodness of Fit (GOF)

The square of the averages of the determination coefficients and shared values is the GOF index. A number between zero and one represents the obtained value. The closer the GOF index is to one, the better the model fit is accepted. Obtained values of 0.01, 0.25, and 0.36 represent low, average, and high GOF, respectively (Hair Jr et al., 2021). As a result, the model was accepted since the overall GOF (see Formula 14.2) was determined to be 0.841.

$$GOF = \sqrt{\text{average (Commonality)} \times \text{average } (R^2)} \qquad (14.2)$$

The mediating role of knowledge sharing was examined by applying the Sobel test, with a result of 3.725; therefore, it was more than the base value of 1.96, which points to the mediating function of knowledge sharing. Given that the independent and mediating variable coefficients were equal to (a = 0.439) and the dependent and mediating variable coefficient was equal to (b = 0.313), the dependent and independent variable path coefficient was equal to (c = 0.309). Furthermore, the dependent and mediating variables' standard errors were (Sb=0.063), while the independent and mediating variables' standard errors were (Sa = 0.078). Lastly, five hypotheses based on Table 14.3 were used to confirm the hypotheses.

Table 14.3. T-test and Influence Coefficients.

Path	Influence Coefficient	T-Test	p value	Result
Hypothesis 1a (H1a): The Local residents' voice has a significant impact on Coopetition in tourism destinations.	0.419	3.819	0.000	Supported
Hypothesis 1b (H1b): The Local residents' voice has a significant impact on the Coopetition in tourism destinations with the mediating role of knowledge sharing.	0.323	2.339	0.007	Supported
Hypothesis 2a (H2a): Social media brand engagement has a significant impact on Coopetition in tourism destinations.	0.199	2.782	0.021	Supported
Hypothesis 2b (H2b): Social media brand engagement has a significant impact on Coopetition in tourism destinations with the mediating role of knowledge sharing.	0.556	4.157	0.000	Supported
Hypothesis 3 (H3): Knowledge sharing has a significant impact on Coopetition in tourism destinations.	0.313	3.201	0.009	Supported

Discussion

This study investigated the impact of residents' voices and social media brand engagement on coopetition between tourism destinations and the mediating role of knowledge sharing using structural equations. The study's first hypothesis results highlight that residents' voices impact the coopetition of tourism destinations and their sub-hypothesis by sharing knowledge. The findings showed that the residents' voice influences tourism because a tourism destination combines different components such as people, products, services, etc. (Kremer et al., 2019). Residents' voices significantly impact coopetition in tourism destinations, as they improve the experience of tourists and encourage them to engage more actively and positively with the place and the local community (Amani, 2022). Promoting residents' voices increases the coopetition in the tourism destinations. Knowledge sharing significantly affects the interactions between residents and tourists, promoting local products and services, active participation of tourists in local activities and projects, and positive interactions between local people and tourists (Azeem et al., 2021). The research results show that knowledge sharing is vital to the local residents' voice. As a result, it creates coopetition between tourism destinations and ultimately leads to the destination's competitive advantage.

The second hypothesis of the research, which states that social media has a positive effect on the coopetition of tourism destinations, has been confirmed, with the mediating role of knowledge sharing. Social media is commonly used for coopetition, communication, and knowledge sharing in the tourism sector (Wang et al., 2021). It facilitates knowledge sharing between businesses in the tourism destination knowledge network, benefiting business owners and managers. Social media interactions can also lead to behavioural motivations such as brand loyalty, commitment, and identification (Senyao & Ha, 2022). Local residents also play a significant role, as they are likely to act as destination advocates in their online social networks. However, addressing potential conflicts and negative consequences of social media, such as spreading misinformation and criticism, is essential. Proper planning and management can help mitigate these issues and strengthen the destination's competitive advantage (Nunkoo et al., 2023). Social media is a powerful tool for active communication, sharing experiences and knowledge, facilitating coopetition, and developing tourism destinations. Sharing knowledge in the context of social media can help strengthen coopetition between tourism destinations and ultimately create a competitive advantage. Overall, the residents' voice and social media brand engagement, with the mediating role of knowledge sharing, play an essential role in promoting the experience of tourists and the success of tourism destinations. By creating knowledge sharing opportunities and directly engaging individuals, social media can contribute to realising tourism goals and strengthening destinations' competitiveness (Senyao & Ha, 2022).

As for confirming the third hypothesis that knowledge sharing positively affects coopetition in tourism destinations, researchers believe tourism is a highly competitive sector (Chong, 2020). Knowledge sharing is valuable when shared among stakeholders, and it can lead to the creation of new knowledge for the better development of tourism destinations and their competitiveness (Donnelly,

2019). Coopetition, a combination of cooperation and competition, can reduce uncertainties, expand the range of opportunities, and disseminate information and knowledge through the organisational structure. Sharing knowledge and experiences of previous travellers about the destination gives more tourists confidence and strengthens coopetition between destinations. Knowledge sharing can play an essential role in promoting sustainable tourism and protecting the natural and cultural resources of the region (Kremer et al., 2019). In order to address the development of sustainable tourism, destination managers must treat residents with respect by sharing information and providing an opportunity to engage residents. Knowledge sharing enables coopetition and teamwork, increasing organisational learning capacity.

Conclusion

Rural tourism in Iran is booming for economic and social development in rural areas. The increase in the number of tourists may lead to changes in the identity and culture of the villages. However, it is essential to maintain a balance between tourism development and preserving the environment and culture. Strategic planning, coordination, raising awareness, and financial support are necessary to tackle challenges. Coopetition in tourism destinations can help strengthen social sustainability in rural society in Iran. This coopetition can help maintain and strengthen the cultural and social identity of the rural society of Iran. Sharing knowledge on social media also allows residents to better understand their community's problems and needs and contribute to the process of collaboration and continued development. Finally, the consistent interaction of these factors with policymakers through social media can help improve the living conditions in villages and achieve tourism goals. In general, the effects of residents' voices, knowledge sharing, and engagement in social media are constantly interacting and communicating with each other, and together, they help to improve the experience of tourists. Develop local partnerships and promote local communities. These interactions create a positive circle that leads to sustainable tourism development between tourists and local communities. This research could help develop coopetition theories for local tourism destinations in Iran. This research, as an extensive study in the field of social media, the residents' voice and knowledge sharing it, can help to develop knowledge in the field of coopetition in tourism destinations and be recognised as a valuable resource for future research in this field. The research results may also provide new patterns and approaches to understand better the role of local communities, knowledge sharing, and the use of social media in attracting tourists to villages. In addition, the combination of influential factors in this research goes beyond one-dimensional approaches to rural tourism issues. Therefore, the mutual analysis of the effects of different aspects in rural tourism in Iran is valuable in providing a new method to improve the tourism experience in this field. Despite the contributions, the current research is not free from limitations. We conducted this research in Iran, so generalising the results to other countries with different cultures may have yet to have distinct and sufficiently reliable results. We suggest conducting a comparative study and comparison with other countries.

References

Amani, D. (2022). Mediation role of destination brand patriotism in social media brand engagement and destination brand value co-creation: Local residents' perspective in the tourism sector in Tanzania. *Journal of Quality Assurance in Hospitality & Tourism*, 1–26. https://doi.org/10.1080/1528008X.2022.2149676

Azeem, M., Ahmed, M., Haider, S., & Sajjad, M. (2021). Expanding competitive advantage through organizational culture, knowledge sharing and organizational innovation. *Technology in Society*, *66*, 101635. https://doi.org/10.1016/j.techsoc.2021.101635

Bacon, E., Williams, M. D., & Davies, G. (2020). Coopetition in innovation ecosystems: A comparative analysis of knowledge transfer configurations. *Journal of Business Research*, *115*, 307–316. https://doi.org/10.1016/j.jbusres.2019.11.005

Braun, E., Kavaratzis, M., & Zenker, S. (2013). My city – My brand: The different roles of residents in place branding. *Journal of Place Management and Development*, *6*(1), 18–28. https://doi.org/10.1108/17538331311306087

Camilleri, M. A. (2018). *Strategic perspectives in destination marketing*. IGI Global.

Chim-Miki, A. F., & Batista-Canino, R. M. (2017). Tourism coopetition: An introduction to the subject and a research agenda. *International Business Review*, *26*(6), 1208–1217. https://doi.org/10.1016/j.ibusrev.2017.05.003

Chim-Miki, A. F., da Costa, R. A., & Oliveira-Ribeiro, R. (2023). Tourism coopetition for a better world: A cycle of creation, appropriation, and devolution of social value. *Current Issues in Tourism*, 1–15. https://doi.org/10.1080/13683500.2023.2254448

Chong, K. L. (2020). The side effects of mass tourism: The voices of Bali islanders. *Asia Pacific Journal of Tourism Research*, *25*(2), 157–169. https://doi.org/10.1080/10941665.2019.1683591

Czakon, W., & Czernek-Marszałek, K. (2021). Competitor perceptions in tourism coopetition. *Journal of Travel Research*, *60*(2), 312–335. https://doi.org/10.1177/0047287519896011

Della Corte, V., & Aria, M. (2016). Coopetition and sustainable competitive advantage. The case of tourism destinations. *Tourism Management*, *54*, 524–540. https://doi.org/10.1016/j.tourman.2015.12.009

Donnelly, R. (2019). Aligning knowledge sharing interventions with the promotion of firm success: The need for SHRM to balance tensions and challenges. *Journal of Business Research*, *94*, 344–352. https://doi.org/10.1016/j.jbusres.2018.02.007

Edwards, D., Cheng, M., Wong, I. A., Zhang, J., & Wu, Q. (2017). Ambassadors of knowledge sharing. *International Journal of Contemporary Hospitality Management*, *29*(2), 690–708. https://doi.org/10.1108/IJCHM-10-2015-0607

Estrada, I., Faems, D., & de Faria, P. (2016). Coopetition and product innovation performance: The role of internal knowledge sharing mechanisms and formal knowledge protection mechanisms. *Industrial Marketing Management*, *53*, 56–65. https://doi.org/10.1016/j.indmarman.2015.11.013

Gowreesunkar, V. G., Séraphin, H., & Morrison, A. (2018). Destination marketing organizations: Roles and challenges. In *The Routledge handbook of destination marketing* (pp. 16–34). Routledge.

Hair Jr, J. F., Hult, G. T. M., Ringle, C. M., Sarstedt, M., Danks, N. P., & Ray, S. (2021). *Partial least squares structural equation modeling (PLS-SEM) using R: A workbook*. Springer Nature.

Hakala, U. (2021). The voice of dwellers – Developing a place brand by listening to its residents. *Journal of Place Management and Development, 14*(3), 277–300. https://doi.org/10.1108/JPMD-12-2019-0111

Hosseini, E., & Ferreira, J. J. (2023). The impact of ethical leadership on organizational identity in digital startups: Does employee voice matter?. *Asian Journal of Business Ethics*, 1–25. https://doi.org/10.1007/s13520-023-00178-1

Kline, R. B. (2023). *Principles and practice of structural equation modeling*. Guilford publications.

Kremer, H., Villamor, I., & Aguinis, H. (2019). Innovation leadership: Best-practice recommendations for promoting employee creativity, voice, and knowledge sharing. *Business Horizons, 62*(1), 65–74. https://doi.org/10.1016/j.bushor.2018.08.010

Leite, H. d. L. K., Binotto, E., Padilha, A. C. M., & Hoeckel, P. H. d. O. (2023). Cooperation in rural tourism routes: Evidence and insights. *Journal of Hospitality and Tourism Management, 57*, 84–96. https://doi.org/10.1016/j.jhtm.2023.09.005

Liu, J., & Yan, J. (2022). Filling structural holes? Guanxi-based facilitation of knowledge sharing within a destination network. *Journal of Organizational Change Management, 35*(2), 264–279. https://doi.org/10.1108/JOCM-11-2020-0358

Ma, X. L., Dai, M. L., & Fan, D. X. F. (2020). Cooperation or confrontation? Exploring stakeholder relationships in rural tourism land expropriation. *Journal of Sustainable Tourism, 28*(11), 1841–1859. https://doi.org/10.1080/09669582.2020.1762622

Madanaguli, A., Kaur, P., Mazzoleni, A., & Dhir, A. (2022). The innovation ecosystem in rural tourism and hospitality – A systematic review of innovation in rural tourism. *Journal of Knowledge Management, 26*(7), 1732–1762. https://doi.org/10.1108/JKM-01-2021-0050

Mariani, M. M. (2016). Coordination in inter-network co-opetitition: Evidence from the tourism sector. *Industrial Marketing Management, 53*, 103–123. https://doi.org/10.1016/j.indmarman.2015.11.015

McLeod, M., Vaughan, D. R., Edwards, J., & Moital, M. (2024). Knowledge sharing and innovation in open networks of tourism businesses. *International Journal of Contemporary Hospitality Management, 36*(2), 438–456. https://doi.org/10.1108/IJCHM-03-2022-0326

Morgan, M., & Ranchhod, A. (2010). *Marketing in travel and tourism*. Routledge.

Nadalipour, Z., Imani Khoshkhoo, M. H., & Eftekhari, A. R. (2019). An integrated model of destination sustainable competitiveness. *Competitiveness Review: An International Business Journal, 29*(4), 314–335. https://doi.org/10.1108/CR-12-2017-0086

Nguyen, T. Q. T., Johnson, P., & Young, T. (2022). Networking, coopetition and sustainability of tourism destinations. *Journal of Hospitality and Tourism Management, 50*, 400–411. https://doi.org/10.1016/j.jhtm.2022.01.003

Nunkoo, R., Gursoy, D., & Dwivedi, Y. K. (2023). Effects of social media on residents' attitudes to tourism: Conceptual framework and research propositions. *Journal of Sustainable Tourism, 31*(2), 350–366. https://doi.org/10.1080/09669582.2020.1845710

Obrenovic, B., Du, J., Godinić, D., & Tsoy, D. (2022). Personality trait of consci-
entiousness impact on tacit knowledge sharing: The mediating effect of eagerness
and subjective norm. *Journal of Knowledge Management, 26*(5), 1124–1163. https://
doi.org/10.1108/JKM-01-2021-0066

Pan, Y., Wang, X., & Ryan, C. (2021). Chinese seniors holidaying, elderly care, rural
tourism and rural poverty alleviation programmes. *Journal of Hospitality and
Tourism Management, 46*, 134–143. https://doi.org/10.1016/j.jhtm.2020.09.010

Rastegar, R., & Ruhanen, L. (2023). A safe space for local knowledge sharing in
sustainable tourism: An organisational justice perspective. *Journal of Sustainable
Tourism, 31*(4), 997–1013. https://doi.org/10.1080/09669582.2021.1929261

Resende, L. M. M. d., Volski, I., Betim, L. M., Carvalho, G. D. G. d., Barros, R. d.,
& Senger, F. P. (2018). Critical success factors in coopetition: Evidence on a
business network. *Industrial Marketing Management, 68*, 177–187. https://doi.org/
10.1016/j.indmarman.2017.10.013

Ritala, P., & Hurmelinna-Laukkanen, P. (2013). Incremental and radical innovation
in coopetition—The role of absorptive capacity and appropriability. *Journal of
Product Innovation Management, 30*(1), 154–169. https://doi.org/10.1111/j.1540-
5885.2012.00956.x

Ritala, P., Kraus, S., & Bouncken, R. B. (2016). Introduction to coopetition and
innovation: Contemporary topics and future research opportunities. *International
Journal of Technology Management, 71*(1–2), 1–9. https://doi.org/10.1504/IJTM.
2016.077985

Roberts, L., Hall, D., & Morag, M. (2017). *New directions in rural tourism.* Routledge.

Romero-Cortes, T., Pérez España, V. H., López Pérez, P. A., Rodríguez-Jimenes, G.
D. C., Robles-Olvera, V. J., Aparicio Burgos, J. E., & Cuervo-Parra, J. A. (2019).
Antifungal activity of vanilla juice and vanillin against Alternaria alternata. *CyTA
- Journal of Food, 17*(1), 375–383. https://doi.org/10.1080/19476337.2019.1586776

Rosalina, P. D., Dupre, K., & Wang, Y. (2021). Rural tourism: A systematic literature
review on definitions and challenges. *Journal of Hospitality and Tourism Management, 47*, 134–149. https://doi.org/10.1016/j.jhtm.2021.03.001

Scott, N., Cooper, C., & Baggio, R. (2008). Destination networks: Four Australian
cases. *Annals of Tourism Research, 35*(1), 169–188. https://doi.org/10.1016/j.annals.
2007.07.004

Seepana, C., Paulraj, A., & Huq, F. A. (2020). The architecture of coopetition:
Strategic intent, ambidextrous managers, and knowledge sharing. *Industrial Marketing Management, 91*, 100–113. https://doi.org/10.1016/j.indmarman.2020.08.012

Senyao, S., & Ha, S. (2022). How social media influences resident participation in
rural tourism development: A case study of Tunda in Tibet. *Journal of Tourism and
Cultural Change, 20*(3), 386–405. https://doi.org/10.1080/14766825.2020.1849244

Stone, L. S., & Nyaupane, G. P. (2020). Local residents' pride, tourists' playground:
The misrepresentation and exclusion of local residents in tourism. *Current Issues in
Tourism, 23*(11), 1426–1442. https://doi.org/10.1080/13683500.2019.1615870

Thomas, R. (2003). *Blending qualitative & quantitative research methods in Theses and
Dissertations.* https://doi.org/10.4135/9781412983525

Tidd, J., & Bessant, J. R. (2020). *Managing innovation: Integrating technological,
market and organizational change.* John Wiley & Sons.

Vasanicova, P., Jencova, S., Gavurova, B., & Bacik, R. (2022). Coopetition of European Union countries within destination management. *Journal of Tourism and Services, 13*(24), 71–89. https://doi.org/10.29036/jots.v13i24.368

Wang, K., Tai, J. C. F., & Chang, H.-L. (2021). Influences of place attachment and social media affordances on online brand community continuance. *Information Systems and e-Business Management, 19*(2), 459–493. http://doi.org/10.1007/s10257-019-00418-7

Werner, K., Dickson, G., & Hyde, K. F. (2015). Coopetition and knowledge transfer dynamics: New Zealand's regional tourism organizations and the 2011 Rugby World Cup. *Event Management, 19*(3), 365–380. http://doi.org/10.3727/152599515X14386220874841

Xiong, L., & King, C. (2019). Aligning employees' attitudes and behavior with hospitality brands: The role of employee brand internalization. *Journal of Hospitality and Tourism Management, 40*, 67–76. https://doi.org/10.1016/j.jhtm.2019.06.006

Yang, Y. (2018). Understanding tourist attraction cooperation: An application of network analysis to the case of Shanghai, China. *Journal of Destination Marketing & Management, 8*, 396–411. https://doi.org/10.1016/j.jdmm.2017.08.003

Yao, G., Zhao, H., Hu, Y., & Zheng, X. (2023). Exploring knowledge sharing and hiding on employees' creative behaviors: A coopetition perspective. *Journal of Innovation & Knowledge, 8*(4), 100447. https://doi.org/10.1016/j.jik.2023.100447

Zehrer, A., & Hallmann, K. (2015). A stakeholder perspective on policy indicators of destination competitiveness. *Journal of Destination Marketing & Management, 4*(2), 120–126. https://doi.org/10.1016/j.jdmm.2015.03.003

Zeng, S. X., Xie, X. M., & Tam, C. M. (2010). Relationship between cooperation networks and innovation performance of SMEs. *Technovation, 30*(3), 181–194. https://doi.org/10.1016/j.technovation.2009.08.003

Zhang, T., Chen, Y., Wei, M., & Dai, M. (2022). How to promote residents' collaboration in destination governance: A framework of destination internal marketing. *Journal of Destination Marketing & Management, 24*, 100710. https://doi.org/10.1016/j.jdmm.2022.100710

Chapter 15

Co-creating Locally Embedded Rural Tourist Experiences Using Coopetition Strategies: Insights From Village Tourism in Portugal

Elisabeth Kastenholz[a] and Mariana Carvalho[b]

[a]University of Aveiro, Portugal
[b]Coimbra Education School - Coimbra Polytechnique Institute, Portugal

Abstract

Rural tourism has become increasingly popular given its opportunities to get to know local traditions and lifestyles, to immerse in appealing cultural and natural landscapes and to enjoy a calm and relaxing atmosphere, contrasting stressful city life. Additionally, visitors seek personalised, unique and memorable experiences and immersion in rural places, which could be fostered by co-creative and authentic multisensory experiences. The co-creation of value resulting from tourists' interaction with rural destinations' multiple local agents and resources calls for articulation and even coopetition amongst these agents who may benefit from joining efforts to compete not against each other but together within a wider competitive context to, thus, achieve a stronger, unique market position. This chapter presents a qualitative, exploratory case study, illustrating the overall rural tourist experience lived and co-created in a Portuguese schist village. Semi-structured interviews were applied to visitors, supply and development agents and to the local community in order to understand their perspective regarding the nature, quality and potential of the village experience. Experience co-creation seemed to have a positive impact on visitors' satisfaction. The coopetition approach was also identified in the discourse of supply and development agents who recognised the importance of cooperation, also within the Schist Village Network yielding a more cohesive and attractive tourism product in the village. Aligning locally embedded co-creation experiences and coopetition amongst local actors seems to be a strategic approach for fostering appealing, competitive and sustainable rural tourism experiences.

Value Proposition to Tourism Coopetition, 219–234
Copyright © 2025 Elisabeth Kastenholz and Mariana Carvalho
Published under exclusive licence by Emerald Publishing Limited
doi:10.1108/978-1-83797-827-420241015

Keywords: Rural tourism; experience co-creation; coopetition; cultural heritage; local community; sustainable development

Introduction

Rural tourist experiences often attract urbanites, nostalgically seeking a closer link to nature, rural landscapes, lifestyles and traditions, including artisan manufacture, small-scale agriculture and food production, small communities, where people are more than numbers, and where tourists may genuinely interact with local culture, people and resources (Carvalho et al., 2016; Kastenholz, 2013; Kastenholz, Carneiro, & Marques, 2012; Kastenholz, Carneiro, Marques, et al., 2012; Kastenholz et al., 2020; Kastenholz & Carneiro, 2023).

It is in this rural context that co-creative tourist experiences may gain value for visitors seeking to escape massification, serial reproduction of culture, globalised lifestyle and daily urban stress, noise and pollution. Mirroring the tensions between the global and the local, the search for rural holiday experiences is also a quest for authenticity, for unique, locally embedded social and cultural experiences, which creative local actors may successfully address through engaging tourist experience opportunities (Carvalho et al., 2016; Lane et al., 2022; Sidali et al., 2015).

Particularly in Portugal, whose rural hinterland still suffers from rural exodus, population ageing and a fragile socio-economic context (Santos, 2023), a vibrant rural tourism sector, involving local actors in experience co-creation may represent important development opportunities and hope for the survival of some local communities (Carvalho et al., 2016; Kastenholz, 2013, 2014; Maziliauske, 2024).

In this context, a comprehensive process of value co-creation, based on the integration of resources of all relevant local/regional, public and private destination stakeholders (Song et al., 2013; Yılmaz & Bititci, 2006), has long been called for overcoming the often-prevailing reality of fragmentation and lack of resources (Beckmann et al., 2023; Wang & Fesenmaier, 2007), through well-articulated and managed network approaches in rural tourism (Komppula, 2014; Lane & Kastenholz, 2015). In this context, the coopetition approach seems particularly adequate suggesting enhanced value creation through competitive cooperation produced between networks, organisations or within organisations, including the relationships between competitors, suppliers, complementary companies, government agencies, local population and customers (Chim-Miki & Batista-Canino, 2018).

This chapter looks at the specificities and evolution of rural tourist demand. It aims at analysing the potential and challenges of coopetition-based, co-creative rural tourist experiences, integrating local resources, products and skills, engaging local communities and their visitors. The conceptual debate will be complemented by an example from a study on rural tourist experiences undertaken in a schist village of Central Portugal. Examples are derived from field observation, interviews with local actors and visitors, within an action–research approach, revealing the types, ingredients and outcomes of such experiences. The chapter concludes with a debate on the role, potential and challenges of co-creation in rural tourism in developing appealing, competitive and sustainable rural tourism destinations, suggesting relevant management interventions as well as future avenues for research in the field.

Literature Review

Rural Tourism, Coopetition and Sustainable Development

Rural tourism, with its multiple connections to nature, traditions, food and wine, 'authenticity,' nostalgically embellished ways of life, has increasingly attracted interest from tourist markets, investors and politicians, due to its experience appeal and, consequently, expected sustainable development opportunities (An & Alarcón, 2021; Lane & Kastenholz, 2015; Quaranta et al., 2016; Ribeiro & Marques, 2002; Sidali et al., 2015). Within an increasingly competitive environment, new experience products as well as more professional market approaches have been developed, largely benefitting from cooperative destination management (Kastenholz, Carneiro, & Marques, 2012; Lane & Kastenholz, 2015; Quaranta et al., 2016). Such approaches may, indeed, deliver well-articulated and regionally embedded, distinctive and appealing place experience products (Kastenholz, Carneiro, Marques, et al., 2012; Lane & Kastenholz, 2015; Quaranta et al., 2016; Saxena et al., 2007; Wondirad et al., 2020), while making the best of scarce resources (Beckmann et al., 2023). This was found, for example, by Pato and Kastenholz's (2017) study in Portuguese hinterland areas, revealing that more successful rural accommodation units, not only used a more systematic and well-designed marketing approach but were also more active in networking. They were thereby able to present more appealing, articulated products, also benefitting regional development. Through a systematic literature review, Maziliauske (2024) concluded that rural SMEs use, indeed, relation-based collaboration as a strategy to respond to the specific challenges characterising many rural areas. The author suggests a conceptual model explaining why rural SMEs should use collaboration as a tool to innovate and access critical resources in otherwise resource-scarce rural territories.

Against this background, Lane et al. (2022) underline the importance of regional governance and the potential of active private–public sector rural development partnerships, including academic institutions, to identify and implement successful and sustainable rural tourism initiatives. Quaranta et al. (2016, p. 1) show in their study of network-based rural tourism development in an Italian national park, '*how the challenge for many rural territories lies in increasing levels of trust and rebuilding social capital as a precondition of developing the tourism sector and fostering socio-economic development as a whole.*' They also highlight the potential role of traditional as well as research institutions.

Zach and Racherla (2011) suggest that the centrality of 'co-opetition' within the tourism system should be recognised, where agents apart from competing for the same market also collaborate to develop complementary offerings (Tsai, 2002) to form an overall, competitive destination product. This context-dependent place product (Kastenholz, 2018) is experienced, perceived, evaluated and later remembered as a complex, meaningful and wholesome experience (Woodside & Dubelaar, 2002; Wang & Xiang, 2007). Therefore, a destination's success depends on a well-coordinated value chain, articulating all players to deliver comprehensive, enjoyable, meaningful and memorable visitor experiences (Zach & Racherla, 2011), while potentially yielding wider social value (Chim-Miki et al., 2023).

Focussing on social sustainability, Chim-Miki et al. (2023) reveal the potential of coopetition at the destination-level to create social value for the destination community. This higher social value is particularly important in peripheral rural areas, as evident when assessing attitudes of local communities regarding tourism development (Kastenholz, Paço, & Nave, 2023). Romão et al. (2023) stress the importance of integrating communities in such coopetition approaches, intensifying the relationships and interactions amongst local actors in the provision of tourism products. This should result in more satisfied visitors, increased destination appeal and competitiveness, enhancing sustainable regional development.

Additionally, Maziliauske (2024) highlights the role of rural tourism SMEs, whose owner-managers often show a true concern about place, community and local heritage. The author explains that by involving different stakeholders in co-creative rural tourism initiatives and by shifting the focus from economic to socio-cultural concerns, long-term sustainability challenges may be successfully addressed. These include depopulation, youth out-migration, lacking social and cultural dynamism and even the risk of disappearance of entire villages. Similarly, Cunha et al. (2020) suggest the idea of sustainable entrepreneurial ecosystems through engaged lifestyle entrepreneurs in rural tourism.

Thus, co-creative rural tourism networks, including communities and community concerns, can be managed according to a coopetition strategy to improve the destination's appeal, while enhancing local development through an interplay based on complementarity and a common vision, while maintaining competition, both between local actors (stimulating quality and innovation) and in face of other destinations.

Co-creation in Rural Tourism – A Fresh Lens on Coopetition

Coopetition may represent a positive stimulus to improve destination stakeholders' performance. Nguyen et al. (2022) point out that in a competitive environment, promoting coopetition may lead to market expansion and the consolidation of destination's brand image. In the tourism experience, co-creation emerges as key to visitors' involvement with the destination through meaningful place experiences, enhancing the destination's differentiation.

Co-creation results from the interaction between two or more actors. As suggested by Prahalad and Ramaswamy (2004), the creation of value may result from the interaction between consumers and enterprises, with high-quality interactions in experience co-creation resulting in a competitive advantage (Campos et al., 2018). Tourists increasingly want to play an active role and live unique local experiences (Binkhorst & Dekker, 2009). Co-creation in tourism is based on actively involved visitors co-creating value through interaction with supply agents, the local community or other tourists (Binkhorst & Dekker, 2009). Besides, visitors look for unique and personalised experiences, through which they actively explore the destination (Carvalho et al., 2022). Campos et al. (2018, p. 391) define co-creation as 'the sum of the psychological events a tourist goes through when contributing actively, through physical and/or mental participation, in activities and interacting with other subjects in the experience environment.' Besides, Carvalho et al. (2023) identified in a literature review key dimensions in co-creative food and wine experiences, namely (a) interaction with human (socialisation between tourists and other experience participants) (Campos et al., 2018) and (b) the physical environment (Binkhorst & Dekker, 2009; Carvalho et al., 2021), (c) active participation (Campos et al., 2018; Carvalho et al., 2016), (d) cognitive (learning involvement) and emotional engagement (personal connection) (Minkiewicz et al., 2014) and (e) personalisation (Minkiewicz et al., 2014).

In rural tourism, visitors seek engagement with both the local hosts and tangible (local natural and cultural resources) and intangible resources (local habits and lifestyle features) (Lian, 2020). Rural destinations benefit from providing immersive experiences that facilitate visitors' personal engagement and active participation in place experiences. Furthermore, tourists' central role in the experience implies the chance of subjective self-expression (Binkhorst & Dekker, 2009; Prebensen et al., 2013). The rural experiencescape is of fundamental importance in this experience co-creation. Natural and cultural resources are crucial, as visitors desire a holistic and authentic experience, in which their active physical and engaged participation ensures memorability (Carvalho et al., 2021; Lian, 2020).

A strategy combining co-creation and coopetition may further enhance experience value, as collaboration amongst stakeholders ensures optimally articulated and more consistent and meaningful overall place experiences. Investing in the design of co-creative experiences based on a coopetition dynamic between different destination stakeholders, distinctly specialised on, integrating and representing diverse resources, place or cultural facets – even if serving the same function (e.g. distinct restaurants with different dishes) – may thereby highlight the distinctive features of territories. According to Machado et al. (2021), destination stakeholders should mobilise joint resources in order to meet shared and individual goals, which in the case of co-creation should also consider visitor goals. In rural tourism, the synergy between co-creation and coopetition may add value to promising, trustful, strategic relationships between supply agents, reinforcing Chim-Miki and Batista-Canino's (2017, p. 1209) perspective of the *'relational component [as] key in applying the concept [coopetiton] to the tourism sector.'*

Aligning co-creation and coopetition in rural experiences suggests rethinking the collaborative roles supply agents and local communities may assume to promote a dynamic and competitive tourism sector in these territories (Machado et al., 2021). According to Abraham and Dixit (2020, p. 567), destinations need to provide great tourism experiences, while *'the stakeholders need to be educated about how to nourish and improve such experiences'* in a joint fashion. The shared value resulting from co-creation may, indeed, further interest in cooperation amongst local agents in their shared ambition to provide memorable and unique experiences of a place, which they jointly represent and whose enhanced market position benefits all. Recognising visitors' increasing quest for unique and differentiated experiences, the design of experience co-creation should not only meet tourists' expectations in single services, but consider the destination's overall value, requiring well-managed and articulated local resource deployment (Carvalho et al., 2021). Destination stakeholders must therefore cooperate with local competitors to yield a shared competitive advantage (Abraham & Dixit, 2020; Chim-Miki & Batista-Canino, 2017; Machado et al., 2021), as illustrated next for a Portuguese schist village.

Empirical Evidence from a Portuguese Rural Area

The Case Study Methodology

The results of the study presented here are based on a qualitative, exploratory study, undertaken in Portuguese rural contexts within the scientific, action-research-inspired project ORTE[1] ('The Overall Rural Tourism Experience and sustainable local community development'). This three-year project (2010–2013) analysed the overall tourism experience in three Portuguese villages (Linhares da Beira, Janeiro de Cima and Favaios). In this chapter, the focus is on the case of Janeiro de Cima, which is part of a Schist Village Network and located in Fundão, in the country's hinterland Central region (Fig. 15.1). The village had 306 inhabitants in 2011 (INE, 2011), being one of the most populated schist villages at that time. It presents several small accommodation units, a restaurant, a coffee-shop/bar, a grocery shop and the 'Weaver's House,' a museum-like institution, where the weaving tradition is presented and recovered through resident-targeted weaving courses. The village is located close to a river and presents a popular river beach.

The Schist Village Network is an interesting regional initiative, created in 2000 with European funding and supervised by the Regional Coordination Commission for the Development of the Central Region, CCDRC, as a regional development project, including a series of villages built with traditional schist materials. It aims at stimulating social and economic development, through heritage-restoration and rural tourism initiatives, encouraging locals to work together. Villages were assisted by specialised interdisciplinary teams to develop 'village plans' and corresponding articulated projects and initiatives. The network of 27 villages reveals a logic of cooperation rather than competition between villages, for example through their joint online promotion, platform suggesting territorial exploration through the diverse villages and even reservation system developed by the non-profit shared development agency ADXTUR (*Agência para*

[1]The ORTE Project (PTDC/CS-GEO/104894/2008) was financed by the Portuguese Foundation for Science and Technology (co-financed by COMPETE, QREN and FEDER).

Fig. 15.1.   Location of Janeiro de Cima. *Source:* Adapted with
permission of Portuguese Directorate General for Territorial Development
(DGT) (2015).

o Desenvolvimento Turístico das Aldeias de Xisto) (for more details Lane et al.,
2013; https://www.aldeiasdoxisto.pt/en/visit-enjoy/).

Regarding the case of Janeiro de Cima, the present chapter analyses the dimensions
of co-creative rural tourist experience, considering the perspectives of the local community, visitors and local supply and development agents, also considering
networking, governance and partnerships. Categories assessed include dimensions of
co-creation experiences in tourism, namely interaction, co-production, active participation (Campos et al., 2018; Carvalho et al., 2023; Minkiewicz et al., 2014); integration
of rural natural and cultural resources (Carvalho et al., 2016; Kastenholz, 2013; Lane
& Kastenholz, 2015); the diverse perspectives of co-creation and cooperation in
developing rural experience according to visitors, supply agents and the local

community (Carvalho et al., 2021; Kastenholz, Carneiro, & Marques, 2012; Lane et al., 2022). This chapter revisits results from semi-structured interviews that were applied to development agents ($N = 8$), tourism suppliers ($N = 7$), residents ($N = 11$) and visitors ($N = 12$). Content analysis was carried out with the support of the qualitative software WebQDA. Additionally, the content of a final project meeting with the local agents of the village, showing and discussing main results of the overall three-year study and reflecting on future avenues of development are considered for this chapter.

Results

In Janeiro de Cima, visitors revealed an interest in exploring a schist village belonging to the nationally renowned network, enjoying close contact with nature, a relaxing experience and escape from the urban home environment. Results revealed high levels of visitor satisfaction with the experience, mainly due to the escape from stressful city life and the possibility to appreciate the aesthetics of the village, its architecture and landscape, as well as the relaxing atmosphere. The multisensory experience was also noteworthy, mainly in terms of sounds (e.g. birds, the wind and the 'sound of silence'), taste (e.g. new flavours associated to regional dishes) and the visual component (e.g. mountains, the rebuilt houses, the architecture and construction materials, typical of this village – the combination of schist and river stone). All these experiences derive from a highly appreciated experiencescape that has naturally evolved but also been carefully preserved by many village actors, who actually engage with local tourism development in many, not always profit-oriented, ways.

A clear concern of involving the local community in the village's tourism development is visible, since the first investments made in this schist village, following the 'village plan.' Indeed, local agents and residents showed a clear support of tourism development, revealing a concern about learning how to welcome visitors and how to collaborate with other supply agents and residents in order to enhance the quality of the tourist experience. Residents frequently reported the pride in they felt in their village and the fact that it attracted visitors. This involvement of the local community was recognised by visitors who were grateful for rich and authentic experiences, where interaction with locals was perceived as unique and very pleasant. In addition, Janeiro's integration in the Schist villages network plays a central role in attracting visitors, strengthening both the territorial brand and local identities through a multiplicity of initiatives (ADXTUR, 2024; Lane et al., 2013).

The development agents interviewed underlined the importance of cooperation between all supply agents and the locals to promote memorable experiences and visitor satisfaction. In the village's Weavers' House, where the region's ancient weaving tradition was recovered, visitors had the opportunity to engage in an exploratory experience of weaving, while learning about historical and cultural traditions related to a unique local product: the linen. In this establishment, visitors could also explore a museum and a handicraft shop, where they could find utilitarian linen craft produced in this space by resident women and regional gastronomic specialties, mainly honey and cheese. According to all local agents, this place is understood as an important asset of the village, mirroring part of its history and identity, but with a potential to develop more dynamism and creative approaches (for example, weaving courses for tourists), possibly involving knowledgeable resident women who would have another income source, while preserving and sharing their craft skills.

In the studied co-creative rural tourist experiences in Janeiro de Cima, coopetition was present when considering supply agents' (restaurant, accommodations and shop) common goals and those of the local community (new job and income opportunities through flourishing village tourism). Locals and visitors already co-created experiences in different contexts, which were not only driven by profit intentions. Locals revealed high satisfaction resulting from the interaction with village visitors. Visitors' appreciation of the village's beauty made residents often feel proud and special. They also recognised the importance of this interaction as an escape from the loneliness and isolation felt by some villagers, but also to promote local culture, endogenous products, and the preservation of local heritage, thereby enhancing the village's identity and the residents' quality of life. At the same time, some residents were also supply agents managing local businesses (e.g. a local bar, a grocery store and a local accommodation) and were aware of their key role as promoters of Janeiro de Cima as an outstanding and competitive schist village, which could be stimulated through a collaborative view.

After confronting local actors and residents, in the final project meeting, with the project's results and study examples from elsewhere, the potential to jointly develop diverse appealing co-creative experiences was identified by all local agents as particularly strong in Janeiro de Cima. As an example, culinary workshops in local accommodations or in the village's restaurant, where visitors could learn with locals how to cook regional dishes, could be an attractive co-creative experience, as mentioned by an older woman. The knowledge transfer through residents would help preserve the region's gastronomic heritage as well as the expertise that could add value to these unique experiences. Visitors, who increasingly seek rich, immersive experiences, would have close contact with local features through an appealing hands-on experience. Agricultural workshops could facilitate coopetition amongst local farmers, giving visitors the possibility to learn about the food production process and (traditional) farming techniques, while facilitating the contact with the land, local products and habits. These appealing, cooperatively designed experiences could promote memorability, while strengthening local identity and cohesion within the community. One agent also suggested linking all the services of Janeiro de Cima to promoting a 'corporate entrepreneurial culture,' which would promote the development of new co-creative, local identity-reinforcing competitive products responding to visitors' expectations. Hence, the coopetition perspective emerged as a strategy these agents wanted to apply in this rural destination.

The local community also underlined the importance of investing in outdoor activities for visitors who, as they correctly understand, appreciate close contact with nature as well as exploring the village and the surroundings. Improving the pedestrian routes, promoting sports, like rock climbing (near the Zêzere river) or biking would add value and make the village more attractive, make people stay longer and get more involved with the place. In these nature-based experiences, the cooperation between locals and supply agents could be especially important. Knowledgeable locals could help visitors explore the village surroundings in a more immersive and authentic way acting as local guides working with specialised local supply agents (e.g. walking or biking tour enterprises).

The local community also highlighted the special value of the river and the village's river beach that could be better explored for leisure activities during all year. One historical feature of Janeiro de Cima is its 'river boat,' that in ancient times served as the main mode of transportation and was originally crafted in the village. Villagers suggested that, apart from presenting guided river tours on this boat, this craft expertise could be also revitalised (similar to the weaving tradition) and made available as artistic workshops also to interested visitors seeking unique, interactive and hands-on handicrafts experiences. The cooperation between all involved in the traditional boat construction process would be of particular interest, not only improving the village's tourism experience but also enhancing a meaningful collaborative attitude in the village, leaving a physical product that may later be used for trips on the river. From the locals' perspective, such engaging and meaningful experiences would also make visitors stay longer, accordingly increase their expenditures, while deepening place and community attachment and stimulating repeat visitation.

Although competition is part of the coopetition strategy, the enhanced value results mainly from cooperation amongst local actors and between locals and visitors, generating a positive impact on the destination's distinctiveness. Coopetition and experience co-creation may, thus, go hand-in-hand in a sustainable strategic destination approach that not only benefits tourism agents but also local residents and visitors, as presented in the Fig. 15.2.

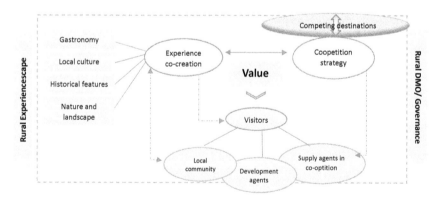

Fig. 15.2.   Co-creation Experiences and Coopetition in Rural Destinations. *Source:* Elaborated by the authors.

Fig. 15.2 presents a model of value co-creation in rural tourism, visualising how the tourists experience co-creation, based on local resources and interaction amongst destination stakeholders and visitors, within the *experience co-creation* and *coopetition strategy* framework generates value for all involved. For visitors, unique value results from integration of endogenous resources and interaction with local stakeholders and in a highly personalised context. These local agents co-create not only with visitors but also with other local agents to develop together appealing tourism experiences that foster the rural destinations' competitiveness through both co-creative and coopetitive approaches. For the local community, value-creation also means the enhancement of local identity, which in turn will ensure preservation of local heritage resources. Coopetition strategies, particularly if well-coordinated through rural tourism governance structures/DMOs, may thus create cohesion and valuable local dynamics within the village, joining forces against competition.

The consequent economic development also benefits residents (some more than others) through additional income and business opportunities. Last but not least, residents recognise the more dynamic social living context they all enjoy through the visitation of people from outside the village. These help keep the village alive and reduce through new economic perspectives, the trends towards rural depopulation. In brief, the quality of life of all village residents and local actors may be critically enhanced by strategies of cooperation and coopetition representing one key to more innovative and dynamic rural destination development and correspondingly more competitive village destinations. In this context, destination management organisations (DMOs) may play an important role in fostering strategic networking and coopetition efforts yielding the design and provision of appealing, unique and sustainability-enhancing co-creative experiences. The adoption of a coopetition strategy in co-creative rural tourist experiences may, consequently, lead to win-win outcomes for all parts involved and to the destinations' competitive distinctiveness.

Conclusion

Coopetition and cocreation in rural tourism may be central to involve diverse community actors in a dynamic, appealing and positively shared social and cultural living context, attracting visitors, boosting local economy and enhancing residents' quality of life through multiple benefits achieved, as presented for the case of Janeiro de Cima. A shared vision of community development and resilience, enhanced through collaborative and engaged entrepreneurship (Cunha et al., 2020; Maziliauske, 2024; Pato & Kastenholz, 2017), may thus lead to sustainable and even regenerative tourism (Becken & Kaur, 2022; Kastenholz, Salgado, & Gomes, 2023). Through co-creation and coopetition strategies, a more dynamic and competitive tourism sector can thus be fostered (Abraham & Dixit, 2020; Chim-Miki & Batista-Canino, 2017; Machado et al., 2021), providing unique, appealing and meaningful experiences, strongly connected with and embedded in local communities, culture and nature. The strategic collaboration between– even locally competing – supply agents and the local community permits the creation of attractive and distinctive tourist experiences, bringing benefits to all parts involved. Through this collaborative approach, locally-embedded value co-creation generates shared economic, social and cultural value as an outcome of engaging, authentic rural tourist experiences, possibly enjoyed by all involved. This case underlines the pertinence and advantages of using a combined co-creation–co-opetition approach, with coopetition enhancing the rural destination's potential in experience-value co-creation. DMOs or other local governance structures play an important role in stimulating and coordinating these co-creative and coopetitive strategies, involving multiple stakeholders, sensitising, developing and making them follow common goals (Lane et al., 2022; Lane & Kastenholz, 2015; Nguyen et al., 2022). Through such coopetition-inspired visions, strategies and actions a destination should boost its competitive position (Abraham & Dixit, 2020), enhancing its sustainability, resilience and regenerative potential (Chim-Miki et al., 2023; Kastenholz, Salgado, & Gomes, 2023).

The connections between co-creation and coopetition were identified in this study regarding the tourism experience only for one Portuguese village destination. Analysing different rural settings (national and international), with distinct geographical scope (regional), diverse co-creative experience offerings and coopetition strategies, involving supply agents, residents and DMOs, should be considered in future studies. In this respect, comparative studies (e.g. comparing distinct degrees of community involvement, experience types or governance structures and dynamics) could also add value to the field.

References

Abraham, A., & Dixit, S. (2020). Tourism experience and destination competitiveness. In S. Dixit (Ed.), *The Routledge handbook of tourism experience management and marketing* (pp. 560–569). Routledge.

ADXTUR (Schist Villages Tourism Development Agency). (2024). *Aldeias do Xisto.* https://www.aldeiasdoxisto.pt/en/

An, W., & Alarcón, S. (2021). From netnography to segmentation for the description of the rural tourism market based on tourist experiences in Spain. *Journal of Destination Marketing & Management, 19.* https://doi.org/10.1016/j.jdmm.2020.100549

Becken, S., & Kaur, J. (2022). Anchoring 'tourism value' within a regenerative tourism paradigm–A government perspective. *Journal of Sustainable Tourism, 30*(1), 52–68. https://doi.org/10.1080/09669582.2021.199030

Beckmann, M., Garkisch, M., & Zeyen, A. (2023). Together we are strong? A systematic literature review on how SMEs use relation-based collaboration to operate in rural areas. *Journal of Small Business and Entrepreneurship, 35*(4), 515–549. https://doi.org/10.1080/08276331.2021.1874605

Binkhorst, E., & Dekker, T. (2009). Agenda for co-creation tourism experience research. *Journal of Hospitality Marketing & Management, 18*(2–3), 311–327. https://doi.org/10.1080/19368620802594193

Campos, A. C., Mendes, J., do Valle, P., & Scott, N. (2018). Co-creation of tourist experiences: A literature review. *Current Issues in Tourism, 21*(4), 369–400. https://doi.org/10.1080/13683500.2015.1081158

Carvalho, M., Kastenholz, E., & Carneiro, M. J. (2023). Co-creative tourism experiences – A conceptual framework and its application to food & wine tourism. *Tourism Recreation Research*, *48*(5), 668–692. https://doi.org/10.1080/02508281. 2021.1948719

Carvalho, M., Kastenholz, E., & Carneiro, M. J. (2021). Interaction as a central element of co-creative wine tourism experiences—Evidence from *Bairrada*, a Portuguese wine-producing region. *Sustainability*, *13*(16), 9374. https://doi.org/10. 3390/su13169374

Carvalho, M., Kastenholz, E., & Carneiro, M. J. (2022). Co-creation experiences and experiencescape. In D. Buhalis (Ed.), *Encyclopedia of tourism management and marketing* (pp. 519–522). Edward Elgar Publishing. 978 1 80037 747 9.

Carvalho, M., Lima, J., Kastenholz, E., & Sousa, A. (2016). Co-creative rural tourism experiences—Connecting tourists, community and local resources. In E. Kastenholz, M. J. Carneiro, C. Eusébio, & E. Figueiredo (eds), *Meeting Challenges for rural tourism through co-creation of sustainable tourist experiences* (pp. 83–106). Cambridge Scholars Publishing. 1-4438-9488-5.

Chim-Miki, A. F., & Batista-Canino, R. (2017). Tourism coopetition: An introduction to the subject and a research agenda. *International Business Review*, *26*, 1208–1217. https://doi.org/10.1016/j.ibusrev.2017.05.003

Chim-Miki, A. F., & Batista-Canino, R. (2018). Development of a tourism coopetition model: A preliminary Delphi study. *Journal of Hospitality and Tourism Management*, *37*, 78–88. https://doi.org/10.1016/j.jhtm.2018.10.004

Chim-Miki, A. F., Costa, R., & Oliveira-Ribeiro, R. (2023). Tourism coopetition for a better world: A cycle of creation, appropriation, and devolution of social value. *Current Issues in Tourism*. https://doi.org/10.1080/13683500.2023.2254448

Cunha, C., Kastenholz, E., & Carneiro, M. J. (2020). Entrepreneurs in rural tourism: Do lifestyle motivations contribute to management practices that enhance sustainable entrepreneurial ecosystems?. *Journal of Hospitality and Tourism Management*, *44*, 215–226. https://doi.org/10.1016/j.jhtm.2020.06.007

INE. (2011). *Resultados provisórios dos Censos 2011* [Provisional results of the 2011 Census]. Instituto Nacional de Estatística (INE).

Kastenholz, E. (2013). Living, sharing and marketing the overall rural tourism experience – A conceptual discussion and first results from a research project in 3 Portuguese villages. In N. Santos & F. Cravidão (eds), *Turismo e Cultura: Destinos e Competitividade* (pp. 371–394). Imprensa da Universidade de Coimbra. 978-989-26-0544-9.Coords.

Kastenholz, E. (2014). A experiência integral de turismo em meio rural – conceptualização na perspetiva do turista e reflexão sobre a natureza da experiência turística, com base em dados recolhidos em 3 aldeias portuguesas. In A. Cristóvão, X. Pereiro, M. de Souza, & I. Elesbão (eds), *Turismo Rural em Tempos de Novas Ruralidades* (pp. 49–78). Editora da UFRGS. Série "Estudos Rurais". (Coords.).

Kastenholz, E. (2018). Tourism and specific localities - Mountains, deserts and coasts. In C. Cooper, S. Volo, W. Gartner, & N. Scott (eds), *Handbook of tourism management* (pp. 493–515). Sage Publishing. ISBN-10: 1473974240.

Kastenholz, E., & Carneiro, M. J. (2023). Co-creating sustainable rural tourism experiences with food & wine, local culture, landscapes, and people. *Editorial note*. *Revista Turismo & Desenvolvimento* [Journal of Tourism & Development], *43*, 7–12. https://doi.org/10.34624/rtd.v43i0.33028

Kastenholz, E., Carneiro, M. J., Eusébio, C., & Figueiredo, F. (2020). Host–guest relationships in rural tourism: Evidence from two Portuguese villages. In A. Artal-Tur & M. Kozak (eds), *Culture and cultures in tourism: Exploring new trends* (pp. 177–190). Routledge. 9780367660925.

Kastenholz, E., Carneiro, M. J., & Marques, C. (2012a). Marketing the rural tourism experience. In R. Tsiotsou & R. Goldsmith (eds), *Strategic marketing in tourism services* (pp. 247–264). Emerald. 9781780520704.

Kastenholz, E., Carneiro, M. J., Marques, C. P., & Lima, J. (2012). Understanding and managing the rural tourism experience—The case of a historical village in Portugal. *Tourism Management Perspectives*, *4*, 207–214. https://doi.org/10.1016/j.tmp.2012.08.009

Kastenholz, E., Paço, A., & Nave, A. C. (2023). Wine tourism in rural areas – Hopes and fears amongst local residents. *Worldwide Hospitality and Tourism Themes*, *15*(1), 29–40. ISSN:1755-4217. https://doi.org/10.1108/WHATT-08-2022-0095

Kastenholz, E., Salgado, M., & Gomes, R. (2023). Resilient and regenerative Rural Tourism: The case of Travancinha Village. *Cadernos de Geografia*, *48*, 81–97. https://doi.org/10.14195/0871-1623_48_6

Komppula, R. (2014). The role of individual entrepreneurs in the development of competitiveness for a rural tourism destination–A case study. *Tourism Management*, *40*, 361–371. https://doi.org/10.1016/j.tourman.2013.07.007

Lane, B., Kastenholz, E., & Carneiro, M. J. (2022). Rural tourism and sustainability: A special issue, review and update for the opening tears of the twenty-first century. *Sustainability*, *14*(10), 6070. https://doi.org/10.3390/su14106070 4

Lane, B., & Kastenholz, E. (2015). Rural tourism: The evolution of practice and research approaches – Towards a new generation concept?. *Journal of Sustainable Tourism*, *23*(8–9), 1133–1156. https://doi.org/10.1080/09669582.2015.1083997

Lane, B., Weston, R., Davies, N., Kastenholz, E., Lima, J., & Majewski, J. (2013). *Industrial Heritage and Agri/Rural Tourism in Europe: a review of their development, socio-economic systems and future policy issues.* European Union. https://doi.org/10.2861/13312 Available at: http://www.europarl.europa.eu/studies

Lian, J. (2020). Developing rural tourism through co-creation of sustainable tourist experiences. In S. Dixit (Ed.), *The Routledge handbook of tourism experience management and marketing* (pp. 473–484). Routledge.

Machado, H., Vareiro, L., Caldas, I., & Sousa, B. (2021). Supply diversification and coopetition in rural tourism. In J. V. de Carvalho, Á. Rocha, P. Liberato & A. Peña (Eds), *Advances in tourism, technology and systems. ICOTTS 2020. Smart tnnovation, systems and technologies* (pp. 192–206), 208. Springer. https://doi.org/10.1007/978-981-33-4256-9_18

Maziliauske, E. (2024). Innovation for sustainability through co-creation by small and medium-sized tourism enterprises (SMEs): Socio-cultural sustainability benefits to rural destinations. *Tourism Management Perspectives*, *50*. https://doi.org/10.1016/j.tmp.2023.101201

Minkiewicz, J., Evans, J., & Bridson, K. (2014). How do consumers co-create their experiences? An exploration in the heritage sector. *Journal of Marketing Management*, *30*(1–2), 30–59. https://doi.org/10.1080/0267257X.2013.800899

Nguyen, T., Johnson, P., & Young, T. (2022). Networking, coopetition and sustainability of tourism destinations. *Journal of Hospitality and Tourism Management*, *50*, 400–411. https://doi.org/10.1016/j.jhtm.2022.01.003

Pato, L., & Kastenholz, E. (2017). Marketing of rural tourism - A study based on rural tourism lodgings in Portugal. *Journal of Place Management and Development, 10*(2), 121–139. doi:10.1108/JPMD-06-2016-0037

Portuguese Directorate General for Territorial Development (DGT). (2015). *Mapas on-line* [On-line maps]. Available at http://mapas.dgterritorio.pt/viewer/index.html

Prahalad, C., & Ramaswamy, V. (2004). Co-creation experiences: The next practice in value creation. *Journal of Interactive Marketing, 18*(3), 5–14. https://doi.org/10.1002/dir.20015

Prebensen, N. K., Vittersø, J., & Dahl, T. I. (2013). Value co-creation significance of tourist resources. *Annals of Tourism Research, 42*, 240–261. https://doi.org/10.1016/j.annals.2013.01.012

Quaranta, E., Citro, E., & Salvia, R. (2016). Economic and social sustainable synergies to promote innovations in rural tourism and local development. *Sustainability, 8*(7). https://doi.org/10.3390/su8070668

Ribeiro, M., & Marques, C. (2002). Rural tourism and the development of less favoured areas: Between rhetoric and practice. *International Journal of Tourism Research, 4*(3), 211–220. https://doi.org/10.1002/jtr.377

Romão, J., Palm, K., & Persson-Fischier, U. (2023). Open spaces for co-creation: A community-based approach to tourism product diversification. *Scandinavian Journal of Hospitality and Tourism, 23*(1), 94–113. https://doi.org/10.1080/15022250.2023.2174183

Santos, R. (2023). Return migration and rural tourism development in Portugal. *Tourism Planning & Development, 20*(4), 636–659. https://doi.org/10.1080/21568316.2021.1953121

Saxena, G., Clark, G., Oliver, T., & Ilbery, B. (2007). Conceptualizing integrated rural tourism. *Tourism Geographies: An International Journal of Tourism Space, Place and Environment, 9*(4), 347–370. https://doi.org/10.1080/14616680701647527

Sidali, K., Kastenholz, E., & Bianchi, R. (2015). Food tourism, niche markets and products in rural tourism: Combining the intimacy model and the experience economy as a rural development strategy. *Journal of Sustainable Tourism, 23*(8–9), 1179–1197. ISSN: 0966-9582. https://doi.org/10.1080/09669582.2013.836210

Song, H., Liu, J., & Chen, G. (2013). Tourism value chain governance: Review and prospects. *Journal of Travel Research, 52*(1), 15–28. https://doi.org/10.1177/0047287512457264

Tsai, W. (2002). Social structure of "coopetition" within a multiunit organization: Coordination, competition, and intra-organizational knowledge sharing. *Organization Science, 13*(2), 179–190. https://doi.org/10.1287/orsc.13.2.179.536

Wang, Y., & Fesenmaier, D. R. (2007). Collaborative destination marketing: A case study of Elkhart county, Indiana. *Tourism Management, 28*(3), 863–875. https://doi.org/10.1016/j.tourman.2006.02.007

Wang, Y., & Xiang, Z. (2007). Toward a theoretical framework of collaborative destination marketing. *Journal of Travel Research, 46*(1), 75–85. https://doi.org/10.1177/0047287507302384

Wondirad, A., Tolkach, D., & King, B. (2020). Stakeholder collaboration as a major factor for sustainable ecotourism development in developing countries. *Tourism Management, 78*, 104024. https://doi.org/10.1016/j.tourman.2019.104024

Woodside, A. G., & Dubelaar, C. (2002). A general theory of tourism consumption systems: A conceptual framework and an experimental exploration. *Journal of Travel Research, 41*(2), 120–132. https://doi.org/10.1177/00472870223741

Yılmaz, Y., & Bititci, U. S. (2006). Performance measurement in tourism: A value chain model. *International Journal of Contemporary Hospitality Management, 18*(4), 341–349. https://doi.org/10.1108/09596110610665348

Zach, F., & Racherla, P. (2011). Assessing the value of collaborations in tourism networks: A case study of Elkhart County, Indiana. *Journal of Travel & Tourism Marketing, 28*(1), 97–110. https://doi.org/10.1080/10548408.2011.535446

Chapter 16

Social Relationships in Coopetition Among Entrepreneurs on Culinary Tourist Routes

Katarzyna Czernek-Marszałek and Dagmara Wójcik

University of Economics in Katowice, Poland

Abstract

Coopetition, that is simultaneous collaboration and competition between organisations, is a significant phenomenon in inter-organisational relations, particularly in the tourism sector. This chapter explores the role of social embeddedness in coopetition dynamics within the tourism sector. Drawing on qualitative research conducted among members of tourism (culinary) routes in various regions of Poland, the study investigates how social relationships affect coopetition among entrepreneurs. The findings indicate that social embeddedness fosters cooperation by facilitating trust and shared norms among route members, leading them to perceive themselves less as competitors and more as collaborators or even only as collaborators. At the same time, social embeddedness makes it possible to clear the market of competitors who do not comply with certain adopted rules or standards, as well as mitigating competition for employees. Thus, the research findings highlight the complex interplay between social embeddedness and coopetition dynamics in a tourism context. Overall, this research contributes to understanding the perceptions underlying coopetition in the tourism sector and sheds light on the importance of social relationships in shaping inter-organisational behaviour within the tourist industry.

Keywords: Social relationships; social embeddedness; coopetition; inter-organizational relations; culinary tourist routes

Value Proposition to Tourism Coopetition, 235–264

Introduction

Coopetition is an important and topical subject area in the literature on inter-organisational relations (Chim-Miki & Batista-Canino, 2017; Corbo et al., 2023) and takes place in various sectors, including tourism. It results from the need to co-create and co-provide tourists with products and services that are part of a comprehensive experience at tourism destinations. Tourism enterprises (mainly SMEs) therefore cooperate with one another, including cooperation with competitors (VonFriedrichs Grängsjö, 2003). Importantly, a common location in tourist destinations is associated not only with geographical proximity but also with cultural and social proximity (Blasi et al., 2022), manifested by the existence of trust, common norms, values and social relationships between cooperating competitors (Kylanen & Mariani, 2012; Czakon & Czernek, 2016; Lascaux, 2020; Raza-Ullah & Kostis, 2020; VonFriedrichs Grängsjö & Gummesson, 2006). Moreover, these social relationships create emotional intimacy and a social sense of belonging (Tsaur & Wang, 2011).

The above-mentioned elements create an important social context for coopetition. Previously, little attention was paid to the close ties between competitors because, as Ingram and Roberts (2000, p. 388) claim, 'personalized modes of interaction between competing organizations long have been viewed as illegitimate.' In recent years, the behavioural antecedents of coopetition and – more broadly – the coopetition social context have become important streams of coopetition research (Chim-Miki & Batista-Canino, 2017; Czakon et al., 2020). In this line of research, attention has been paid so far, for example, to trust between competitors (e.g. Czakon & Czernek, 2016; Lascaux, 2020), the set of values shared among competitors (VonFriedrichs Grängsjö, 2003) and associations relating to the number of relationships a tourism firm maintains and coopetition (Della Corte & Aria, 2016). Grauslund and Hammershøy (2021) claim that co-location can be a contributing factor to building trust between coopetitors and strengthening their relationships. Thus, in tourist destinations, the above-mentioned elements are interconnected. The theoretical perspective that allows us to look at them is the concept of social embeddedness (relational and structural), which indicates that entrepreneurs make decisions and business activities through the prism of the social relationships in which they are embedded (Granovetter, 1985).

It has been shown that close social relations promote cooperation, e.g. they facilitate the flow of information, the transfer of knowledge, and reduce transaction costs, etc. (Czernek-Marszałek et al., 2023; Uzzi, 1996). However, while there are tourism studies on the importance of such ties for promoting cooperative performance (e.g. Kallmuenzer et al., 2021; Tortoriello et al., 2011; VonFriedrichs Grängsjö & Gummesson, 2006) or some papers on mitigating competition (e.g. by avoiding conflict – Yuan et al., 2020), they rarely involve analysis of these relations simultaneously. Moreover, the concept of social embeddedness itself has been used in coopetition literature to a limited extent, for example, it was applied to analyse cooperation in tourist destinations (Czernek-Marszałek, 2021). However, coopetition as a completely different form of relationship (related to certain contradictions and tensions) has still not been sufficiently studied in this context. Moreover, an approach where coopetition is conceptualised through a multi-level perspective – interpersonal and inter-firm – is claimed to be limited, while at the same time it strongly contributes to our knowledge of coopetition mechanisms (Bengtsson & Raza-Ullah, 2016; Wolff et al., 2020). A multi-level perspective is used in this chapter, which aims to show how tourism entrepreneurs' social embeddedness affects their coopetition by strengthening cooperation and/or mitigating competition. We present the findings of qualitative research conducted among entities belonging to culinary routes located in tourism destinations in various parts of Poland.

Theoretical Background

The Concept of Social Embeddedness

Social embeddedness is understood in general as the nature, depth or degree of the bond of a given entity with the community (Czernek-Marszałek, 2020b). The author of the concept of social embeddedness is Mark Granovetter, who stated that all business relationships are embedded in a network of social relationships, i.e. specific interpersonal contacts, that entrepreneurs have with other market players (Granovetter, 1985). The sources of such relationships can vary. Czernek-Marszałek's (2021) research has shown that in tourism destinations, especially in small towns, the sources are often family ties, friendships, previous jobs, neighbourhood location, background and even religion. Social and business relationships are therefore intertwined, and one results from the other. Indeed, not only do social relationships lead to business relationships, but strictly business relationships can also give rise to social relations (Granovetter, 1985; Uzzi, 1997).

Social embeddedness conceptualisation is usually done on the basis of Granovetter's (1973) comparison between so-called strong and weak ties. The first are based on frequent communication, reciprocity, emotional intensity and trust, while the latter – weak ties – are their opposite, i.e. they are ad hoc in nature, often leading to one-off market transactions that are not emotionally charged. Their establishment does not require the existence of trust between the parties and certainly not in the affective dimension (Uzzi, 1997). As the conceptualisation of social embeddedness is most often based on the distinction between strong and weak ties, strong ties or strong social/interpersonal/informal relationships or socially embedded relationships are often used as interchangeable terms (see more in Czernek-Marszałek et al., 2023).

There are different types of social embeddedness – relational and structural (Granovetter, 1992). This is important from the point of view of the purpose of this work, because when analysing the role of social embeddedness in coopetition in tourist destinations or trails, one can talk about relational embeddedness – i.e. strong ties between any two actors from the route but also structural embeddedness – reflected in the form of the bond that a given actor from the trail has with a group of other actors from the trail, as well as with the trail/organisation as a whole or with the entire tourist destination where the route is located.

According to Uzzi (1997), social relationships understood in this way (being the result of social embeddedness of business actors) regulate partners' mutual expectations and behaviour, resulting in the parties achieving economic benefits. This is due to the components of social embeddedness, which, as shown by the results of research on relationships built in tourism destinations, are trust, close personal relations, emotional bond, respect for a partner, the willingness to help, reciprocity and so-called 'local patriotism' (Czernek-Marszałek, 2021). For example, trust allows one to enter into a business relationship, e.g. cooperation or coopetition, as trust involves positive expectations of the other party. Close personal relationships, emotional bonding, respect or the willingness to help further strengthen the relationship, allowing, for example, for the transfer of tacit knowledge, creativity and, as a result, increased innovativeness of activities or assistance in crisis situations (Jack, 2005; Uzzi, 1997). In turn, local patriotism, i.e. a bond with a place often found in the case of tourism sector entities – especially in small towns – allows for activities for the development of a given place that go beyond mere market actions serving the development of one's own enterprise (Czernek-Marszałek, 2021; VonFriedrichs Grängsjö, 2003). As empirical research to date has shown (but so far mainly in relation to cooperation per se and not cooperation with competitors i.e. coopetition) all of this serves the initiation, development and results of cooperation in tourism destinations.

Coopetition and Competitors Identification

Coopetition means 'a paradoxical relationship between two or more actors simultaneously involved in cooperative and competitive interactions, regardless of whether their relationship is horizontal or vertical' (Bengtsson & Kock, 2014, p. 182). This relationship therefore refers to cooperation between competitors, i.e. entities that are characterised by market commonality and resource similarity (Chen, 1996).

Market commonality is 'the degree of presence that a competitor manifests in the markets where it overlaps with a focal firm' (Chen, 1996, p. 106). It is determined by two factors: the strategic importance of the market and the share of competitors in those markets. The greater the number of markets where competitors are jointly involved, the higher the degree of market commonality (Dagnino & Rocco, 2009). Importantly, the market is a complex construct and can be understood through the prism of the products (services) provided, the customers served and, crucially in the case of tourism, the geographic area (Day, 1981). In this view, competitors are entities operating in the same sector and offering similar products (services), targeting similar customers and possibly operating in a common geographic area. Importantly, features of competition understood in this way are the subjective perceptions of competitors, the possible asymmetry in these perceptions and the uniqueness of each type of competitive relationship, which is very entity-specific (Czakon & Czernek-Marszałek, 2021).

In turn, resource similarity, the second criterion for identifying competitors, is 'the extent to which a given competitor possesses strategic endowments comparable, in terms of both type and amount, to those of the focal firm' (Chen, 1996, p. 107). A unique set of resources and their proper use determines achieving a competitive advantage. Organisations with similar strategic resources are likely to have similar strategic capabilities and also be characterised by similar competitive weaknesses in the market.

The presented criteria for identifying competitors are important for further considerations in the chapter. As will be shown, social relationships – influencing coopetition – can both stimulate cooperation between competitors and mitigate competition by reducing the commonality of the market and/or reducing the similarity of resources.

The Role of Social Relationships in Inter-Organizational Competitor Relations

Strengthening Cooperation Among Competitors Through Social Relationships

There are papers in the literature on how social relationships affect cooperation – as one of the two key relationships of coopetition (e.g. Grauslund & Hammershøy, 2021; Ingram & Roberts, 2000; Wolff et al., 2020). In addition to negative consequences such as price collusion, which Ingram and Roberts (2000) argue has previously dominated the literature, or the disadvantages of strong ties that can hinder or prevent cooperation, e.g. personal conflicts, limited innovativeness or greater exposure to opportunistic behaviour (Czernek-Marszałek, 2020b; Mitręga & Zolkiewski, 2012; Uzzi, 1997), overall, numerous positives of social relationships for cooperation are mentioned (an overview of these is presented in Czernek-Marszałek et al., 2023).

With regard to the importance of social relations for the cooperation of competitors in the tourism sector, Ingram and Roberts (2000), for example, emphasise the better transfer of information regarding market conditions e.g. price and occupancy information on a daily basis and strategic possibilities and operations (e.g. regarding planning the entry of a new hotel). Also, Tsaur and Wang (2011) argue that social relationships between competitors can foster cooperation. This is because they not only enable or facilitate the formation of various forms of strategic alliances but also influence their performance.

VonFriedrichs Grängsjö (2003), on the other hand, shows that there are generally two different sets of values represented by entrepreneurs in a tourist destination (so-called Gemeinschaft and Gesellschaft). They decide to what extent an entity (more or less related to a given destination) wants to act for its benefit and to what extent it wants to act only for its own business. These values also determine what kind of relationships, including competition and cooperation (based on social or strictly business relationships), an organisation establishes with other market players. The results of the study show that 'the longer an entrepreneur has been involved in the destination the greater the number of personal relationships, even with regard to company contacts. The closer companies come to each other the more personal the relationships become' (VonFriedrichs Grängsjö, 2003, p. 438).

The importance of social embeddedness for cooperation in tourism is summarised by Czernek-Marszałek (2020a, 2020b, 2021). She points to the following benefits of strong ties occurring between entities belonging to a Destination Management Organisation (DMO), being both competitors and non-competitors: faster and easier access to key resources, flexibility of business activities, reduction of transaction costs, easier acquisition and transfer of knowledge, building partners' common identity, positive 'domino effects' in the whole destination, elimination of dishonest entities from the market and limiting inappropriate market behaviour (Czernek-Marszałek, 2020a). Generating these benefits is made possible by trust, which accelerates and facilitates the flow of information, while reducing the transaction costs involved. In addition, reciprocity is also important as it implies a certain commitment to positive behaviour in the future towards a partner. Moreover, an emotional bond and affection for the partner (in the case of relational embeddedness) and for the place (in the case of structural embeddedness), which involve a willingness to act for its (the partner's/destination's) benefit, are also very useful (the way in which strong ties are used in cooperation is described more extensively in Czernek-Marszałek, 2021).

Mitigating Competition Among Competitors Through Social Relationships

Far less often – compared to analyses of cooperation – is literature emphasising the impact of social relationships on coopetition through the lens of the competitive behaviour of partners.

For example, Yuan et al. (2020) argue that the existence of strong ties between competitors implies conflict avoidance in the relationship between them. This tendency to avoid conflict stems from fears that a close relationship will end and partners' trust will be violated. It may also have a broader cause – when an entity operates in an environment where relationship-oriented values prevail, while avoiding direct confrontation in conflict situations (the literature indicates that this may be characteristic of Chinese companies and less typical of Western companies) (Gao et al., 2010). Yuan et al. (2020) show how strong ties between competitors leading to conflict avoidance can weaken a firm's active practice of competitive actions. In doing so, the firm's market orientation is also weakened, leading – as their research results finally showed – to a decline in innovative performance.

Ingram and Roberts (2000) show that friendships formed between competing hotel managers in Sydney can improve the performance of organisations (measured by revenue per available room of a given hotel). This is done not only through the previously mentioned mechanisms of enhanced cooperation (which may create value for customers) but also through mitigation of competition and information exchange, with the latter selected by the authors as a separate element.

In the context of mitigation of competition, Ingram and Roberts (2000) highlight (1) tacit norms against aggressive competitive behaviour and (2) strategic awareness among competitors. The first element is about using strong ties to create common norms and codes of behaviour, according to which entities behaving inappropriately will be punished by the community (group of competitors) and excluded from it. In the second– strategic awareness – it is about building awareness of so-called 'strategic dispositions' among competitors. Through social relations, competitors form a group of mutually understanding entities with a common identity. A feature of such groups is better sharing of information and higher levels of collective actions. Interlocutors in the Ingram and Roberts (2000) study indicated that the awareness of strategic dispositions was instrumental in avoiding bidding wars between hotels.

The authors additionally found that the benefits of social relationships between competitors are best achieved when competitors 'are embedded in a cohesive network of friendships (i.e. one with many friendships among competitors), since cohesion facilitates the verification of information culled from the network, eliminates the structural holes faced by customers, and facilitates the normative control of competitors' (Ingram & Roberts, p. 387). The authors also analysed the structure of friendship ties among hotel managers and showed that friendships are more likely between managers who are close competitors.

Affecting Coopetition Through Social Relationships

In contrast, studies on the importance of social relationships for coopetition broken down into its two simultaneously occurring components – cooperation and competition – are virtually absent in the literature. These studies are dominated by works whose authors refer to coopetition as an independent relationship. There are also works in which the considerations are only theoretical or where the influence is analysed of only selected components of social relations on coopetition, such as trust.

Here we should mention the previously cited studies by VonFriedrichs Grängsjö and Gummesson (2006) or Ingram and Roberts (2000), where it was found that social relationships (including community feelings) serve coopetition since they facilitate cooperating effectiveness and efficiency in a strategic competitor alliance. The positive association between social relationships (measured by the number of relationships that a tourism firm maintains) and coopetition has also been empirically substantiated by Della Corte and Aria (2016).

It is also worth pointing out the findings of Kallmuenzer et al. (2021). The authors address the topic of coopetition in SME hospitality family firms in western Austria. Their research findings show that for family-run hospitality SMEs, social relationships are a significant antecedent to coopetition. As they claim, 'family firms focus on long-term relationships with tight emotional binding and trustworthy personal contacts' (Kallmuenzer et al., 2021, p. 8).

Meanwhile, Tsaur and Wang (2011) studied senior executives of tour companies in Taipei as competitors participating in horizontal strategic alliances and presented the role of social relationships in such coopetition. They analysed competitive intensity in the relationship between personal ties and performance in the travel industry. The results of their research indicate that competitive intensity moderates this relationship. Personal ties affect the performance of a horizontal strategic alliance positively in the condition of low competition, but they become insignificant when competition is high (i.e. when there is a high degree of partner market commonality and partners are direct or immediate competitors (Das & Teng, 2003)).

In turn, Grauslund and Hammershøy (2021) investigated patterns of coopetition in a merged tourism destination in North Denmark. Their findings show that coopetition takes place on two levels (inter-firm and interpersonal/informal). The actors in the three towns show different motivations (patterns) for engaging in coopetitive relationships: passive, reactive and proactive. Moreover, co-location is a crucial factor in coopetition. This is an important conclusion from the point of view of the role of social relationships in coopetition, since it was co-location and the informal ties that came with it that, according to Grauslund and Hammershøy (2021), created the best conditions for frequent communication and thus for competitors to undertake and develop cooperation. They also created the foundation for unplanned cooperation between competitors.

In addition, a number of works refer to the role of social relationships in coopetition and emphasise this role, but the studies either do not have accompanying empirical research, or they only look at certain components of social relationships, e.g. trust or reciprocity (e.g. Tsaur & Wang, 2011) and their impact on coopetition.

Research Methodology

This study presents the findings of qualitative research placed in an interpretive paradigm, in accordance with the methodology proposed by Eisenhardt and Graebner (2007). Research of this type allows for the identification of new phenomena, concepts or relationships, contributing to filling gaps in existing knowledge (Graebner et al., 2012).

The research context of this study was broader – it was conducted in four different creative sectors, one of them being tourism. The sector was represented by cultural tourism entities, that is members of different types of culinary routes in Poland (restaurants, producers of food, etc – see Table 16.1). The findings presented in this study relate only to the tourism sector. The research was completed in two stages – in the first stage, 19 individual in-depth interviews (IDIs) were conducted and in the second – one focus group interview (FGI) with five people. The IDIs were conducted between February and March 2020 and the FGI in June 2021.

To achieve the research aim, we deliberately selected entities that (1) represent members of different culinary routes in Poland; (2) are diverse regarding: (a) type of services/products (gastronomy, accommodation, farming, etc.), (b) length of presence on the market (the oldest of the companies was established in 1926, and the youngest in 2019), (c) location (the entities were located in big cities, e.g. Poznań, Wrocław, Katowice, Gdańsk as well as smaller towns – e.g. Lipka,

Table 16.1. Characteristics of Entities From IDIs and FGI.

No.	Code	Interlocutor's Position	Year of Firm Establishment	Location-City	Company Size (No. of Employees)	Voivodeship	Range of Activity	Type of Activity
IDIs								
1.	T1	Owner	2004	Koniaków	Small	Małopolskie	European	Providing tourist attractions, handicrafts (providing local cultural products)
2.	T2	Manager	2014	Poznań	Small	Wielkopolskie	Regional	Gastronomy (restaurant, bar, cafe, confectionery, etc.); Accommodation (accommodation facility)
3.	T3	Manager	2006	Katowice	Small	Śląskie	Regional	Gastronomy (restaurant, bar, cafe, confectionery, etc.)
4.	T4	Owner	2017	Gdańsk	Small	Pomorskie	Regional	Gastronomy (restaurant, bar, cafe, confectionery, etc.)
5.	T5	Owner	2019	Długie	Micro	Podkarpackie	Regional	Gastronomy (restaurant, bar, cafe, confectionery, etc.); providing tourist attractions; production/breeding

(Continued)

Table 16.1. (*Continued*)

No.	Code	Interlocutor's Position	Year of Firm Establishment	Location-City	Company Size (No. of Employees)	Voivodeship	Range of Activity	Type of Activity
6.	T6	Head chef	1999	Wrocław	Big	Dolnośląskie	Global	Gastronomy (restaurant, bar, cafe, confectionery, etc.); accommodation (accommodation facility); providing tourist attractions
7.	T7	General manager	2008	Gdynia	Small	Pomorskie	Regional	Gastronomy (restaurant, bar, cafe, confectionery, etc.)
8.	T8	Manager	2000	Uniejów	Middle	Łódzkie	Regional	Gastronomy (restaurant, bar, cafe, confectionery, etc.)
9.	T9	Owner	1962	Karnice	Micro	Dolnośląskie	Nationwide	Production/breeding
10.	T10	Owner	1990	Jaworze	Micro	Śląskie	Local/regional	Gastronomy (restaurant, bar, cafe, confectionery, etc.)
11.	T11	Manager	2009	Świętoszówka	Small	Śląskie	Regional	Gastronomy (restaurant, bar, cafe, confectionery, etc.); accommodation (accommodation facility)
12.	T12	Owner	1994	Biała Góra	Middle	Łódzkie	Regional	Production/breeding

No.	Code	Position	Year	Location	Size	Voivodeship	Range	Business activity
13.	R1	Manager	1990	Klementów	Small	Łódzkie	Regional	Production/breeding
14.	R2	Owner	2003	Kombrownia	Small	Podkarpackie	Nationwide	Gastronomy (restaurant, bar, cafe, confectionery, etc.); accommodation (accommodation facility); providing tourist attractions; production/breeding
15.	R3	Owner	2019	Gdynia	Small	Pomorskie	Regional	Gastronomy (restaurant, bar, cafe, confectionery, etc.)
16.	R4	Owner	1999	Żegocina	Micro	Małopolskie	Global	Accommodation (accommodation facility); providing tourist attractions
17.	R5	Owner	1991	Iwkowa	Micro	Małopolskie	European	Gastronomy (restaurant, bar, cafe, confectionery, etc.); accommodation (accommodation facility); providing tourist attractions; production/breeding; handicrafts (providing local cultural products)
18.	D1	Director	2014	Opole	Middle	Opolskie	Global	Providing tourist attractions; handicrafts (providing local cultural products);

(Continued)

Table 16.1. *(Continued)*

No.	Code	Interlocutor's Position	Year of Firm Establishment	Location-City	Company Size (No. of Employees)	Voivodeship	Range of Activity	Type of Activity
19.	D2	Director	1998	Ustroń	Big	Śląskie	European	Gastronomy (restaurant, bar, cafe, confectionery, etc.); accommodation (accommodation facility)
FGIs								
1.	R1	Owner	1926	Pawłów	Micro	Świętokrzyskie	European	Production, breeding: apple orchards, pear orchards, large-fruited hazel
2.	R2	Owner	2009	Dolistowo Stare	Micro	Podlaskie	Nationwide	Accommodation (accommodation facility)
3.	R3	Owner	1996	Lipka	Micro	Wielkopolskie	Nationwide	Fishing farm
4.	R4	Owner	2017	Wrocław	Micro	Dolnośląskie	Regional	Gastronomy, providing tourist attractions, handicrafts
5.	R5	Employee	2013	Stara Wieś, gm. Końskowola	Micro	Lubelskie	Regional	Production of preserves from rosehip and quince petals and fruits

Source: own elaboration.

Jaworze, Świętoszówka, Koniaków), (d) size (most companies were micro-, small- or medium-sized firms, but at the same time, there were also firms of European or even global reach) (Krampus-Sepielak et al., 2020) – see details in Table 16.1. The majority of the interviewees were company owners, while some were managers or other employees, but all research participants had knowledge about the entity's relationships, i.e. cooperation or competition with other entities.

The study used a semi-structured interview containing 17 questions. These questions concerned, among others: understanding the very concept of social relationships; their types, sources and characteristics (building blocks); positive and negative aspects of maintaining and developing social relationships as well as their importance for business activity and inter-organisational relations (including coopetition with competitors and non-competitors). In total, all the IDIs conducted with culinary route entities lasted approximately 27 hours.

In the second stage (FGI), a group interview guide was used. It included open-ended questions and instructions for the interview moderator. The aim of this stage was to expand the knowledge acquired after the implementation and analysis of the IDIs, to explore the examined issues and to discuss them with a larger group of people, which allowed for mutual interactions and group processes to be triggered. The FGI with the representatives of the culinary routes lasted 2 hours and 22 minutes. Both the IDIs and FGI were recorded and then fully and faithfully transcribed.

The entire empirical material (IDIs and FGI) was later coded using abduction, i.e. a combination of deductive codes emerging from the literature review, supplemented with inductive codes resulting from analyses of the content of the interviews (Auerbach & Silverstein, 2003). The codes used in the study are presented in Table 16.2.

It is worth mentioning that in order to increase the credibility of our research (Guba, 1981), the following activities were undertaken: (1) conducting the interviews in places indicated by the interlocutors themselves so as to create conditions for comfortable and free conversation (only the FGI was carried out remotely due to the COVID-19 pandemic); (2) the use of thick description (Geertz, 1973) for the analysed phenomena, the use of field notes, and the development of full and faithful transcriptions; (3) establishing a detailed code list to ensure the reliability of the coding process; (4) the use of triangulation (various: type of interviews – IDIs, FGI; type of entities and their specificity as well as size, location and time of existence on the market) in order to ensure different views and perceptions regarding the analysed issues.

The whole material was analysed and then interpreted according to three interrelated activities: data collection, display and verification (Miles & Huberman, 1994). The findings of both stages made it possible to obtain a coherent picture of the issue under study, which allowed the authors to better and more fully understand it. The findings, along with quotes from the interviews, are presented in the next part of the chapter. These quotes enrich the description of

Table 16.2. Deductive (D) and Inductive (I) Codes Used in the Empirical Analysis.

No.	Type of Code	Code
1.	*D*	*Social embeddedness mitigates competition by:*
1.1.	D	Sharing the market
1.1.a	D	Sharing customers/resigning from a given customer group
1.1.b	D	Differentiation of products/services they offer; resignation from a given product
1.1.c	D	Sharing the geographical area in which they operate/opting out of doing business in a given area
1.2.	I	Market expansion
1.3.	I	New products, innovations, competitiveness on the market
1.4.	D	Diversifying existing tangible and intangible resources/ transferring own resources to a competitor
1.4.a	I	Transfer of information, experience, mutual assistance
1.5.	D	Subjective lack of perception of competitors as competitors, but only as cooperators
1.6.	I	Division of areas of cooperation and competition
2.	*D*	*Social embeddedness strengthens cooperation through:*
2.1.	D	Establishing new forms of cooperation
2.2.	D	Development of existing forms of cooperation
2.3.	I	Maintaining relationships for future cooperation
2.4.	I	Development of firms' activities, and thus also the development of cooperation
3.	*D*	*Cooperation and competition relations:*
3.1.	D	Establishing cooperation eliminates competition
3.2.	D	The development of cooperation eliminates competition
3.3.	I	Strengthening cooperation (also with competitors) thanks to social relations (also social embeddedness)
3.	*D*	*Social relations (embeddedness) of competitors – features e.g. trust, reciprocity*
4.	*D*	*The importance of social relations in tourism – in general*

Source: own elaboration.

the research findings and allow the interviewees themselves to speak, which allows the reader to better understand the studied reality (Eisenhardt & Graebner, 2007; Miles & Huberman, 1994).

Research Findings

The Importance of Social Relationships Between Competitors

The research findings indicate the important role of social relationships in the activities of entities belonging to culinary routes. Our interviewees emphasised that interpersonal relationships are the foundation of business development, also influencing decisions regarding establishing inter-organisational relationships, including the selection of business partners. The importance of social relationships between competitors was described by one of our interlocutors as follows:

> The restaurant or hotel itself is just a building, exactly in the sense of the word. And in fact, in this case, the company itself is created by people, so interpersonal or social relationships are the basis for developing this business [. . .]. These relationships often influence the choices of our clients and our business partners [. . .]. In our case, relationships are the basis. **[IDI-D1]**

Moreover, as the participants stated, an organisation is made up of people, and changing people in the organisation may affect the dynamics of social relations and lead to difficulties in implementing specific business ideas. The lack of continuation of interpersonal relationships based on sympathy, a kind of 'chemistry' or a good 'climate for cooperation' may make it difficult to achieve the intended goals:

> If you like someone, you want to work with them and come up with some additional ideas together. If you want to work with someone, if you like someone, if you know that – well, I don't know – that they will understand the topic, that I feel the atmosphere with them, then let's organize another festival, let's organize some nice fairs or events here, that is, then as much as you want, yes. And when everything goes like it did in December, you can't do it, it's too difficult and it will be complicated, then you don't want to, yes. We had a great team at the Lower Silesian Agricultural Advisory Center [...], specific people changed – someone retired, someone moved to another job and so on, and suddenly these specific people are no longer there [...]. For me, there is no such thing as an organization, because organizations are made up of people. And it depends on these individual people what this organization will act on and do. These individual people in one organization, when they get along with individual people from the other organization, then something cool will work, or it won't work if they don't get along. **[IDI-T9]**

Participants also indicated that many private relationships, including those with competitors, gradually evolved into business relationships, which contributed to both personal and business benefits:

> These relationships may have been my private ones at first, and then they became company relationships, because one is from my group of friends, and secondly, it also brought a lot of benefits for the company itself, so we combined it as a partnership and good cooperation. **[IDI-T11]**

Perceiving Competitors Through the Prism of Market Commonality, Resources and Social Relations

The interlocutors declared that for various reasons they do not treat each other as competitors. In some cases, the reason for this state of affairs was operating on a different market (including a geographic market); in other cases, it resulted from occupying a leading position in the market and the belief that the entity had no real competitors. This group of interlocutors – indicating the reasons for such a perception of competitors – did not refer to social relations with rivals:

> There are different types [of events] – fairs, where we even get to know the competition, because they are, well, everyone is scattered at one end and the other. It is not a competition either, because everyone operates regionally, just like we do in our own region [...]. **[IDI-T12]**

> I'm going to sound a little proud now, but I don't think that [name of the company] has any competition on the market in this city right now. **[IDI-T7]**

The participants also did not perceive themselves as competitors when they knew, firstly, that there were few of them on the local market and, second, that they satisfied the needs of slightly different customer groups and had different strategic resources. Then, they declared that they were connected by cooperation rather than competition, as if cooperation eliminated or prevented simultaneous competition:

Moderator: Do you have competitors on the market?

Interviewee: Sure, yes.

Moderator: Do you cooperate with them?

Interviewee: Locally, we do not treat each other as competition. We cooperate. Everyone has some specificity. I have families with children, someone there has one for disabled people. Other accommodation units have, for example, small rooms with bathrooms. So, it's like there's a different target group. We rather try to cooperate. I can't imagine us competing here and somehow lowering our prices. There were such practices in other regions, but these were probably places where there were a lot of accommodations. There is a psychological factor at work here – when there are a lot of us on the market, we start to fight harder. There were five facilities here, now there are even fewer. **[IDI-R4]**

One interlocutor additionally declared that she cares about the development of local tradition and industry; hence, she is happy with the increase in the number of competitors in the region with whom she cooperates rather than competes:

We have gingerbread makers scattered throughout Lower Silesia, which I am very happy about, because we want gingerbread to come back to life here, but really we cooperate more than compete with each other. **[IDI-R2]**

There was also a group of participants who declared that they did not perceive rivals as competitors and, as in the previous cases, the fact of cooperation with them puts rivals in the role of partners rather than competitors. At the same time, they were aware of the fact that they operated in the same market and served a similar group of customers, which objectively made them competitors. However, this group of entities admitted that the fact that they have long-standing social relationships based on understanding and willingness to help each other plays a significant role in this perception of competitors:

These contacts with other restaurants are based more on the fact that I know someone who works there – it is more in the sense that I treat them more as people than as business entities, because of course competition is competition, but also people who, whether they used to work here, or we know each other professionally or privately and work in other places somewhere, whether it's some kind of cooperation or exchange, it may turn out that we are missing some goods and they are nearby. However, sometimes we exchange, give or borrow something (. . .). **[IDI-T2]**

Social Relations as a Factor Mitigating Competition

Our research has also shown that social relationships play an important role in 'clearing the market' of partners who behave inappropriately – aggressively and rudely towards others. In this context, social relations in the environment served to eliminate such entities from the market. One of the interlocutors described such a situation. During one of the events, he organised – based on a formal agreement – he made it possible for a tourist entrepreneur to present his own offer. The entrepreneur represented a big company operating on a large scale. At the same time, based on social relations with another small entrepreneur from the local market (which he did not perceive as a competitor to the first one and which he wanted to help promote his offer), he also allowed him to participate in the same event. As a result, the former entrepreneur demanded that the latter be removed from the event, considering him to be his competitor. However, he did it in a very arrogant and aggressive way. The words of our interlocutor, presented below, show the effect of both positive social relations in the environment (allowing to 'clean' the market), as well as negative social relations between entrepreneurs that arise as a result of failure to comply with certain standards related to kindness, culture or honesty in running a business:

> If we had a positive, mutual relationship [with the "aggressive entrepreneur"], I would help him even more. However, because he behaved like a total boor, he started shouting at me and doing who knows what, [...] in the end the guy disappeared from the market, even though he was in ten companies and came here on purpose, within a month he stopped coming [...]. The guy drove me crazy [...] and it just took one call to a few of my colleagues and the guy wasn't on the market. There is no mercy [...]. It's not about showing our strength, I'm just saying how these negative relationships later affect your career, earnings or something like that. As the old saying goes, it's better to have a hundred friends than one enemy, yes. That's how it works. **[IDI-T6]**

Moreover, our research showed that thanks to social relationships it was also possible to limit competition in the form of transferring one's own customers to a competitor in a situation where it was not possible to serve them (e.g. due to an overbooked facility), while at the same time, they were competitors with whom good social relations were maintained and who provided an offer at a similar and appropriate level (hence there was trust that the customer would be served appropriately):

> When we are unable to do something, we sometimes recommend the competition or contact the competition because we know that they can do what we cannot, or we could, but we have an exclusive restaurant or a booked date, and I know they can. **[IDI-T2]**

Interestingly, the interlocutors pointed out that thanks to social relations between competitors, they managed to develop a kind of 'code of good practices.' Thanks to existing long-term private relationships, trust between competitors and reciprocity in relationships, compliance with such a code may limit competition, not so much for the customer but for the employee. At the same time, the exchange of tacit knowledge in this area allows entities to make important decisions, e.g. regarding the employment of new employees. This is how one of the chefs of one of the hotels described the importance of social relations with competitors in this context:

> Five hotels open every year, so it's macabre [...]. I regret to say that for at least five years there have been people who have a completely different view. So let's say, we have had relationships with these people since 2010 and they are paying off [...], these are my friends, as I said earlier, I have positive, proven relationships with them. These are reliable people, not people who might make trouble [...]. So, you can say that we are closed in some kind of group of mutually accepting people, chefs or cooks, well, who value these relationships [...]. With my colleagues, chefs, there is no situation where, I don't know, a chef comes to me from [name of the hotel] and I employ him without my friend's knowledge. So we do not steal employees, it is based on such a code. Of course, if an employee says: "I'm leaving because I don't want to continue" and then says that he wants to work somewhere else, and then the chef says: "listen, an employee has come to me, what's going on?" I say: "listen, he's already here, I don't know, he's burned out, he's coming to you, I'm giving you my blessing" [...]. That's why I say, these relationships between us, the ones that are positive, that we have developed, will pay off later, because I won't get burned anymore, right? Even if it's someone from a completely different company, yes, so he's not from my circle, but I call them my, let's say, colleagues and ask: "have you had contact with him?" What can you say about him? Is he worth investing in?" **[IDI-T6]**

Social Relations as Conducive to Cooperation Between Competitors

The analysis of the research findings also showed that social relationships between competitors often make them cooperate. The interlocutors cited many such examples, and we cannot present them all in this chapter. However, we will focus on the most important ones.

The interlocutors pointed out, for example, that competitors – thanks to the social relations existing between them, including kindness, sympathy, respect, understanding and reciprocity as important elements of these relations – provide each other with mutual support expressed, for example, by lending each other resources needed in current activities, but also in crisis situations when quick help is necessary:

> Maintaining these social relations, when it comes to management, definitely, all the restaurant managers know each other and if we cooperate often – as I said earlier – for example, replacing equipment, for example, my fridge broke down today, and God forbid, I call my friend Paweł from a restaurant at Aleja 40 and I say: "Paweł, lend me a fridge", so they lend it, such an example, yes. So we all try to support each other and not undermine each other. Such relationships work well in this sense. **[IDI-T7]**

In addition to equipment, participants also indicated the exchange of promotional materials or valuable information (concerning customers or contractors) as a form of cooperation, stimulated by the existence of social relationships based on a high level of trust, a willingness to help and mutual kindness:

> Development is easier because we help each other, because we cooperate, we also exchange our data – in the sense of contacts with customers – listen, it's worth going there, they are a nice store, or the store asks: do you know any good cheese or flour producer? We also say it's very nice, we recommend it, so there it is, it's priceless yes. **[IDI-T9]**

The research findings also show that thanks to the cooperation among entities from the culinary trail; it is possible for the trail members to exchange experiences (which is especially valuable for new members), and, consequently, to introduce new ideas, techniques and products to their own farms or restaurants. Strong social relationships fostering cooperation can contribute to improving the quality of services and the development of the local community by promoting local cuisine and culinary traditions. As the interviewee's exemplary statement shows, cooperation on the Podlasie Culinary Trail not only strengthens individual enterprises but also builds a strong community and supports the development of the entire catering industry in the region:

> Cooperation meant a lot to me. Our Podlasie Culinary Trail is very young, we founded it in 2017 with over 50 members, but I think we are quite dynamic. As my friend mentioned study trips, from each trip I bring some experience to my farm, which I try to implement here, and at the same time, as we said, trips to some fairs, showing what we have, what products we have, what dishes we have. Such a well-functioning culinary trail is also an experience for those who are just starting out. We can share [experience] with those who have been operating for longer [...] and we exchange these experiences together. I think this is a very good thing. **[FGI-R3]**

The participants also indicated that thanks to the existing trust between competitors; there is no need to 'spy on each other,' and maintaining social relations serves the purpose of organising events in which direct competitors – chefs of several restaurants – take part:

> I call, we get along, we have some kind of relationship, there is no need to spy on each other, there is trust [. . .]. And then we do some joint events like, I don't know, Europe on the Fork, there are, I don't know, 10 or 15 of us chefs who have to cooperate with each other. **[IDI-T6]**

The interlocutors also indicated that thanks to acquaintances from the past, e.g. from school, they have long-term acquaintance with their competitors, and thanks to honesty and trust, they not only exchange tacit knowledge about running a business, but also recommend each other. All this is greatly facilitated by the close geographical location:

> We have competitors, until recently we were very happy because we simply had – so to speak – a monopoly in our niche segment, but the competition is growing [...]. When it comes to our products, there is a lot of sauerkraut on the market [. . .]. This is where we know each other, we cooperate with each other based on helping each other, letting each other know what's going on, and if someone – just like us, wanted to see what pasteurization looks like at their place, what their halls look like, they invited us – or if we have any contacts, someone wants something, needs to buy something, and we know they can produce it, we recommend them. And it's very cool, it's so sincere, honest. It all came about because we established such a deeper relationship because Michał – my brother, who runs the farm – and Tomek, who took over from my father in Ścinawa, went to school together. Today it's going well and Ścinawa is also geographically close to us and that's cool. **[IDI-T9]**

Referring more broadly to the issue of location, the research results indicate that cooperation between competitors based on strong social relationships takes place mainly at the local level. A common location makes it easier to build trust because it allows you to get to know your competitors as both entrepreneurs and private individuals. It promotes frequent and long-term contacts, which in turn strengthens such elements of social relationships as trust, reciprocity and sympathy. At the same time, a common location is associated with so-called local patriotism – the existence of common norms and principles and the willingness to act for the benefit of the local or regional community. All this facilitates coopetition at the municipal or regional level but makes it much more difficult or impossible in the case of 'outside' competitors. One of the interlocutors even indicated that she was afraid of competition from 'foreigners,' especially larger companies that do not operate locally, due to their greater opportunities to expand and promote their products on a larger scale, which may pose a threat to the small, local business she runs:

> If we had competition that is very close to us, but we know each other, we can cooperate, talk, there is greater trust, but when a competitor enters Lower Silesia under the title [name of the company] – a company that comes from the north, by the sea and tells such stories that they are a small family company and they are starting and opening their own stores in shopping malls and all over Poland, we are afraid, because they have large capital, it is clearly visible, yes. We will never open a [name of interviewee's company] store in a shopping mall in Radom, we simply don't have the budget for it, and here we have one with an offer, active on the Internet, a lot of positive opinions and so on, so we have to be careful and watch. **[IDI-T9]**

Finally, one of the interlocutors emphasised that thanks to social relationships, it is easier for competitors to define areas of cooperation and competition and to stick to established boundaries, which facilitates better functioning in the industry and avoids unnecessary conflict:

> If there are higher-level issues, they need to be sorted out. You need to explain to yourself, to others that at this level we just cooperate, at this level we do not cooperate, and you can say that in this environment it is automatic, because some people like each other very much, cooperate, and some know that they have this advantage [...], it's not like they don't shake hands, but they don't necessarily have to cooperate with each other. **[IDI-T1]**

Discussion and Conclusion

The Importance of Social Relationships, Their Sources and Components in Coopetition

The aim of the chapter was to show how tourism entrepreneurs' social embeddedness affects their coopetition by strengthening cooperation and/or mitigating competition. To achieve this aim, we fill a few gaps in the literature. We not only use the concept of social embeddedness, which has very rarely been used to date to analyse coopetition but also we analyse coopetition relationships at two levels i.e. interpersonal and inter-organizational, which is highly recommended in the literature (Bengtsson & Raza-Ullah, 2016; Wolff et al., 2020). In addition, to date, the role of social relationships has not often been analysed in relation to coopetition, including in tourism.

Our research findings demonstrate that the role of social relationships for coopetition is crucial. They are, as our research participants stated, the basis of running a business, and some even called them 'priceless' in this regard. Their importance is also demonstrated by the difficulties described by the interviewees due to the inability to continue important and valuable business projects in the event of a change of people in positions in the companies with which one cooperates.

Our research confirms the results of other previous findings on the components of tourism entrepreneurs' embeddedness in a network of social relations (Czernek-Marszałek, 2021; Jack, 2005; Tsaur & Wang, 2011). Although the literature has so far focused on the components of social relations of tourism entrepreneurs (both competitors and non-competitors), our research has found that social relations between direct competitors are also primarily based on trust, close personal relations, an emotional bond, respect for a partner, a willingness to help, reciprocity and so-called 'local patriotism' (Czernek-Marszałek, 2021). As for the extent to which – compared to non-competitors – these features characterise the social relations of competitors, it would be worth conducting separate empirical studies. However, these findings allow us to conclude that when strategic resources were not at stake, while there was a shared sense of local identity and proximity of location conducive to the building and development of social relationships, these relationships were strong enough to both limit competition in areas that were considered undesirable or unfavourable to the industry and to stimulate cooperation in areas considered desirable and necessary for both the industry and the route or tourist destination. Interestingly, none of our interviewees stated that they had hostile relations with a competitor, only one admitted that she was afraid of such competition, and others at worst stated that they did not have social relations with competitors (but this was never the case, for example, with entities located in close proximity). All of this leads to confirmation of the very important role of location as a factor conducive to building and developing social relations among tourism entrepreneurs (Chim-Miki & Batista-Canino, 2017; Grauslund & Hammershøy, 2021; Kylanen & Mariani, 2012). It is worth noting that entrepreneurs did not treat these social relationships instrumentally. Rather, they saw these relationships as a value in themselves and were aware that treating this type of relationship instrumentally does not make sense in the long run. This is in line with the research of Ingram and Roberts (2000) about social relationships among competitors in the Sydney hotel industry.

The sources of the social relationships of the coopetitors were, in addition to shared location, membership in common organisations (including the culinary trail, but also the DMO), and graduating from school or workplaces together (former employees, supervisors or co-workers) (Czernek-Marszałek, 2021; Jack, 2005; Uzzi, 1997).

Social Relationships as Stimulating Cooperation

Moreover, the findings of the study show that social relationships between participants in culinary trails affect coopetition by both stimulating cooperation and reducing competition (see Fig. 16.1).

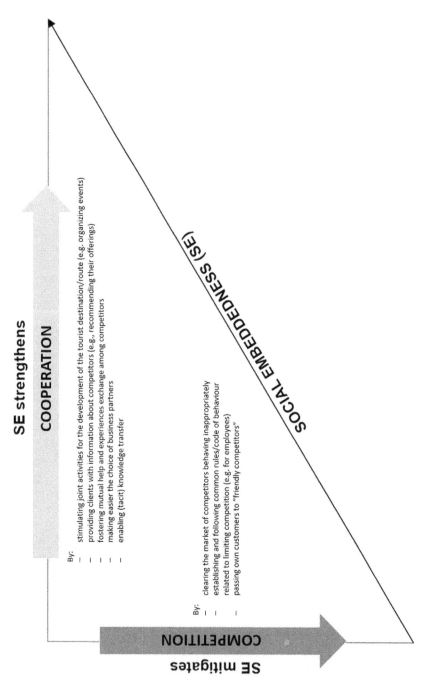

Fig. 16.1.   Actor's Social Embeddedness and Its Impact on Cooperation and Competition.

In the case of stimulating cooperation, our research is consistent with other works on the subject, which have shown that social relationships (Czernek-Marszałek, 2020a; Jack, 2005; Ingram & Roberts, 2000; VonFriedrichs Grängsjö, 2003):

- determine the choice of business partners;
- foster mutual assistance between competitors e.g. lending resources to each other in more or less urgent situations, including emergencies;
- serve to provide information about competitors (e.g. recommending their offerings to customers);
- serve mutual promotion;
- enable knowledge transfer, including tacit knowledge about, for example, contractors or employees;
- serve to exchange experience, especially for the benefit of less experienced entrepreneurs (e.g. from a common culinary trail or located in close proximity);
- foster the organisation of events;
- stimulate joint activities for the development of the tourist destination (including strengthening the tourist and cultural offer and the sense of local identity, in the case of structural social embeddedness) and
- facilitate the establishment of areas of cooperation and competition and their respecting.

It should be acknowledged that the importance of social relations for coopetition in the form of facilitating its establishment (selection of partners) or the development of cooperation in a tourist destination is quite similar to that emphasised for entities that are not necessarily competitors (Czernek-Marszałek, 2020a). Our research identified one key reason for this. Namely, the way our participants perceived other entities in terms of competitors or non-competitors. Their subjective perceptions of market rivals were most often at odds with the objective perceptions of competitors resulting from the fulfilment of the conditions of the market and resource community (Chen, 1996). Among other things, our interviewees, due to their social relationships with other entrepreneurs, did not perceive many of them (objectively market competitors) as their rivals. This was not necessarily due to their limited perception capacity. In some cases, they recognised that they were operating in the same market and, for example, providing similar products aimed at similar customer groups. However, when there were few of them on the market, they recognized that the emergence of more similar businesses was not a threat to them – it was even necessary for, e.g. the survival of local cultural heritage (including culinary) or the development of local/regional attractions and thus the entire tourist destination (this local patriotism as a component of structural social embeddedness therefore played a significant role in this regard).

One interviewee even admitted that given the circumstances in which she operates (the lack of entities providing similar services to hers), she was glad to see an increasing number of competitors. In the perception of the interviewees, this combination of mitigating the commonality of the market and/or resources with the need to act for the benefit of a partner or the local community as a whole (thanks to relational or structural social embeddedness), either did not position competitors as market rivals at all or positioned them more as partners than competitors. In such situations, interviewees declared that they were 'cooperating rather than competing with each other' as it were, recognising that cooperation precludes competition or that increased cooperation must entail reduced competition. This view corresponds with perceiving coopetition as antagonistic phenomena of cooperation and competition where they are operationalised as two opposite extremes on a continuum, where one increases at the expense of a reduction in the other (Ricciardi et al., 2022). Importantly, however, the lack of perception of each other as competitors was also due to the existence of often long-standing social relations between them and, as was stressed by participants, the perception of organisations mainly through the prism of acquaintances with people who manage or work in them. Often these were previous employees or people representing organisations located in close proximity with whom the interviewees also maintained friendly relations on a personal level. At the same time, a strong sense of belonging to a route and destination favoured the perception of entities outside the route or destination (not socially embedded in a given location) as competitors.

Social Relationships as Mitigating Competition

Referring to mitigating competition, we did not identify examples of competition being mitigated by avoiding conflict (Yuan et al., 2020) – none of our interviewees stated this directly. However, our research is consistent with the work of Ingram and Roberts (2000), which emphasises the role of social relations in terms of a kind of 'market cleansing.' According to an interview with one of the inter-viewees, when entrepreneurs do not follow certain tacit rules and norms in operating on the market and behave arrogantly and aggressively, social relations with competitors that make up the industry can serve to eliminate such players from the market. According to our interviewee, one phone call from him to a few acquaintances with a lot of clout in the industry was enough for the entrepreneur to be eliminated from the market.

The research also showed that due to existing social relationships, competition was reduced, as entities passed on their customers to 'friendly competitors.' This happened when, due to limited resources, they could not serve a particular customer. So, they referred the client to a competitor providing a similar level of service in whom they trust, while hoping for reciprocity – that is, the same behaviour towards them when a similar situation arose for a competitor.

The interviewees also pointed to the interesting role of social relations in developing a kind of code regarding behaviour towards potential and current employees. They said that their competition for employees takes place within boundaries that do not violate jointly established rules, i.e. they do not take each other's employees, and they use social relations to pass on tacit knowledge about former, current and potential employees. As a result, they are able to make better hiring decisions, while a lack of social relations can result in decisions that are in perspective unfavourable to themselves as employers.

Practical Implications, Limitations and Future Research

Our research also identified some recommendations of a practical nature. Recognising the importance of social relationships in shaping inter-organizational relations can help in enhancing overall business performance. Understanding the role of social relationships in coopetition can guide businesses in selecting suitable partners. Prioritising relationships built on trust, shared values and mutual assistance can lead to more fruitful collaborations, ultimately benefiting the entire tourism industry. This is because coopetition – driven by social embeddedness – can foster a sense of local identity and contribute to the overall attractiveness and sustainability of tourist destinations. Thus, recognising the multifaceted impact of social relationships on coopetition allows businesses to strategically navigate competitive landscapes, fosters meaningful cooperation and contributes to the sustainable growth of the whole tourism sector. All this means that competitors should treat social relations among themselves as a valuable resource allowing them to stay competitive and adapt to changing market dynamics. At the same time, due to the specific nature of the relationship between competitors (mainly due to tensions), they should build and develop social relationships with the competitor with special attention and care.

Our research has some limitations. The research findings are not representative in nature, so no universal conclusions can be drawn from them. The research is strongly contextual, although it was not conducted in a single region, and the subjects of the culinary trails were located in both small and large cities across Poland. However, it is always the social and cultural context in which the interviewees operate that strongly determines their feelings, as well as their decisions – especially when it comes to the topic of social embeddedness, which is already contextual by definition. However, this does not change the fact that many of the collected statements were similar, which indicates that to some extent the conclusions of the research can be considered more general and therefore more broadly useful. This could provide a starting point for further research in this area – perhaps in relation to other tourist destinations, other types of tourism and other countries and using different research methods, including quantitative ones. Moreover, in the context of future research, it is also worth emphasising that our research focused on the positive role of social relationships for cooperation and on limiting competition. However, social relationships may also have a negative impact on cooperation (too strong ties) and may also favour competition. Such an effect of coopetition should be analysed in future empirical research.

Acknowledgements

The authors would like to thank the book's Editors and Reviewers for the valuable comments helpful in preparing the final version of the chapter.

The project was financed from sources of the National Science Centre, Poland, according to decisions: UMO-2017/27/B/HS4/01051 and 2021/43/B/HS4/01823.

References

Auerbach, C. F., & Silverstein, L. B. (2003). *Qualitative data: An introduction to coding and analysis.* New York University Press.
Bengtsson, M., & Kock, S. (2014). Coopetition – Quo vadis? Past accomplishments and future challenges. *Industrial Marketing Management, 43*(2), 180–188.
Bengtsson, M., & Raza-Ullah, T. (2016). A systematic review of research on coopetition: Toward a multilevel understanding. *Industrial Marketing Management, 57,* 23–39.
Blasi, S., Fano, S., Sedita, S. R., & Toschi, G. (2022). A network perspective of cognitive and geographical proximity of sustainable tourism organizations: Evidence from Italy. *International Journal of Contemporary Hospitality Management, 36*(2), 478–504.
Chen, M. J. (1996). Competitor analysis and interfirm rivalry: Toward a theoretical integration. *Academy of Management Review, 21*(1), 100–134.
Chim-Miki, A. F., & Batista-Canino, R. M. (2017). The coopetition perspective applied to tourism destinations: A literature review. *Anatolia, 28*(3), 381–393.
Corbo, L., Kraus, S., Vlačić, B., Dabić, M., Caputo, A., & Pellegrini, M. M. (2023). Coopetition and innovation: A review and research agenda. *Technovation, 122,* 102624.
Czakon, W., & Czernek, K. (2016). The role of trust-building mechanisms in entering into network coopetition: The case of tourism networks in Poland. *Industrial Marketing Management, 57,* 64–74.
Czakon, W., & Czernek-Marszałek, K. (2021). Competitor perceptions in tourism coopetition. *Journal of Travel Research, 60*(2), 312–335.
Czakon, W., Klimas, P., & Mariani, M. (2020). Behavioral antecedents of coopetition: A synthesis and measurement scale. *Long Range Planning, 53*(1), 101875.
Czernek, K., & Czakon, W. (2016). Trust-building processes in tourist coopetition: The case of a Polish region. *Tourism Management, 52,* 380–394.
Czernek-Marszałek, K. (2020a). Social embeddedness and its benefits for cooperation in a tourism destination. *Journal of Destination Marketing & Management, 15,* 100401.
Czernek-Marszałek, K. (2020b). The overembeddedness impact on tourism cooperation. *Annals of Tourism Research, 81,* 102852.
Czernek-Marszałek, K. (2021). The sources and components of social embeddedness as determinants of business cooperation in a tourist destination. *Journal of Destination Marketing & Management, 19,* 100534.
Czernek-Marszałek, K., Klimas, P., Juszczyk, P., & Wójcik, D. (2023). Social relationships: The secret ingredient of synergistic venture cooperation. In *Bleeding-edge entrepreneurship: Digitalization, blockchains, space, the ocean, and artificial intelligence* (pp. 51–90). Emerald Publishing Limited.
Dagnino, G. B., & Rocco, E. (Eds.). (2009). *Coopetition strategy: Theory, experiments and cases* (Vol. Vol. 47). Routledge.

Das, T. K., & Teng, B. S. (2003). Partner analysis and alliance performance. *Scandinavian Journal of Management, 19*(3), 279–308.

Day, G. S. (1981). Strategic market analysis and definition: An integrated approach. *Strategic Management Journal, 2*(3), 281–299.

Della Corte, V., & Aria, M. (2016). Coopetition and sustainable competitive advantage. The case of tourist destinations. *Tourism Management, 54*, 524–540.

Eisenhardt, K. M., & Graebner, M. E. (2007). Theory building from cases: Opportunities and challenges. *Academy of Management Journal, 50*(1), 25–32.

Gao, H., Ballantyne, D., & Knight, J. G. (2010). Paradoxes and guanxi dilemmas in emerging Chinese–Western intercultural relationships. *Industrial Marketing Management, 39*(2), 264–272.

Geertz, C. (1973). *The interpretation of cultures: Selected essays.* Basic Books.

Graebner, M. E., Martin, J. A., & Roundy, P. T. (2012). Qualitative data: Cooking without a recipe. *Strategic Organization, 10*(3), 276–284.

Granovetter, M. S. (1973). The strength of weak ties. *American Journal of Sociology, 78*(6), 1360–1380.

Granovetter, M. (1985). Economic action and social structure: The problem of embeddedness. *American Journal of Sociology, 91*(3), 481–510.

Granovetter, M. (1992). Problems of explanation in economic sociology. In N. Nohria & R. G. Eccles (Eds.), *Networks and organizations* (pp. 25–56). Harvard Business School Press.

Grauslund, D., & Hammershøy, A. (2021). Patterns of network coopetition in a merged tourism destination. *Scandinavian Journal of Hospitality and Tourism, 21*(2), 192–211.

Guba, E. G. (1981). Criteria for assessing the trustworthiness of naturalistic inquiries. *Educational Technology Research & Development, 29*(2), 75–91.

Ingram, P., & Roberts, P. W. (2000). Friendships among competitors in the Sydney hotel industry. *American Journal of Sociology, 106*(2), 387–423.

Jack, S. L. (2005). The role, use and activation of strong and weak network ties: A qualitative analysis. *Journal of Management Studies, 42*(6), 1233–1259.

Kallmuenzer, A., Zach, F. J., Wachter, T., Kraus, S., & Salner, P. (2021). Antecedents of coopetition in small and medium-sized hospitality firms. *International Journal of Hospitality Management, 99*, 103076.

Krampus-Sepielak, A., Rodzinska-Szary, P., Bobrowski, M., Śliwiński, M., & Gałuszka, D. (2020). *Kondycja Polskiej Branży Gier 2020.* Ministry of Culture and National Heritage in Poland and Cracow Technology Park [access: June 30, 2021. https://www.kpt.krakow.pl/wp-content/uploads/2020/12/kpbg2020.pdf].

Kylanen, M., & Mariani, M. M. (2012). Unpacking the temporal dimension of coopetition in tourism destinations: Evidence from Finnish and Italian theme parks. *Anatolia, 23*(1), 61–74.

Lascaux, A. (2020). Coopetition and trust: What we know, where to go next. *Industrial Marketing Management, 84*, 2–18.

Miles, M. B., & Huberman, A. M. (1994). *Qualitative data analysis: An expanded sourcebook.* Sage.

Mitręga, M., & Zolkiewski, J. (2012). Negative consequences of deep relationships with suppliers: An exploratory study in Poland. *Industrial Marketing Management, 41*(5), 886–894.

Raza-Ullah, T., & Kostis, A. (2020). Do trust and distrust in coopetition matter to performance?. *European Management Journal, 38*(3), 367–376.

Ricciardi, F., Zardini, A., Czakon, W., Rossignoli, C., & Kraus, S. (2022). Revisiting the cooperation–competition paradox: A configurational approach to short-and long-term coopetition performance in business networks. *European Management Journal, 40*(3), 320–331.

Tortoriello, M., Perrone, V., & McEvily, B. (2011). Cooperation among competitors as status-seeking behavior: Network ties and status differentiation. *European Management Journal, 29*(5), 335–346.

Tsaur, S. H., & Wang, C. H. (2011). Personal ties, reciprocity, competitive intensity, and performance of the strategic alliances in Taiwan's travel industry. *Service Industries Journal, 31*(6), 911–928.

Uzzi, B. (1996). The sources and consequences of embeddedness for the economic performance of organizations: The network effect. *American Sociological Review, 61*(4), 674–698.

Uzzi, B. (1997). Social structure and competition in interfirm networks. *Administrative Science Quarterly, 42*(1), 37–69.

VonFriedrichs Grängsjö, Y. (2003). Destination networking: Co-opetition in peripheral surroundings. *International Journal of Physical Distribution & Logistics Management, 33*(5), 427–448.

VonFriedrichs Grängsjö, Y., & Gummesson, E. (2006). Hotel networks and social capital in destination marketing. *International Journal of Service Industry Management, 17*(1), 58–75.

Wolff, G., Wältermann, M., & Rank, O. N. (2020). The embeddedness of social relations in inter-firm competitive structures. *Social Networks, 62*, 85–98.

Yuan, X., Guo, Z., & Lee, J. W. (2020). Good connections with rivals may weaken a firm's competitive practices: The negative effect of competitor ties on market orientation practices and innovative performance. *Asia Pacific Journal of Management, 37*, 693–718.

Chapter 17

Fostering a Better Spatial Distribution of Tourism: Using Geotagged Photos to Shape the Coopetition Network

Márcio Ribeiro Martins[a]*, Rui Augusto da Costa*[b,c]
and André Pedrosa[d]

[a]Instituto Politécnico de Bragança, Portugal; Tansdisciplinary Research Center in Education and Development (CITED), Portugal; Centre for Tourism Research, Development and Innovation (CITUR), Portugal
[b]Department of Economics, Management, Industrial Engineering and Tourism, University of Aveiro, Portugal
[c]GOVCOPP Research Unit, Portugal
[d]University of Aveiro, Portugal

Abstract

This study examines network coopetition strategies to promote the spatial distribution of tourists and their importance for Destination Management Organisations (DMOs). Geotagged photos from the municipality of Porto, Portugal ($n = 152,312$) uploaded to the Flickr social network between 2010 and 2022 were utilised, and thematic maps were produced using geographic information systems (GISs). Residents and visitors were identified and separated, employing a heuristic approach with a five-day threshold between the first and last photo of each user. The findings indicate an uneven distribution of tourists within the destination, with a notable concentration of accommodation, attractions and visitors in the historic centre. The establishment of a coopetition network could contribute to the dispersion of activity.

Keywords: Coopetition; tracking technologies; Flickr; visitors' spatial behaviour; tourism destination

Value Proposition to Tourism Coopetition, 265–278
Copyright © 2025 Márcio Ribeiro Martins, Rui Augusto da Costa and André Pedrosa
Published under exclusive licence by Emerald Publishing Limited
doi:10.1108/978-1-83797-827-420241017

Introduction

Tourism has been growing during the last years. Urban tourism destinations face several constraints regarding the increase of visitors and its implications for sustainable management and planning while enabling the creation of places to visit and reside. By analysing the spatial behaviour of visitors, DMOs can enhance destination planning and management (Beeco et al., 2013; Ferrante et al., 2016). This analysis enables the development of strategies for dispersing tourist from highly concentrated areas, thereby contributing to the redistribution of tourism income in the local economy, the management of flows and the reduction of the negative environmental impacts of tourism (Hall, 2005 cit. by Le-Klähn et al., 2015). DMOs can also adapt the destination to the tourists, maximising the opportunities offered to them and increasing their satisfaction with attractions, tourist services, public spaces, transportation, signage and strategic information (Ferrante et al., 2016; Lew & McKercher, 2006).

Technologies play a significant role in the analysis of tourists' spatial behaviour, allowing the collection of high-resolution georeferenced information on their movements. The utilization of geotagged photos from social networks, such as Flickr, has several advantages. This approach is non-intrusive, providing a high sample size with a large amount of associated data, and it is a low-cost source of information with virtually unlimited scope for studies across various geographical scale (local, regional, national and global). It uses technological advances but requires less effort in data processing.

The management and planning of tourism destinations are a collective effort, as diverse activities, institutions and firms need to work together to create the tourism offering. DMOs become a manager of a mosaic of sub-networks composed of players that cooperate and compete within the tourism destinations (Chim-Miki & Batista Camino, 2017a; Nguyen et al., 2022). Coopetition has been studied in some tourism destinations and represents an essential strategy to tourism, as indicated by previous studies. For instance, it is observed as a behaviour within supply chains or business networks in tourism destinations (Nguyen et al., 2022). However, to the best of our knowledge, little attention has been paid in the relationship between coopetition networks and the spatial behaviour of tourists, despite its importance for DMOs in establishing mechanisms to improve the distribution of tourism flows in tourism destinations (Kirillova et al., 2020; Nguyen et al., 2022).

This chapter addresses the importance of coopetition network to promote a balanced distribution of tourism flows and examines the use of tracking technologies, i.e. geotagged photos, in developing strategies for tourism destination planning. This study shows how Geotagged Photos can support efforts to disperse visitors across destination areas, thereby mitigating issues of overtourism in certain locations. The municipality of Porto, Portugal, is analysed with data collected from the popular photo-sharing platform, Flickr. Photos uploaded by both residents and visitors are identified and separated, and thematic maps are produced using GISs.

This chapter is structured as follows: after the introduction, Section 2 presents the objective and discusses the importance of coopetition for tourism destinations. It is also outlining how tracking technologies can aid in analysing the spatial distribution of visitors to develop strategies for a better management and planning of tourism destinations. In Section 3, the methodology is presented, focussing on the analysis of Flickr photos, and the study area is described. Section 4 delves into the analysis of the results and the discussion, considering the literature review. Finally, the conclusion presents the main results of the study.

Literature Review

Coopetition and Tourism Destinations

The coopetition concept emerged from game theory and the resource-based view (Meena et al., 2024) and has gained significant importance within the domain of strategic management research and practice (Klimas et al., 2024). It is now considered a distinct theory (Czakon & Czernek, 2016) with applicability in diverse contexts, such as strategic alliances and networks (Klimas et al., 2024). Tourism destinations have become a focal point of coopetition research. Companies located in a specific geographical area must collaborate for destination marketing and planning, as well as for product co-creation, to achieve sustained development in the tourism industry. However, despite the relevance of coopetitive strategies in the tourism sector, research in tourism management is still in its initial stages (Czernek & Czakon, 2016; Nguyen et al., 2022).

According to Chim-Miki and Batista-Canino (2017a, b), coopetition can occur at four levels, such as intra-organizational (micro-level), inter-organizational (meso-level), inter-networks (macro-level) and regional coopetition (meta-level). Moreover, in tourism coopetition research, five levels are identified: individual, intra-organisational, inter-organisational, network and inter-network or inter-destination level (Bengtsson et al., 2010; Butler & Weidenfeld, 2011; Mariani, 2016).

From a network perspective, stakeholders in tourism destinations can simultaneously compete for benefits or resources while cooperate to create value. The diverse array of stakeholder relationships in a tourism destination, including competitors, suppliers, complementary businesses, government offices, visitors and residents, gives rise to the emergence of coopetition networks for value creation (Czakon & Czernek, 2016). Stakeholders may engage in value networks for various purposes, such as sharing resources (Kylanen & Mariani, 2012), addressing challenges, managing risks (Chim-Miki & Batista-Canino, 2017a; Damayanti et al., 2013), attracting customers and engaging in co-marketing (Chim-Miki & Batista-Canino, 2017a; Damayanti et al., 2013; Wang & Krakover, 2008). Coopetition can facilitate the achievement of sustainability goals and sustainable tourism in terms of social, economic and environmental aspects (Bramwell et al., 2017; Sharpley, 2020). It contributes to develop destination competitiveness (Della Corte & Aria, 2016) and enable a better customer experience focused on a customer-oriented service delivery (Kylänen & Mariani,

2014). Moreover, at network level, coopetition can improve the performance and success of marketing tourism destinations (Friedrichs Grangsjo, 2003).

In the tourism sector, coopetition also arises when destination stakeholders cooperate and compete among networks in a regional context (Wang & Krakover, 2008). The escalating competition among tourism destinations is a stark reality and is becoming increasingly relevant over time (Chim-Miki et al., 2020). While competition among tourism destinations is notably intensifying, competitive advantage is typically sustained on a shorter period. Consequently, the emergence of coopetition strategies (collaboration and cooperation between stakeholders) within a tourism destination is increasingly important for a destination to achieve a competitive advantage based on its resources and capabilities.

The resource-based theory (RBV) posits that competitive advantage is contingent upon the resources and capabilities of the firm or destinations (Peteraf, 1993; Wernerfelt, 1984). According to Barney (1991), the critical attributes of resources are value, rarity, imperfect imitability and lack of substitutability. In tourism destinations, in accordance with the RBV theory, competitive advantage can arise from natural and cultural resources, infrastructures and tourism attractions or from inter-organisational alliances that cooperate and compete to create value (Crick & Crick, 2020). This implies that tourism stakeholders can cultivate coopetitive advantages.

DMOs and tourism associations play several significant roles in tourism destinations, including leadership and coordination. This coordination role enables DMOs to bring together various stakeholders for planning and research purposes. DMOs are responsible for preparing the plans and strategies, developing products, conducting promotional efforts and creating new tourism products. They also market and promote the destination as an integrated product. All these activities are based on the establishment of local partnerships, which poses a challenge for DMOs and tourism associations, aiming to foster collaboration among tourism firms and create a coopetition network (Chim-Miki et al., 2024).

The tourist is recognized as a co-creator of the destination (Buonincontri et al., 2017; Nguyen et al., 2022), and from the viewpoint of the value network proposed by Brandenburger and Nalebuff (1996), the tourist serves as the customer – one of the players in the coopetition. A similar perspective is echoed in the work of Chim-Miki and Batista-Canino (2018), where the tourist is also regarded as part of the tourism destination's coopetition network. However, tourists engage in co-creation through various means, actively and passively, with one of these ways being through the consumer behaviour and the spatial analysis of their movements.

Tracking Technologies Using Geotagged Photos

Studying the spatiotemporal behaviour of tourists, which involves tracking their physical movements in space and time, implies the use of a set of techniques enabling such tracking (Xia et al., 2011). Recent technological advances in information and communication technologies (ICTs) have led to the emergence and progressive adaptation of a wide array of tracking techniques the collection of high-resolution georeferenced information on tourists' movements. This information can then be processed within in a GIS environment, offering the advantage of exploring and interpreting increasingly large and complex databases (Martins & Costa, 2022). These modern techniques encompass the use GPS (Global Positioning System) devices (Caldeira & Kastenholz, 2018), telephone tracking systems (Raun et al., 2016), business cards/passes (Zoltan, 2014), smartphone applications (Apps) (Martins et al., 2022; Yun & Park, 2014), Bluetooth (Versichele et al., 2014) and georeferenced data shared on social networks such as X (formerly Twitter) (Solazzo et al., 2022), Flickr (Kádár & Gede, 2021) among others. When employing some of these data collection techniques, the researcher exerts no influence on the data selection process, thereby making them less intrusive. Generally, these techniques are more efficient and accurate compared to traditional tracking techniques, reducing participants' responsibilities as they are not reliant on their enthusiasm and memory. Consequently, they enable the generation of high-resolution spatiotemporal information facilitating the analysis of individual spatial and temporal behaviour (Grinberger et al., 2014).

The sharing of photos from social networks such as Flickr or Instagram has garnered tourism researchers. Geotagged photos, in particular, have proven to be valuable for various research purposes within the field: studying visitors' spatio-temporal behaviour (Paulino et al., 2022), classifying and quantifying visitors (Kádár & Gede, 2022; Wood et al., 2013), exploring itineraries and providing attractions recommendation (Noorian et al., 2022), analysing brand and/or destination image(Cho et al., 2022), ranking tourism attractions/destinations (Al-Sultany, 2018), analysing tourism activity in protected areas with a focus on sustainability and climate change (Barros et al., 2020; Kádár & Gede, 2022; Pickering et al., 2020), studying specific types of tourism such as wine tourism (Sottini et al., 2019), coastal tourism (Teles da Mota et al., 2022) or cultural tourism (Payntar, 2022), and analysing post-disaster tourism recovery (Yan et al., 2017) or the relationship between tourism and crime (Paliska et al., 2020). In this chapter, photos from Flickr were utilised to analyse the distribution of visitors in the city of Porto.

Methodology

Methods

Flickr is a widely used photo-sharing platform, hosts approximately 13 billion photos contributed by 122 million users across 72 countries, with notable concentration in the USA (31.03%), the UK (9.83%) and Germany (5.26%). The platform sees a staggering 25 million photos uploads each day (Broz, 2022). Recognized as a valuable research database for tourism studies, Flickr has been utilised by researchers to measure tourism demand and provide comparable data on visitor flows across diverse regions of the globe (Kádár & Gede, 2021; Mou et al., 2022; Thomee et al., 2016).

This chapter utilises photos from Flickr taken in the municipalities of Porto and Vila Nova de Gaia, spanning from 1 January 2010 and 31 December 2022. Vila Nova de Gaia was included due to its significant attractions, notably the Port wine cellars, which are highly popular for visitors to Porto. Utilising the Flickr Metadata Downloader plug-in within QGIS software, a total of 152312 photos were downloaded.

Following data collection, photos were categorised into those taken by residents and visitors. Various approaches have been employed by tourism researchers to distinguish tourists from locals, including heuristic methods, supervised machine learning (ML) algorithms and Shannon entropy (SHEN) (Derdouri & Osaragi, 2021). In this study, a heuristic approach was adopted, wherein a five-day threshold was applied to identify visitors. This threshold was selected based on the minimum length of stay deemed characteristic of visitors in urban destinations (Kádár & Gede, 2013). This decision is supported by previous research indicating short-term stays for city trips, with Balińska (2020) noting that visits to cities typically span a maximum of three nights. Consequently, 66,754 photos (43.83%) from visitors were identified, uploaded by 12,957 users/visitors.

Cartography was created using ArcGIS Pro 3.2. Georeferenced photographs were leveraged to generate a map depicting visitor intensity, utilising the kernel density tool. Additionally, the map illustrates the distribution of tourist accommodation, including local accommodation and tourist establishments), sourced from the using TravelBI Open Data – Georeferenced Open Data Platform of Turismo de Portugal (https://dadosabertos.turismodeportugal.pt/).

Key tourist resources within the city were also incorporated into the analysis. This approach enables the identification of primary tourist hotspots and facilitates the analysis of visitor distribution in Porto, allowing for comparisons with the locations of accommodation and attraction.

Study Area: Porto Municipality

Situated in the north-west of Portugal, the municipality of Porto spans an area of 41.42 square kilometres. As of 2022, it boasts a population of 238,298 residents (Pordata, 2024c). Porto is further divided into seven parishes, namely Bonfim, Campanhã, Paranhos, Ramalde, the Union of the parishes of Aldoar, Foz do Douro and Nevogilde, the Union of the parishes of Cedofeita, Santo Ildefonso, Sé, Miragaia, São Nicolau and Vitória,and the Union of the parishes of Lordelo do Ouro and Massarelos.

In terms of tourist resources, Porto is renowned for its cultural tourism, gastronomy and wine and religious tourism. A highlight among these is Porto's historic centre, which earned UNESCO World Heritage Site status in 2001. The city's competitive positioning, as outlined by Turismo de Portugal e Norte de Portugal, emphasises not only its diverse natural resources and rich historical and cultural heritage but also on the harmonious blend of tradition and innovation, quality service provision, proximity to major European destinations, and intangible qualities such as hospitality and authenticity (Turismo do Porto e Norte de

Portugal, 2015). Costa et al. (2014) note that the tourism landscape of Porto and Northern Portugal have been shaped by promotional campaigns, territorial marketing initiatives, the establishment of new accommodation facilities, and the strategy positioning of Francisco Sá Carneiro airport as a regional hub.

In 2022, the municipality of Porto boasted a tourist accommodation capacity of 25,936 beds, representing 5.7% of the national total, 31.9% of the total for the northern region, and 60.9% of the Porto Metropolitan Area (Pordata, 2024a). The growth trajectory of tourist activity has surpassed both national and regional average, evidenced in the 61.8% increase in bed capacity (Pordata, 2024a) and a 46% surge in overnight stays (Pordata, 2024b) between 2016 and 2022. Of the existing tourist accommodation, 173 establishments fall under the category of tourism establishments (such as hotels, resorts and camping sites), boasting a combined capacity of 20,753 beds (Turismo de Portugal, 2024a). Additionally, there are 10,327 local accommodation options (i.e. rooms, flats, villas, lodging establishments and hostels), accommodating up to 44,755 guests (Turismo de Portugal, 2024b).

Porto has earned notable acclaim within the travel community, underscored by its recognition as the best European destination by consumers on the www.europeanbestdestinations.com platform in 2014, 2016, and 2017. This acknowledgement was further bolstered by its inclusion in Lonely Planet's prestigious list of the top 10 European destinations in 2013 (Costa et al., 2014). Subsequently, Porto made significant strides in global tourism, securing a place among the 100 most visited cities worldwide in 2018 (Geerts, 2018). Further accolades followed, with Porto receiving acclaim from the travel platform Culture Trip in 2018, which bestowed upon it the title of the best European destination and ranked it second globally for visits in 2019. This recognition underscores Porto's enduring appeal and popularity among international travellers.

Analysis and Discussion

The map (Fig. 17.1) illustrates a notable concentration of tourist activity in the area corresponding to the historic centre of Porto. This concentration is evident in terms of tourist density, as evidenced by the results of kernel density analysis of the Flickr photos, as well as in the distribution of accommodations and attractions; that is, there is a large concentration of attractions and accommodation in the city's historic centre, particularly in the area classified by UNESCO as a World Heritage Site. Other city areas have the potential for further development, as indicated by the data, however, the number of photos taken by visitors is very low, suggesting a low level of visitation. In this context, the western area of Porto stands out, where there is currently a lower concentration of tourists, accommodation services, and attractions. In contrast to the historic centre, which is oriented towards gastronomy, wine and cultural heritage products, this area of the city can offer a range of other tourist resources, including the *Jardins de Serralves*, *Parque da Cidade do Porto*, beaches, and the mouth of the Douro River.

Indeed, a comprehensive understanding of visitor's spatial behaviour in Porto offers several advantages. This understanding allows public institutions to engage in

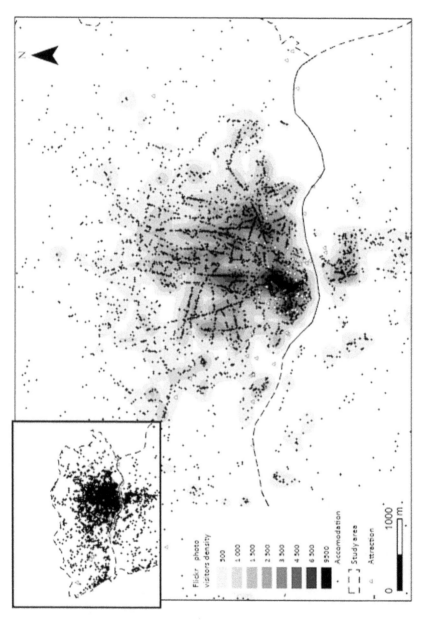

Fig. 17.1.   Visitor's Intensity in Porto.

more effective destination planning, while enabling tourism providers to tailor their products and services to match observed demand patterns. Moreover, it will provide DMOs with insights into the nature of visitor activities during their time in the city, thereby supporting destination management and decision-making processes.

DMOs play a pivotal role in facilitating tourism businesses and coordinating the process of coopetition among members of the destination network (Chim-Miki et al., 2024; Wang & Krakover, 2008). They can facilitate knowledge exchange, align activities, formulate collaborative strategies, including marketing initiatives, and work towards common objectives, thereby enabling the planning and development of new products and the promotion of the destination (Wang & Krakover, 2008).

The process of coopetition, based on a joint effort to diversify the tourist products offered to visitors in Porto, could contribute to the redistribution of visitor flows. Coopetition has the potential to significantly benefit the destination by enhancing its competitiveness (Della Corte & Aria, 2016; Wang & Krakover, 2008) and improving the performance and success of tourism destinations and stakeholders (Friedrichs Grangsjo, 2003) as well as promoting the sustainable development of tourism across social, economic, and environmental dimensions (Bramwell et al., 2017; Sharpley, 2020). This could be achieved by engaging both public and private stakeholders in the development of marketing activities and the promotion of the local resources, as well as in the hosting of events in less touristic or less crowded areas. For instance, the Municipal Council of Porto has implemented a strategy designated as the 'Tourist District,' which aims to decentralise tourist activity away from the historic centre to other areas of the city with touristic potential (Município do Porto, 2024). This initiative has the potential to yield several positive outcomes. It aims to enhance both infrastructure and sustainability conditions for tourists and residents, while improving the visitor experience by reducing the impact of overtourism. The anticipated economic benefits include an increase in hotel occupancy rates, leading to an expansion of tourism tax revenues and income for tourism stakeholders, as well as an augmented number of employees, expenditure, and tax revenues. Furthermore, the strategy aspires to reinforce Porto's reputation as a sustainable tourist destination and to enhance the efficacy of budget allocations for territorial and tourism marketing initiatives. Finally, it aims to consolidate the levels of tourist inflow, consumption, length of stay and accommodation capacity.

Conclusion

There is an uneven spatial distribution of tourism activities in Porto, characterised by a clustering of accommodation, attractions and visitors in the historic centre. The creation of a coopetition network aims to promote the spatial distribution of tourism activities throughout the city. The role of DMOs in promoting these networks is highlighted, with these organizations in charge of coordinating and promoting their development in collaboration with private stakeholders, residents and tourists. The analysis of the spatial behaviour of visitors may assist DMOs in the decision-making process. Suggested actions include the promotion of resources beyond the historic centre and the development of new products and services, such as the 'Tourist District' project. The literature suggests that this can benefit not only the competitiveness of the destination and tourism business (Della Corte & Aria, 2016; Friedrichs Grangsjo, 2003; Wang & Krakover, 2008), but also its social, environmental and economic development (Bramwell et al., 2017; Sharpley, 2020), benefiting both crowded and less touristic areas.

Theoretically, this work introduces the tourist spatial behaviour into the process of building coopetition network from the perspective of DMO's. Technology can be used to identify the most relevant players who should belong to a stakeholders' network, defining the ideal composition for a destination coopetitive network with common goals and complementarity. In practice, it is expected to lead to an improvement in the quality of the destination experience for tourists as well as for the community.

References

Al-Sultany, G. A. (2018). Semantic based geotagged photos similarities for location's ranking purposes. *Journal of Engineering and Applied Sciences, 13*(18), 7716–7720. https://doi.org/10.3923/jeasci.2018.7716.7720

Balińska, A. (2020). City break as a form of urban tourism. *Zeszyty Naukowe Małopolskiej Wyższej Szkoły Ekonomicznej w Tarnowie, 2020*(2), 85–95. https://doi.org/10.25944/znmwse.2020.02.8595

Barney, J. (1991). Firm resources and sustained competitive advantage. *Journal of Management, 17*(1), 99–120. https://doi.org/10.1177/014920639101700108

Barros, C., Moya-Gómez, B., & Gutiérrez, J. (2020). Using geotagged photographs and GPS tracks from social networks to analyse visitor behaviour in national parks. *Current Issues in Tourism, 23*(10), 1291–1310. https://doi.org/10.1080/13683500.2019.1619674

Beeco, J. A., Huang, W.-J., Hallo, J. C., Norman, W. C., McGehee, N. G., McGee, J., & Goetcheus, C. (2013). GPS tracking of travel routes of wanderers and planners. *Tourism Geographies, 15*(3), 551–573. https://doi.org/10.1080/14616688.2012.726267

Bengtsson, M., Eriksson, J., & Wincent, J. (2010). Coopetition: New ideas for a new paradigm. In S. Yami, S. Castaldo, G. B. Dagnino, & F. L. Roy (eds), *Coopetition: Winning strategies for the 21st century* (pp. 19–39). Edward Elgar Publiching Limited.

Bramwell, B., Higham, J., Lane, B., & Miller, G. (2017). Twenty-five years of sustainable tourism and the journal of sustainable tourism: Looking back and moving forward. *Journal of Sustainable Tourism, 25*(1), 1–9. https://doi.org/10.1080/09669582.2017.1251689

Brandenburger, A. M., & Nalebuff, B. J. (1996). *Co-opetition: A revolutionary mindset that combinescompetition and cooperation in the marketplace.* Harvard Business School Press.

Broz, M. (2022). *Flickr statistics, user count, & facts (September 2022).* Phototutorial. Com.

Buonincontri, P., Morvillo, A., Okumus, F., & van Niekerk, M. (2017). Managing the experience co-creation process in tourism destinations: Empirical findings from

Naples. *Tourism Management*, *62*, 264–277. https://doi.org/10.1016/j.tourman. 2017.04.014

Butler, R., & Weidenfeld, A. (2011). *Cooperation competition spatial Proximity and Stage of Development of tourist destinations CAUTHE 2011: Tourism: Creating a brilliant blend*. Adelaide.

Caldeira, A. M., & Kastenholz, E. (2018). Tourists' spatial behaviour in urban destinations: The effect of prior destination experience. *Journal of Vacation Marketing*, *24*(3), 247–260. https://doi.org/10.1177/1356766717706102

Chim-Miki, A., & Batista-Canino, R. (2017a). The coopetition perspective applied to tourism destinations: A literature review. *Anatolia*, *28*(3), 381–393. https://doi.org/ 10.1080/13032917.2017.1322524

Chim-Miki, A., & Batista-Canino, R. (2017b). Tourism coopetition: An introduction to the subject and a research agenda. *International Business Review*, *26*, 1208–1217. https://doi.org/10.1016/j.ibusrev.2017.05.003

Chim-Miki, A. F., & Batista-Canino, R. M. (2018). Development of a tourism coopetition model: A pre-liminary Delphi study. *Journal of Hospitality and Tourism Management*, *37*, 78–88.

Chim-Miki, A. F., da Costa, R. A., & Okumus, F. (2024). Investigating the strategic role of business associations in willingness toward tourism coopetition. *Current Issues in Tourism*, 1–18. https://doi.org/10.1080/13683500.2024.2333910

Chim-Miki, A., Medina-Brito, P., & Batista-Canino, R. (2020). Integrated management in tourism: The role of coopetition. *Tourism Management & Development*, *17*(2), 127–146. https://doi.org/10.1080/21568316.2019.1574888

Cho, N., Kang, Y., Yoon, J., Park, S., & Kim, J. (2022). Classifying tourists' photos and exploring tourism destination image using a deep learning model. *Journal of Quality Assurance in Hospitality & Tourism*. https://doi.org/10.1080/1528008X. 2021.1995567

Costa, J., Moreira, M., & Vieira, F. (2014). Profile of the tourists visiting Porto and the North of Portugal. *Worldwide Hospitality and Tourism Themes*, *6*(5), 413–428.

Crick, J. M., & Crick, D. (2020). Coopetition and COVID-19: Collaborative business-to-business marketing strategies in a pandemic crisis. *Industrial Marketing Management*, *88*, 206–213.

Czakon, W., & Czernek, K. (2016). The role of trust-building mechanisms in entering into network coo-petition: The case of tourism networks in Poland. *Industrial Marketing Management*, *57*, 64–74.144.

Czernek, K., & Czakon, W. (2016). Trust-building processes in tourist coopetition: The case of a polish region. *Tourism Management*, *52*, 380–394. https://doi.org/10. 1016/j.tourman.2015.07.009

Damayanti, M., Scott, N., & Ruhanen, L. (2013). A review of the concept of coopetition: Application in tourism.*CAUTHE 2013: Tourism and global change: On the edge of something big*.

Della Corte, V., & Aria, M. (2016). Coopetition and sustainable competitive advantage. The case of tourist destinations. *Tourism Management*, *54*, 524–540. https:// doi.org/10.1016/j.tourman.2015.12.009

Derdouri, A., & Osaragi, T. (2021). A machine learning-based approach for classifying tourists and locals using geotagged photos: the case of Tokyo. *Information Technology and Tourism*, *23*(4), 575–690. https://doi.org/10.1007/s40558-021-00208-3

Ferrante, M., De Cantis, S., & Shoval, N. (2016). A general framework for collecting and analysing the tracking data of cruise passengers at the destination. *Current Issues in Tourism*, 1–32. https://doi.org/10.1080/13683500.2016.1194813

Friedrichs Grangsjo, Y. (2003). Destination networking—Co-opetition in peripheral surroundings. *International Journal of Physical Distribution & Logistics Management*, *33*(5), 427–448.

Geerts, W. (2018). *Top 100 city destinations 2018.* http://go.euromonitor.com/rs/805-KOK-719/images/wpTop100CitiesEN_Final.pdf?mkt_tok=eyJpIjoiTURFeE56TTBOVlJrTW1GaSIsInQiOiJ0Tk5ibkJYZ3JFd2t5eWh1Qll6YjJMNjVjVabFdnWlRhbTRVZlI5czNwNnhDRm02dFlEcjV3T1krMDc3bjN5YXpkUnJ3J3QnNpSm9xUkkV0aHpnWkdJUWpvbWUzS0Y5ZXhhcHcQ4ZTBG

Grinberger, a. Y., Shoval, N., & McKercher, B. (2014). Typologies of tourists' time–space consumption: A new approach using GPS data and GIS tools. *Tourism Geographies*, *16*(1), 105–123. https://doi.org/10.1080/14616688.2013.869249

Kádár, B., & Gede, M. (2013). Where do tourists go? Visualizing and analysing the spatial distribution of geotagged photography. *Cartographica*, *48*(2), 78–88. https://doi.org/10.3138/carto.48.2.1839

Kádár, B., & Gede, M. (2021). Tourism flows in large-scale destination systems. *Annals of Tourism Research*, *87*, 103113. https://doi.org/10.1016/j.annals.2020.103113

Kádár, B., & Gede, M. (2022). The measurable predominance of weekend trips in established tourism regions—The case of visitors from Budapest at Waterside Destinations. *Sustainability*, *14*(6). https://doi.org/10.3390/su14063293

Kirillova, K., Park, J., Zhu, M., Dioko, L., & Zeng, G. (2020). Developing the coopetitive destination brnd for the Greater Bay Area. *Journal of Destination Marketing & Management*, *17*, 1–12. https://doi.org/10.1016/j.jdmm.2020.100439

Klimas, P., Gadomska-Lila, K., & Sachpazidu, K. (2024). Operationalization of coopetition performance: Challenge accepted. *Review of Managerial Science*. https://doi.org/10.1007/s11846-024-00746-0

Kylanen, M., & Mariani, M. M. (2012). Unpacking the temporal dimension of coopetition in tourism destinations: Evidence from Finnish and Italian theme parks. *Anatolia*, *23*(1), 61–74.

Kylänen, M., & Mariani, M. M. (2014). Cooperative and coopetitive practices: Cases from the tourism industry. In M. M. Marcello, R. Baggio, D. Buhalis, & C. Longhi (Eds.), *Tourism Management, marketing, and development* (pp. 149–178). Palgrave Macmillan Books. https://doi.org/10.1057/9781137354358_9

Le-Klähn, D.-T., Roosen, J., Gerike, R., & Hall, C. M. (2015). Factors affecting tourists' public transport use and areas visited at destinations. *Tourism Geographies*, *17*(5), 738–757. https://doi.org/10.1080/14616688.2015.1084527

Lew, A., & McKercher, B. (2006). Modeling tourist movements. *Annals of Tourism Research*, *33*(2), 403–423. https://doi.org/10.1016/j.annals.2005.12.002

Mariani, M. M. (2016). Coordination in inter-network coopetition: Evidence from the tourism sector. *Industrial Marketing Management*, *53*, 103–123. https://doi.org/10.1016/j.indmarman.2015.11.015

Martins, M., & Costa, R. (2022). Tracking technologies in tourism: A bibliometric and content review. *Smart Innovation, Systems and Technologies*, *284*. https://doi.org/10.1007/978-981-16-9701-2_18

Martins, M. R., Costa, R. A. da, & Moreira, A. C. (2022). Backpackers' space – Time behaviour in an urban destination: The impact of travel information sources. *International Journal of Tourism Research*, 2021, March, 1–16. https://doi.org/10. 1002/jtr.2514

Meena, A., Dhir, S., & Sushil, S. (2024). Coopetition, strategy, and business performance in the era of digital transformation using a multi-method approach: Some research implications for strategy and operations management. *International Journal of Production Economics*, *270*, 1–18. https://doi.org/10.1016/j.ijpe.2023.109068

Mou, N., Jiang, Q., Zhang, L., Niu, J., Zheng, Y., Wang, Y., & Yang, T. (2022). Personalized tourist route recommendation model with a trajectory understanding via neural networks. *International Journal of Digital Earth*, *15*(1), 1738–1759. https://doi.org/10.1080/17538947.2022.2130456

Município do Porto. (2024). *Estratégia de base para a dispersão dos fluxos turísticos do destino Porto e a criação de quarteirões no concelho do Porto.*

Nguyen, T., Johnson, P., & Young, T. (2022). Networking, coopetition and sustainability of tourism destinations. *Journal of Hospitality and Tourism Management*, *50*, 400–411. https://doi.org/10.1016/j.jhtm.2022.01.003

Noorian, A., Harounabadi, A., & Ravanmehr, R. (2022). A novel Sequence-Aware personalized recommendation system based on multidimensional information. *Expert Systems with Applications*, *202*. https://doi.org/10.1016/j.eswa.2022.117079

Paliska, D., Mušič, K., Ćeklić, J., & Mekinc, J. (2020). Theft crimes against tourists and visitors in Slovenia. *Tourism and Hospitality Management*, *26*(1), 15–32. https://doi.org/10.20867/thm.26.1.2

Paulino, I., Domènech, A., & Bassols, N. (2022). Do visitors visit what the tours industry supplies? Sightseeing tours versus first-timers' photos. *Tourism Planning and Development*. https://doi.org/10.1080/21568316.2021.2023206

Payntar, N. D. (2022). Archaeological heritage 'on-the-rise': Detecting emerging tourist attractions in Peru using machine learning and geotagged photographs. *Journal of Heritage Tourism*, *17*(2), 222–244. https://doi.org/10.1080/1743873X.2021.2007254

Peteraf, M. (1993). The cornerstones of competitive advantage: A resource-based view. *Strategic Management Journal*, *14*(3), 179–191.

Pickering, C., Walden-Schreiner, C., Barros, A., & Rossi, S. D. (2020). Using social media images and text to examine how tourists view and value the highest mountain in Australia. *Journal of Outdoor Recreation and Tourism*, *29*. https://doi. org/10.1016/j.jort.2019.100252

Pordata. (2024a).Capacidade nos alojamentos turísticos: Total e por tipo de alojamento. *Capacidade Nos Alojamentos Turísticos: Total e Por Tipo de Alojamento Onde Existem Mais e Menos Hotéis e Outros Alojamentos Turísticos?.*

Pordata. (2024b).Dormidas nos alojamentos turísticos: Total e por tipo de alojamento. *Dormidas Nos Alojamentos Turísticos: Total e Por Tipo de Alojamento Onde Pernoitam Os Turistas, Mais e Menos, Nos Hotéis e Outros Alojamentos Turísticos?.*

Pordata. (2024c). *População residente: Total*. Pordata, Estatísticas Sobre Portugal e Europa.

Raun, J., Ahas, R., & Tiru, M. (2016). Measuring tourism destinations using mobile tracking data. *Tourism Management*, *57*, 202–212. https://doi.org/10.1016/j. tourman.2016.06.006

Sharpley, R. (2020). Tourism, sustainable development and the theoretical divide: 20 years on. *Journal of Sustainable Tourism*, *28*(11), 1932–1946. https://doi.org/10. 1080/09669582.2020.1779732

Solazzo, G., Maruccia, Y., Lorenzo, G., Ndou, V., Del Vecchio, P., & Elia, G. (2022). Extracting insights from big social data for smarter tourism destination management. *Measuring Business Excellence, 26*(1), 122–140. https://doi.org/10.1108/MBE-11-2020-0156

Sottini, V. A., Barbierato, E., Bernetti, I., Capecchi, I., Fabbrizzi, S., & Menghini, S. (2019). Winescape perception and big data analysis: An assessment through social media photographs in the Chianti Classico region. *Wine Economics and Policy, 8*(2), 127–140. https://doi.org/10.1016/j.wep.2019.07.001

Teles da Mota, V., Pickering, C., & Chauvenet, A. (2022). Popularity of Australian beaches: Insights from social media images for coastal management. *Ocean & Coastal Management, 217*, 1–13. https://doi.org/10.1016/j.ocecoaman.2021.106018

Thomee, B., Shamma, D. A., Friedland, G., Benjamin Ni, K., Poland, D., Borth, D., & Li, L.-J. (2016). YFCC100M: The new data in multimedia research. *Communications of the ACM, 59*(2), 64–73. https://doi.org/10.1145/2812802ElizaldeKarl.

Turismo de Portugal. (2024a). Empreendimentos Turísticos | Oferta. *Empreendimentos Turísticos | Oferta (RNET - Registo Nacional de Empreendimentos Turísticos) | Dashboard.*

Turismo de Portugal. (2024b). *SIGTUR - Sistema de Informação Geográfica Do Turismo.*TravelBI.

Turismo do Porto e Norte de Portugal. (2015). *Estratégia de Marketing Turístico do Porto e Norte de Portugal.*

Versichele, M., de Groote, L., Claeys Bouuaert, M., Neutens, T., Moerman, I., & Van de Weghe, N. (2014). Pattern mining in tourist attraction visits through association rule learning on Bluetooth tracking data: A case study of Ghent, Belgium. *Tourism Management, 44*, 67–81. https://doi.org/10.1016/j.tourman.2014.02.009

Wang, Y., & Krakover, S. (2008). Destination marketing: Competition, cooperation or coopetition?. *International Journal of Contemporary Hospitality Management, 20*(2), 126–141.

Wernerfelt, B. (1984). A resource-based view of the firms. *Strategic Management Journal, 5*(2), 171–180.

Wood, S. A., Guerry, A. D., Silver, J. M., & Lacayo, M. (2013). Using social media to quantify nature-based tourism and recreation. *Scientific Reports, 3*. https://doi.org/10.1038/srep02976

Xia, C., Zeephongsekul, P., & Packer, D. (2011). Spatial and temporal modelling of tourist movements using Semi-Markov processes. *Tourism Management, 32*(4), 844–851. https://doi.org/10.1016/j.tourman.2010.07.009

Yan, Y., Eckle, M., Kuo, C.-L., Herfort, B., Fan, H., & Zipf, A. (2017). Monitoring and assessing post-disaster tourism recovery using geotagged social media data. *ISPRS International Journal of Geo-Information, 6*(5). https://doi.org/10.3390/ijgi6050144

Yun, H. J., & Park, M. H. (2014). Time–space movement of festival visitors in rural areas using a smart phone application. *Asia Pacific Journal of Tourism Research,* 1–20. https://doi.org/10.1080/10941665.2014.976581

Zoltan, J. (2014). Understanding tourist behaviour in terms of activeness and intra-destination movement patterns for managing tourism experience. *Università della Svizzera italiana.*

Chapter 18

Conclusion: The Footprint of Coopetition in Tourism

Rui Augusto da Costa[a,b] *and Adriana Fumi Chim-Miki*[c]

[a]Department of Economics, Management, Industrial Engineering and Tourism, University of Aveiro, Portugal
[b]GOVCOPP Research Unit, Portugal
[c]Federal University of Campina Grande, Brazil

Abstract

This concluding chapter examines the footprint of coopetition within the tourism domain, drawing upon existing literature to present a comprehensive overview of its evolution to date. To achieve this, the authors conducted a literature review of 94 articles published on coopetition in tourism and hospitality, sourced from esteemed databases such as Scopus and Web of Science. Each article was meticulously categorised based on its thematic focus, geographical scope and the sample of respondents employed to elucidate the dynamics of coopetition. The findings underscore the concerted efforts of researchers to delineate the contours of coopetition within the tourism and hospitality sectors. Through diverse lenses and methodologies, these studies collectively contribute to the burgeoning discourse surrounding coopetition, illuminating its multifaceted implications and applications in different contexts. This chapter presents a systematic analysis that serves as a testament to the growing momentum behind the coopetition paradigm in tourism. It shows how researchers on coopetition are paving the road towards the coopetition paradigm in tourism and hospitality.

Keywords: Tourism coopetition footprint; coopetition paradigm; coopetition approach; tourism and hospitality; literature review

Understanding researchers' pathway on a particular topic analysis is a collaborative effort that shapes the field and its future directions. This book, a testament to this collaborative spirit, is dedicated to cases and tools demonstrating the

Value Proposition to Tourism Coopetition, 279–292
Copyright © 2025 Rui Augusto da Costa and Adriana Fumi Chim-Miki
Published under exclusive licence by Emerald Publishing Limited
doi:10.1108/978-1-83797-827-420241018

applicability of coopetition strategy in tourism. In their respective chapters, the authors have presented examples that foster a sense of community in destination and tourism management, all rooted in the concept of coopetition. These studies not only add to the existing literature but also pave a new trail, building the coopetition paradigm. It is a collaborative footprint. Therefore, to conclude this book, we aim to provide a comprehensive overview of the footprint of coopetition in tourism up to the present date according to the literature.

There are already some articles that are literature reviews or bibliometrics studies that assist the overview of coopetition in tourism (e.g. Chim-Miki & Batista-Canino, 2017; Crick & Crick, 2021; Fong et al., 2018; Köseoğlu et al., 2019; van der Zee & Vanneste, 2015). However, in this final chapter, we want to summarise the focus on coopetition in tourism. We indicated the published studies' geographic dispersion, thematic, focal and participant perspectives. We provided an objective analysis to identify the footprint that coopetition scholars are leaving in tourism. Therefore, as part of the group of scholars in tourism coopetition, we wrote this concluding chapter to answer, in terms of the coopetition perspective: *Where do we look? Why do we look? What do we see? And, who do we listen to?*

We employed the combination of the words 'tourism or hospitality or hotel' and 'coopetition or co-opetition' as Boolean search terms in the Scopus and Web of Science databases. Subsequently, we conducted a content analysis to ensure that the focus of the article was on coopetition in Tourism and hospitality. We obtained a sample of 94 articles up to mid-April 2024. This set of studies demonstrates the directions and focus attributed to coopetition in tourism.

Where Do We Look?

Empirical analyses of coopetition in tourism have been conducted around the world. As expected, the affiliation locations of the coopetition scholars received particular attention in the early stages of applied research in tourism coopetition. However, the same scholars have diversified their research locus for empirical investigations. Researchers analysed tourism destinations from 25 countries, with 44% of studies focused on European countries, 31% in Asia, 13% in the Americas, 8% in Oceania and 4% in Africa (Fig. 18.1). China and Brazil had the most studies applying coopetition in tourism. Additionally, five studies focused on entire regions or groups of countries, such as the Nordic region of Europe, Mediterranean countries or the World.

Publications on coopetition in tourism have evolved significantly since their inception in 2003. Over the course of 20 years, the field has seen a shift from theoretical propositions to systematic literature reviews, contributing to the identification of trends and gaps for future studies on tourism coopetition. *Sofia Almeida and João Domingues*, in Chapter 13, join these literature review studies by bringing an essay on coopetition in tourism that helps to translate knowledge from strategic management based on game theory to tourism. *Marcia Mariluz Amaral, Luiz Carlos Da Silva Flores, and Sara Joana Gadotti Dos Anjos*, in Chapter 11, also contributed to a literature review focussing on tourism having synergy with other industries, which ultimately is coopetition.

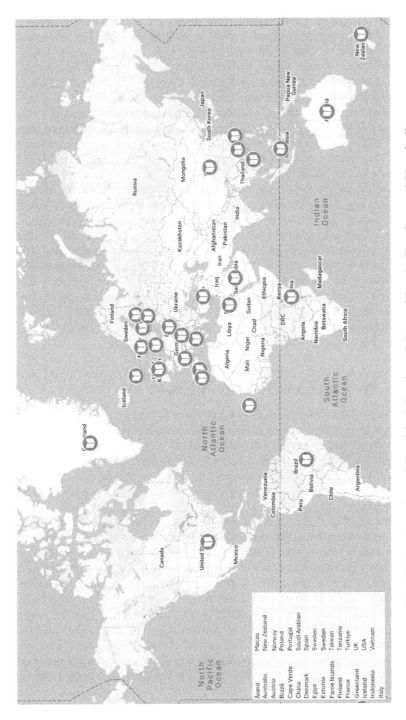

Fig. 18.1. Location of Empirical Studies of Coopetition in Tourism and Hospitality.

The vast majority of published empirical studies on coopetition focus on the tourism destination or sector without detailing a specific tourism modality. However, 26 articles directed towards a tourism typology, with attention given to Cruise tourism, Cultural tourism, Event tourism, Gastronomy tourism, Geotourism, Mountain Tourism, Nautical Tourism, Religious Tourism, Rural Tourism, Sports Tourism, Theme parks tourism, Wine tourism and Winter tourism.

Understanding the locus of application of studies contributes to the advancement of this theory because factors such as cultural influence still need to be understood in the context of coopetition. Indeed, geographical effects require further studies, as authors have focused on co-location (Czakon & Czernek, 2016) and characteristics of sharing natural tourist resources (Kylänen & Rusko, 2011). However, some geographic configurations have not been the subject of studies. For example, how does isolation affect the level of coopetition? Do islands have a higher propensity for intra-destination coopetition and lower inter-destination coopetition? Does belonging to remote mountainous or rural areas influence the propensity to coopete in tourism? Many questions still need to be answered, but the literature is moving in this direction. For instance, *Anna-Emilia Haapakoski, Juulia Tikkanen and Rauno Rusko*, in Chapter 7, discussed facts related to co-location and provided insights into the geographical influence on coopetition. Petra *Vašaničová*, in Chapter 3, also addressed how differences between countries can simultaneously be heterogeneous and homogeneous, which promote coopetition from the perspective of cross-border tourism coopetition.

Why Do We Look? And What Do We See?

To understand why researchers study coopetition in tourism, we extracted the articles' focuses and clustered them into approaches to coopetition (Table 18.1). The authors studied tourism from the coopetition perspective with diverse motivations, focussing on different outcomes. We grouped by study approaches and observed that some research' focuses repeat across categories, such as the focus on Regional Development, motivators and barriers, co-marketing, and innovation (Table 18.1).

The most significant research focus is on business networks and SME networks. These studies focus on firms' alliances and organisational networks, often analysing SMEs, for instance, the study conducted by Jooss et al. (2023). It reflects the tourism sector's context, primarily composed of SMEs. There is a diversity of perspectives in this category. Still, they converge to a consensus among scholars that coopetition networks are motivated to generate competitive advantages, that is, coopetitive advantages (Della Corte & Sciarelli, 2012; Webb et al., 2021). In this line, some research focuses on identifying the different network structures, creating taxonomies of coopetition (Lorgnier & Su, 2014; Chim-Miki & Batista-Canino, 2017), network configurations (Nguyen et al., 2022), and analysing the degree of formalisation of networks (Damayanti et al., 2017). Della Corte and Sciarelli (2012) argued that, in tourism, the competition level among players contributes more to consolidating the coopetition network than the level of cooperation. This assumption was confirmed

Table 18.1. Categories of Coopetition Approaches in Tourism and Hospitality Based on the Study Focus.

Study Approach on Coopetition	Study Focus	
Business networks and SME networks	• Competitive intelligence • Coopetition disadvantages • Coopetition taxonomy • Dynamic capabilities • Firm performance • Governance • Innovation • Knowledge management • Formalisation • Informal business	• Motivators and barriers • Network structure • Organisational practices • OTAs and online coopetition • Regional development • Sustainability • Tourism satisfaction • Trust-building mechanisms • Co-evolution • Digital transformation
Associationism	• Co-marketing • Knowledge sharing • Motivators and barriers • Drivers to coopetition	• Governance • Integrative management • Participation • Regional development
Coopetition models	• Coopetition indicators • Coopetition scale • Community participation • Synergy among industries	• Regional development • Co-marketing • Innovation
Cross-border coopetition	• Co-marketing • Co-location and natural shared attractions • Co-evolution	• Trust-building mechanisms • Synergy among industries • Regional development

(Continued)

Table 18.1. *(Continued)*

Study Approach on Coopetition	Study Focus	
Value creation and coopetitive advantages	• Synergy among industries • Firm performance • Sustainability • Social value creation	• Social ties • OTA • Regional development

by Chim-Miki et al. (2023), whose research results demonstrated that interdependence and complementarity are not always variables with the most significant weight in the coopetition model. In this book, *Maya Damayanti, Mohd Alif Mohd Puzi, Sari Lenggogeni and Hairul Nizam Ismail*, in Chapter 6, also built knowledge about coopetition in tourism SMEs by studying actions conducted by small accommodation establishments.

Other studies on tourism coopetition within the business networks category have directly analysed the outcomes of coopetition, such as effects on innovation (Dambiski et al., 2020), firm performance (Abdalla et al., 2022; Crick et al., 2021), tourist satisfaction or sustainability (Nguyen et al., 2022). Examining coopetitive practices among tourism stakeholders provided insights into competitive intelligence (Köseoğlu et al., 2021), dynamic capabilities, governance and organisational practices (Silva et al., 2023). From this perspective, governance becomes a system whose foundation is coopetition, as both a behaviour of the players and a strategy of centralised and participative management (Mariani, 2016). Learning the mindset of cooperating and competing simultaneously, like a win-win game, and applying it in the practices of tourism organisations paves the way towards a new perspective on the dynamic capabilities of organisations in tourism (Fong et al., 2018; Werner et al., 2015). In this book, *Joice Denise Schäfer and Rogério João Lunkes*, in Chapter 8, contributed to this perspective by demonstrating the relationship between co-entrepreneurship, coopetition and governance mechanisms in tourism destinations.

Still, within the category of business networks, many studies focus on the barriers and motivators of coopetition, paving the way to a better understanding of how to implement a coopetition strategy (Cortese et al., 2021). It included insights into the advantages and disadvantages of this strategy (Della Corte, 2009) and the trust-building mechanisms necessary for coopetitive alliances (Pesämaa et al., 2013; Czernek & Czakon, 2016). Coopetition networks focussing on regional development, co-evolution and governance have shown that this strategy is the foundation for building a better distribution of tourism outcomes (Kirillova et al., 2020). Scholars also included the examination of operations in virtual networks, which was a reassessment of tourism marketing platforms as a coopetition network (Bahar et al., 2022a, 2022b; Bilbil, 2019) and how this strategy can help firms towards digital transformation or coopetition among online travel agencies (Guo et al., 2014). In this book, *Magnus Emmendoerfer and Elias Mediotte*, in Chapter 5, showed that governance is shaped by multi-level networks and understanding and managing these multi-networks of coopetition can be the key to better management.

In the same way, governance and associationism came to be seen through the lens of coopetition and received the same reinterpretation. We categorised the articles that focused on how business associations, DMOs, Convention and Visitor Bureaus (CVBs) and other types of partnering represent hubs of sectoral and intersectoral coopetition, producing co-marketing for destinations (Bourdages, 2022), modes of integrated management (Chim-Miki et al., 2020), improvements on the players participation of tourism destination and the promotion of shared knowledge (Chaudhry et al., 2023; Romão et al., 2023). As formal institutions, associations promote mediated coopetition, reducing tension between competitors and acting on drivers and barriers, accelerating the coopetition strategy and governance systems in destinations (Chim-Miki et al., 2024).

In this path towards building the paradigm of coopetition, researchers have paid attention to proposing and validating models, determinants, indicators and scales (Chim-Miki & Batista-Canino, 2018; Hermawan & Hutagalung, 2020). Models and monitors for coopetition are topics that scholars need to develop to create general and specific models for various tourism modalities. Contributing to this, in Chapter 9, *Adriana F. Chim-Miki and Rosa M. Batista-Canino* indicate a model for monitoring coopetition in tourism, with its measurement variables and determinants bringing an applied contribution. It is important to note that coopetition is not an end in itself but a strategy to achieve a result, which in some scholars is related to co-marketing (Wang & Krakover, 2008), regional development (Grauslund & Hammershøy, 2021) or innovation (Yavuz & Çemberci, 2022). Competition has become a new perspective on tourism competitiveness. Tourism destinations are a social construction and, therefore, collective. Its consolidation depends on relational capacity and managing multiple public and private networks that cooperate and compete simultaneously in creating and appropriating advantages (Song et al., 2022). In the Chapter 14, *Elahe Hosseini, Milad Ebrahimi and Aidin Salamzadeh* showed how the resident's voice contributes to this collective construction of the tourist destination from the coopetition perspective, creating value through co-marketing.

Studies that focus on the interplay between different industries and tourism also are in the category of coopetition models, as some scholars analysed regions or clusters, particularly with studies of the synergy between the wine industry and tourism (Crick et al., 2020). The cooperative mindset makes us realise that tourism has synergies with a wide range of sectors and industries. That establishes a win-win game, which is the formula for successful interactions. In the Chapter 12, *Jefferson Marlon Monticelli, Tatiane Pellin Cislaghi and Kettrin Farias Bem Maracajá* dedicated themselves to the interplay between tourism and the wine industry, highlighting how coopetition has shaped an important global success case in wine tourism.

The category named cross-border coopetition, although not the one with the largest number of topics, has been a growing category in the literature. It began with the seminal studies by Grängsjö (2003), Kylänen and Rusko (2011) and

Kylänen and Mariani (2012), which focused on neighbouring destinations with touristic attractions. These studies catalysed the analysis of regional destinations, for instance, the case study on the Foz do Iguaçu Destination located in the triple border region of Brazil, Paraguay and Argentina (Chim-Miki et al., 2020). Other examples are the studies of Czakon and Czernek (2016) on trust-building mechanisms among co-located destinations in Poland and regional co-marketing (Wu & He, 2022). In the Chapter 16, *Katarzyna Czernek-Marszałek and Dagmara Wójcik* also contributed to understanding the cross-border coopetition, studying its effect on establishing culinary tourist routes.

The role of tourists and residents as co-creators of value and players in coopetition is a topic that requires a change of thinking within strategic management. We've grouped some studies in the category of value creation and Competitive advantages to concentrate attention on this mindset. It was exemplified by *Elisabeth Kastenholz and Mariana Carvalho* in Chapter 15, demonstrating how tourists co-create experiences and generate competitive and coopetitive advantages for two economic sectors, agribusiness and tourism. The performance of tourism firms is also a focus of study in this category. Mainly, scholars focused on hotels. For example, Webb et al. (2021) presented three types of benefits derived from cooperative relationships in the hotel industry. Other examples of studies on coopetition and performance are from Wu and He (2022), who studied the intermediate role of coopetition on the performance of thematic parks, and Liu et al. (2020), who studied the coopetitive advantage derived from networks and relational capability among travel agencies. Social ties play a relevant role in coopetition networks. The study by Kallmuenzer et al. (2021) indicated that family involvement indirectly and positively moderates the effect of environmental conditions and social relationships on coopetition.

Tourism's generation of value has motivated governments to plan tourism competitiveness as it helps improve conditions for achieving social progress. However, tourism competitiveness has been reinterpreted in the coopetition paradigm. The social value of tourism that allows social progress encompasses social, economic and environmental benefits (Chim-Miki et al. 2023), as well as the blend between them, for instance, the social–environmental value created by coopetition (Volschenk et al., 2016). In the Chapter 4, *Jako Volschenk, Wojciech Czakon, Adriana F. Chim-Miki, and Rui Augusto da Costa* illustrate these interrelations and value generation at the tourism destination, reinforcing these new perspectives that broaden the viewpoint of tourism coopetitive advantage generation. How technology can assist in identifying standards to shape cooperation networks to generate more value for tourism destinations and their stakeholders is a topic that has yet to be explored in the literature. In the Chapter 17, *Marcio Martins, Rui Augusto da Costa and André Pedrosa* demonstrated a destination co-creation process through consumer behaviour and how this becomes a tool to shape coopetition networks that can create a better dispersion of tourist flows, generating benefits for a more significant number of players in the destination.

Sustainability is the generation of value for society and a competitive advantage for destinations; thus, it is a focus of study within coopetition. In the literature, few scholars analysed the coopetition strategy for the sustainability of tourism destinations. Phi and Waldesten (2021) studied coopetition for sustainability education in hospitality. Nguyen et al. (2022) focused on networking processes of collective actions for specific sustainability goals in two popular destinations in Vietnam. Filimonau (2021) proposes potential strategies to manage waste in the hospitality sector in a post-pandemic world based on coopetition. In the Chapter 10, *Nadine Leder, Maria Saju Abraham and Jin Hooi Chan* contributed to studies on coopetition and sustainability. They demonstrated ways for coopetition to be the strategy to create and run shared schemes that lead to more sustainable production and consumption behaviours in the tourism sector.

There are many focuses of studies on coopetition in tourism and authors' approaches in the literature. All of them provided details and directions to guide this paradigm, that is, footprints on the path of tourism coopetition.

Who Do We Listen to?

Among the 94 articles on coopetition, the authors used 107 different types of respondents in the empirical studies, covering stakeholders from the public and private sectors, non-profit organisations and society in general (Table 18.2).

Table 18.2. Types of Respondents in the Coopetition Studies.

Sample Group	Respondents	N	Frequence
Business	Tourism firms, accommodation, providers, entrepreneurs, family-firms, hoteliers, managers, OTA, owners of tourism firms, SMEs, tour operators, wine producers.	55	51.4%
Associations and governments	Business associations, DMOs and NGO ou RTO managers, members of co-operatives, members of CVBs, non-profits organisations, and public officers	15	14.0%
Stakeholders	Several stakeholders of tourism	13	12.1%
Scholars	Experts in tourism and students	6	5.6%
Tourists	visitors, and tourists TripAdvisor comments	5	4.7%
Secondary data	Secondary government sources or from world organisations	5	4.7%
Practitioners	Event organisers, pedicab drivers, tourism practitioners, street vendors and wellbeing professionals	4	3.7%
Residents	Host society	2	1.9%
Employees	Travel agents, employees of tourism firms	2	1.9%

Scholars primarily seek answers to their studies among companies (55%), which coincides with the largest category of studies of business and SME business networks. Second, the research used the associations as respondents (14%). It is the focus on mediated coopetition. A general look at the various stakeholders has also been a preference for researchers to hear what the tourism sector has to say to build the coopetition paradigm. Research with scholars as respondents was used to validate models, for example, in Chim-Miki and Batista-Canino (2018) and Chen et al. (2024). Tourists, as part of the coopetition network and residents, are still low on the agenda of coopetition researchers. Studies on intra-organisational coopetition are fewer in the literature in general and in tourism almost non-existent, which is demonstrated by the low number of studies that used employees as respondents (1.9%). Another factor to highlight from this analysis of who the coopetition scholars are listening to is that few studies have used secondary sources (4.7%). It is indicative of variables on the presence of collaborative alliances and organisational and institutional arrangements that indicate cooperative-competitive arrangements are not yet monitored. This is a point that must be improved by governments and global organisations, as many studies have already demonstrated coopetition generates collective individual and collective advantages of different types, including improvements in performance, innovation, sustainability and the generation of social value.

The type of respondent directly depends on the objective of the study, therefore, a variety of participants in the articles was expected. There must be different coopetition networks according to the objective established by the players. To contribute to the creation of these networks in tourism, in the Chapter 2, *Adriana F. Chim-Miki and Rui Augusto da Costa* presented a Roadmap to build Tourism Coopetition with a series of tools that assist the manager.

In synthesis, researchers are leaving a footprint of coopetition in tourism with a multi-dimensional perspective, which makes it possible to study the transversality of tourism as its extensive value chain that permeates other industries in an intricate cooperation-competitive network. This coopetition footprint expresses a path that seeks to understand the phenomenon as a behaviour of society and a development strategy towards social progress from tourism.

References

Abdalla, M. J., Mwesiumo, D., Ozturen, A., & Kilic, H. (2022). Perceived threat of informal players: Enhancing the operational performance of inbound tour operators through coopetition. *International Journal of Tourism Research*, 24(6), 775–785. https://doi.org/10.1002/jtr.2544

Bahar, V. S., Nenonen, S., & Starr Jr, R. G. (2022a). Coopetition with platforms: Balancing the interplay of cooperation and competition in hospitality. *Tourism Management*, 88, 104417. https://doi.org/10.1016/j.tourman.2021.104417

Bahar, V. S., Nenonen, S., & Starr Jr, R. G. (2022b). On the same boat but singing a different tune: Coopetition between hotels and platforms close to customers. *Industrial Marketing Management*, 107, 52–69. https://doi.org/10.1016/j.indmarman.2022.09.020

Bilbil, E. T. (2019). Platform coopetition in the tourism industry: Conflicts and tensions caused by the closure of Booking.com in Turkey. *Current Issues in Tourism*, *22*(13), 1617–1637. https://doi.org/10.1080/13683500.2018.1461199

Bourdages, É. (2022). Key problems of interorganizational collaborations: A multilevel and temporal analysis. *Journal of Inter-Organizational Relationships*, *28*(3–4), 84–111. https://doi.org/10.1080/26943980.2023.2217500

Chaudhry, S., Crick, D., & Crick, J. M. (2023). I'll be there for you: Coopetition and competitor-oriented activities among South Asian restaurants in two UK regional clusters. *International Journal of Entrepreneurial Behavior & Research*, *29*(9/10), 1973–2004. https://doi.org/10.1108/IJEBR-08-2022-0694

Chen, H., Lu, C., Wang, Y., & An, L. (2024). Competitiveness evaluation and cooperation network analysis of tourist attractions from the perspective of coopetition in the Yangtze River Delta (YRD). *Sustainability*, *16*(2), 834.

Chim-Miki, A. F., & Batista-Canino, R. M. (2017). Tourism coopetition: An introduction to the subject and a research agenda. *International Business Review*, *26*(6), 1208–1217. https://doi.org/10.1016/j.ibusrev.2017.05.003

Chim-Miki, A. F., & Batista-Canino, R. M. (2018). Development of a tourism coopetition model: A preliminary Delphi study. *Journal of Hospitality and Tourism Management*, *37*, 78–88. https://doi.org/10.1016/j.jhtm.2018.10.004

Chim-Miki, A. F., da Costa, R. A., & Okumus, F. (2024). Investigating the strategic role of business associations in willingness toward tourism coopetition. *Current Issues in Tourism*, 1–18.

Chim-Miki, A. F., da Costa, R. A., & Oliveira-Ribeiro, R. (2023). Tourism coopetition for a better world: A cycle of creation, appropriation, and devolution of social value. *Current Issues in Tourism*, *0*(0), 1–15. https://doi.org/10.1080/13683500.2023.2254448

Chim-Miki, A. F., Medina-Brito, P., & Batista-Canino, R. M. (2020). Integrated management in tourism: The role of coopetition. *Tourism Planning & Development*, *17*(2), 127–146. https://doi.org/10.1080/21568316.2019.1574888

Cortese, D., Giacosa, E., & Cantino, V. (2021). Knowledge sharing for coopetition in tourist destinations: The difficult path to the network. *Review of Managerial Science*, *15*(2), 275–286. https://doi.org/10.1007/s11846-018-0322-z

Crick, J. M., & Crick, D. (2021). Market-oriented activities and communal wine consumption events: Does coopetition make a difference?. *Journal of Wine Research*, *32*(3), 161–187. https://doi.org/10.1080/09571264.2021.1971642

Crick, J. M., Crick, D., & Tebbett, N. (2020). Competitor orientation and value co-creation in sustaining rural New Zealand wine producers. *Journal of Rural Studies*, *73*, 122–134. https://doi.org/10.1016/j.jrurstud.2019.10.019

Crick, J. M., Karami, M., & Crick, D. (2021). The impact of the interaction between an entrepreneurial marketing orientation and coopetition on business performance. *International Journal of Entrepreneurial Behaviour & Research*, *27*(6), 1423–1447. https://doi.org/10.1108/IJEBR-12-2020-0871

Czakon, W., & Czernek, K. (2016). The role of trust-building mechanisms in entering into network coopetition: The case of tourism networks in Poland. *Industrial Marketing Management*, *57*, 64–74. https://doi.org/10.1016/j.indmarman.2016.05.010

Czernek, K., & Czakon, W. (2016). Trust-building processes in tourist coopetition: The case of a Polish region. *Tourism Management, 52,* 380–394. https://doi.org/10.1016/j.tourman.2015.07.009

Damayanti, M., Scott, N., & Ruhanen, L. (2017). Coopetitive behaviours in an informal tourism economy. *Annals of Tourism Research, 65,* 25–35. https://doi.org/10.1016/j.annals.2017.04.007

Dambiski, G. C., Alisson Westarb Cruz, J., Gomes de Carvalho, H., Carlos Duclós, L., & Oliveira Corrêa, R. (2020). Innovativeness and coopetition in tourism SMEs: Comparing two coopetitive networks in Brazil. *Journal of Hospitality and Tourism Insights, 3*(4), 469–488. https://doi.org/10.1108/JHTI-12-2019-0134

Della Corte, V. (2009). The light side and the dark side of inter-firm collaboration: How to govern distrust in business networks. *Corporate Ownership and Control, 6*(4), 407–426. https://doi.org/10.22495/cocv6i4c3p6

Della Corte, V., & Sciarelli, M. (2012). Can coopetition be source of competitive advantage for strategic networks?. *Corporate Ownership and Control, 10*(1), 363–379. https://www.scopus.com/inward/record.uri?eid=2-s2.0-84883328809&partnerID=40&md5=49d1a81dc3a271d661fde0937fae6b23

Filimonau, V. (2021). The prospects of waste management in the hospitality sector post COVID-19. *Resources, Conservation and Recycling, 168,* 105272. https://doi.org/10.1016/j.resconrec.2020.105272

Fong, V. H. I., Wong, I. A., & Hong, J. F. L. (2018). Developing institutional logics in the tourism industry through coopetition. *Tourism Management, 66,* 244–262. https://doi.org/10.1016/j.tourman.2017.12.005

Grängsjö, Y. V. F. (2003). Destination networking: Co-opetition in peripheral surroundings. *International Journal of Physical Distribution & Logistics Management, 33*(5), 427–448. https://doi.org/10.1108/09600030310481997

Grauslund, D., & Hammershøy, A. (2021). Patterns of network coopetition in a merged tourism destination. *Scandinavian Journal of Hospitality and Tourism, 21*(2), 192–211. https://doi.org/10.1080/15022250.2021.1877192

Guo, X., Zheng, X., Ling, L., & Yang, C. (2014). Online coopetition between hotels and online travel agencies: From the perspective of cash back after stay. *Tourism Management Perspectives, 12,* 104–112. https://doi.org/10.1016/j.tmp.2014.09.005

Hermawan, D., & Hutagalung, S. S. (2020). Coopetition as a model of tourism participation management in south Lampung Indonesia. *Journal of Environmental Management and Tourism, 11*(6), 1571–1580. https://doi.org/10.14505/jemt.v11.6(46).27.

Jooss, S., Lenz, J., & Burbach, R. (2023). Beyond competing for talent: An integrative framework for coopetition in talent management in SMEs. *International Journal of Contemporary Hospitality Management, 35*(8), 2691–2707. https://doi.org/10.1108/IJCHM-04-2022-0419

Kallmuenzer, A., Zach, F. J., Wachter, T., Kraus, S., & Salner, P. (2021). Antecedents of coopetition in small and medium-sized hospitality firms. *International Journal of Hospitality Management, 99.* https://doi.org/10.1016/j.ijhm.2021.103076

Kirillova, K., Park, J., Zhu, M., Dioko, L. (Don), & Zeng, G. (2020). Developing the coopetitive destination brand for the Greater Bay Area. *Journal of Destination Marketing & Management, 17.* https://doi.org/10.1016/j.jdmm.2020.100439

Köseoğlu, M. A., Yick, M. Y. Y., & Okumus, F. (2021). Coopetition strategies for competitive intelligence practices-evidence from full-service hotels. *International Journal of Hospitality Management*, *99*. https://doi.org/10.1016/j.ijhm.2021.103049

Köseoğlu, M. A., Yildiz, M., Okumus, F., & Barca, M. (2019). The intellectual structure of coopetition: Past, present and future. *Journal of Strategy and Management*, *12*(1), 2–29. https://doi.org/10.1108/JSMA-07-2018-0073

Kylanen, M., & Mariani, M. M. (2012). Unpacking the temporal dimension of coopetition in tourism destinations: Evidence from Finnish and Italian theme parks. *Anatolia*, *23*(1), 61–74. https://doi.org/10.1080/13032917.2011.653632

Kylänen, M., & Rusko, R. (2011). Unintentional coopetition in the service industries: The case of Pyhä-Luosto tourism destination in the Finnish Lapland. *European Management Journal*, *29*(3), 193–205. https://doi.org/10.1016/j.emj.2010.10.006

Liu, C.-H., Chang, A. Y., Horng, J.-S., Chou, S.-F., & Huang, Y.-C. (2020). Co-competition, learning, and business strategy for new service development. *Service Industries Journal*, *40*(7), 585–609. https://doi.org/10.1080/02642069.2019.1571045

Lorgnier, N., & Su, C.-J. (2014). Considering coopetition strategies in sport tourism networks: A look at the nonprofit nautical sports clubs on the northern coast of France. *European Sport Management Quarterly*, *14*(1), 87–109. https://doi.org/10.1080/16184742.2013.876436

Mariani, M. M. (2016). Coordination in inter-network co-opetitition: Evidence from the tourism sector. *Industrial Marketing Management*, *53*, 103–123. https://doi.org/10.1016/j.indmarman.2015.11.015

Nguyen, T. Q. T., Johnson, P., & Young, T. (2022). Networking, coopetition and sustainability of tourism destinations. *Journal of Hospitality and Tourism Management*, *50*, 400–411. https://doi.org/10.1016/j.jhtm.2022.01.003

Pesämaa, O., Pieper, T., Vinhas da Silva, R., Black, W. C., & Hair, J. F. (2013). Trust and reciprocity in building inter-personal and inter-organizational commitment in small business co-operatives. *Journal of Co-operative Organization and Management*, *1*(2), 81–92. https://doi.org/10.1016/j.jcom.2013.10.003

Phi, G. T., & Waldesten, T. (2021). Educating sustainability through hackathons in the hospitality industry: A case study of Scandic hotels. *Scandinavian Journal of Hospitality and Tourism*, *21*(2), 212–228. https://doi.org/10.1080/15022250.2021.1879669

Romão, J., Palm, K., & Persson-Fischier, U. (2023). Open spaces for co-creation: A community-based approach to tourism product diversification. *Scandinavian Journal of Hospitality and Tourism*, *23*(1), 94–113. https://doi.org/10.1080/15022250.2023.2174183

Silva, L. M. da, Silveira, A. B. da, Monticelli, J. M., & Kretschmer, C. (2023). Microfoundations of dynamic coopetition capabilities in firms from a micro-brewery cluster. *REGE Revista de Gestão*, *30*(2), Artigo 2. https://doi.org/10.1108/REGE-04-2021-0064

Song, X., Mo, Z., Liu, M. T., Niu, B., & Huang, L. (2022). Cooperator or supporter: How can cross-boundary Macau-Zhuhai metropolis promote regional tourism together?. *Asia Pacific Journal Of Marketing And Logistics*, *34*(10), 2207–2236. https://doi.org/10.1108/APJML-02-2021-0137

van der Zee, E., & Vanneste, D. (2015). Tourism networks unravelled; a review of the literature on networks in tourism management studies. *Tourism Management Perspectives*, *15*, 46–56. https://doi.org/10.1016/j.tmp.2015.03.006

Volschenk, J., Ungerer, M., & Smit, E. (2016). Creation and appropriation of socio-environmental value in coopetition. *Industrial Marketing Management, 57,* 109–118. https://doi.org/10.1016/j.indmarman.2016.05.026

Wang, Y., & Krakover, S. (2008). Destination marketing: Competition, cooperation or coopetition?. *International Journal of Contemporary Hospitality Management, 20*(2), 126–141. https://doi.org/10.1108/09596110810852122

Webb, T., Beldona, S., Schwartz, Z., & Bianco, S. (2021). Growing the pie: An examination of coopetition benefits in the US lodging industry. *International Journal of Contemporary Hospitality Management, 33*(12), 4355–4372. https://doi.org/10.1108/IJCHM-03-2021-0340

Werner, K., Dickson, G., & Hyde, K. F. (2015). Coopetition and knowledge transfer dynamics: New Zealand's regional tourism organizations and the 2011 Rugby World Cup. *Event Management, 19*(3), 365–380. https://doi.org/10.3727/152599515X14386220874841

Wu, M., & He, J. (2022). Horizontal tourism coopetition strategy for marketing performance—Evidence from theme parks. *Frontiers in Psychology, 13.* https://doi.org/10.3389/fpsyg.2022.917435

Yavuz, F., & Çemberci, M. (2022). The moderator role of trust in the relationship between coopetition and incremental innovation: Evidence from tourism industry. *Geojournal of Tourism and Geosites, 44*(4), 1292–1299. https://doi.org/10.30892/gtg.44413-945

Index

www.ingramcontent.com/pod-product-compliance
Lightning Source LLC
Jackson TN
JSHW011916131224
75386JS00004B/215